Green Crimes and International Criminal Law

Edited by
Regina M. Paulose
International Criminal Law Attorney

Series in Law

VERNON PRESS

www.vernonpress.com

In the Americas:
Vernon Press
1000 N West Street, Suite 1200
Wilmington, Delaware, 19801
United States

In the rest of the world:
Vernon Press
C/Sancti Espiritu 17,
Malaga, 29006
Spain

Series in Law

Library of Congress Control Number: 2021930376

ISBN: 978-1-64889-109-0

Cover design by Vernon Press. Cover image by Sagina Vadakal and Tess M. Paulose.

Table of contents

Foreword *v*

Introduction *vii*

Regina Menachery Paulose

International Criminal Law Attorney

List of Abbreviations *xi*

Chapter 1 **Green Criminology: A rights-based approach** 1

Dr. Zoi Aliozi

International Human Rights Lawyer

Chapter 2 **Environmental Personhood Towards a Rights Based Approach for Nature and Humanity** 35

Prayank Jain

The Fletcher School of Law and Diplomacy, Tufts

Chapter 3 **Addressing Environmental Harm in Conflicts within Africa: Scope for International Criminal Law?** 65

Damian Etone

University of Stirling

Chapter 4 **Legal challenges to the inclusion of a crime of ecocide in the Rome Statute of the International Criminal Court** 107

Beatrice L. Hamilton

Rolin-Jaequemyns International Law Institute Ghent and Edinburgh Centre for Global and International Law

Chapter 5	**The International Court for the Environment – Could the International Court for the Environment offer a solution for the problem of international environmental crimes?** David Krott, LL.M. *Vrije Universiteit Brussels*	141
Chapter 6	**Dakota Access Pipeline a Case of Cultural Genocide? Through an Indigenous Data Sovereignty Lens** Leo Mukosi *James E Rogers College of Law (Indigenous Peoples Law and Policy) University of Arizona*	183
Chapter 7	**Ecosystem Destruction in the Kole Wetlands in India** Dr. Dayana Maliyekkal Kunjachan *Government Law College, Ernakulam*	231
Chapter 8	**Crouching Tiger, Hidden Dragon: Hydropower and Crimes against Humanity** Regina Menachery Paulose *International Criminal Law Attorney*	257
Chapter 9	**To infinity and beyond: Finding an adequate approach to protect against Environmental Damages in Outer Space – prevention or remediation?** Tamara Blagojević *Independent Researcher*	295
	Index	*347*

Foreword

As a human rights lawyer, I welcome this compilation of in-depth articles written on green crimes and international criminal law by outstanding lawyers and scholars. Although the range of variety is wide from environmental personhood to crimes in outer space, I am particularly keen on the indigenous perspective. This perspective needs more attention.

Indigenous peoples around the world are living in harmony with nature and often see their livelihood destroyed for profit from timber, mining or otherwise. "You have ate my body. Which part that you have not eaten?" Mama Yosepha Alomang, an elderly woman of the Amungme tribe in the Indonesian province Papua, cried out to express the deeply felt connection with the land.[1] The land destroyed is by a US company Freeport McMoran (Freeport), through the exploitation of the biggest gold and copper mine in the world. From 1967 up until this very day, Freeport exploits the Grasberg mountain and its surroundings. In 2019 alone, Freeport's revenue was 3,232 million US dollars.[2] Deforestation, pollution of the rivers and change of current through sediment settlings have led to an ecological disaster. Moreover, the indigenous people have been killed and tortured for protesting against these crimes.

In fact, Freeport is seen as the root cause for the fact that Papuan people are being oppressed and denied a free exercise of their right of self-determination. After World War II, West Papua, being the Western half of the island New Guinea, became subject of a conflict between the new Republic Indonesia and The Netherlands. The Netherlands wished that West Papua would be an independent state. However, Indonesia seized control over West Papua in 1963. The promising revenues from a large gold mine played an important role. The contracts for the exploitation of the Grasberg between Freeport and the Indonesian government were signed in 1967 without any involvement of the Papuan people. In 1969 a sham referendum was held in which 1025 Papuans, representing 800,000 Papuans at that time, were forced

---

1 Mama Ypsepha Alomang, Markus Haluk, *You have ate my body. Which part that you have not eaten, An overview of Humanity Crimes and Ecological Destruction by Freeport McMoran Copper and Gold in Timika West Papua, Timika - West Papua,* (May 20, 2018).

2 FREEPORT -MCMORAN, *On Building Strength,* (2019), https://www.annualreports.com/HostedData/AnnualReports/PDF/NYSE_FCX_2019.pdf.

to vote in favor of annexation to Indonesia.[3] Since then, the Papuan people, outnumbered by newcomers from other parts of Indonesia through well-organized transmigration programs, are discriminated against and marginalized. Human rights organizations like Human Rights Watch, Amnesty International, and the International Coalition for Papua have reported gross human rights violations throughout the years.

Therefore, it is of great importance that international companies like Freeport, which commit these crimes, will be prosecuted and will be held accountable for their actions. In 2016 I had the great fortune of meeting Polly Higgins, lawyer of the Earth, who dedicated her life until her passing in April 2019 to establish ecocide as a crime at the International Criminal Court. Beatrice L. Hamilton will explain more about the crime of ecocide in her chapter. Criminalization is an important first step in reducing green crimes. In situations where perpetrators are aware of possible prosecution, they will start changing their behavior. This is the reason I am very motivated to be part of the Stop Ecocide Campaign and continue the work of Polly Higgins.

Hopefully, this book can guide lawyers and equip them to fight the battle for indigenous peoples in order to preserve the Earth and our future.

Leiden, November 22, 2020

Mrs. F.R. Schouten-Korwa, human rights lawyer

Ancillary activities:
Member of the Advisory Board of the Stop Ecocide Campaign
Pro bono counselor of Papua Support Foundation, The Netherlands
Member of the Preparatory Body of the Congress of Nations and States, scheduled for 2022

---

[3] P.J. Drooglever, *An Act of Free Choice*, BOOM, Amsterdam-The Netherlands, (2005), http://resources.huygens.knaw.nl/indonesischebetrekkingen1945-1969/DekolonisatieVanIndonesieEnHetZelfbeschikkingsrechtVanDePapoea/papers_pdf/summary_afc.

Introduction

Regina Menachery Paulose

International Criminal Law Attorney

Since the 1980s, the Narmada Bachao Andolan (NBA) movement has been raising awareness concerning the destructive impact hydropower dams continue to create in the Narmada River Valley in India.[1] In the 1990s, campaigns launched by the NBA focused on human rights violations hydropower projects created - forced displacement, ecosystem destruction, and the erasure of Peoples and cultures. Eventually, the World Bank, which planned to finance the construction of the Sardar Sarovar Dam, withdrew, citing human rights concerns.[2] While they are not given credit, it was movements like the NBA which inspired the creation of the World Bank Inspection Panel in 1993. The Inspection Panel allows communities to challenge World Bank projects in their localities.[3]

In 2013 I wrote an article that focused on the NBA's attempt to gain redress through the Indian legal system, specifically focusing on the 2000 Indian Supreme Court judgment *Narmada Bachao Andolan v. Union of India and others.*[4] Despite the subsequent judgments ordering people displaced by the dams to be rehabilitated (compensated and relocated) to date, the people of the Narmada Valley are still ignored.

---

[1] The Indian Express, *A short history of the Sardar Sarovar Dam on river Narmada,* (September 17, 2017), https://indianexpress.com/article/research/a-short-history-of-the-sardar-sarovar-dam-on-river-narmada-4847807/.

[2] *See* Narula, Smita, *The Story of Narmada Bachao Andolan: Human Rights in the Global Economy and the Struggle Against the World Bank* (December 12, 2008), in Human Rights Advocacy Stories, Deena R. Hurwitz, Margaret L. Satterthwaite, Douglas B. Ford, eds., West, 2009, NYU School of Law Public Law Research Paper No. 08-62, Available at SSRN: https://ssrn.com/abstract=1315459.

[3] *Id. See also* The World Bank, The Inspectional Panel, available at: https://www.inspectionpanel.org/.

[4] Regina M. Paulose, *Water politics: Narmada Bachao Andolan vs. Union of India and others,* LEX-Warrier, (January 5, 2013), http://www.journal.lex-warrier.in/?s=narmada+dam.

The NBA movement continues to operate with the same goals. As I write this, 500 victims, whose homes were submerged in water because of the Sardar Sarovar Dam on the Narmada River in Madhya Pradesh, staged a sit-in at the Grievance Redressal Authority's office.[5] The victims and survivors are *still* asking for various court orders to be fulfilled by state governments. Rohini Mohan eloquently reported, "[t]he Narmada valley is an unbearable spectre of displacement today, the losses largely hidden from the rest of the country. To witness the process of forced displacement is like watching the beginnings of a terminal illness. It's ugly, and you know it's going to get worse."[6]

I am mortified that after all this time, governments, despite national, regional, and international commitments to protect human rights *and* the environment, cannot create coherent policies that can do both. The Narmada Valley and other ecological disasters where people are raising awareness about damage and fighting for redress are the inspiration behind this volume.

This volume explores how green crimes fit within international criminal law. Green crimes have a harmful impact on humans, wildlife, and ecosystems. After reading this text, the reader may be pleasantly surprised to find that international criminal law is not the solution in some cases, but it may be a useful tool in other cases.

The movement to recognize green crimes within the international criminal law community has been slow but appears hopeful. In 2016 the International Criminal Court's Office of the Prosecutor issued a policy paper that mentioned the contours of green crimes. This policy paper is discussed throughout this volume in different contexts.[7] To date, there are no cases involving green crimes which have been prosecuted under the Rome Statute. Although, there are victims who have filed a communication with the Office of the Prosecutor alleging that illegal dispossession of their lands is taking place

---

[5] PTI, *Dam-affected persons stage protest in Indore,* (November 19, 2020), https://www.devdiscourse.com/article/politics/1314064-dam-affected-persons-stage-protest-in-indore.

[6] Rohini Mohan, *Madhya Pradesh villagers displaced by Sardar Sarovar Dam wait in tin sheds for new life,* THE HINDU, (October 6, 2019), https://www.thehindu.com/society/madhya-pradesh-villagers-displaced-by-sardar-sarovar-dam-wait-in-tin-sheds-for-new-life/article29596657.ece.

[7] "[T]he Office will give particular consideration to prosecuting Rome Statute crimes that are committed by means of, or that result in, inter alia, the destruction of the environment, the illegal exploitation of natural resources or the illegal dispossession of land." The Office of the Prosecutor, *Policy paper on case selection and prioritisation,* ¶41, INTERNATIONAL CRIMINAL COURT, (September 15, 2016), https://www.icc-cpi.int/items Documents/20160915_OTP-Policy_Case-Selection_Eng.pdf.

in Cambodia.[8] While there are many lessons that can be gleaned from this text, the biggest take away is that the international criminal law community must create space for *meaningful action* around environmental crimes so that environmental justice can take root. The current effort by a coordinating panel on the crime of ecocide to be included within the Rome Statute is a positive step to that creating space,[9] although it could have come sooner had the state parties to the Rome Statute listened to Polly Higgins.

The volume begins with the philosophical underpinnings of green crimes. What are green crimes, and who has the right to pursue redress? Has the time come for the environment to be given legal personality? What rights are there for nature? After this discussion, the volume moves on to an examination of how courts and tribunals are handling green crimes, the crime of ecocide, environmental crimes in conflict, and whether it is time for us to consider the idea of an international environmental criminal court. Finally, the volume examines ongoing and diverse situations in the status quo and questions whether international criminal law can respond to perceived environmental injustices. The cases presented in this volume explore discussions on cultural genocide, ecocide, and space pollution. Every discussion in this text likely deserves its own book. My goal in creating this volume was to start the conversation, and hopefully, it will blossom and continue in many iterations and forms by all those who are committed to stopping the wanton destruction of Peoples and the environment.

The authors who I asked to contribute to this volume are passionate about these topics. The authors have, where possible, worked together to discuss and consider each other's viewpoints. I imagine if all the authors were to sit in a room together, it is unlikely a consensus would be reached on how to address all the issues presented in this book, but I am sure that everyone would agree that more attention needs to be given to the idea of marrying certain green crimes with international criminal law. I wholeheartedly believe that these authors are the right people to light the way for that discussion to evolve into something deeper and, more importantly, actionable.

---

[8] FIDH AND GLOBAL DILIGENCE, *Questions and Answers: Crimes against Humanity in Cambodia from July 2002 until Present,* https://static1.squarespace.com/static/5bf447e7365f02310e09e592/t/5eb176ba9e5da97b82efe15f/1588688581121/qanda_cambodia_icc-2.pdf (last visited November 28, 2020).

[9] Owen Bowcott, *International lawyers draft plan to criminalise ecosystem destruction,* THE GUARDIAN, (November 30, 2020), https://www.theguardian.com/law/2020/nov/30/international-lawyers-draft-plan-to-criminalise-ecosystem-destruction.

With that in mind, I want to thank the contributors for indulging my invitation to participate. The cover for this text was drawn by my family members, Tess M. Paulose and Sagina Vadakal. I am grateful that both of them for their patience with me in describing what I had in mind and their artistic abilities. As with all art, it is best to leave the interpretation up to the person who views it, but I will note that the cover was inspired by the Dark Hedges in Northern Ireland.

Special thanks also go to Mrs. F.R. Schouten-Korwa, Anne Watanabe, Tim Franklin, Dr. Corinne Lewis, and Tamara Olsen for their valuable feedback. Pats on the head go to Bowser and Dolce, my four-legged friends who know about this book but will never read it. Finally, my appreciation goes out to the extremely responsive staff at Vernon Press for working closely with me despite the difficulties COVID 19 presented during the course of this publication.

I am constantly inspired by the determination of victims, survivors, defenders, and engaged citizens who mobilize for recognition of their rights and justice. I am also inspired by the lawyers who also work on these issues, which enables us to have discussions like the ones contained in this book. I look forward to hearing from those of you who work in this space and engaging in further dialogue on these issues.

List of Abbreviations

AU	African Union
EIA	Environmental Impact Assessment
EU	European Union
ECHR	European Convention of Human Rights
ECtHR	European Court of Human Rights
ICC	International Criminal Court
ICCPR	International Covenant on Civil and Political Rights
ICESCR	International Covenant on Economic, Social and Cultural Rights
ICJ	International Court of Justice
ICTR	International Criminal Tribunal for Rwanda
ICTY	International Criminal Tribunal for the Former Yugoslavia
ILC	International Law Commission
UN	United Nations
UNEP	United Nations Environmental Programme
UNGA	United Nations General Assembly
UNDRIP	United Nations Declaration on the Rights of Indigenous Peoples
UNGPBHR	United Nations Guiding Principles on Business and Human Rights
UNICRI	United Nations Interregional Crime and Justice Research Institute
UNSC	United Nations Security Council

Chapter 1

Green Criminology: A rights-based approach

Dr. Zoi Aliozi

International Human Rights Lawyer

Abstract: This chapter is an introduction to green criminology, enhanced by an analysis of the definition of green crimes. Green criminology involves the study of green crimes, which is the modern term for environmental crimes. Green crimes are an integral part of climate justice, and there is a vital need to illuminate this link and their role in global justice, in empowering environmental advocacy and in practically applying environmental ethics. Green crimes from a rights-based angle have strong links with human rights, with inter-generational equity and the rights of future generations, and these linkages reveal their critical connection to climate justice. The chapter is based on a multi-disciplinary methodology designed through the merging of law with philosophy and aims to describe: 'What is Green Criminology?'; 'What are Green Crimes?'; and 'How international law, criminal law, human rights, and eco-philosophy inform our conception of green crimes and fuel the development of green criminology?'. The author introduces the reader to the field of green criminology by looking into green crimes through a cosmopolitan rights-based perspective and a critical legal studies prism.

Keywords: Green crimes, green criminology, legal philosophy, environmental ethics, eco-philosophy, ecocide, ecocentrism, climate justice, animal rights, greenwashing, criminal law.

***

I. Introduction

Green Criminology is the study of environmental harms from a criminological perspective. It is the art of applying criminological thought to ecological issues and thus "greening"[1] criminology. In this distinct, multi-disciplinary, and colorful area of criminological studies, there is one protagonist that requires our full attention, and that is the special legal category of harms against nature, labeled as 'green crimes'.

Green criminology's whole ontological existence is based on studying, analyzing, and decoding this important legal category of crimes. To gain a better understanding of this area, consider the case of ecocide,[2] which has inspired a movement of citizens and international lawyers wanting to make 'harming the environment' a crime. A legally enforceable green crime of ecocide[3] that will criminalize the destruction of our world's ecosystems, is a much-needed addition to our international criminal justice system. The case of ecocide is a representative example of a unique green criminological term, describing mass-scale environmental harms, which are still waiting to be recognized, legitimized, and punished by law. It is essential to clarify that the harms falling within this classification must be caused by human action, while the fault must signify individual, governmental, or corporate[4] responsibility. Considering the enormous size of corporate environmental damages, it is more likely for ecocide to be applicable to corporate or governmental environmental damages, since it is in cases like that where the damages are so large and widespread that they could amount to ecocide. An international crime of ecocide, as an essential component of green criminology, can be beneficial and a great addition to criminal justice due to the important regulatory impact it can have on both individual and state responsibility, and ideally in achieving the much-needed balance between the anthropocentric and ecocentric theories[5] of environmental law for the survival of both humanity and nature. This is not a small matter, and any discussion about the justifications that can fuel the evolution of this body of

---

[1] *See* Matthew Hall et al., eds. GREENING CRIMINOLOGY IN THE 21ST CENTURY, London: Routledge, (2017).

[2] Mark Allan Gray, *The International Crime of Ecocide*, CALIFORNIA WESTERN INTERNATIONAL LAW JOURNAL 215, (1996).

[3] Anastacia Greene, *The Campaign to Make Ecocide an International Crime: Quixotic Quest or Moral Imperative?* FORDHAM ENVIRONMENTAL LAW JOURNAL, Vol. 30, No. 3, (2019).

[4] Consider that "[o]ver half of global industrial emissions since human induced climate change was officially recognized can be traced to just 25 corporate and state producing entities." *See* THE CDP CARBON MAJORS REPORT, at 8, (2017), available at: https://www.cdp.net/en/articles/media/new-report-shows-just-100-companies-are-source-of-over-70-of-emissions.

[5] Ronald E. Purser et al., *Limits to Anthropocentrism: Toward an Ecocentric Organization Paradigm?* ACADEMY OF MANAGEMENT REVIEW, 20(4) at 1053-89, (1995).

law belongs to a different era. Wasting words in debating whether strong justifications exist to protect the environment from anthropogenic criminal damages legally is at least unnecessary; since, if there is one thing that the whole international community can agree on, it is the urgent need to jointly take action to protect our home planet, which means that there is a great opportunity for the global justice system to fulfill its promise of universal justice and do so through the complete –and not selective — criminalization of environmental harms. Indeed, taking action to save our planet and ensure the sustainability of our environment depends deeply on the criminalization of such environmental harms and the establishment of a genuinely green economy that will safeguard future living conditions, the rights of future generations, and the sustainability of our home planet.

Nonetheless, it should be made clear that ecocide is not a recognized green crime in today's international legal order. Ecocide is not prescribed by law, just like many other criminal harms to nature that are not legally codified as green crimes. The case of ecocide is a useful case-study for understanding green criminology and green crime challenges. For instance, although ecocide is not acknowledged by law, it does not mean that the law is turning a blind eye to this kind of environmental harm. It is reassuring, to a certain degree, to know that there is one provision in the Rome Statute of the ICC, which makes it a crime to damage the environment. Article 8(2)(b)(iv) makes it a crime to: "Intentionally launch an attack in the knowledge that such attack will cause... widespread, long-term and severe damage to the natural environment..." Due to its ecocentricity, this Article signifies an important breakthrough in international law.[6] It may seem plausible to argue at this point that ecocide is implicitly included –between the lines— in this legal prohibition since it is a "widespread, long-term and severe damage to the natural environment" that is producing ecocide. Unquestionably, there is a great need for a legal definition of 'ecocide' as a possible international crime that could carry as much legal value and force as war crimes, genocide, and crimes against humanity. As a term and concept, Ecocide is representative of the challenges surrounding the application of green crimes and the paradoxes that stream from linguistics to inform the application of legal theories with "voiceless victims,"[7] or seemingly "victimless crimes."[8]

---

[6] Kevin J. Heller and Jessica C. Lawrence, *The Limits of Article 8(2)(b)(iv) of the Rome Statute, the First Ecocentric Environmental War Crime.* GEORGETOWN INTERNATIONAL ENVIRONMENTAL LAW REVIEW (GIELR), Vol. 20, (2007).

[7] Rob White, *Green Victimology and Non-Human Victims,* INTERNATIONAL REVIEW OF VICTIMOLOGY, 24(2) at 239-55, (2008).

Consider, for example, that the claim to protect the rights of future generations also implies that the criminal activities that are punishable and described by law today *de jure* can have long-term effects and harm the environment in future instances, which makes the allocation of damages and blame a rather complicated enterprise. On the same train of thought go the arguments for the invisibility of damages and thus the problem of constituting the *actus reus* and *mens rea* of a green crime, which is the most important criminal legal test in proving the criminality of a conduct and the justification for the moral condemnation and ultimately of the criminal punishment. In simple terms, it is these two elements of criminal law's theory, the *actus reus* and the *mens rea* (referring to the guilty act and the guilty mind), that make or break a crime. Keep in mind that these two elements serve as the test used by judges in deciding whether a conduct can be tried as a crime. The debates about the invisibility of harms, victimless crimes, and all these unregulated territories that may blow our legal minds to think about regulating as green crimes (e.g., agriculture, animal exploitation, natural resources, fishing, outer space, to name but a few) require a pathbreaking legal attitude and a disconnection from the comfort zone that anthropocentrism provides to the global legal order.

Green crimes are prescribed and punished by law; however, not every possible act that can harm the environment is prohibited and punished as a green crime. Arguably, it may be impossible in certain cases to connect the *actus reus* of a green crime to the damages caused or to the victim's suffering. It should be highlighted that until the day international law views and deals with 'crimes against the environment' as carrying equal value, severity and urgency as 'crimes against humanity', we will still have a long road to cover in the development of green criminology, green crimes, and climate justice. In our attempt to grasp the complexities of green criminology and green crimes, it can be useful to consider the 'speciesism'[9] and 'anthropocentrism'[10] that block the development of this body of law, since these topics are essential in environmental ethics that inform the development of the relevant law and

---

[8] *See* Intelligence Project on Environmental Crime, *Report on Environmental Crime in Europe*, EnviCrimeNet, The Hague, (Feb. 20, 2015), available at: http://www.envicrimenet.eu/images/docs/ipec_report_on_environmental_crime_in_europe.pdf (last visited October 30, 2020).

[9] Onora O'Neill, *Environmental Values, Anthropocentrism and Speciesism*, ENVIRONMENTAL VALUES, 6(2) at 127-42, (1997).

[10] Kyle Burchett, *Anthropocentrism as Environmental Ethic.* 10.13023/ETD.2016.259, THESES AND DISSERTATIONS—PHILOSOPHY, Dec. 2016, available at: https://uknowledge.uky.edu/philosophy_etds/12 (last visited March 15, 2020).

direct the moral compass of society. Similarly, there is utility in underlining the essential truth about green crimes and green criminology, and that is that green crimes are about the environmental harms that are caused by human-related activity or action. We are not concerned with environmental catastrophes in general, but only with the anthropogenic damages that could be classified as green crimes. Just like climate justice is about the anthropogenic harms that contribute to climate change and not about the natural changes in the environment, analogously, green crimes are about the criminal human actions that cause criminal damages to nature. According to this simple definition of green crimes, any harm against the environment caused by human action with the necessary intention could theoretically be classified as a crime against the environment, an environmental crime, or a green crime.

This chapter starts with asking what green criminology is, and through a legal and philosophical prism, looks into the state of green crimes. The main discussion on green criminology and anthropogenic environmental damages is facilitated through the methodological support and epistemological guidance of the legal theories behind criminal law, international law, human rights, and their inter-connection to environmental ethics. This introduction to green criminology will discuss the main debates that move change in environmental justice. In the essence of these legal developments lie the justifications provided by climate justice, inter-generational equity, and the rights of future generations, as well as the moral and legal duty to protect the environment. As an inter-disciplinary rights-based approach to green criminology, it is about law, crime, sociology, philosophy, ethics, and the morality of law in relation to environmental harms. Through the methodological support of law and philosophy, the author's main aspiration is to explain in a descriptive manner: 'What green criminology is;' balanced by an attempt to define green crimes and their relationship to criminal law.

In this rights-based approach, the reader will be introduced to the main debates around this field of criminal studies and will be presented to the relevant international law through a critical legal study's lens to green criminology.

II. Green Criminology

Green criminology studies the concepts of crimes, wrongdoings, damages, offenses, harms, and injurious behaviors against the environment and recently began to examine how organized societies, including corporations and states, are committing environmental crimes. Criminology recognizes the criminally harmful impact of humans on the environment and analyzes the ways law enforcement agencies and the judiciary bodies evaluate these damages to nature and apply criminal sanctions to the wrongdoers.[11] What is of pivotal importance to understand at this point is that green crime does not affect only the land, water, air; it also affects the health of humans, including children and the health of future generations, so it enters in the realm of inter-generational equity, human rights, and climate justice. Green criminology is a fairly new branch of criminology, as the "term came into existence in the 1990s."[12]

So, the term, as we know it, was born only some decades ago, and it has been used by different academic disciplines —and not just law— to denote mainly criminal activities that harm the environment, human and non-human components of our ecosystems. There is still a great need for advanced criminological research and clearer legal rules with enforceability in a court of law because the legal world has a long way to go and a lot of work to do for ensuring that the criminalization of all relevant human activities that result in environmental harms are legally codified through positive law. Green criminology is not as developed as the criminology of terrorism, for example, but on the bright side, environmental criminology is steadily and rapidly progressing reciprocally at the national and international levels. Criminology, by definition, is an integral part of the global criminal justice project both in the theoretical and practical arenas.

A simple etymological examination and analysis of the term can be proven to be very effective in getting introduced to this field of crime studies. For example, 'crimino-*logy*' is a polysynthetic term comprised of two synthetic words: (a) crimino, and (b) logy. It derives from (a) 'crimen' which in Latin meant "accusation" "to be judged", and (b) the Ancient Greek word 'logos' meaning: "word, reason, language". Etymologically then, crimino-logy is the study of crime and the motivations behind criminal behavior. Green criminology is the branch of criminology that studies environmentally-related crime and the intentions of the criminal minds. It is important to understand that the scope and systematic methodologies that green criminology can adopt may vary since they depend on the specific disciplines the criminologists are choosing to employ and their respective fields of expertise. This means that green criminology can be employed by various disciplines, either in a multi-disciplinary scheme or for specific research questions that could break new

---

[11] Rob White, *Environmental Issues and the Criminological Imagination*, THEORETICAL CRIMINOLOGY, 7(4) at 483-506, (2003).

[12] Michael Lynch, *The Greening of Criminology: a Perspective on the 1990s*, THE CRITICAL CRIMINOLOGIST 2(3) at 1–4, (1990).

scientific ground or create new research styles. It is critical to highlight the essential role that linguistics and language play in jurisprudence and law, from the terminological formation and grammatical constructions codifying green crimes to the practical application of criminal law.

Criminology is an interdisciplinary field of study, which can be found in both the behavioral and social sciences. The field is being developed predominantly upon the research of lawyers, sociologists, psychologists, philosophers, psychiatrists, biologists, anthropologists and as in our case, scholars of law, academia, civil society, and so on, and so forth. In examining and presenting what green criminology is all about in a descriptive manner, this critique will seek answers from eco-philosophy, environmental ethics, human rights, and social values. In this inter-disciplinary methodological journey, there is one underlying question that informs the flow of the information and relevant rights-based analysis. This question is: 'what is of value in law and society?' To anticipate the answer, one needs to take a look at the way human society is treating animals and the disregard for their right to life. By looking at the value of an animal's life and the ways in which law values nature, a green criminologist can reach deeper conclusions and examine through a new lens the legal prohibitions relevant to environmental harms, or the lack of criminal legal codification of relevant green crimes, due to the problematic anthropocentric tradition of the lawmaking process. There is *prima facie* evidence that criminal exploitation of the world's natural resources affects our everyday lives, from the water we drink to the air we breathe. We know well today that natural resources are finite, which makes the regulation of the exploitation of nature necessary and provides for an urgent justification for developing the relevant legal body since it is beyond debate that we must combat environmental crimes for the present and future generations and the survival of our planet. According to Interpol, which has been fighting green crimes for the last decade, "environmental crime has a direct impact on climate change, harms the livelihoods of millions of people, results in forced migration and can trigger the spread of animal-to-human viruses (zoonotic diseases)."[13] This is a perfect time and point to connect green crime with climate justice since the prosecution of green crimes is a necessary condition for ensuring climate justice.

---

[13] See INTERPOL, *Interpol marks a decade of tackling serious organized environmental crime*, https://www.interpol.int/News-and-Events/News/2020/INTERPOL-marks-a-decade-of-tackling-serious-organized-environmental-crime (last visited November 1, 2020).

Climate justice[14] is about dealing with environmental harms and damages from a legal and ethical perspective while ensuring that human rights claims are included, safeguarded, and fully protected in this process. Criminal law is an integral part of climate justice since it is the body of law that deals with crime and punishment. Although criminalization of a certain act does not guarantee the decline of criminal activities due to the deterrent effect of punishment, however, the deterrent effect as a justification for criminal punishment is still used in criminal justice reform and lawmaking;[15] this view is based on the theory that it is the knowledge of possible punishment that acts as a preventive of wrongdoing that causes damages. It is on this fact that we can distill the first justification for the necessity to empower the legal enforceability of green crimes and ensure the deterrence and punishment of environmental offenses.

Law as a human-made creation tries to protect our general safety mainly from anthropogenic harms, and in doing so, needs to regulate human-to-human conduct. This simplified view of our legal systems is representative of the anthropocentrism of law (or anthropo-nomo-centrism to be more precise)[16], which awards more value to the anthropo (Greek for human) and places the human in the center of the legal entitlement. This can be said to be one of the main reasons that the international legal community and the UN have been unable to create a legally binding agreement protecting the environment. The ideal future would include a special court for the environment, able to hear legal questions that require special considerations and attention while offering a *de jure* protection to the environment, addressing climate justice, and providing for the full process of law to be carried out up to the stage of punishment for environmental harms and green crimes.

---

14 Zoi Aliozi, *Climate Justice: Climate Change and Human Rights,* in Denialism And Human Rights, Roland Moerland et al., eds., at 403, (2016).

15 *See* Herbert Lionel, et. al, Punishment and Responsibility: Essays in the Philosophy of Law, 2nd Edition, Oxford University Press, USA, (2008).

16 Anthropo-nomo-centrism, trans: Anthropo=human, nomo=law, centrism; can be understood in reference to 'Logocentrism' and 'Logonomocentrism'. *See* Jacques Derrida, OF GRAMMATOLOGY, G. Spivak trans., Baltimore, The J.H. University Press, (1974.) Under the light that 'Logo-nomo-centrism,' as a theory, provides the "logos" (words) is what is of importance for law (Greek for law: Nomo); so, the necessity to have meaningful words that reflect the whole spectrum of any given phenomenon in need of a legal regulation is celebrated within this term. The central power is invested in "logos," in language, since law is essentially connected to language and constructed within the terms of a logocentric tradition. *See* Costas Douzinas, et. al, POSTMODERN JURISPRUDENCE: THE LAW OF TEXTS IN THE TEXTS OF THE LAW, London: Routledge, at 9, (1991).

Green criminology concentrates on green crimes, and it is an interdisciplinary field of legal research that is an integral part of the international criminal justice project. In this descriptive introduction of green criminology, accompanied by an analysis of the available legal definition of green crimes and an assessment of their value for criminal law, we will be able to take a glimpse at the essence of this field and thus achieve a deeper understanding of the issues at stake.

Green criminology is the study of green crime from a social perspective, including examining who commits crimes, why they commit them, their impact, and how to prevent them. In simple terms, it is the systematic and methodical study of law-making, law-breaking, and law enforcing. Criminology is a self-explanatory term. Language in science is in many ways used as a code, just like in law and the legal codification of concepts of law through language and linguistics; and let us not forget that lawmakers use language to make law,[17] so language is one of the integral parts of the law and one of its most useful and important tools.

Criminology, although a newly recognized term, is rooted in a long intellectual history of ideas and early thinking about crime and punishment. Early thinking about crime and punishment goes as back as the first philosophers in ancient Greece, with Aristotle, who maintained that societal responses to crime could be preventive or repressive. In his *Nicomachean Ethics*, Aristotle defined crime as the act of free will, stimulated by desire. Thus, he argued that children, idiots, the mentally ill, and individuals in a state of ecstasy should not be held responsible for criminal actions. Aristotle dealt with what today we call *mens rea* and stated that if there is no "malice aforethought"[18] or immoral calculated intentions to harm and commit the crime, then the perpetrator should not be held a criminal. At this point, it will be useful to consider Plato's (429–347 B.C.) analysis of the basis of law, which argued that what is fundamental and essential is the prevailing social morality rather than the laws of the gods.[19] So, the idea of dealing with crime from a sociological perspective is very well rooted in philosophy, and it is a recipe that seems to work. Green criminology, in essence, is about the study of crime through a sociological prism, and these great thinkers' body of work illustrates in the best possible way; the long intellectual tradition that informed the

---

[17] *See* Andrei Marmor and Scott Soames, *PHILOSOPHICAL FOUNDATIONS OF LANGUAGE IN THE LAW*, Oxford: Oxford University Press, (2011).

[18] Aristotle, NICOMACHEAN ETHICS, Kitchener, Ont, Batoche Books at 121, (1999).

[19] Plato, BOOK I, 344C. PLATO REPUBLIC. Indianapolis: Hackett, (2004).

creation of green criminology and still supports today the further development of the field.

III. Green Crimes

Green crimes include local and global damages like pollution, ecological destruction, poaching and wide-ranging harms such as anthropogenic climate change and species loss. It is important to take a step back and see that the numerous active victims of this special category of crimes include all species, human and non-human animals, but also the environment at large. The question of victimology in green crimes is one that poses some thought-provoking questions. Green crimes are crimes committed against the environment, but this broad definition can be better understood if we consider some specific paradigms of green crimes, such as air pollution, water pollution, deforestation, species decline, and the dumping of hazardous waste. The most common green crimes include animal cruelty and abuse, wild animal trafficking, electronic waste mismanagement, finning, dumping in rivers, illegal fishing, illegal logging and trade in timber.

Green crime is defined as "an act that is destructive to the environment and that has been criminalized by statute."[20] Environmental crimes cover acts that violate national or international law and cause significant harm or risk to the environment and human health. This definitional approach was provided by the European Commission who adopted a proposal for a directive aiming to ensure the protection of the environment through criminal law.[21] Other attempts to define environmental crimes, worthy of mentioning, include Europol's[22] definition of environmental crimes, which states that "[e]nvironmental crime covers the gamut of activities that breach environmental legislation and cause significant harm or risk to the environment, human health, or both."

A wider viewpoint is offered by Interpol's[23] definition of environmental crimes, which opens the frame from the single criminal act of the individual

---

[20] *See* MERRIAM-WEBSTER LEGAL DICTIONARY, *environmental crime*, https://www.merriam-webster.com/legal/environmental%20crime (last visited 24 November 2020).

[21] Directive 2008/99/EC on the Protection of the Environment Through Criminal Law was formally adopted by the EU on October 24, 2008 and had to be transposed by EU Member States by December 2010.

[22] EUROPOL, *Environmental Crime*, https://www.europol.europa.eu/crime-areas-and-trends/crime-areas/environmental-crime (last visited February 10, 2020).

[23] INTERPOL, *Environmental Crime*, https://www.interpol.int/en/Crimes/Environmental-crime (Last visited February 10, 2020).

offender to the real transnational dimensions of this category of crimes. Interpol's designation of environmental crimes concentrates on the fact that criminal exploitation of the world's natural resources affects our everyday lives. Interpol emphasizes that all forms of environmental crime are organized and global in nature, and as such, require an equally organized and global response. Interpol's view of environmental crime focuses on the essential fact that green crime is no different from traditional organized crime. The same routes used to smuggle environmentally sensitive products across countries are used to traffic people, weapons, and drugs.

On the same train of thought is the UNICRI, who considers that environmental crime is strongly "linked with other forms of crime, and is a serious and growing danger for development, global stability and international security."[24]

Green crime refers to a violation of environmental law that was created to protect the environment.

Generally speaking, green crimes signify forbidden acts that can establish a crime in a court of law and directly cause environmental damage, while it is noteworthy that they are also discussed as 'crimes against the environment.'[25] In theory, all wrongdoings in violation of environmental laws could classify as green crimes; however international bodies such as the UNICRI, G8, Interpol, EU, and the UNEP have recognized some specific offenses that originate from the environmental crime classification. These well recognized green crimes include activities like the dumping of industrial wastes into water bodies, illicit trade in hazardous waste in contravention of the 1989 Basel Convention on the Control of Transboundary Movement of Hazardous Wastes and Other Wastes and their Disposal[26] and Illegal fishing, which is in breach of laws and rules of various national, regional, and international fisheries regulations. Well recognized and punishable green crimes include dealing with endangered species, which is in violation of the Convention on International Trade in Endangered Species of Fauna and Flora (CITES); smuggling of Ozone-depleting substances, which is in contravention to the 1987 Montreal Protocol on Substances that Deplete the Ozone Layer; and illegal logging and trade in violation of the wildlife laws.

---

[24] UNICRI, *Environmental Crimes*, http://www.unicri.it/topics/environmental (last visited March 12, 2020).

[25] Neil Hawke, *Crimes against the Environment*, ANGLO-AMERICAN LAW REVIEW, 16(1) at 90-96, (1987).

[26] THE CONVENTION ON THE CONTROL OF TRANSBOUNDARY MOVEMENT OF HAZARDOUS WASTES AND THEIR DISPOSAL, 1673 U.N.T.S. 126, (March 22, 1989).

It is interesting to note that over the past decades, "the discovery of severe environmental damage caused by unregulated waste has become a widespread concern in America."[27] Green crime as a state-corporate offense has been developing strongly on the litigation front both nationally and internationally. The spring of climate justice trials around the world concerning climate change and natural catastrophes caused by corporate negligence is noteworthy. "More recently, green criminologists, have begun to examine the connection between genocide and ecocide, or how the human destruction of ecosystems and people are inter-related, and reflect features of state-corporate crime."[28] The environmental pollution and health risks caused by this have been a common topic in relevant environmental lawsuits and caselaw.[29] The corporate liability issues that arise from this type of green crime have also brought to light attempts from the industry to 'greenwash' their harmful kind of business. 'Greenwashing' refers to a company spending more time, money and resources on marketing themselves as eco-friendly than on actually minimizing their environmental impact and avoid environmental damages. This is another important area where green criminology has a crucial role in highlighting these newly emerging attempts to change the narrative and dislocate or disassociate the criminal blame from the wrongdoer's business activities. The employment of the word green in the case of greenwashing has a negative connotation and rather sarcastic utility; however, it is interesting to reflect on the multi-dimensional 'meaning of green'[30] since it is central in our discussion and clarify that green is meant to represent the environment and all that the fauna and flora it entails.

What do all these human-inflicted harms to the environment have in common, apart from the criminal damage and harm to nature caused by human action and activities? All these crimes are punishable because they have been recognized and codified by law. So, in order for a green crime to be

---

[27] Kenneth A. Hodson et al. *The Prosecution of Corporations and Corporate Officers for Environmental Crimes: Limiting One's Exposure for Environmental Criminal Liability*, 34 AMUZ. L. REV. 553, (1992).

[28] *See* Michael J. Lynch et al., eds. *Green Criminology and State-Corporate Crime: The Ecocide-Genocide Nexus with Examples from Nigeria*, JOURNAL OF GENOCIDE RESEARCH, (2020).

[29] As an example of the litigation that is occurring many law schools have resources highlighting environmental cases. One example can be found here: PACE LAW SCHOOL, *Environmental Crimes: Federal and State Cases*, https://libraryguides.law.pace.edu/c.php?g=319401&p=2134065 (last visited May 1, 2020).

[30] *See* Michael Lynch and Paul Stretesky, *The Meaning of Green: Contrasting Criminological Perspectives*. THEORETICAL CRIMINOLOGY 7. 217-238, (2003).

punishable by law, it needs to be treated by the law, codified through legal language and then explicitly forbidden by law. The logical question that arises is what happens if a harmful conduct to the environment is not prescribed by law; is it not possible to be tried and punished as in any other unlawful criminal act? Well, in law, things are not always black or white, sometimes things are green. For example, it is useful for the purposes of this introduction to green crimes to consider that the lawmaking power of our organized societies does not stop in the parliament, or the court of law, since there is also a role for society and its citizens in affecting the lawmaking process by pushing for positive legal change, for instance, through the moral condemnation of offensive wrongdoings that harm our ecosystems, and by utilizing all the methods and tools that environmental advocacy has to offer.

Observe, for example, how criminal law follows the commands of society in developing its rules with respect to society's morality. In Greece, for instance, during 2020, the Greek law 4039/2012[31] received a practical boost and upgrade if you like, in the criminal justice system, since the crime of animal cruelty and abuse became a felony with harsher punishment and greater sentencing. What is interesting for our analysis, is to look at two specific animal cruelty cases in the country; since after these two horrific cases of criminal animal abuse, Greece moved to make animal cruelty a felony carrying a minimum of 10 years imprisonment. As pointed out, this upgrade of the criminal sanctions for animal abuse was prioritized by the government due to many shocking animal abuse cases committed in the country. In one case, a dog was hanged and brutally tortured in front of the house he was living in and was brutally abused by his own caretaker, while the neighbors turned a blind eye to the screams and suffering of the animal; there is a common sense in this European society that an animal's life has less value than a human's, and hence, it is morally tolerable to do with them as you wish if you are their owner, which is also indicative of how the normalization of wrongdoings for achieving other utilitarian ends happens in our societies.

Similarly, to the customs of a society that become the law of a country, if we reverse the roles, we can observe that the criminalization of certain actions can affect the moral systems of a society in such a way as to be compatible and in line with the legal prohibitions. Law and society are inter-connected and inter-dependent, and this case demonstrates this in a rather revealing way. What the author means by that example can be understood by looking at

---

[31] *See* Law 4039/2012: For dominant and stray pets and the protection of animals from exploitation or use for profit, https://www.e-nomothesia.gr/kat-zoa-suntrophias-prostasia-zoon/n-4039-2012.html (last visited November 1, 2020).

another wide-spread green crime committed in different parts of Greece almost every day; the mass killings of stray animals in the city centers of the country through food-based poisoned baits.

This green crime is being observed in every part of the country throughout the whole year; however, only in recent years, we have seen some cases reaching the stage of sentencing and punishment for the wrongdoers, which is another contributory factor for these green crimes to continue being committed with society's tolerance as an accomplice. So, to make it easier to understand, the possibility of a dog eating poison that someone intentionally placed on the street, in order to kill the stray animals who are plenty in the Greek streets and form dangerous herds, and in that way "clean" the roads from these unwanted, by some living beings, is an everyday threat for any animal that walks on the asphalt streets of this organized European society. The fact that this outrageous and sinister green crime goes unpunished is because the law was not as strong as to enforce these rules, the law enforcement is not trained to enforce these regulations, and the justice system lacks the necessary resources to prioritize these prosecutions, with the result being, for years, numbers of criminals going unpunished and continuing to commit green crimes by criminally targeting vulnerable, innocent animals that happen to live in their neighborhoods. For this discussion, we should not miss acknowledging the important role of education and animal rights advocacy, which by raising awareness of these issues can turn society's tolerance for these green crimes into moral condemnation, and consequently mobilize the legal machine for restoring justice by prosecuting and punishing these green criminals. The publicity that these 2020 Greek cases received due to social media, and the mobilization that animal rights groups around the country promoted, left the government no choice but to revamp the justice system in a way as to punish the criminals, ensure the law is enforced, and restore justice as an example to the rest of society, sending the message that animal abuse is a crime.

However, another case of animal cruelty took place in a short period of time in another part of Greece, where a man attacked a dog with a knife and almost took its life. Again, the united voices of civil society and animal rights organizations, in combination with the previous outrageous crime of animal abuse, contributed to the relevant Ministry of Greece developing the necessary bill and legal supplements to quickly and efficiently upgrade the law in such a way as to add severity in the punishment and sentencing stages of the criminal procedure to animal cruelty and abuse.

This is a demonstration of how laws change to reflect society's morality. This is why civil society and citizens share part of the duty through their individual responsibility to protect our planet and take climate action. However, the real responsibility lies with the state who is the legitimate protector of human rights. International law places the obligation to protect human rights on states, while the obligation to fulfill this requires that states take positive and in line with the values supporting human rights action to facilitate the gratification of human rights. The state's duty to act, be prepared for crises, and protect the environment through policies and green crime prosecutions are all interlinked with the human rights project and ultimately with climate justice. As discussed above, green crimes refer to harms against the environment caused by human action. It should not be difficult to understand that the environment as a whole becomes a legal person who is entitled to legal protection. Green crimes are important components of climate justice and ensuring that human rights with the rule of law are the primary consideration when assessing, evaluating, and regulating human society's contact with our ecosystem.

On the same train of thought, we need to bring into the scene the fact that climate justice needs powerful laws that can ensure that human rights, animal rights, the rights of nature, the rule of law and justice are served equally and efficiently. Numerous green crimes are being committed and will never have their day in court. Hundreds of thousands of crimes go unreported, and countless harms are committed by humans who will never be held accountable nor punished for their wrongdoings. As a preliminary clarification, we need to understand that green crimes, in this instance, refer to wrongdoings that are forbidden by law, which means that if an action is not codified by law, then it cannot be classified as a green crime. It is the role of green criminology to create the necessary legal research that will require the creation of new legal rules and will expand the list of green crimes. It is equally important to understand that most human activity linked to agriculture, livestock, or any business that is making a profit by using the planet's resources and by using animals as tools; will not be able to continue doing so if complete protection of the rights of animals and the environment is constitutionally established in the future.

In summary, green crimes refer to crimes committed against the environment, and the investigation of green crime is the focus of "green criminologists." According to Interpol, "criminal exploitation of the world's natural resources affects our everyday lives, from the food we eat to the air we breathe."[32] It is important to stress that green crimes refer to environmental harms. For the purpose of this introduction, green crimes and environmental crimes will mean the same thing and will be used interchangeably to refer to

---

[32] INTERPOL, *supra* note 23.

and denote the same type of crimes and harms. It is worth highlighting that not every harm can be classified as a crime according to criminal law's theory, since there is the prerequisite of proving the necessary *actus reus* and *mens rea* of the alleged crime in a court of law, as well as the main elements that constitute a crime like causation, concurrence, harm, and attendant circumstances.[33]

Pragmatically speaking, green crimes are crimes that are coded through criminal law, and if one action is not prescribed by law, criminal justice is unable to name the charge and activate all the legal and procedural tools available in criminal hearings. From a legal perspective, there can be no enforceability of these legal claims, nor strong legal protection. Legal scholarship requires certain methodological systems and rules to be reliable and religiously followed. That brings the question of the choice of "green" in the term green criminology, which some may argue makes the term sound "lighter" or less serious than it should. However, on the other side of the coin, the counter-arguments hold that the word "green" makes this category separate, distinct and recognizable; it is a shorter and all-inclusive term. So, one fundamental issue that requires clarification is the ambiguous definition of "green." Green is used in an inclusive manner and is meant to include the environment as a whole, with all the components that make up nature included, like human and non-human animals, equally valued. Green crimes refer to human-caused harms to the environment, or simply put, crimes damaging the environment. Interestingly the focus of international criminal justice is mainly on transnational environmental crimes since it is an industry worth billions.

IV. International Law

Green crime as a global challenge requires a global response. An organized industry that functions within transnational organized criminal networks that commit environmental crimes is estimated to worth up to billions a year[34] , with wildlife crime, for example, coming in shortly after illicit activities like illegal drugs or human and weapons trafficking, which are traditionally the most profitable criminal activities.

Take a look at these numbers to understand the size of the "green crime" organized industry: "wildlife (estimated annual value: USD 7.8 to 10 billion);

---

33 INTERNATIONAL CRIMINAL COURT, *Elements of Crimes*, (2011), https://www.icc-cpi.int/NR/rdonlyres/336923D8-A6AD-40EC-AD7B-45BF9DE73D56/0/ElementsOfCrimesEng.pdf.

34 Jeremy Haken, *Transnational Crime in The Developing World*, GLOBAL FINANCIAL INTEGRITY at 56, (2011).

timber (estimated annual value: USD 7 billion); fish (estimated annual value: USD 4.2 to 9.5 billion)."[35] The rise of green crime has brought these issues to the foreground as top priorities in governmental agendas around the globe. Threats and wrongdoing are being treated by lawmakers as serious international crimes of great harmful impact to the environment and human life. An illustrative example is how Interpol and Europol admit the connection of green crime and transnational organized crime with international terrorism. According to Interpol, "the exploitation of natural resources by criminal networks, often in conflict areas, poses a threat to peace and security."[36]

The EU included environmental crime as an offense under the 6th EU Anti-Money Laundering Directive[37] , while it is hopeful to see that the new Financial Action Task Force (FATF)[38] priorities for 2020 are focused on the illegal wildlife trade. Despite the increased focus on green crime, the sentences and punishment aimed at controlling these crimes are much less than those linked to anti-money laundering and terrorism.

These inconsistencies pose the urgent need to re-evaluate the reach of international criminal law and re-assess the existing judicial and implementation regimes by considering the harm caused by these crimes, the violations of human rights, and the risk they present for future generations. The effective enforcement of green crimes requires a well-functioning and efficient prosecution service and an independent judiciary. This will ensure that offenders are kept accountable for their actions, and the rights of all stakeholders are protected. Judicial responses to green crimes can broadly be classified into five recognized categories. Not every crime that can satisfy the requirements for being classified as green crime enjoys the protection of the international criminal law; however, in most cases, there are national laws in place to prosecute these offenses through different legal routes. The

---

[35] *Id.*

[36] INTERPOL-UN ENVIRONMENT REPORT, *Environmental Crime Threatening Peace and Security, (December 8, 2016),* https://www.interpol.int/en/News-and-Events/News/2016/Environmental-crime-threatening-peace-and-security-finds-new-INTERPOL-UN-Environment-report.

[37] EUR-LEX, *Directive (EU) 2018/1673 of the European Parliament and of the Council of 23 October 2018 on combating money laundering by criminal law,* https://eur-lex.europa.eu/legal-content/EN/TXT/?uri=uriserv:OJ.L_.2018.284.01.0022.01.ENG (last visited October 14, 2020).

[38] FINANCIAL ACTION TASK FORCE, *Priorities for the Financial Action Task Force (FATF) under German Presidency,* https://www.fatf-gafi.org/media/fatf/documents/German-Presidency-Priorities.pdf (last visited May 26, 2020).

magnitude of the international organized green crime "cartels" demands a special mention and treatment by international law.

The international agreements between states play an important complementary role in the whole climate justice project, and their utility cannot be emphasized enough. For example, CITES has been a priceless tool in bringing together almost the entire global community in an attempt to protect endangered species by restricting trade. It is observable that the rules and language employed in international law dealing with green crimes are better associated with trade offenses and the super profitable transnational organized crime, which should be noted that it also depends on the market's demands. All these factors are relevant in a sociological examination of the green-related criminal activities; however, it cannot serve as an inclusive legal definition because it limits the reach of the law in specific offenses while overseeing or renders invisible other harms that should be addressed for the further development of green crimes. By examining the relevant green crimes case law and international legal rules pertaining to this area of criminal conduct, one can observe that the crimes that enjoy complete and strong protection from the criminal justice system are mainly connected to transnational organized crime, and we are talking about activities that are part of an organized industry worth of billions according to relevant research from the UN, Interpol, and the EU. It seems that it has been more effective to push for legal change when powerful economic interests are affected in our capitalist world.

The lack of political will, in combination with the huge economic interests involved, has proven to be more effective than the pleas of legal scholars and activists for preventing these types of harms and criminal wrongdoings. This could partly explain the reasons for having only specific green crimes being recognized, prohibited, and punished by law. The more profitable businesses at the current economic system have to do with waste management, pollution crimes, emission levels, and other mass global crimes that recent climate change conferences and caselaw have identified. It is worth mentioning that the UN's work should not be under-estimated in light of the system's failings to ensure the basic goals of its mandate due to its susceptibility to political factors. It is easy to critique the inadequacies of the United Nations system when it comes to restoring criminal justice; however, the supplementary role of all these climate actions reflects back on the law-making process of criminal law and informs the further development of criminal justice. Environmental concerns belong at the top of the priorities list of every governmental agenda, while they currently enjoy unprecedented publicity through the online world and civil society's environmental advocacy, while it is fair to acknowledge that climate change, environmental protection, and climate justice remains a sizzling topic of deep legal, philosophical, political, and public debates.

This is why environmental law is broadly acknowledged as the rapidly developing area of global jurisprudence and international law. In addition, with the rise of environmental agreements and policies, the greening of international law has created a flourishing field of judicial regimes. As a result of civil society, the legal, political, and philosophical developments on these environmental demands were advanced and contributed greatly to the enforcement of the green penalties. It is observable that the judicial processing of green crimes is steadily developing across many jurisdictions. Take, for example, the Special Prosecutor in Spain. Spain is a prodigy in tackling green crimes. It is one of the first and few countries with a special police unit dedicated to dealing with environmental crime; the Servicio de Protecci6n de la Naturaleza. SEPRONA is part of the Guardia Civil, the Spanish police force, which is generally entrusted with combating specific types of crime. However, an effective judiciary depends on suitable organization.

Another useful example for this discussion is to be found in the creation of the National Green Tribunal of India, discussed further in this volume. India's judiciary has repeatedly called for the establishment of a system of specialized environmental courts. In 2010, the National Green Tribunal Act was passed to set up dedicated environmental courts. India's judiciary played a central role in shaping this legislation, and the drafters of the Act were mindful of addressing the specific needs that had been identified by judges and others working in the judicial system.[39] Another example is the Court of Environment and Agrarian Issues in the State of Amazonas, Brazil. This Court is an example of a substantially independent environmental court and has one of the widest and most innovative ranges of remedies available to address environmental crimes. A unique policy is a 'night school for environmental law violators', which won Brazil's 2013 Prize of National Quality in the Judiciary.[40]

Green crimes should be viewed and dealt with by law as being a category and type of crime by itself. The harms involved and the effects of the offense can be of an immeasurable magnitude and the reparation impossible, so making sure this dimension of green crimes is reflected in the punishment

---

[39] Domenico Amirante, *Environmental Courts in Comparative Perspective: Preliminary Reflections on the National Green Tribunal of India'* 29, PACE ENVIRONMENTAL LAW REVIEW 441, (2012).

[40] UNODC, *Prosecution and Judiciary*, https://www.unodc.org/e4j/en/wildlife-crime/module-3/key-issues/prosecution-and-judiciary.html (last visited May 1, 2020).

and sentencing stages is not an easy enterprise. Green crimes could be so severe and impactful that the harm can initiate a chain of harms in the environment, which can potentially damage the whole of humanity, planet, flora and fauna. The harm and impact of the crime on victims can be huge. Just like hate crime can affect a whole community, a green crime can contribute to the destruction of our planet and climate, while in reality, these kinds of crimes affect and have an impact on humanity as a whole and at the same time violate the rights of future generations. For example, advocates of such a view argue that global warming should be classified as a global crime. On the same train of thought, an ecocide law could contribute greatly to bringing an end to environmental destruction. Ecocide refers to the deliberate destruction of ecosystems, which satisfies all the requirements for being classified as the worst crime against humanity and nature. This crime has not been recognized by the UN or any other lawmaking body, but it is worth mentioning to illustrate the ways law stays silent when there is a lack of political will to ensure justice at all costs.

V. Criminal Law

A green crime is an act or omission that breaks the law and is consequently a matter for criminal prosecution. To better understand what is at stake here, consider the Latin legal maxim: *dictum nullum crimen, nulla poena sine lege,* which is applicable to our analysis of green crimes and means that there can be no crime and no punishment except as the law prescribes. Environmental criminal law defines green crimes and sets the scene for green criminology's topics of interest. In criminal law, we know that the significance of the *mens rea* element is crucial in addressing the definitional challenges concerning what can classify as criminal conduct in the context of environmental law.[41] *Mens rea* establishes whether the conduct is subject to moral condemnation.[42] The damage produced is relevant, mainly to the degree that the defendant in a criminal trial wanted to cause the green crime violation or had knowledge that s/he was causing or generating the threat of this harm. Causation of harm by itself is not enough to trigger criminal sanction absent the accompanying culpable *mens rea.* The establishment of the guilty

---

[41] Richard J. Lazarus, *Mens Rea in Environmental Criminal Law: Reading Supreme Court Tea Leaves,* 7 FORDHAM ENVTL. L. REV. 861, (2011).

[42] Martin R. Gardner, *The Mens Rea Enigma: Observations on the Role of Motive in the Criminal Law Past and Present,* UTAH L. REV. 635, (1993).

intention to cause harm to the environment is a prerequisite for constituting a crime according to the theory of criminal law.[43]

An overview of criminal law's theory is necessary at this point in order to expose certain issues that block the strong and actual environmental legal protection of the green crime's regime. Some legal scholars argue that the sole function of criminal law is to deliver justified punishment[44] , otherwise known as the punitive view. Other theorists tend to support the curial[45] view, which is justifying the calling for exemplar of suspected offenders to account in criminal courts. This view puts the criminal trial at the center not just of criminal proceedings but criminal law as a whole. While the communitarian view[46] conceives criminal law as an instrument of the community and focuses on the available ways for ensuring that the community gets what it is owed from wrongdoers. Criminal law's theory is the most developed set of legal rules there is in existence. In every legal system around the world, there is a strong penal organization in place, meaning that a legal researcher can find plenty of bodies of law that deal with judging someone's action, intention, and balancing it with the damages on a victim. As pointed out at the beginning of this chapter, even the word crime derives from a Latin word meaning to judge.

The inclusion of green crimes in the criminal justice system and theory and the enhancement of their theoretical foundations through the development of green criminology is a positive evolution of the law as a living organism. In defense of the effectiveness and impact of criminal law's involvement in ensuring justice, it is important to highlight that criminal law is developed in a co-dependent relationship with societal morality, and as such, it discharges duties of interest to other areas like politics, sociology, philosophy and not just criminal law alone. The imperfectionist view, for example, looks at how criminal law enables duties, shapes the moral compass of a society and further promotes the prevention of wrongdoings of general interest. According to this view, what is characteristic of criminal law is not its role but its method of performing: the modus in which it satisfies utilities shared with other bodies of law or sciences. What is special in criminal law is that it openly

---

[43] John C. Coffee, *Does "Unlawful" Mean "Criminal"?: Reflections on the Disappearing Tort/Crime Distinction in American Law,* 71 B.U. L. REV. 193, 201, 223-33, (1991).

[44] Michael S. Moore, *PLACING BLAME: A THEORY OF CRIMINAL LAW,* Oxford: Oxford University Press, 28–29, (1997).

[45] John Gardner, OFFENCES AND DEFENCES, Oxford: Oxford University Press, 80, (2007).

[46] Antony Duff, *Relational Reasons and the Criminal Law,* in OXFORD STUDIES IN PHILOSOPHY OF LAW, Leslie Green and Brian Leiter eds., (2013).

prohibits, criminalizes, condemns, and punishes the worst wrongdoings. This significant role is mainly associated with criminal punishment.

In summary, the punitive view asserts that criminal law's value consists in delivering justified punishment, while the preventive view argues that the value of criminal law is to be found in preventing criminal wrongs. However, none of these views aid us in determining what the value of fulfilling each function actually is. For example, the punitive view does not provide justifications as to criminal punishment; nor the preventive view offers any useful information about the effectiveness or value of preventing crime. A broad justification of criminal law satisfies this descriptive hole. It should be no matter of debate, but in legal science, we still need to justify the inclusion of newly constructed legal terms, even if their birth through language and law fills an unjustified gap in criminal justice and serves the purpose of justice as a positive addition.

Green crimes describe wrongdoings as old as humanity on this planet. It may be a newly constructed legal term, but every sound legal mind "will know them when" s/he "sees them."[47] Criminal justice is essentially the application of criminology. While criminology is the study of crime, criminal justice describes the societal response to crime. For example, police officers and investigators are integral components of the criminal justice system. The inter-connectedness of criminology with criminal law requires no further justification or proof. In essence, green criminology is the study of environmental crimes, and although it is a relatively new branch of criminology and a new term, however, it describes the oldest undocumented type of crime in humanity's history that managed to go unpunished for centuries while entering the realm of invisible[48] crimes. Scholars argue that even if something is criminalized, powerful actors are able to keep these crimes and harms hidden. Consider, for example, how greenwashing is being used by the corporate business world, and you discover many examples of powerful actors trying to keep environmental harms hidden by promoting alternative greener narratives. To be more precise, consider these seven features that contribute according to criminologists to the invisibility of crimes – they are: no knowledge, no statistics, no theory, no research, no control, no politics, and no panic."[49] Undeniably, there is no better medicine for restoring justice in this case other than supporting the further development of

---

[47] As Justice Stewart held about definitional difficulties, in *Jacobellis vs Ohio*, 378 U.S. 184 (1964).

[48] *See* Victor Jupp et al., *Features of Invisibility*, in INVISIBLE CRIMES: THEIR VICTIMS AND THEIR REGULATION, Pamela Davies, ed., (1999).

[49] *Id.*

green criminology while moving towards a preventive criminal legal theory about green crimes.

Green crimes refer to the criminal harms committed by humans against the environment that may harm the environment and human life. A useful and necessary legal exercise is to look into the *actus reus* and problematic *mens rea* of the crimes in question and assess the epistemological validity of the theoretical requirements for constituting a crime. From a criminological perspective: the importance of those issues is evident, and this is why they are at the core of studying green criminology. One of the ways law can overcome some of these challenges is to create a special international court for the environment.[50] An international court for the environment is a welcome addition to our global criminal justice system since it will fill the existing gap with a legal institution dedicated solely to prosecuting and punishing green crimes. It is worth mentioning that in September 2016, the ICC announced that it would prosecute government and individuals for environmental crimes. According to the Case Selection Criteria announced in the ICC Policy Paper on "Case Selection and Prioritisation" in September 2016, the Office will give particular consideration to prosecuting Rome Statute crimes that are committed by means of, or that result in, "inter alia", the destruction of the environment, the illegal exploitation of natural resources or the illegal dispossession of land.[51] Prosecuting polluters like war criminals for the crime of ecocide is inevitable, and it is the duty of the international lawmaking community to fuel the concrete development of the relevant green crimes legal procedures.

The fundamental idea behind green criminology is that human action harms the environment, and by the environment, green criminologists mean the whole ecosystem and species that inhabit the environment. What is included in the environment is a question that the author suggests we leave open, since outer space may not be a habitable environment, but it is part of our ecosystem, and there are a number of related ecological harms that

---

50 For a more detailed discussion about an international court for the environment see David Krott's chapter later in this book, where he argues that: "The International Court for the Environment is a welcome addition to this net of international jurisdictional entities to fill the existing gap."

51 OFFICE OF THE PROSECUTOR ICC, *Policy Paper on Case Selection and Prioritisation*, (September 15, 2016), https://www.icc-cpi.int/itemsDocuments/20160915_OTP-Policy_Case-Selection_Eng.pdf.

humans are causing to outer space[52] like for example pollution crimes, emissions, waste dumping to name some of the most obvious ones. By proceeding with our analysis, the main problem with green criminology and green crimes comes down to the simple fact that most of the harms are defined as crimes under law, while a significant amount of these harms are yet to be demarcated as illegal. There is a strong debate over which behaviors ought to be illegal in this area, as well as unanswered questions about specific green harms and problematic methodologies in studying and examining the legal systems enforcing environmental regulations. One of the purposes of this chapter is to expose you to a wide range of crimes that criminologists ordinarily fail to examine. Topics include crimes against animals, forests, and water and the ways in which these crimes can be addressed.

VI. Human Rights

When we start exploring green crimes through topics such as equality, human rights, collective rights, intergenerational equity, and the historical responsibilities for climate change, we enter the world of climate justice. "A fundamental proposition of climate justice is that those who are least responsible for the anthropogenic climate change suffer its gravest consequences, with animals being the less fortunate in this case, since even in the climate justice terrain their suffering is not efficiently acknowledged to date."[53] Human rights expose the deeper harms of green crime cases and offer the strongest possible justifications for mobilizing positive change in the legal realm. Human rights cases, relevant to green criminology and green crimes, present critical case studies which illustrate that natural resources exploitation is one of the major causes of human rights abuses. Land-grabbing, the destruction and pollution of lands and water essential to indigenous and other vulnerable communities, are the direct consequences of oil extraction, logging, and industrial agriculture, for example.

The main trend in green criminology is classifying green crimes into two categories: (a) anthropocentric, which as the term dictates, is about green crimes harming humans, and as such, the human is central to this category. For example, pollution is a problem because it harms humans and violates a number of rights, while climate change is a problem because of its impact on people, their rights and the rights of future generations. The second category

---

[52] For a detailed analysis of these topics see Tamara Blagojević's chapter later in this book, where she discusses in detail the topic of environmental damages in outer space.

[53] Zoi Aliozi, *Climate Justice: Human Rights and Animal Rights*, THE RESOLUTION JOURNAL 112, (2020).

of green crimes is (b) ecocentric. As the term suggests, it is based on a nature-centered system of values driven by environmental ethics, eco-philosophy, and climate justice. This category of green crimes does not distinguish between humans, non-human animals, and the rest of the ecosystem; it offers a lens through which green criminologists view harm to any part of the environment as harm to all of it. Consequently, green crimes like animal abuse or deforestation are green crimes, regardless of whether or not there is any specific human cost.[54] In this latter category, we would also find ecocide if it was recognized by international criminal law as a green crime.

The majority of human rights law was created before environmental protection became a subject of global concern. For example, the Universal Declaration of Human Rights was adopted in 1948, which means that it was built in the aftermath of WWII and dealt with the known injustices which resulted from the barbarities of war, which can partly explain the lack of environmental protection language in early productions of human rights law. The most obvious exceptions are found in the 1976 Covenant's rights to life and health, which have some references to the environment. For example, article 12 of the ICESCR[55] expressly calls on state parties to take steps to improve all aspects of environmental and industrial hygiene and the prevention, treatment and control of epidemics and other diseases. This article demonstrates the link between human rights and environmental protection, as well as the need for legal action to ensure the progressive realization of human rights.

To proceed, it will be useful to consider that human rights and science are becoming the main protagonists in climate change litigation. There is a steady development of the global trends in climate change litigation, which in practice has the effect of strengthening the connection between climate change and human rights under the all-inclusive umbrella of climate justice. There is also an increase in the number of important recent climate justice cases against governments and/or private entities, which have employed rights-based arguments, marking a "rights turn"[56] in climate change litigation. For example, *Ashgar Leghari v. Federation of Pakistan*[57] was the first case where a human

---

[54] Daan P. van Uhm, *A green criminological perspective on environmental crime: the anthropocentric, ecocentric and biocentric impact of defaunation*, REVUE INTERNATIONALE DE DROIT PÉNAL. 87, 323-40, (2017).

[55] *See* ICESCR, Art. 7 b and Art. 10-3, December 16, 1966.

[56] Jacqueline Peel and Hari Osofsky, *A Rights Turn in Climate Change Litigation?* TRANSNATIONAL ENVIRONMENTAL LAW, 7(1), 37-67, (2018).

[57] *See* Leghari v. Federation of Pakistan, (2015) W.P. No. 25501/201.

rights basis for litigation on climate change was accepted, notwithstanding the obstacles presented by the problematic causality and extra-territoriality. In this 2015 case, a Pakistani court produced a ground-breaking decision by accepting claims that it was the government's failure to address climate change that caused the violations of the claimant's rights.

The term "climate justice" was originally defined as actual legal action on climate change. It is interesting to see the numbers of the relevant case law, which according to a 2017 UN report[58] there were, at the time, 894 identified ongoing legal actions globally. A human rights basis for litigation on climate change has had increasing significance for courts in case law, despite the problems that arise from the need to establish causality. The new lawsuits that recent reports are analyzing are also illustrative of these advancements in the process of establishing a causal link between a particular source of emissions and climate-related harms of environmental crimes. Climate change litigation continues to evolve with the demands of our time, and we can observe a continuous geographic expansion of these legal cases. There are now cases all around the globe, with their majority being filed in the Americas, alongside Asia, the Pacific region, and Europe. In a very recent climate case, which serves as a reminder that failure on climate commitments is actionable in a court of law, and which is also illustrating the interconnected roles of political agreements with the law— the Irish Supreme Court found that the Irish government's climate plan fell short and heard a case where terms and concepts such as derived rights, constitutional rights, right to life, to health, and bodily integrity were heard. In this historic case, *Friends of the Irish Environment v. The Government of Ireland, et al.*,[59] the applicants claimed that they are:

> entitled to rely on rights, said to be guaranteed both under the Constitution and under the ECHR, to put forward its claim that the Plan fails to vindicate the rights concerned such that the adoption of the Plan is unlawful. So far as the Constitution is concerned, FIE placed reliance on the right to life and, in particular, on what is said to be the obligation of the State to seek to protect persons against a future threat

---

[58] *See* UNITED NATIONS ENVIRONMENT PROGRAMME AND COLUMBIA LAW SCHOOL'S SABIN CENTER FOR CLIMATE CHANGE LAW, *The Status of Climate Change Litigation: A Global Review, 2007,* http://wedocs.unep.org/handle/20.500.11822/20767?show=full (last visited June 28, 2020).

[59] The Supreme Court [Appeal No: 205/19], Judgment of Mr. Justice Clarke, Chief Justice, delivered the 31st of July 2020. Judgement: https://www.courts.ie/acc/alfresco/681b8633-3f57-41b5-9362-8cbc8e7d9215/2020_IESC_49.pdf/pdf.

> to life arising from climate change. Likewise, FIE placed reliance on the constitutional right to bodily integrity, as also guaranteed by the Constitution. It was again said that the consequences of climate change will significantly impact on the health and bodily integrity of persons thus infringing that right.

It is interesting to point out that the Government, in this ground-breaking case, raised a question over whether it can be said that there is a so-called unenumerated right to an environment consistent with human dignity. The High Court has recognized such a right in the judgment *of Barrett J. in Friends of the Irish Environment v. Fingal County Council* [2017] IEHC 695. These so-called "derived rights" are a very interesting hypothesis from a legal perspective and an inevitable question of law for the appropriate courts.

VII. Conclusion

If humanity as a whole can reach a consensus and collectively agree on one thing, the environment should be protected through strong laws. It is because we are all part of nature, and our existence is dependent on the health of the environment and the sustainability of our planet. This chapter's discussion has exposed that the criminalization of such environmental harms and the establishment of a genuinely green economy that will safeguard future living conditions, the rights of future generations, and the sustainability of our ecosystems by respecting eco-philosophy, environmental ethics, safeguarding human rights, and climate justice are crucial for overcoming the climate crisis. Climate justice offers a unique opportunity to the global justice project to step forward in designing powerful legal institutions and international law that can ensure the protection of nature and tackle the existential threats to humanity due to climate change and pandemics. Green criminology and green crimes are rapidly developing areas due to the urgent necessity that drives their evolution.

The current state of affairs and climate change negotiations can be described by this metaphor "our house is on fire", and we continue to negotiate who will get the silverware. What needs to be emphasized is that history has proven over and over again that the lack of political will can be trumped and counter-acted by the stronger will of the people. The force of the climate action movement needs to be acknowledged at this point because understanding green criminology and the evolution of green crimes is necessary to grasp the pivotal role the climate action movement has played in moving positive social and legal change. The fact that laws are changing, and the protection of the environment is on the top of any governmental agenda around the world as an urgent issue, is another way to see the achievements of the current state of environmental crimes and climate justice. The problem green criminologists are called to work against is about the difficulties in constituting a clear actus reus and, worse than that, the impossibility in most cases of connecting the intention and *mens rea* to the relevant *actus reus*, in order for the theory of criminal law to be satisfied in constituting a crime. This, however, is the oldest struggle of the judicial body, and these conflicts are part of the legal exercise a judge needs to overcome since it is up to the judge to decide case-by-case whether a criminal act against the environment was committed; connect this act and *actus reus* to a legal entity, whether human or company, and then depending on the facts of each case, it will be up to the judge to decide whether the *mens rea* is sufficiently and legally established in a court of law.

That being said, the full inclusion of green crimes in the international criminal justice system is crucial, with ecocide, for example, sitting side-by-side having equal status, value, and legal enforceability, as genocide, war crimes and crimes against humanity. Ecocide, as a green crime, has the potential to achieve a de facto universal legal status through, for example, international laws protecting the environment, since it is in the best interest of every nation and member of the human family to protect the ecosystems that sustain our lives, provide all the necessary conditions for realizing the Universal Declaration of Human Rights and live a life in dignity within a healthy environment free from fear and existential threats. It is a matter of time for ecocide[60] to be classified and legally defined as an international green crime and fill the gap that lingered for too long in climate justice's legal mandate.

In conclusion, the societal morality that enables the legal prohibitions to be punishable is where preventing green crimes should focus. This means that in addition to the legal work required to include green crimes in the global criminal justice system, we will also need to re-evaluate the worth of life of non-human animals and our human footprint on the environment. The urgent need for empowering green criminology through further scientific research and projects is now more evident than ever.

Criminology as the study of crime is also a branch of sociology, and it involves research and analysis of who commits crimes, why they commit them, their impact, and how to prevent them. The goal of criminology is to determine the root causes of criminal behavior and develop effective and humane means to

---

[60] Ricardo Pereira, *After the ICC Office of the Prosecutor's 2016 Policy Paper on Case Selection and Prioritisation: Towards an International Crime of Ecocide?* CRIM LAW FORUM 31, 179–224, (2020).

address and prevent it. As a concluding remark, it will be useful to point out that criminology is related, but is not identical, to the field of criminal justice. Green criminology is a new, fresh and extremely useful addition to criminal justice. As a special branch of criminology, it offers research prospects that can translate into improving criminal law, criminal justice, and climate justice. Notwithstanding the plethora of interconnected disciplines offering their distinct methodological systems and tools, green criminology is a distinct and priceless device for studying law and green crime.

There are many factors that deserve acknowledgment in describing green criminology since it should be made clear that a number of different disciplines can offer methodological tools to this colorful branch of criminology, like sociology, psychology, law, philosophy, and political sciences, to name but a few; however, green criminology although a newly born concept and field of study, has deep roots in the history of ideas, and its origin can be found in the first philosophers reflecting on crime, prevention, punishment, and law. Acknowledging that philosophy, law, and political thought, were developed by philosophers in ancient Greece while observing nature and natural laws exposes the obvious realization that eco-philosophy is not really a new concept, rather the original and oldest form of philosophy.

Ideally, any harm to the environment that is linked to human action should be punishable by law and should be prohibited by criminal law. This theoretical rule is more of an outline rather than the essence of the crimes in question. In the theory of criminal law, we know that for a crime to come into existence, it should be codified by law, and lawyers should prove that the two elements of the crime are present in the case in question. The *actus reus* meaning the guilty act, and the *mens rea* meaning guilty mind and referring to the intention to commit the wrongdoing and inflict harm. So, these two very important to criminal law components: (a) the criminal act and (b) the intention to commit the act; are the two elements that constitute a crime, and if proven in a court of law, then punishment and sentencing should follow. The main 'problem' with green crime theory and practice is that, customarily, these kinds of harms were not viewed with the same moral value as harms against person and property, and thus were viewed as 'victimless'. Due to this reason, green crimes were rendered invisible in the eyes of justice for a long time. On the bright side, the raising of awareness about climate justice and the promotion of society's understanding of the environment brings a natural re-evaluation of what the environment can and cannot sustain and creates new duties on the lawmakers to move from the anthropocentric understanding of the function of law, into serving the essential function of law and justice which is about protecting the vulnerable and restoring injustices in an unbiased manner. The recognition that ecologically damaging human activities need to be strictly regulated and criminalized is the fuel that is needed to move towards a fairer and better-protected world.

Through a critical legal studies lens, this chapter aspired to present the reader to this newly born scientific area and, in doing so, to shed light on the shortcomings of the international criminal justice project. The methodology used in developing this chapter is a mixture of legal and philosophical research tools, with legal analysis walking hand-in-hand with philosophical questioning. As pointed out above, green criminology is a branch of criminology that involves the study of crimes against the environment, including the study of environmental law and policy, plus the study of corporate crimes against the environment and climate justice. In conclusion, green crimes are an essential part of climate justice, and there is an urgent need to clarify, highlight and acknowledge the essential role they should play in international criminal justice. There are many open questions in the field of green criminology, and these legal challenges can serve as another justification for the necessity to develop green criminology further. The important role of green criminology in exploring the social perception of environmental harms while humanity is facing a climate crisis cannot be emphasized enough. Finally, it is the vital and important job of this multi-disciplinary branch of criminology in tackling the greenwashing dangers that add negatively to the already inadequate environmental protection since it is the only appropriately skilled field of study that can analyze this phenomenon in a holistic and comprehensive manner. Green crimes and green criminology are integral parts of our legal systems, and it is a matter of time for crimes against the environment to legally evolve in such a way as to take their rightful place next to international crimes carrying as much value as crimes against humanity and war crimes.

Bibliography

Zoi Aliozi, *Climate Justice: Human Rights and Animal Rights,* The Resolution Journal, (2020).

Zoi Aliozi, *Climate Justice: Climate Change and Human Rights,* in Denialism and Human Rights, Moerland Roland et al. eds., 403, (2016).

Domenico Amirante, *Environmental Courts in Comparative Perspective: Preliminary Reflections on the National Green Tribunal of India,* 29 Pace Environmental Law Review 441, (2012).

Aristotle, Nicomachean Ethics, Kitchener, Ont, Batoche Books at 121, (1999).

Kyle Burchett, *Anthropocentrism as Environmental Ethic.* 10.13023/ETD.2016.259, Theses and Dissertations—Philosophy, (Dec. 2016), https://uknowledge.uky.edu/philosophy_etds/12.

THE CDP CARBON MAJORS REPORT, (2017), https://www.cdp.net/en/articles/media/new-report-shows-just-100-companies-are-source-of-over-70-of-emissions.

John C. Coffee, *Does "Unlawful" Mean "Criminal"?: Reflections on the Disappearing Tort/Crime Distinction in American Law,* 71 B.U. L. REV. 193, 201, 223-33, (1991).

THE CONVENTION ON THE CONTROL OF TRANSBOUNDARY MOVEMENT OF HAZARDOUS WASTES AND THEIR DISPOSAL, 1673 U.N.T.S. 126, (March 22, 1989).

Jacques Derrida, OF GRAMMATOLOGY, G. Spivak trans., Baltimore, The J.H. University Press, (1974).

Directive 2008/99/EC on the Protection of the Environment Through Criminal Law.

Costas Douzinas, et. al, POSTMODERN JURISPRUDENCE: THE LAW OF TEXTS IN THE TEXTS OF THE LAW, London: Routledge, at 9, (1991).

Antony Duff, *Relational Reasons and the Criminal Law,* in OXFORD STUDIES IN PHILOSOPHY OF LAW, Leslie Green and Brian Leiter eds., (2013).

EUR-LEX, *Directive (EU) 2018/1673 of the European Parliament and of the Council of 23 October 2018 on combating money laundering by criminal law,* https://eur-lex.europa.eu/legal-content/EN/TXT/?uri=uriserv:OJ.L_.2018.284.01.0022.01.ENG.

EUROPOL, *Environmental Crime,* https://www.europol.europa.eu/crime-areas-and-trends/crime-areas/environmental-crime.

FINANCIAL ACTION TASK FORCE, *Priorities for the Financial Action Task Force (FATF) under German Presidency,* https://www.fatf-gafi.org/media/fatf/documents/German-Presidency-Priorities.pdf.

John Gardner, *OFFENCES AND DEFENCES,* Oxford: Oxford University Press. (2007).

Martin R. Gardner, *The Mens Rea Enigma: Observations on the Role of Motive in the Criminal Law Past and Present,* UTAH L. REV. 635, (1993).

Mark Allan Gray, *The International Crime of Ecocide,* CALIFORNIA WESTERN INTERNATIONAL LAW JOURNAL 215, (1996).

Anastacia Greene, *The Campaign to Make Ecocide an International Crime: Quixotic Quest or Moral Imperative?* FORDHAM ENVIRONMENTAL LAW JOURNAL, Vol. 30, No. 3, (2019).

Jeremy Haken, *Transnational Crime in The Developing World,* GLOBAL FINANCIAL INTEGRITY at 56, (2011).

Matthew Hall et al., eds. GREENING CRIMINOLOGY IN THE 21ST CENTURY, London: Routledge, (2017).

Neil Hawke, *Crimes against the Environment,* ANGLO-AMERICAN LAW REVIEW, 16(1) at 90-96, (1987).

Kevin J. Heller and Jessica C. Lawrence, *The Limits of Article 8(2)(b)(iv) of the Rome Statute, the First Ecocentric Environmental War Crime,* GEORGETOWN INTERNATIONAL ENVIRONMENTAL LAW REVIEW (GIELR), Vol. 20, (2007).

Kenneth A. Hodson et al. *The Prosecution of Corporations and Corporate Officers for Environmental Crimes: Limiting One's Exposure for Environmental Criminal Liability,* 34 AMUZ. L. REV. 553, (1992).

Douglas Husak, *OVERCRIMINALIZATION,* Oxford: Oxford University Press, 92-95, (2008).

ICESCR, Art. 7 b and Art. 10-3, December 16, 1966.

Intelligence Project on Environmental Crime, *Report on Environmental Crime in Europe*, EnviCrimeNet, The Hague, (Feb. 20, 2015), http://www.envicrimenet.eu/images/docs/ipec_report_on_environmental_crime_in_europe.pdf.

INTERNATIONAL CRIMINAL COURT, *Elements of Crimes*, (2011), https://www.icc-cpi.int/NR/rdonlyres/336923D8-A6AD-40EC-AD7B-45BF9DE73D56/0/ElementsOfCrimesEng.pdf.

INTERPOL, *Interpol marks a decade of tackling serious organized environmental crime*, https://www.interpol.int/News-and-Events/News/2020/INTERPOL-marks-a-decade-of-tackling-serious-organized-environmental-crime.

INTERPOL, *Environmental Crime*, https://www.interpol.int/en/Crimes/Environmental-crime.

INTERPOL-UN ENVIRONMENT REPORT, *Environmental Crime Threatening Peace and Security, (December 8, 2016)*, https://www.interpol.int/en/News-and-Events/News/2016/Environmental-crime-threatening-peace-and-security-finds-new-INTERPOL-UN-Environment-report.

Jacobellis vs Ohio, 378 U.S. 184 (1964).

Victor Jupp et al., *Features of Invisibility*, in INVISIBLE CRIMES: THEIR VICTIMS AND THEIR REGULATION, Pamela Davies, ed., (1999).

Law 4039/2012 (Greece).

Richard J. Lazarus, *Mens Rea in Environmental Criminal Law: Reading Supreme Court Tea Leaves*, 7 FORDHAM ENVTL. L. REV. 861, (2011).

Leghari v. Federation of Pakistan, (2015) W.P. No. 25501/201.

Herbert Lionel, et. al, PUNISHMENT AND RESPONSIBILITY: ESSAYS IN THE PHILOSOPHY OF LAW, 2nd Edition, Oxford University Press, USA, (2008).

Michael Lynch, *The greening of criminology: a perspective on the 1990s*, THE CRITICAL CRIMINOLOGIST 2(3), (1990).

Michael J. Lynch et al., eds. *Green Criminology and State-Corporate Crime: The Ecocide-Genocide Nexus with Examples from Nigeria*, JOURNAL OF GENOCIDE RESEARCH, (2020).

Michael Lynch and Paul Stretesky, *The Meaning of Green: Contrasting Criminological Perspectives*. THEORETICAL CRIMINOLOGY 7. 217-238, (2003).

Andrei Marmor and Scott Soames, *PHILOSOPHICAL FOUNDATIONS OF LANGUAGE IN THE LAW*, Oxford: Oxford University Press, (2011).

Michael S. Moore, *PLACING BLAME: A THEORY OF CRIMINAL LAW*, Oxford: Oxford University Press, (1997).

Office of the Prosecutor, *Policy Paper on Case Selection and Prioritisation*, ICC, (September 15, 2016), https://www.icc-cpi.int/itemsDocuments/20160915_OTP-Policy_Case-Selection_Eng.pdf.

Onora O'Neill, *Environmental Values, Anthropocentrism and Speciesism*, ENVIRONMENTAL VALUES, 6(2) at 127-42, (1997).

Jacqueline Peel and Hari Osofsky, *A Rights Turn in Climate Change Litigation?* TRANSNATIONAL ENVIRONMENTAL LAW, 7(1), 37-67, (2018).

Ricardo Pereira, *After the ICC Office of the Prosecutor's 2016 Policy Paper on Case Selection and Prioritisation: Towards an International Crime of Ecocide?* CRIM LAW FORUM 31, 179–224, (2020).

Plato, BOOK I, 344C. PLATO REPUBLIC. Indianapolis: Hackett, (2004).

Ronald E. Purser et al., *Limits to Anthropocentrism: Toward an Ecocentric Organization Paradigm?* ACADEMY OF MANAGEMENT REVIEW, 20(4) at 1053-89, (1995).

The Supreme Court [Appeal No: 205/19], Judgment of Mr. Justice Clarke, Chief Justice, delivered the 31st of July 2020. Judgement: https://www.courts.ie/acc/alfresco/681b8633-3f57-41b5-9362-8cbc8e7d9215/2020_IESC_49.pdf/pdf.

Daan P. van Uhm, *A green criminological perspective on environmental crime: the anthropocentric, ecocentric and biocentric impact of defaunation*, REVUE INTERNATIONALE DE DROIT PÉNAL. 87, 323-40, (2017).

UNITED NATIONS ENVIRONMENT PROGRAMME AND COLUMBIA LAW SCHOOL'S SABIN CENTER FOR CLIMATE CHANGE LAW, *The Status of Climate Change Litigation: A Global Review, 2007*, http://wedocs.unep.org/handle/20.500.11822/20767?show=full.

UNICRI, *Environmental Crimes*, http://www.unicri.it/topics/environmental.

UNODC, *Prosecution and Judiciary*, https://www.unodc.org/e4j/en/wildlife-crime/module-3/key-issues/prosecution-and-judiciary.html.

Rob White, *Green Victimology and Non-Human Victims*, INTERNATIONAL REVIEW OF VICTIMOLOGY, 24(2) at 239-55, (2008).

Rob White, *Environmental Issues and the Criminological Imagination*, THEORETICAL CRIMINOLOGY, 7(4) at 483-506, (2003).

Further Reading

Peirs Beirne and Nigel South, ISSUES IN GREEN CRIMINOLOGY: CONFRONTING HARMS AGAINST ENVIRONMENTS, HUMANITY AND OTHER ANIMALS, Willan Publishing, Devon, (2007).

Robert Bullard, THE QUEST FOR ENVIRONMENTAL JUSTICE: HUMAN RIGHTS AND THE POLITICS OF POLLUTION, Sierra Club Books, San Francisco, (2005).

Pamela Davies, et al, INVISIBLE CRIMES THEIR VICTIMS AND THEIR REGULATION, Basingstoke: Macmillan, (1999).

Hannah Graham and Rob White, INNOVATIVE JUSTICE, London: Routledge, (2015).

Myrna Hall, VICTIMS OF ENVIRONMENTAL HARM: RIGHTS, RECOGNITION AND REDRESS UNDER NATIONAL AND INTERNATIONAL LAW, London: Routledge, (2013).

H. L. A. Hart, PUNISHMENT AND RESPONSIBILITY, Oxford: Oxford University Press, (1968).

H. L. A. Hart, THE CONCEPT OF LAW, 2nd edition, Oxford: Oxford University Press, (1994).

Nigel South, *A green field for criminology? A proposal for a perspective*, THEOR CRIMINOL 2(2):211–233, (1998).

Reece Walters and Diane Westerhuis, *Green crime and the role of environmental courts*, CRIME, LAW AND SOCIAL CHANGE, 59 (3), (2013).

Rob White, CRIMES AGAINST NATURE: ENVIRONMENTAL CRIMINOLOGY AND ECOLOGICAL JUSTICE, Willan Publishing, Devon, (2008).

Rob White, TRANSNATIONAL ENVIRONMENTAL CRIME: TOWARD AN ECO-GLOBAL CRIMINOLOGY, Routledge, London, (2011).

Rob White and Diane Heckenberg, GREEN CRIMINOLOGY: AN INTRODUCTION TO THE STUDY OF ENVIRONMENTAL HARM, London: Routledge, (2014).

Rob White and Hannah Graham, *Greening Justice: Examining the Interfaces of Criminal, Social and Ecological Justice*, BRITISH JOURNAL OF CRIMINOLOGY, (2015).

Rob White, ENVIRONMENTAL CRIME: A READER, Cullompton: Willan Publishing, 200-22, (2009).

Chapter 2

Environmental Personhood Towards a Rights Based Approach for Nature and Humanity

Prayank Jain

The Fletcher School of Law and Diplomacy, Tufts

Abstract: Climate change as an anthropogenic phenomenon demands conservation and sustainable use of natural resources. In the face of overwhelming human-induced ecological disruption and biodiversity loss, there is moral as well as socio-political imperative to revisit the principles that have defined mankind's relationship with nature. For all its fascinating and myriad forms, nature has had the legal status of property across jurisdictions. It is subject to ownership, control, and protection for the benefit of natural persons and corporations. To meet the challenges of our time and the needs of future generations, it is essential for nature's identity to undergo an *activist reconstruction* that can enable it to be a holder of rights. Environmental Personhood is an emerging doctrine that has legal potential to shape a systematic global response to the status quo. Several jurisdictions have applied this doctrine and have recognized rivers and other ecosystems as legal persons. Through legal innovation and adaptation, international and national law systems can expand the jurisprudence and legal character of nature and accrue it the identity and entitlements of a legal person. Environmental personhood is a necessary precursor for achieving climate justice.

In this chapter, the author makes the international legal argument for Environmental Personhood and examines its possible effects. Specific focus is given to the root of the problem in legal philosophy and how mankind has taken steps forward from anthropocentrism to ecocentrism. The chapter explains the development towards nature's rights approach in select jurisdictions and the linkages between environmental rights and the human right to a healthy environment, both of which are developing in parallel at the international level. The author suggests that pursuing an integrated rights-based approach will aid the development of this doctrine and highlights the key voices and movements that will play a role in the future.

Keywords: Environmental Personhood, climate change, legal philosophy, *Res Nullis, Res Communis,* Rights of Nature, common heritage of mankind, human rights to a healthy environment.

***

I. Introduction

Climate change as an anthropogenic phenomenon demands conservation and sustainable use of natural resources. In the face of human-induced ecological disruption and biodiversity loss, there is moral as well as *socio-political* imperative to revisit the principles that have defined *mankind's* eternal relationship with nature.

As early societies evolved into civilizations, humans have seemed to be on a never-ending quest to conquer the world. This adventure has led to discovery, innovation, and conflict- yielding the provision of 21st century necessities, the essentials of which are recognized entitlements for the fulfillment and enjoyment of the right to life. At the heart of this advancement in human history has been our access and processing of Earth's resources. However, it has not been an equitable process that has met the needs and concerns of all stakeholders. We find ourselves in a world full of environmental inequity. Corporate exploitation and aggressive industrialization have pushed us to the brink of biodiversity collapse.

This may seem to be an unusual concern. In a global society with plurality and differences, our understanding and management of nature have been a model of solid consensus amongst the power brokers.

Why is it necessary?

Earth's biological frameworks are falling apart drastically. In 2018, a major report from the UN found that twenty to thirty percent of evaluated species are likely to be at an expanded chance of termination within the occasion of a temperature increment of 1.5-2.5°C, with the rate expanding to forty to seventy percent of species at a 3.5°C increase.[1] The report too highlighted the

---

[1] INTERGOVERNMENTAL PANEL ON CLIMATE CHANGE, *Climate Change 2007: Synthesis Report of IPCC Fourth Assessment Summary for Policymakers,* 13-14, (Nov. 2007).

rising water emergency, with seven to seventy-seven million individuals anticipated to encounter water stress due to climate alter impacts by the 2020s.[2] As per a 2014 World Wellbeing Organization Report, more than 250,000 yearly deaths may happen between 2030 and 2050 due to climate alter impacts.[3] Analysts caution that our warming world may be a few years close to a "point of no return."[4]

This environmental emergency expands beyond climate change. Earth has now crossed more than four of the nine planetary boundaries, or natural tipping points.[5] Recent studies appraise a forty percent decay in insect populations, which play a basic role in various ecological processes such as fertilization, bug control, and decomposition.[6] The anthropogenic annihilation of approximately eighty percent of the world's local forests, especially within the tropics, has brought about deplorable results for these biological systems and the worldwide climate and has caused a fracture of the basic environment and expanded the spread of tropical diseases.[7] A 2019 UN report on biodiversity found that human action is driving mass termination and worldwide biodiversity loss, with critical consequences for human well-being and society. This report cautioned that "transformative change" is required to spare humankind and nature.[8]

The environmental crisis is caused by a misjudgment of value; protecting environmental entities because of their intrinsic value rather than utility to humans is not an academic distinction; it shows in every balancing of

---

[2] *Id.*

[3] WORLD HEALTH ORGANIZATION *Climate Change and Health*, (Feb. 1, 2018), https://www.who.int/news-room/fact-sheets/detail/climate-change-and-health.

[4] See e.g. Matthias Aengenheyster et al., *Risk and the Point of No Return for Climate Action*, EARTH SYST. DYNAM. (2018), https://pdfs.semanticscholar.org/3520/dc9ae7a5599d38a12e587b477dd58c032542.pdf.

[5] THE STOCKHOLM RESILIENCE CENTRE, *The Nine Planetary Boundaries*, (Sept. 17, 2009), https://www.stockholmresilience.org/research/planetary-boundaries/planetary-boundaries/about-the-research/the-nine-planetary-boundaries.html.

[6] Damian Carrington, *Plummeting Insect Numbers Threaten Collapse of Nature*, THE GUARDIAN (Feb. 10, 2019), https://www.theguardian.com/environment/2019/feb/10/plummeting-insect-numbers-threaten-collapse-of-nature.

[7] WHO *supra* note 3.

[8] E.S. Brondizo et al., *Global Assessment Report on Biodiversity and Ecosystem Services of the Intergovernmental Science-Policy Platform on Biodiversity and Ecosystem Services*, IPBES (May 2019), https://ipbes.net/global-assessment.

interests.[9] The time has come for the wheel of international legal thought to turn again.

II. Personhood in Law and Philosophy

Personhood cannot exist without having personality. Legal personality is a specific term in public international law with specific connotations to rights and obligations. For legal identity, there should be character. What is the meaning of legal character, and why is it essential for legal identity? Character creates a framework for certainty in predicting the actions of a party. When parties deviate from expected legal conduct or act in line with their personal specific interest, it is because of character. Every subject of law has a particular character that aligns with specific values that is part of their personality.

When we talk about the environment, however, there is no character, at least within the traditional perspective of legal thought and philosophy. This lack of characterization of nature is an impediment to defining and framing its legal identity.

The first step is to identify character for to environment. An identity that has existed, but it is only now, on account of climate imperatives, that the international system must recognize (not grant) it an independent personality. Possible application of the contractual principle of estoppel – by giving all of humanity with resources and opportunities to build human civilization and everything we need, we are bound to take and ensure that our actions are in furtherance of nature's interests of conservation and ecological continuity.

Person is a moral term in philosophy. A person is a being who is the pot of our moral community. Some non-human animals' beings are also considered person. What must one process to be a part of a modern community? What factors should determine the essentials for an environment person? What qualifying criteria should an environmental cluster pose?

a. Diagnosing the problem in the root – traditional philosophy

Several legal difficulties that we face in global law and policy today stem from foundational principles inherited from the classical period of international law. Principals and thinking frameworks that were developed to meet current

---

[9] Klaus Michael Meyer-Abich, Wege Zum Frieden, *Mit Der Natur*, PRAKTISCHE NATURPHILOSOPHIE FIR DIE UMWELTPOLITIK, 11 (Mfinchen 1986).

problems of that time period, which in their basic design and imagination could not pre-empt and account for the consequences of industrial civilization.[10]

Today, the global community is simply continuing the fragile process of adjusting and updating these traditional frameworks. In a turf dominated by nation states and heavily invested by private stakeholders, the international environmental regime is struggling for legal means of control in the face of an exploding competition for limited natural resources and its systemic inability to control and prevent their exploitation.

In this frame, the search for options and inspiration for the next phase of international environmental regulation becomes more intelligible when viewed in a historical context.[11]

b. Classic international law and nature

In line with the basic underpinnings of international legal theory, environmental-decision making has naturally been centered around nation-states as the key players of international law. Historically, early discussions on the legal status, character, and treatment of the environment have been premised on the seas. For it was the natural resource vastly available to nations. The primary issues of concern have been those related to jurisdiction: *who* should control and be responsible for the international environment.[12]

This is the traditional thought this chapter challenges**:** that the environment ought not to be controlled or owned for others to be responsible for it. What does this mean in practical terms? Of course, responsibility and accountability will continue to be perennial contours of this discussion. It is the division of rights and consequent obligations that needs rethinking.

As far as the worldwide climate, classic theorists concentrated on the utilization and protection of the assets of the ocean, basically fishing. They saw fish, fowl, and wild creatures as *res nullius*, an idea taken from old Roman law. The Romans had an expand lawful arrangement conspire for each "thing" (res). The way of thinking of the law depended on the suggestion that everything at first had a place with nobody (*res nullius*); yet as man dealt with his current circumstance, fluctuating ideas of property were created. Fish, fowl, and wild creatures were things impervious to possession; however, they could be asserted by an individual on the off chance that he could catch them.

---

[10] Forest L. Grieves, *Classical Writers of International Law and the Environment*, 4 B.C. ENVTL. AFF. L. REV. 309 (1975), http://lawdigitalcommons.bc.edu/ealr/vol4/iss2/5.
[11] *Id.*
[12] *Id.*

The importance of the *res nullius* idea is that nobody possesses the thing in its wild state; it is basically there, free for the taking.[13]

In the seventeenth century, Pufendorf addressed a growing problem of increased national interest in "international" resources. He stated, "the moral reason why ownership is not suitable to the sea is drawn from the consideration that its use is inexhaustible and therefore sufficient for the general service of all, so that it is idle to wish to assign parts of it to individuals."[14] He continued, "we would certainly consider this the final argument if it were established that the sea in all its use is sufficient for all men in every part; for the purpose of introducing the right of property over things is to preserve peace in human society."[15] Peace between humans has been an overriding factor in environmental decision-making.

Much of man's encounter with the international environment, as with the domestic environment, has raised questions of: Who owns what? Who controls what? Who gets the use of what?[16]

The genesis of Roman property concepts is not entirely clear, but the predominant view was that man's history revolved around the progressive assertion of ownership claims to the world in which man found himself.[17] *Res nullius* areas became subjected to property claims to the extent that discovery, occupation, and contemporary technology permitted. For those areas not apparently susceptible to occupation, the Roman jurists devised the concept of res communis, or community property, open to use by all. In this category were air, running water, the sea, and the shores of the sea.[18]

i. Conceptual difficulty of international common property versus national interest

It would not be wrong to infer that the environment has never been analyzed and treated by legal philosophers as a subject of its own self and design. Not disregarding the challenges of their time, the philosophical view of the environment has primarily been concerned with man's interests and how

---

[13] P. Fenn, *Justinian and the Freedom of the Sea,* 19 AM. J. OF INTERNATIONAL LAW 716 (1925).
[14] S. Pufendorf, DE JURE NATURAE ET GENTIUM, LIBRI OCTO 567 (1688 ed. C. and W. Oldfather transl. 1934)
[15] *Id.*
[16] Grieves, *supra* note 10.
[17] Francis Stephen Ruddy, *Res Nullius and Occupation in Roman and International Law,* 36 U. MO. AT KANSAS C.L. REV. 274 (1968).
[18] Samuel C. Wiel, *Natural Communism: Air, Water, Oil, Sea and Seashore,* 47 HARV. L. REV. 425.

natural resources can be used to further those interests. Furthermore, it is interesting to note that the idea of common property was considered primitive and that private ownership of resources was looked upon as the next step of civilization, irrespective if it was the right one or not. Vattel, Pufendorf, Grotius and others all did recognize that the special conservation status of certain exhaustible resources (fish, shells, pearls, and amber, for example) might allow for national claims. As means and opportunity to exploit the sea expanded, so did nations' interest in asserting claims over it.

> As the earth, in its uncultivated state, did not furnish the human race, when it had multiplied greatly, with all necessary and useful products, it was found convenient to introduce the right of ownership, so that each one might apply himself with greater success to cultivate the share which fell to his lot, and to increase by his industry the various necessities of life. That is why the natural law approves of the rights of private ownership, which put an end to the common property of primitive times.[19]

c. Res Nullis and Res Communis - Problem with creating a regime to address issues of pollution and conservation

Roman jurists drew a distinction between imperium and dominium, but the theoretical quagmire of ownership versus jurisdiction can be avoided simply by regarding the issue as one of authority over an international area.[20]

The ancient lawful ideas of *res communis* and *res nullius* offer a system inside which the universal environment can be directed. For self-evident political reasons, countries within the past have attempted to back both concepts. Bolster of the *res communis* position was simple when countries had no capability to or were intrigued in involving the oceans. Countries might safeguard their rights of free "get" to the oceans by demanding that they be treated as a common asset. At the same time, a solid component of *res nullius* runs through the thinking about international ranges just like the oceans.

The *res nullius* concept implies susceptibility to occupation or ownership. It has been the rationale for claiming a license to exploit the living resources of the sea and for expanding national control over the seas. The cavalier attitudes of some states to further their "right" in protected areas show that

---

[19] Emer de Vattel, *Le Droit Des Gens, Ou Principes De La Loi Naturelle,* APPLIQUES A LA CONDUITE ET AUX AFFAMES DES SOUVERAINS 106 (1758 ed. C. Fenwick transl. 1916).

[20] Grieves, *supra* note 10.

international attitudes on the *res communis/ res nullius* status to international areas have not been solidified.

The *res nullius* concept recommends self-evident consequences; the weaker, less created countries will lose out in any future "get" for the seas, and the capable, innovatively progressed countries may conclusion up battling. The *res communis* concept, on the other hand, sets that worldwide zones cannot be subject to select apportionment by any state, which misuse of such zones must drop beneath a few kinds of worldwide authorization. The difficulty with the community concept is that community ventures all too often yield to dominant national interests. Nations have become increasingly urgent in advocating the *res communis* status for international areas. The Treaty on Principles Governing the Activities of States in the Exploration and Use of Outer Space, Including the Moon and Other Celestial Bodies, which went into force in October 1967, is one example.

The common heritage of the mankind emerged as a guiding principle to essentially address concerns over international maritime resources between nations. It fundamentalized the international legal understanding of 'common resources' and as goods defined by their utility to human interests in trade, development, manufacturing, etc.

The thought of *res communis,* the "common heritage of mankind," can help in modern endeavors to unravel the worldwide issue of keeping up global order. Until the "property" status of the seas is clarified and acknowledged by all, there will be ceaseless potential for universal instability. We cannot bargain coherently with contamination and preservation, whereas the taking from and dumping into the "no man's land" of the seas are "free" and uncontrolled. The *res communis* concept gives us a vehicle for stabilizing and directing the utilize of worldwide regions since it militates against the one-sided and regularly uncontrolled abuse of "universal" assets, extricated from and beneath the oceans.[21]

The conception of humankind's relation to nature depends upon whatever theory we have with regard to the natural order and our place in it.[22] This theory then becomes our environmental paradigm when we think about nature. A paradigm shift, therefore, includes a re-evaluation of our relationship with the rest of nature.[23]

---

[21] *Id.*

[22] *See* John Rawls, A THEORY OF JUSTICE (1971).

[23] Susan Emmenegger and Axel Tschentscher, *Taking Nature's Rights Seriously: The Long Way to Biocentrism in Environmental Law,* 6 GEO. INT'L ENVTL. L. REV. 545 (1994).

d. Environmental Ethics

Ethics mainly deals with what humans ought to do regarding each other. Environmental ethics represent the part of environmental philosophy that discusses how we should act concerning nature. These are "sets of principles, which would guide our treatment of wild nature, constitute an environmental ethic in the most general sense."[24]

There is a variety of competing, including partly overlapping, environmental ethics."[25] Environmental ethics remains crucial for providing us with the means to evaluate the extent to which we should protect nature's rights.[26] The arguments of the ethical discussion must be reconsidered in the light of the lesser-known position that environmental law already acknowledges the rights of nature.

e. Paradigm Shifts in International Environmental Policy

Thomas Kuhn's theory of paradigm shifts explains a sequence of events that lead to revolutions with an effect on people's conceptualization and information processing. Paradigm shifts are multidimensional and affect different areas of society, knowledge, and value at the same time.[27]

The environmental paradigms include how we see our relationship to nature, if and how we control nature, and whether we limit our actions because of nature.[28] The broad change these shifts envisage is the recognition of the special responsibility of humans as representatives of all interests and formulates criteria for equal protection of natural entities.

Taking nature's rights seriously is a paradigm shift in international environmental law whose present expressions reveal only the tip of an iceberg. So far, the legal acknowledgment of nature's intrinsic value construes no more than the legal background for the application and interpretation of international law. The formulation of detailed rights of nature in enacting this new legal dimension is yet to come.[29]

---

[24] Robert Elliot, *Environmental Ethics,* A Companion To Ethics 284, 285 (Peter Singer ed. 1993).

[25] *Id.* 285.

[26] J. Baird Callicott, *The Search for an Environmental Ethic,* MATTERS OF LIFE AND DEATH 420 (Tom Regan ed., 2nd ed. 1986).

[27] Thomas S. Kuhn, THE STRUCTURE OF SCIENTIFIC REVOLUTIONS 111-35 (2d ed. 1970).

[28] Emmenegger, *supra* note 33.

[29] *Id.*

Biocentrism is the relevant new paradigm in environmental law, protecting animals and plants as right-holders but leaving non-living natural entities and compounds without protection if such protection does not derive from their function as a natural habitat for living beings.[30]

f. International Environmental Legal Regime and the Nature's Rights Approach

Professor Christopher Stone's pivotal work on rights of nature, "Should Trees Have Standing?"[31] has been the leading thought on the issue. In 1994, legal scholars working on nature's rights approach mapped out the stage-wise development of international environmental law. While the protection of nature remains subordinated to the interests of humankind throughout the early stages, environmental instruments, both hard and soft non-binding texts, signal a progressive trend towards non-anthropocentrism and acknowledging nature's rights in a biocentric perspective.

In stage-wise development in international law – classifying the instruments according to whose interest is protected – we can distinguish three stages of development. The progression in language and scope of successive international environmental instruments indicates an evolution consisting of three different stages. The first stage is a purely anthropocentric vision (protecting nature for the good of presently living humans). Essentially, utilitarianism and human rights as the ethical perspectives informing the first step. Both ethical concepts are restricted to purely anthropocentric considerations and extend this consideration only to the interest of the present generation of humans. Utilitarianism and human rights theory together provide a comprehensive rationale for the first stage purposes of maximizing natural resources and protecting humans from international pollution.

The second stage is encompassing the interests of future generations.[32] Intergenerational equity can explain environmental provisions reaching beyond the interest of currently living humans, but it cannot give meaning to the protection of nature's own interest independent of humankind's needs and wants.

---

[30] *Id.*

[31] Christopher D. Stone, *Should Trees Have Standing? - Toward Legal Rights For Natural Objects,* 45 S. CAL. L. REV. 450, 456 (1972).

[32] Edith Brown Weiss, *Our Rights and Obligations to Future Generations for the Environment,* 85 AM. J. INT'L L. 198 (1990).

The final stage is to acknowledge an intrinsic value of nature and adopting a nature's rights approach.[33] The interest of humans is not congruent with the interest of nature as a whole, "anthropocentrism is too limited a world view to grasp the new reality."[34]

Acknowledging an intrinsic value of nature means acknowledging the value of natural entities, i.e., of animals and other so-called "natural objects."[35] It subsequently avoids any prohibitive definition of value in terms of utility for display or future generations of people.[36] The recently recognized lawful position beyond human interest we call "nature's rights." The nature's rights approach is an expansion of the chronicled concept of rights.[37] Humans are no longer seen as 'apart from nature' but as 'a part of nature'.

Not as it were people, but each substance of nature, carries the potential to have rights on its claim. Within the strict refinement of lawful subjects and legitimate objects, common substances are moving from the question status to the status of potential right-holders, i.e., lawful subjects. Rather than being at the free transfer of people, common substances presently pick up a status that requires a particular defense for each activity influencing their judgment as right-holders - they are prima facie non-disposable. The annihilation of the Brazilian rain forest and the extinction of the African elephant, for example, are not only dangerous since for their impacts on worldwide temperatures and African tourism; they are also destructive since they reduce the differences of the earth's natural life and thereby will eventually influence mankind; instead, we have to see them as an infringement of rights - rights belonging to creatures and plants as substances of nature.[38]

III. Precedents and developments

Various jurisdictions have offered protection to the natural environment through substantive environmental protection laws and the granting of standing to human beings who allege environmentally-related harms. Most

---

[33] Stone, *supra* note 31 at 456.

[34] Laurence H. Tribe, *Ways Not To Think About Plastic Trees: New Foundations for Environmental Law,* 83 YALE L.J. 1315, 1343 (1974).

[35] Stone, *supra* note 31 at 456.

[36] J. Baird Callicott, *Traditional American Indian and Traditional Western European Attitudes Towards Nature: An Overview,* ENVIRONMENTAL ETHICS, Vol 4, Issue 4, (Winter 1982), https://doi.org/10.5840/enviroethics1982443.

[37] Clarence Morris, *The Rights and Duties of Beasts and Trees: A Law Teacher's Essay for Landscape Architects,* 17 JOURNAL OF LEGAL EDUCATION 189, 190, 191 (1964).

[38] Emmenegger, *supra note* 23.

constitutions worldwide have provisions for the protection of features of the environment.

Environmental personhood has been concretized as an applicable doctrine through a rights of nature approach in select jurisdictions. Several nations have developed versions of rights of nature regimes, including Ecuador, Bolivia, New Zealand, India, Bangladesh, Uganda, and local jurisdictions in the United States. Not all of these rights of nature regimes take nature as a whole to be a juridical person; in some cases, parts of nature—a river, a species—become named as persons or otherwise equipped to litigate their own rights.[39]

This section focuses on highlighting the normative developments of environmental personhood and how it has developed in different jurisdictions through constitutional amendments, legislative enactments, and judicial decisions. The efficacy and impact of these measures are not discussed in detail.

a. Ecuador

The Rights of Nature movement has won extensive recognition in Ecuador, where rights were constitutionally codified in 2008. Under the Ecuadorian constitution, Pachamama (nature) has rights "to exist, persist, maintain and regenerate its vital cycles, structure, functions and its processes in evolution." Every person and every community has the right to advocate on its own behalf. Pachamama here escapes direct personification. Instead, it is the bearer of rights as "nature," as distinct from "persons, people, communities and nationalities" and "natural and judicial persons."

In 2008, Ecuador became the first country in the world to recognize the Rights of Nature in its national constitution. Articles 71-74 of the national constitution, which binds both state and non-state actors, provide grounds for the protection of nature through recognition of its rights and entitlements. This has led to some important cases for the conservation of rivers, particularly *The Vilcabamba River Case* and *The Goldminers' Case.*

Ecuador has been instrumental in forming the International Rights of Nature Tribunal (IRNT). It is a civil society initiative created in 2014 by the Global Alliance for the Rights of Nature.[40] It followed on from the Universal Declaration of the Rights of Mother Earth, which was passed at a conference

---

[39] Gwendolyn Gordon, *Environmental Personhood* (March 7, 2017), http://dx.doi.org/10.2139/ssrn.2935007.

[40] RIGHTS OF NATURE TRIBUNAL, https://www.rightsofnaturetribunal.com/.

attended by thousands of civil society delegates from around the world.[41] Although the IRNT does not have legal authority, it issues recommendations to improve the protection of the Rights of Nature.

b. Bolivia

The Bolivian legal recognition of "Mother Earth" is in the nature of collective public interest. Rather than directly granting legal personhood to nature, Bolivia's law instead strips human persons of their dominance over all of the other bits and pieces of nature. The Bolivian Rights of Nature measures finding their conceptual grounding in Indigenous Kwecha jurisprudence and particularly the concepts of Pacha Mama (Mother Earth) and Sumac Kawsay (Living Well).[42] Furthermore, Rights of Nature in Bolivia are viewed as encoding socialist alternatives to capitalism.[43]

Bolivia enacted its first Rights of Nature statute in 2010. The Law of the Rights of Mother Earth, Law 71 of 2010. Art. 3, states that Pacha Mama/Mother Earth is a dynamic living system with legal personality, comprising an indivisible community of all living things and organisms.[44] Specifically, it states that: Mother Earth is the dynamic living system formed by the indivisible community of all life systems and living beings, interrelated, interdependent and complementary, that share a common destiny. Mother Earth is considered sacred, according to the worldviews of nations and original Indigenous peoples and peasant communities.[45] Article 7 of the law establishes that the rights of Mother Earth include rights to life, diversity of life, water, clean air, equilibrium, restoration, and pollution-free living.[46]

The 2012 Law links the Rights of Nature to the further concepts of "holistic development" and "living well" (Sumac Kawsay). Article 1 states its purpose is

---

41 World People's Conference on Climate Change and the Rights of Mother Earth, *Universal Declaration of the Rights of Nature*, (April 2010), https://therightsofnature.org/universal-declaration/.

42 Paola Villavicencio Calzadilla and Louis J. Kotze, *Living in Harmony with Nature? A Critical Appraisal of the Rights of Mother Earth in Bolivia*, 7 Transnational Env. L. 397 (2018).

43 Cyrus R. Vance Center for International Justice, Earth Law Center, and International Rivers, *Rights of Rivers*, (October 2020), https://www.internationalrivers.org/resources/reports-and-publications/rights-of-river-report/.

44 Bolivia Mother Earth Law 071 of 2010 (Ley (Corta) de Derechos de Madre Tierra), Article 3.

45 *Id.*

46 Bolivia Mother Earth Law, *supra* note 44, Article 7.

to "establish holistic development and life systems of Mother Earth to regenerate, strengthening ancestral knowledge."[47] Significantly, art. 4.2 establishes an enforceable right to climate justice, which can be brought by victims of climate change who have been denied their right to "live well."[48]

Bolivia has been a lead state actor in the Rights of Nature movement at the international level. Bolivia has been instrumental in putting together the draft Universal Declaration of the Rights of Nature.[49] The Bolivian government led negotiations that resulted in the 2009 Proclamation, and has since contributed both diplomatic energy and funding to the development of the Harmony with Nature program at the UN.[50]

c. New Zealand

In Aotearoa/New Zealand, Rights of Nature are framed as rights of legal personhood, which are vested in a particular representative body (with strong input from Māori communities). Instead of granting rights for the whole of nature, particular natural features have been named as persons pragmatically. The Whanganui River and the forest Te Urewera have been granted the status of a person under law.[51]

In the case of New Zealand, environmental personhood jurisprudence draws heavily on Indigenous concepts, particularly the notion of kaitiakitanga (guardianship; that humans are stewards, and not owners, of the natural environment).

These rights of nature enactments have been primarily advanced through legislation rather than judicial decisions. The legislation is the product of a negotiation between the Aotearoa/New Zealand government and Māori Iwi (tribes) resolving historic breaches of the Treaty of Waitangi, New Zealand's founding document.[52] This has resulted in the recognition of the legal personhood of a national park (Te Urewera Act 2014), a river (Te Awa Tupua/

---

[47] La Ley Marco de la Madre Tierra y Desarrollo Integral para Vivir Bien, Gaceta Oficial del Estado Plurinacional de Bolivia, Ley No. 300 del (15 de Octubre de 2012), http://web.madretierra.gob.bo/sites/default/files/2018-01/ley_nro_300.pdf.

[48] *Id.*

[49] World People's Conference on Climate Change and the Rights of Mother Earth, *supra* note 41.

[50] United Nations Harmony with Nature Programme, www.harmonywithnatureun.org.

[51] Liz Charpleix, *The Whanganui River as Te Awa Tupua: Place based law in a legally pluralistic society*, 184(1) The Geographical Journal 19 (2017), https://onlinelibrary.wiley.com/doi/full/10.1111/geoj.12238.

[52] TE UREWERA ACT 2014 s 11(1) (NZ).

Whanganui River Settlement Act 2017), and pending legislation to recognize legal personhood in a mountain (Mt. Taranaki).[53]

d. India

Rights of Nature in India has been driven primarily by the judiciary. There have been two landmark decisions by the High Court of Uttarakhand in 2014 that conferred a legal personhood upon rivers Ganga, Yamuna, and the Himalayan ecosystem. Both of these decisions, however, have been stayed by the Supreme Court of India.

These developments resemble those in New Zealand, with discrete natural features being considered for rights, against a granular legal background supportive of the protection of nature, rather than broad protection for nature as a whole.

In 2014, the High Court utilized recognition of legal personhood as the basis for its further remedial orders. Analogizing to family law and acting with its *parens patriae* jurisdiction, the court declared three state government officials to be acting in "loco parentis, as the human face to protect, conserve and preserve the Rivers Ganga and Yamuna and their tributaries."[54] These officials were instructed to "uphold the status, promote the health, and to represent the rivers Ganges and Yamuna at all legal proceedings to protect the interest."[55]

That same year, the High Court of Uttarakhand adjudicated a similar petition which sought the protection of the Himalayan ecosystem of glaciers, streams, and forests. Acting under its *parens patriae* jurisdiction, the court formally declared that the Himalayan ecosystem was a full legal person with rights equivalent to those of human beings; that appointed officers from the state government, judicial and local bar would act in loco parentis; and that there must be mandated governance representation from local villages. It also issued a direction for strict compliance with its earlier judgments.[56] The court held that:

> (1) Rivers and Lakes have [the] intrinsic right not to be polluted. Polluting and damaging the rivers, forests, lakes, water bodies, air and

---

[53] Cyrus R. Vance Center, *supra* note 43.

[54] Mohd Salim v. State of Uttarakhand and Others (Writ Petition (PIL)No. 126 of 2014 (High Court of Uttarakhand, Dec. 5, 2016).

[55] *Id.*

[56] Miglani v. State of Uttarakhand, Writ. Petition PIL No. 140 of 2015 (High Court of Uttarakhand, March 30, 2017).

> glaciers will be legally equivalent to harming, hurting and causing injury to [a] person. (2) Rivers, Forests, Lakes, Water Bodies, Air, Glaciers and Springs have a right to exist, persist, maintain, sustain and regenerate their own vital ecology system. The rivers are not just water bodies. They are scientifically and biologically living. (3) The rivers, forests, lakes, water bodies, air, glaciers, human life are unified and are [an] indivisible whole. The integrity of the rivers is required to be maintained from Glaciers to Ocean. (4) The Himalayan Mountain Ranges, Glaciers, rivers, streams, rivulets, lakes, jungles, air, forests, meadows, dales, wetlands, grasslands and springs were declared as the legal entity/ legal person/juristic person/juridical person/moral person/artificial person for their survival, safety, sustenance and resurgence.[57]

From a jurisprudential perspective, it is particular to note the court's observations that "for a bigger thrust of socio-political-scientific development, evolution of a fictional personality to be a juristic person becomes inevitable. This may be any entity, living [or] inanimate, objects or things may impel the courts to recognize it. This recognition is for subserving the needs and faith of the society. All the persons have a constitutional and moral responsibility to endeavor to avoid damage or injury to nature (*in damno vitando*). Any person causing any injury is liable to be proceeded against."[58]

These two decisions of the High Court of Uttarakhand were stayed by the Supreme Court of India in 2017 on the grounds of difficulty in ascertaining liability in case of floods and adjusting the federal division of powers between the central and the state governments.[59] The Ganges and Yamuna Rivers case is majorly centered in Hindu spirituality and religious attachment to the rivers,[60] while the Himalayan ecosystem case is more secular and universal in language. Much of the holding in the Himalayan ecosystem case, such as the indivisible nature of the Himalayan ecosystem and the need for guardianship representation from the local community, does bear strong coherence with legislative and judicial developments in Aotearoa/New Zealand and Colombia.[61]

---

57 *Id.*

58 *Id.*

59 Order of the Supreme Court, Special Leave Petition No. 16879/2017, 7 July (India).

60 Bhadra Sinha, SC *puts on hold Uttarakhand HC order declaring river Ganga a living entity*, HINDUSTAN TIMES, (Jul. 7, 2017), https://www.hindustantimes.com/india-news/sc-puts-on-holduttarakhand-high-court-order-declaring-ganga-a-living-entity/story-IYqkaehoLhAyWfjAP8GYOO.html.

61 Cyrus R. Vance Center, *supra* note 43.

The Indian judiciary has been a pioneer in the development of the Polluter Pays Principle and the strict liability doctrine. Their sensitive response for protecting freshwater sources and critical ecosystems is an ideal progression in national jurisprudence. Considering the degree of political challenges in achieving environmental justice on substantive issues in the country, the judiciary remains best placed to develop the pathway for recognizing and implementing rights of nature.

Rights of Animals

Complimenting these developments, Indian appellate courts have developed a body of jurisprudence recognizing the legal rights of sentient animals, going so far as to declare them to have independent legal personae and imposing human guardianship duties.[62]

A 2012 Indian Supreme Court case established the legitimacy of the Court's consideration of non-anthropocentric views of the protection of nature. In 2014 court allowed that the Indian constitution's Article 21 (right to life) could be extended to non-human animals and guaranteed the 'five freedoms' of animals which includes; freedom from hunger and thirst; freedom from discomfort; freedom from pain, injury, and disease; freedom from fear and distress and freedom to express normal behavior.[63] In 2013, India's Ministry of Environment and Forests declared cetaceans "non-human persons" in a bid to protect them from harm.

e. Bangladesh

In 2019, the High Court of Bangladesh issued a landmark decision finding all rivers in Bangladesh to have legal personhood.[64] The case was brought by a non-governmental organization, which challenged encroachments of individuals, businesses, and government entities on the Turag River. The court recognized all rivers as "living entities" and appointed the National River Protection Commission (NRPC) as their guardian.

---

[62] Narayan Dutt Bhatt v. Union of India and others, Writ Petition (PIL) No. 43 of 2014, (High Court of Uttarakhand); T.N. Godavarman Thirumulpad v. Union of India (2012), I.A. Nos. 1433 and 1477 of 2995 in Writ Petition No. 202 of 1995, (Supreme Court of India); Center for Environment Law and WWF-India v. Union of India (2013), I.A. No. 100 in Writ Petition No. 337 of 1995 (Supreme Court of India).

[63] Animal Welfare Board of India vs. A. Nagaraj and Ors. (2014) 7 SCC 547.

[64] Writ Petition 3839 of 2016 (Supreme Court of Bangladesh, High Court Division).

The High Court also ordered that: all encroachments be removed within six months of the verdict; the government compile a list of all encroachers (subsequently published on the NRPC website); such encroachers be barred from running in elections or receiving certain bank loans; "river grabbing" be criminalized; the government amend relevant legislation within six months to prescribe punishment and fines for encroachment; all industrial workplaces and academic institutions offer compulsory education on rivers; and the NRPC strengthen its independence and enforcement powers.[65] The 2019 decision was upheld by the Supreme Appellate Division of Bangladesh in February 2020 (Bangladesh's highest court).[66]

f. Uganda

In 2019, after an extensive campaign by civil society groups, Uganda enacted environmental legislation that explicitly enshrines Rights of Nature.[67] The National Environment Act 2019[68] provides in section 4:

> (1) Nature has the right to exist, persist, maintain and regenerate its vital cycles, structure, functions and its processes in evolution; (2) A person has a right to bring an action before a competent court for any infringement of rights of nature under this Act; (3) Government shall apply precaution and restriction measures in all activities that can lead to the extinction of species, the destruction of the ecosystems or the permanent alteration of natural cycles; (4) The Minister shall, by regulations, prescribe the conservation areas for which the rights in subsection (1) apply.

The 1995 Constitution and the National Environment Act 1995 provided that every Ugandan has a right to a clean and healthy environment, and the

---

[65] THE DAILY STAR, *Can the historic High Court judgement save our rivers?* (Feb. 5, 2019), https://www.thedailystar.net/environment/news/can-thehistoric-high-court-judgement-save-our-rivers-1697419.

[66] DHAKA TRIBUNE, *Appellate Division upholds HC order on Turag land recovery*, (Feb. 4, 2020), https://www.dhakatribune.com/bangladesh/court/2020/02/04/appellate-division-upholds-hc-order-on-turag-land-recovery.

[67] Frank Tumusiime, *Recognising Rights of Mother Earth: Entrenching Earth Jurisprudence in Uganda*, ANARDE, (2018), https://anarde.org/img/pdf/Earth-Jurisprudence-in-Uganda.pdf.

[68] NATIONAL ENVIRONMENT MANAGEMENT AUTHORITY, *National Environment Act 2019*, https://nema.go.ug/sites/all/themes/nema/docs/National%20Environment%20Act,%202019%20(1).pdf.

Constitution further obligated the state to protect essential natural resources on behalf of the people of Uganda. However, this legal position did not provide for nature to hold, enjoy, and enforce its rights. Through the 2019 legislation, Uganda has given universal rights to both humans and nature to enjoy a clean and healthy environment.[69]

The Ugandan Parliament's Committee on Natural Resources' reasoning to promote rights of nature is a clear example of the legal innovation needed to achieve transformational change. It has recognized that laws have treated nature as property and drawn the direct link between the human right to a healthy environment and the environment's right to be healthy.

This legal right addresses the challenge of legal standing, often described as the ability to sue and be sued, which enables "nature" to go to court to protect its rights. Legal rights are not the same as human rights, and so a "legal person" does not necessarily have to be a human being. Corporations, for example, are also treated in law as "legal persons," as a way to endow companies with particular legal rights and to treat the company as legally distinct from its managers and shareholders. Ugandan lawmakers and society have taken a major step forward in applying the practice and frameworks to nature.[70]

This legislative enactment towards recognizing the rights of nature is a powerful step forward, particularly as the first in Africa where there is serious potential to protect existing natural resources from exploitation and destruction. The Committee cited developments from India and New Zealand to support its decision-making. This jurisprudential exchange of ideas offers the hope for other African jurisdictions to adopt and develop similar policies.

g. United States

In 2006, a small Pennsylvania community named Tamaqua Borough worked with a group called Community Environmental Legal Defense Fund (CELDF) to draft legislation that would protect the community, and the environment, from the dumping of toxic sewage. Since the events in Tamaqua Borough, local government bodies throughout the United States have taken up some form of rights for nature provision. These include ordinances in Pennsylvania, Maine, New Hampshire, and California, and a proposed amendment to the constitution of the Ho-Chunk Nation.

---

[69] BENCH PARLIAMENT OF UGANDA, *Report of the Committee on Natural Resources on The National Environment Bill 2017,* ¶ 3.2 (2018), https://www.parliament.go.ug/cmis/views/365548fd-c4a8-4498-aa0d-8d4492ad574d%253B1.0.

[70] *Id.*

In 2010, a high-profile case, *Citizens United v. Federal Election Commission,* strongly asserted corporation's status as a (legal) person while rejecting local he ordinance that recognized the legal identity of nature.

IV. What came first- Law or Humanity?

Law as a pillar of humanity is, by design, an evolutionary thought. It continues to be in motion, developing and growing with time. Our actions make it interesting by continuing to shape it. This relationship is strengthened by practice and precedent at every layer of the legal ecosystem, starting at the individual level and moving from local to national and regional level, and then at the international level between states, organizations, and corporations.

Did humanity create law?

Law, as we have discovered, defined and developed, continues to be conveniently designed to suit the interests of humanity. In practice, at every layer of this ecosystem, power play of social, economic, or political shades alters the meaning of justice for those from weaker positions. However, these voices play a critical role in legal thought and its development. The result of unfulfilled guarantee of basic rights is a signal which suggests that law is not effective enough to meet the needs of all; it must evolve.

A. Progressive Development in Public International Law

International legal development of rights has many pathways. A new norm of international law could develop as a custom, a treaty, a general principle, or through a judicial decision. Central to these technicalities is the requirement for any norm to have widespread acceptance amongst nations, where state and non-state actors recognize a norm as binding and shape their conduct accordingly.

"The existence of a rule of customary international law requires that there be 'a settled practice' together with opinio juris."[71] National legislation, domestic court decisions, and statements of States can be considered as evidence of customary international law. However, these have to be of a significant level that convey a consistent practice and policy amongst international actors. In order to ascertain a rule of customary international law, the Court "has to direct its attention to the practice and opinio juris of States; it is, of course, axiomatic that the material of customary international

---

[71] ICJ, *Germany v. Italy* 2012, ¶ 55; See also Asylum 1950 at 276-77; North Sea 1969, ¶ 77; Nuclear Weapons GA 1996, ¶ 64.

law is to be looked for primarily in the actual practice and opinio juris of States, even though multilateral conventions may have an important role to play in recording and defining rules deriving from custom, or indeed in developing them."[72]

At this moment in history, it cannot be suggested that we are witnessing the emergence of a new rule of customary international law towards recognizing the natural environment as a person. However, it is pertinent to suggest that we can indeed notice legal developments that, with time and momentum, can render the possibility for the international community to accord special status to the rights of nature doctrine.

Such a possibility would substantively add voice to the recognition of green crimes as a separate new category of international law violations. There is a harmonious overlap in the scope and application of these two doctrines. Recognizing the environment as a person or select natural clusters as a person would first address challenges of legal representation and standing in courts. Secondly, it would pave the way for a new body of reparations to the environment in nature of damage control, improvement, and betterment of biodiversity.

Following domestic pronouncements for the right of nature in select jurisdictions, the next step for the progressive development of this doctrine at the international legal level is the bilateral and regional codification of rights of nature. That would lend credibility in terms of state practice of a kind that can be considered to be the practice of highly affected states. Rivers offer that perfect opportunity. Rivers connect geographies and nations through their steam and flow. For example, the Ganga river in India has a different name, 'Tsangpo' in China, and there may be a possibility for these two nations to develop a comprehensive protection regime that is centered around the legal rights of the river.[73] Similarly, regional pacts and legal instruments that seek to protect natural resources within closely located nations by adopting a rights of nature approach would lend more credibility and weight to the emergence of the doctrine of environmental personhood.

Other factors that have and will continue to play a key role in this pathway of progressive development are the existing international environmental doctrine

---

[72] ICJ, *Continental Shelf (Libyan Arab Jamahiriya/Malta)*, I.C.J. REPORTS 1985, 29-30, ¶ 27.) (Nicaragua Merits 1986, ¶ 183; *See also Germany v. Italy* 2012, ¶ 55; Nuclear Weapons GA 1996, ¶ 64).

[73] More of this topic and some criticism can be found in Regina M. Paulose's chapter on hydropower dams.

of the Polluter Pays and Precautionary Principle. At the heart of these principles lies innate respect and value for the natural environment. The Precautionary Principle suggests that in the case of scientific uncertainty concerning the activity that may harm the environment, the benefit of doubt must be given to science and that activity must not be undertaken; as a result, conducting an EIA is a mandatory step for all developmental and construction activities.[74]

Indigenous customs have a normative value and are playing a key role in the development of jurisprudence. Indigenous principles reframe exploitative or damaging relationships between individuals and Nature. For illustration, in Aotearoa/New Zealand and South America, the environmental personhood statute draws intensely on Indigenous ideas of "kaitiakitanga" or guardianship, which sees people as stewards, instead of proprietors, of the environment.[75] In both Ecuador and Bolivia, regard for the rights of nature coincided with a rise in political power for indigenous groups.

B. Human Rights and Environmental Rights: Jurisprudential relationship

The discussion on rights of the environment has not grown in isolation from new human rights trends and developments. Essential to this discussion is another parallel and connected stream of developments concerning the strongly emerging *right to a healthy and clean environment.*

The right of humans to have a healthy, safe, and clean environment is an upside way of affirming the environment's right to exist in good health. The discussion on the development of both of these rights has emerged in the last decade. It signals a larger shift towards increasing the importance or necessity of maintaining a healthy environment and creating legal safeguards to protect and enforce these rights.[76]

At the international level, the UN has still not formally recognized the human right to a healthy environment. Former UN Special Rapporteur on Human Rights and Climate Change, John Knox, developed 16 Framework Principles that set out basic obligations of the States under human rights law as they relate to the enjoyment of a healthy environment. These principles illustrate the inter-linkages between human rights and environment and how

---

[74] Dispute Regarding Navigational and Related Rights (*Costa Rica v. Nicaragua*), Judgment, I.C.J. REPORTS 2009, 242, ¶ 64.

[75] CYRUS R. VANCE CENTER, *supra* note 43.

[76] David Boyd, *The Constitutional Right to a Healthy Environment*, ENVIRONMENT: SCIENCE AND POLICY FOR SUSTAINABLE DEVELOPMENT, (July 13, 2012).

they are closely connected to fulfill the objectives of international rights instruments.[77]

The right to a healthy environment continues to develop at international, regional, and national levels, both as an implicit and explicit right along three major paths. Through the process of "greening" human rights, treaty bodies, regional tribunals, special rapporteurs, and other international human rights bodies have elaborated on the fundamental importance of a healthy environment for the full enjoyment of other human rights, such as the rights to life, health, food, water, and sanitation.[78]

Pursuing an integrated approach that incorporates rights-based strategies for human beings and the environment is essential. The international human rights system has the benefit of widespread codification and uptake by nations, and principles have been elaborated over time to specific groups of rights holders and duty bearers.[79] Environmental degradation is a human rights issue. Recognition by the UN of the human right to a healthy environment will have a measurable impact on everything from curbing emissions to preserving ecosystems to protecting human health.

This recognition is essential for the era of environmental rights and biocentrism. Rights of Nature entails a fundamental shift from the anthropogenic assumptions in these legal fields to an ecocentric approach that views nature not as an object or property but as a "subject of rights." Strategic litigation and judicial decisions have played a critical role in moving

---

[77] UNITED NATIONS GENERAL ASSEMBLY, *Report of the Special Rapporteur on the issue of human rights obligations relating to the enjoyment of a safe, clean, healthy and sustainable environment,* A/HRC/37/59 (24 January 2018), https://undocs.org/A/HRC/37/59.

[78] For example, the Convention on the Rights of the Child states that in the course of pursuing the right of the child to the enjoyment of the highest attainable standard of health, Parties must take appropriate measures to provide nutritious foods and clean drinking water, taking into consideration the dangers and risks of environmental pollution. Art. 24, ¶ 2 (c). The Committee on Economic, Social and Cultural Rights has interpreted the ICESCR to include the need to ensure "adequate supply of safe and potable water and basic sanitation; [and] the prevention and reduction of the population's exposure to harmful substances such as radiation and harmful chemicals or other detrimental environmental conditions that directly or indirectly impact upon human health." Committee on Economic, Social and Cultural Rights, general comment No. 14, ¶ 15. Decisions by the African Commission on Human and Peoples' Rights, the ECtHR, and the Inter-American Commission and Court of Human Rights have found environmental harm can violate human rights.

[79] Cyrus R. Vance Center, *supra* note 43.

the dial forward.[80] Court decisions can inform the development of legislation, institutions, and environmental planning while strengthening the recognition of, and the linkages between, the human rights to a healthy environment and the environment's right to be healthy.

V. Next Steps

Rivers are a critical focal point within the environmental personhood landscape. All inclusive, river systems are under extraordinary pressure. Numerous of the world's rivers endure from uncommon over-exploitation—through extraction, contamination, damming, change of normal stream administrations, loss of water quality, and changes to riverine environments, living spaces and watersheds. As a result, freshwater vertebrate species are declining more than twice as quickly as land-based and marine vertebrates.[81]

Rivers have the subject of most of the national precedents that signal an emerging jurisprudence for rights of nature in New Zealand, India, and Ecuador. The cases outline the critical part that waterways have played inside both the Rights of Nature thoughts and the broader development to bolster these rights. They offer assistance to bring legitimate shape to the ways in which rivers are valued and understood.[82]

In many cases, Rights of Nature remedies have involved the creation of a guardianship body responsible for particular natural phenomena—a river, forest, or an entire ecosystem. Guardianship bodies are often advised by experts and required to regularly report on their progress. Experience shows the critical importance of guardianship bodies that are robust, well-funded, and unbiased in order to hold the government accountable and put landmark court decisions into practice.[83]

Remedies for violations of Rights of Nature may include both restitution and preventive measures. Alongside the creation of new guardianship bodies, courts have ordered environmental action plans, demarcation of protected areas, data collection and studies, judicial oversight and monitoring, and awarded damages, rehabilitation, and restoration.[84]

---

80 *Id.*

81 Tickner et al, *Bending the Curve of Global Freshwater Biodiversity Loss: An Emergency Recovery Plan,* 70(4) BIO SCIENCE 330 (2020).

82 CYRUS R. VANCE CENTER, *supra* note 43.

83 *Id.*

84 *Id.*

A. Environmental Personhood as a means to achieve Climate Justice[85]

Climate justice "insists on a shift from a discourse on greenhouse gases and melting ice caps into a civil rights movement with the people and communities most vulnerable to climate impacts at its heart."[86] Climate justice links human rights and development to achieve a human-centered approach, safeguarding the rights of the most vulnerable people and sharing the burdens and benefits of climate change and its impacts equitably and fairly. Climate justice is informed by science, responds to science and acknowledges the need for equitable stewardship of the world's resources.[87]

Environmental personhood not only asks for Rights of Nature, but this doctrine also seeks to create equity and balance in the relationship between human beings and nature. This relationship as it exists today is severely affected by the social, political, economic interests of a select few, which places the majority of the world in an environmentally vulnerable position. The climate justice movement does not only seek to address these inequalities but also give nature its due respect and position in the global society.

Furthermore, linking with the understanding of climate litigations, that with the onset of climate change, traditional cases of nuisance and environmental degradation now occupy a greater space aiming at corporate and governmental accountability for violations, inaction, and consequent damage.

Green crimes have occurred nationally and internationally in the past, but there has been no recognition of these acts as serious violations against the environment and the communities that depend on it for their sustenance. What used to be the extractive normal for the 20th century, such as setting up

---

[85] Why does the author use the term climate justice and not environmental justice? While these terms can be complementary, environmental justice is broader in scope and may include foundational aspects of climate justice in its ambit. The author uses climate justice here because of the premise that we have lost the opportunity address a glaringly large amount of environmental injustice and what shall be able to achieve with now with operationalizing environmental personhood will be more survival induced and thus more apt to be climate induced. Using climate justice is more conducive for the development of the doctrine, particularly because environmental justice has a more regional/geographic scope and climate justice will allow for third parties and indigenous groups living in other parts of the world, facing adverse impacts to also be able to connect.

[86] UN SUSTAINABLE DEVELOPMENT GOALS, *Climate Justice*, (May 2019), https://www.un.org/sustainabledevelopment/blog/2019/05/climate-justice/.

[87] MARY ROBINSON FOUNDATION, *Climate Justice*, https://www.mrfcj.org/principles-of-climate-justice/.

new coal-fire-powered plants or changing the soil ecology of a region, is today a flagrant climate justice issue. Environmental personhood is technically at the heart of the climate justice movement as both the issues arise from a common problem of misjudgment of the value of our natural environment.

Climate justice calls for inclusivity in decision-making at the political level. Achieving climate justice in specific sectors and regions creates more favorable conditions for legislators and judges to recognize and enact nature's rights.

The idea of supportive action draws on the concept of affirmative action in that it looks to counterbalance past injustice imposed on nature. Supportive action transcends the idea of "affirmative duties" to pursue the conservation and restoration of endangered species without any specific non-anthropocentric background.

What rights are we talking about? The Right to Flourish, Regenerate, and Evolve. *Ecological amnesia*: when people do not remember that there used to be trees or fish on this land before. Historical amnesia in the West has been a catalyst for ecological amnesia. For nature to be a person, it is essential that it can preserve and carry its identity. There has to be a continuation of its eternal identity in the minds of others. *Indigenous worldview*: when you take care of things and beings, they return. But when you live in a state of transience (every generation in a family moving to a new place to live and settle), there is no taking care of the land or its beings. Extractive traditions of the West: the right to regenerate is essential for nature.

We need to think futuristic and account for the discernible and identifiable crises glaring upon the planet and the international community with increasingly worrying statistics every year. The global water crisis is one such example. It is a result of a broken/western legal understanding of nature. Environmental personhood is a way to address the impending global water crisis. From a strategic perspective, the Amazon forest and the Arctic region are the next most ideal candidates for being recognized as legal persons. Both of these natural ecosystems are transnational and would require legal cooperation between nations.

Rights of Nature jurisprudence is still in its infancy as courts and legislators continue to develop and define concepts and approaches. Any comprehensive assessment of its success would be premature.[88]

---

[88] Cyrus R. Vance Center, *supra* note 43.

VI. Conclusion

With time, humanity's understanding of its relationship with nature has matured. Arguments for the intrinsic value of nature are a class of arguments completely different from arguments for the instrumental value founded on the usefulness of nature for humankind. The role of philosophy will always be important, but now is the time for a more harmonious and ecocentric approach. The Rights of Nature movement is growing. It is led by Indigenous peoples, civil society, legal experts, and youth, who all demand systemic reform of our treatment of nature.

A Rights of Nature approach offers an opportunity for transformative change. First, it recognizes that nature is not mere human property but instead possesses basic rights. These rights can be established by defining nature as a "subject of rights," as a "legal person," as a "rights-bearing entity," or through other terminology. Nature's rights may include rights to exist, to thrive, and the right to restoration. Second, Rights of Nature typically gives nature legal standing, which means its rights can be directly defended in a court of law. Third, a Rights of Nature approach creates duties for humans to act as guardians or stewards of the natural world. Many Rights of Nature laws and decisions create guardianship bodies—a group of people or an entity with a legal duty to uphold the rights and interests of nature.

Rights of Nature is already a transnational jurisprudence. There is growing acknowledgment of such rights within the UN system, and they are enshrined in numerous UN General Assembly resolutions. Countries from New Zealand, Bangladesh, and Uganda have cited one another's decisions and analysis in passing new laws and deciding cases. As Rights of Nature develops, concepts and approaches will continue to travel across and between international and domestic legal systems. An important role for the movement is to continue to support this exchange, both within and across countries.

"The precise meaning and effects of recognizing the rights of nature will be worked out through community conversations, scholarly dialogue, public and political debates, negotiation, and, where necessary, litigation, just as all novel legal concepts evolve."[89] From an international legal perspective, the widespread acceptance amongst nations of this progressive development will take time and happen in due course. This development is very much linked with the recognition and development of the jurisprudence on green crimes. Legal innovation and ecocentrism will offer the pathway forward.

---

[89] David R. Boyd, *Recognizing the Rights of Nature: Lofty Rhetoric or Legal Revolution?*, 32 NAT. RESOURCES AND ENV. 13, 17 (2018).

Bibliography

Matthias Aegenheyster, et al., *Risk and the Point of No Return for Climate Action*, EARTH SYST. DYNAM. (2018), https://pdfs.semanticscholar.org/3520/dc9ae7a5599d38a12e587b477dd58c032542.pdf.

Animal Welfare Board of India vs. A. Nagaraj and Ors. (2014) 7 SCC 547.

Appellate Division upholds HC order on Turag land recovery, Dhaka Tribune, (Feb. 4, 2020), https://www.dhakatribune.com/bangladesh/court/2020/02/04/appellate-division-upholds-hc-order-on-turag-land-recovery.

BENCH PARLIAMENT OF UGANDA, Report of the Committee on Natural Resources on The National Environment Bill 2017, ¶ 3.2 (2018), https://www.parliament.go.ug/cmis/views/365548fd-c4a8-4498-aa0d-8d4492ad574d%253B1.0.

Narayan Dutt Bhatt v. Union of India and others, Writ Petition (PIL) No. 43 of 2014, (High Court of Uttarakhand).

Bolivia Mother Earth Law 071 of 2010 (Ley (Corta) de Derechos de Madre Tierra).

David Boyd, *The Constitutional Right to a Healthy Environment*, ENVIRONMENT: SCIENCE AND POLICY FOR SUSTAINABLE DEVELOPMENT, (July 13, 2012).

David R Boyd, *Recognizing the Rights of Nature: Lofty Rhetoric or Legal Revolution?*, 32 NAT. RESOURCES AND ENV. 13, 17 (2018).

E.S. Brondizo et al., *Global Assessment Report on Biodiversity and Ecosystem Services of the Intergovernmental Science-Policy Platform on Biodiversity and Ecosystem Services*, IPBES (May 2019), https://ipbes.net/global-assessment.

J. Baird Callicott, *The Search For an Environmental Ethic*, in MATTERS OF LIFE AND DEATH 420 (Tom Regan ed., 2nd ed. 1986).

J. Baird Callicott, *Traditional American Indian and Traditional Western European Attitudes toward Nature*, ENVIRONMENTAL ETHICS, Vol 4, Issue 4, (Winter 1982).

Paola Villavicencio Calzadilla and Louis J. Kotze, *Living in Harmony with Nature? A Critical Appraisal of the Rights of Mother Earth in Bolivia*, 7 TRANSNATIONAL ENV. L. 397 (2018).

Damian Carrington, *Plummeting Insect Numbers 'Threaten Collapse of Nature,'* THE GUARDIAN (Feb. 10, 2019), https://www.theguardian.com/environment/2019/feb/10/plummeting-insect-numbers-threaten-collapse-of-nature.

Center for Environment Law and WWF-India v. Union of India (2013), I.A. No. 100 in Writ Petition No. 337 of 1995 (Supreme Court of India).

Liz Charpleix, *The Whanganui River as Te Awa Tupua: Place based law in a legally pluralistic society*, 184(1) THE GEOGRAPHICAL JOURNAL 19 (2017), https://onlinelibrary.wiley.com/doi/full/10.1111/geoj.12238.

THE DAILY STAR, *Can the historic High Court judgement save our rivers?* (Feb. 5, 2019), https://www.thedailystar.net/environment/news/can-thehistoric-high-court-judgement-save-our-rivers-1697419.

DHAKA TRIBUNE, *Appellate Division upholds HC order on Turag land recovery*, (Feb. 4, 2020), https://www.dhakatribune.com/bangladesh/court/2020/02/04/appellate-division-upholds-hc-order-on-turag-land-recovery.

Dispute Regarding Navigational and Related Rights (Costa Rica v. Nicaragua), Judgment, I.C.J. REPORTS 2009, p. 242, ¶ 64).

Robert Elliot, *Environmental ethics*, in A COMPANION TO ETHICS, (Peter Singer ed. 1993).

Susan Emmenegger and Axl Tschentscher, *Taking Nature's Rights Seriously: The Long Way to Biocentrism in Environmental Law*, 6 GEO. INT'L ENVTL. L. REV. 545 (1994).

P. Fenn, *Justinian and the Freedom of the Sea*, 19 AM. J. OF INTERNATIONAL LAW, 716 (1925).

Gwendolyn Gordon, Environmental Personhood (March 7, 2017), http://dx.doi.org/10.2139/ssrn.2935007.

Forest L. Grieves, *Classical Writers of International Law and the Environment*, 4 B.C. ENVTL. AFF. L. REV. 309 (1975).

ICJ, Continental Shelf (Libyan Arab Jamahiriya/Malta), I.C.J. REPORTS 1985, pp. 29-30, ¶ 27.)' (Nicaragua Merits 1986, ¶ 183; See also Germany v. Italy 2012, ¶ 55; Nuclear Weapons GA 1996, ¶ 64).

ICJ, Germany v. Italy 2012, ¶ 55; See also Asylum 1950, pp. 276-277; North Sea 1969, ¶ 77; Nuclear Weapons GA 1996, ¶ 64.

Intergovernmental Panel on Climate Change (IPCC), *Climate Change 2007: Synthesis Report of IPCC Fourth Assessment Summary for Policymakers*, 13-14 (Nov. 2007).

Thomas S. Kuhn, THE STRUCTURE OF SCIENTIFIC REVOLUTIONS, 111-35 (2d ed. 1970).

Miglani v. State of Uttarakhand, Writ. Petition PIL No. 140 of 2015 (High Court of Uttarakhand, March 30, 2017).

Clarence Morris, *The Rights and Duties of Beasts and Trees: A Law Teacher's Essay for Landscape Architects*, 17 JOURNAL OF LEGAL EDUCATION, 189, 190, 191 (1964).

NATIONAL ENVIRONMENT MANAGEMENT AUTHORITY, *National Environment Act 2019*, (2019), https://nema.go.ug/sites/all/themes/nema/docs/National%20Environment%20Act,%202019%20(1).pdf.

S. Pufendorf, DE JURE NATURAE ET GENTIUM, LIBRI OCTO, (1688 ed. C. and W. Oldfather transl. 1934).

Stephen Francis Ruddy, *Res Nullius and Occupation in Roman and International Law*, 36 U. MO. AT KANSAS C.L. REV. 274 (1968).

Mohd Salim v. State of Uttarakhand and Others (Writ Petition (PIL)No. 126 of 2014 (High Court of Uttarakhand, Dec. 5, 2016).

Bhadra Sinha, *SC puts on hold Uttarakhand HC order declaring river Ganga a living entity*, HINDUSTAN TIMES, (Jul. 7, 2017), https://www.hindustantimes.com/india-news/sc-puts-on-holduttarakhand-high-court-order-declaring-ganga-a-living-entity/story-IYqkaehoLhAyWfjAP8GYOO.html.

THE STOCKHOLM RESILIENCE CENTRE, *The Nine Planetary Boundaries*, (Sept. 17, 2009), https://www.stockholmresilience.org/research/planetary-boundaries/planetary-boundaries/about-the-research/the-nine-planetary-boundaries.html.

Christopher D. Stone, *Should Trees Have Standing? - Toward Legal Rights For Natural Objects*, 45 S. CAL. L. REV. 450, 456 (1972).

Te Urewera Act 2014 s 11(1) (NZ).

Tickner et al, *Bending the Curve of Global Freshwater Biodiversity Loss: An Emergency Recovery Plan*, 70(4) BIO SCIENCE 330 (2020).

T.N. Godavarman Thirumulpad v. Union of India (2012), I.A. Nos. 1433 and 1477 of 2995 in Writ Petition No. 202 of 1995, (Supreme Court of India).

Laurence H, Tribe, *Ways Not To Think About Plastic Trees: New Foundations for Environmental Law*, 83 YALE L.J. 1315, 1343 (1974).

Frank Tumusiime, *Recognising Rights of Mother Earth: Entrenching Earth Jurisprudence in Uganda*, ANARDE, (2018), https://anarde.org/img/pdf/Earth-Jurisprudence-in-Uganda.pdf.

UNITED NATIONS GENERAL ASSEMBLY, *Report of the Special Rapporteur on the issue of human rights obligations relating to the enjoyment of a safe, clean, healthy and sustainable environment*, A/HRC/37/59 (24 January 2018), https://undocs.org/A/HRC/37/59.

Edith Brow Weiss, *Our Rights and Obligations to Future Generations for the Environment*, 85 AM. J. INTL'L L. 198 (1990).

Samuel C Wiel, *Natural Communism: Air, Water, Oil, Sea and Seashore*, 47 HARV. L. REV. (Jan 1934), https://doi.org/10.2307/1331877.

Writ Petition 3839 of 2016 (Supreme Court of Bangladesh, High Court Division).

World Health Organization, *Climate Change and Health*, (Feb. 1, 2018), https://www.who.int/news-room/fact-sheets/detail/climate-change-and-health.

WORLD PEOPLE'S CONFERENCE ON CLIMATE CHANGE AND THE RIGHTS OF MOTHER EARTH, *Universal Declaration of the Rights of Nature*, (April 2010), https://therightsofnature.org/universal-declaration/.

Chapter 3

Addressing Environmental Harm in Conflicts within Africa: Scope for International Criminal Law?

Damian Etone

University of Stirling

Abstract: International criminal law has flourished in recent years, emerging with several international criminal tribunals and developing a substantial body of jurisprudence, substantive, and procedural rules, but there is no existing international criminal tribunal with special jurisdiction over environmental crimes. While several international criminal law scholars have questioned the utility of international criminal law in relation to environmental harm, this chapter argues that international criminal law has an important role in environmental protection. Various international criminal tribunals have, in the past, either been reluctant to investigate major environmental and cultural crimes or have adopted a cautious approach in the interpretation of these crimes. However, in 2016, the ICC Office of the Prosecutor released a new policy which broadened the focus of its investigations to give particular consideration to crimes relating to the "destruction of the environment," "exploitation of natural resources," and the "illegal dispossession" of land. This chapter has two key parts. The first undertakes a careful analysis of the jurisprudence from various international criminal tribunals to determine the extent to which they addressed environmental harm in conflicts within the African region. This is followed by an examination of the Protocol on the Statute of the African Court of Justice and Human Rights (Malabo Protocol) and its potential to enshrine international criminal accountability for damage to the environment. At the core of this chapter is the question to what extent can international criminal law accommodate and effectively address environmental crimes committed within the context of armed conflicts in Africa? The chapter contends that international criminal law provides a potential means for addressing environmental harm indirectly through progressive interpretation of genocide, war crimes, and crimes against humanity, and directly within Africa through the provisions of the Malabo Protocol.

Keywords: Malabo Protocol, African Union, International Criminal Court, Special Court for Sierra Leone, International Criminal Tribunal for Rwanda, Additional Protocols Geneva Convention, War Crimes, Crimes against Humanity.

***

I. Introduction

The effects of modern war on biodiversity and the environment have been increasingly well-documented.[1] In Africa, illegal exploitation of natural resources such as oil, diamonds, timber and minerals has fueled several conflicts in the region, including Sierra Leone, Liberia, Congo, and Sudan.[2] The conflict in the Democratic Republic of Congo (DRC) between 1995 and 2006 resulted in the decimation of the elephant and hippopotamus populations slaughtered by the Mai Mai rebel militia on an industrial scale.[3] The impact of armed conflicts in DRC and the Central African Republic between the 1970s-1990s was so severe on the elephant populations that the previously estimated population of about 10,000 is now reported to have essentially disappeared.[4] Some of the negative environmental impacts of conflicts in Africa include deforestation, loss of wildlife and biodiversity, arms

---

[1] Michael J. Lawrence et al., *The Effects of Modern War and Military Activities on Biodiversity and the Environment*, 23(4) ENVIRONMENTAL REVIEWS 443 (2015).

[2] In its judgment on the *Lubanga* Case, the ICC determined that the exploitation of natural resources in the Itura region fanned the flames of the armed conflict in the DRC. See Prosecutor v. Thomas Lubanga Dyilo, Case No. ICC- 01/ 04- 01/ 06- 2842, Judgment Pursuant to Article 74 of the Statute (March 14, 2012); *See also* Rene L. Beyers et al., *Resource Wars and Conflict Ivory: The Impact of Civil Conflict on Elephants in the Democratic Republic of Congo - The Case of the Okapi Reserve*, 6(11) PLoS ONE (2011); Janet Nackoney et al., *Impacts of Civil Conflict on Primary Forest Habitat in Northern Democratic Republic of the Congo 1990–2010*, Biol. Conserv. (2014), https://langint.pri.kyoto-u.ac.jp/ai/intra_data/JanetNackoney/NackoneyJ2014-BC.pdf.

[3] Kevin Bales, Blood and Earth: *Modern Slavery, Ecocide, and the Secret to Saving the World*, 39-41 (2016).

[4] U. C. Jha, *Armed Conflict and Environmental Damage*, 103 (2nd ed. 2014).

production pollution, and soil and water pollution.[5] UN Security Council Resolution 1856 on the Situation Concerning the Democratic Republic of Congo recognized the link between illegal exploitation of natural resources and the proliferation and trafficking of arms as key factors exacerbating conflicts in the Great Lakes regions of Africa.[6] In 2009, a study on the impact of armed conflicts on the environment by the UNEP concluded that lack of governance is a major reason why armed conflicts have continued to cause significant damage to the environment.[7] As a result of armed activities, 23 national parks and nature reserves in Africa have been listed by UNESCO to be in danger.[8] There is, therefore, a need to address environmental crimes in the context of armed conflict in Africa, given the *erga omnes* obligation that arises from some environmental crimes.[9]

International criminal law has flourished in recent years, with the emergence of several international criminal tribunals and developing a substantial body of jurisprudence, substantive and procedural rules. It has been able to achieve a track record of application to non-international armed conflicts in Africa with successful convictions entered for crimes including war crimes, crimes against humanity, and genocide by the ICC, ICTR, and SCSL.[10] However, there is no existing international criminal tribunal with special jurisdiction over environmental crimes. The framers of the ICC Statute limited the scope of the court's jurisdiction to genocide, war crimes, and crimes against humanity. According to Frédéric Mégret, some of the impediments to the emergence of an international environmental crime include the nature of the context (international law), the nature of the protected interest (environment) and the nature of the project (criminal

---

[5] Negasi Solomon et al., *Environmental Impacts and Causes of Conflict in the Horn of Africa: A Review,* 177 EARTH-SCIENCE REVIEW 284-290 (2018); Rene L. Beyers et al., *Resource Wars and Conflict Ivory: The Impact of Civil Conflict on Elephants in the Democratic Republic of Congo - The Case of the Okapi Reserve,* 6(11) PLoS ONE (2011).

[6] *See* United Nations Security Council, *Resolution 2136 - Democratic Republic of* Congo (30 January 2014) 2, UN Doc S/RES/2136 (2014).

[7] UNITED NATIONS ENVIRONMENTAL PROGRAMME, *Protecting the Environment During Armed Conflict: An Inventory and Analysis of International Law,* 8, (2009).

[8] See UNESCO website, at http://whc.unesco.org/en/ danger/ (accessed 4 July 2020).

[9] See Ulrich Beyerlin and Thilo Marauhn, *International Environmental Law,* 282-89 (1st ed. 2011).

[10] *See* Prosecutor v. Issa Hassan Sesay et al, Case No. SCSL-04-15-T, Judgment (Mar. 2, 2009); Prosecutor v. Thomas Lubanga Dyilo, Case No. ICC- 01/ 04- 01/ 06- 2842, Judgment Pursuant to Article 74 of the Statute (March 14, 2012); Prosecutor v. Germain Katanga, Case No. ICC- 01/ 04- 01/ 07, Judgment Pursuant to Article 74 of the Statute (Mar. 7, 2014); Prosecutor v. Ferdinand Nahimana, Case No. ICTR- 99- 52- T, Judgment (Dec. 3, 2003).

law).[11] While many sympathize with the need to address environmental harm, some are critical of the idea of incorporating the crime of ecocide into the Statute of the ICC.[12] International human rights law has made a lot more progress in addressing environmental harm, including creating a framework for environmental harm by corporations,[13] than international criminal law.

Despite the above challenges, the ICC has a limited ability to prosecute environmental criminal offenses as part of war crimes where an attack causes "widespread, long-term and severe damage to the natural environment which would clearly be excessive in relation to the concrete and direct overall military advantage anticipated."[14] This limits the ICC's jurisdiction to wartime environmental harm. In addition, the above provision only applies to international armed conflicts and does not offer any protection for non-international armed conflicts, which have mostly been the case in Africa. Therefore, there is a need for this provision to be amended to apply to non-international armed conflicts, and this chapter argues that international criminal law has an important role in environmental protection in Africa. Various international criminal tribunals have in the past been either reluctant to investigate major environmental and cultural crimes or have adopted a cautious approach in the interpretation of these crimes. However, in 2016, the ICC Office of the Prosecutor released a new policy which broadened the focus of its investigations to give particular consideration to crimes relating to the

---

[11] Frédéric Mégret, *The Challenge of an International Environmental Criminal* Law 1-22 (5 April 2010), https://papers.ssrn.com/sol3/Delivery.cfm/SSRN_ID1583610_code372721.pdf?abstractid=1583610&mirid=1

[12] Mark Notaras, *Should Ecocide Be Deemed a Crime against Peace?*, OUR WORLD (3 May 2010), https://ourworld.unu.edu/en/should-ecocide-be-deemed-a-crime-against-peace; Peter Sharp, *Prospects for Environmental Liability in the International Criminal Court*, 18 VA. ENVTL. LJ 217 (1999); Mohammed Saif-Alden Wattad, *Rome Statute and Captain Planet: What Lies between Crime against Humanity and the Natural Environment*, 19 Fordham Environmental Law Review 266 (2009).

[13] *See* Nadia Bernaz, *Enhancing Corporate Accountability for Human Rights Violations: Is Extraterritoriality the Magic Potion?* J. BUS. ETHICS 117, 493–511 (2013); Jernej Černič, *Corporate Accountability for Human Rights in The Business and Human Rights Landscape: Moving Forward, Looking Back* 193-218 (Jena Martin and Karen Bravo 2015); See also *Legally Binding Instrument To Regulate, In International Human Rights Law, The Activities Of Transnational Corporations And Other Business Enterprises* (OEIGWG Chairmanship Revised Draft 2019), https://www.ohchr.org/Documents/HRBodies/HRCouncil/WGTransCorp/OEIGWG_RevisedDraft_LBI.pdf.

[14] ROME STATUTE OF THE INTERNATIONAL CRIMINAL COURT (last amended 2010) art. 8(2)(b)(iv), July 17, 1998, 2187 U.N.T.S. (entered into force on July 1, 2002).

"destruction of the environment," "exploitation of natural resources," and the "illegal dispossession" of land.

This chapter adopts the conceptualization of the environment by Patricia Birnie and Allan Boyle, which refers to flora, fauna, soil, water (fresh and sea), landscape, cultural heritage, ecosystems, and the climate, and includes dependent human socio-economic systems, health, and welfare.[15] I engage with the concept of the environment as understood in several legal regimes that address natural resources, biodiversity, pollution and wastes, deforestation and endangered species. Part II undertakes a careful analysis of the jurisprudence from various international criminal tribunals to determine the extent to which they addressed environmental harm in conflicts within the African region. I focus on the jurisprudence of three key tribunals: The ICC, the Special Court for Sierra Leone and the International Criminal Tribunal for Rwanda. The analysis in this paper is limited only to the subject matter jurisdiction of the Courts. Part III examines the Protocol on the Statute of the African Court of Justice and Human Rights (Malabo Protocol) and its potential to enshrine international criminal accountability for damage to the environment. At the core of this paper is the question to what extent can international criminal law accommodate and effectively address environmental crimes committed within the context of armed conflicts in Africa? The paper contends that international criminal law provides a potential means for addressing environmental harm indirectly through progressive interpretation of genocide, war crimes and crimes against humanity, and directly within Africa through the provisions of the Malabo Protocol.

II. International Criminal Law and Environmental Crimes

There are several international treaties that seek to protect the environment during armed conflict. However, most of these treaties only attract state responsibility under international law rather than individual criminal responsibility.[16] Also, these treaties are, in general, philosophically

---

[15] Patricia Birnie and Allan Boyle, *International Law and the Environment* 3-4 (2002).

[16] Some examples include U.N. CONVENTION ON THE LAW OF THE SEA, 1833 U.N.T.S. 397 (opened for signature Dec. 10, 1982, entered into force Nov. 16, 1994); PROTOCOL OF 1978 RELATING TO THE INTERNATIONAL CONVENTION FOR THE PREVENTION OF POLLUTION FROM SHIPS, 1973, 1340 U.N.T.S (entered into force Oct. 2, 1983); AFRICAN CONVENTION ON THE CONSERVATION OF NATURE AND NATURAL RESOURCES (REVISED), adopted March 7, 2017, https://au.int/en/treaties/african-convention-conservation-nature-and-natural-resources-revised-version; CONVENTION ON CIVIL LIABILITY FOR DAMAGE RESULTING FROM ACTIVITIES DANGEROUS TO THE ENVIRONMENT, ETS No.150 (opened for signature June 21, 1993).

anthropocentric by focusing on protecting human beings from atrocities and only incidentally protect the environment for its utilitarian survival benefits to human beings.[17] This is in contrast to the eco-centric view, which seeks to protect the environment in its own right, independent of the use for which human beings may exploit it.[18] Nevertheless, several international treaties, cases from international criminal tribunals, and the prospects of an "African Criminal Court" are emerging, albeit limited, avenues for prosecuting damages to the environment under international criminal law. The analysis here will focus on those international treaties that attract some individual criminal responsibility.

2.1. Additional Protocols to the Geneva Conventions

Article 35 of Protocol Additional to the Geneva Conventions (Protocol I) prohibits methods and means of warfare that is intended or expected to cause 'widespread, long-term and severe damage to the natural environment.'[19] Similarly, Article 55 of Protocol I prohibits attacks against the natural environment as a means of retaliation and protects it against "widespread, long-term and severe damage."[20] However, the applicability of these provisions to conflicts within Africa is very limited given that they apply only to international armed conflicts, whereas the conflicts in Africa are mostly of a non-international nature or civil war.[21]

Article 14 of Protocol Additional to the Geneva Conventions (Protocol II) prohibits attacks that would "destroy, remove or render useless … foodstuffs, agricultural areas for the production of foodstuffs, crops, livestock, drinking

---

[17] See Rosemary Mwanza, Enhancing Accountability for Environmental Damage Under International Law: Ecocide as a Legal Fulfilment ff Ecological Integrity, 19(2) MELBOURNE JOURNAL OF INTERNATIONAL LAW 589-97 (2018). See also Louis J. Kotzé and Duncan French, The Anthropocentric Ontology of International Environmental Law and the Sustainable Development Goals: Towards an Ecocentric Rule of law in the Anthropocene, 7 GLOBAL JOURNAL OF COMPARATIVE LAW 5 (2018).

[18] Louis J. Kotzé and Duncan French, *The Anthropocentric Ontology of International Environmental Law and the Sustainable Development Goals: Towards an Ecocentric Rule of law in the Anthropocene,* 7 GLOBAL JOURNAL OF COMPARATIVE LAW 5 (2018).

[19] PROTOCOL ADDITIONAL TO THE GENEVA CONVENTIONS OF 12 AUGUST 1949, AND RELATING TO THE PROTECTION OF VICTIMS OF INTERNATIONAL ARMED CONFLICTS (PROTOCOL I) art. 35, 1125 U.N.T.S (opened for signature June 8, 1977, entered into force Dec. 7, 1978).

[20] *Id.* art. 55.

[21] *See* Linus Nnabuike Malu, *The International Criminal Court and Peace Processes: Côte d'Ivoire, Kenya and Uganda* 75-91 (2019).

water installations and supplies and irrigation works."[22] However, not only does this provision not qualify as a grave breach,[23] but also only applies anthropocentrically when connected to the starvation of civilians as a method and means of warfare.[24] An eco-centric view for the protection of the environment was rejected during the treaty negotiations for AP II in 1975. Australia's proposal to introduce a specific provision for protecting the natural environment and prohibit the destruction of the environment in both international and non-international armed conflict was unsuccessful.[25]

The Protocols to the Geneva Conventions provide very limited protection for the environment. Nevertheless, these provisions impose individual criminal responsibility, and subsequent treaties and international law cases have increasingly referred to the need to protect the environment in the context of armed conflict, as examined below.

2.2. Article 8 (2)(b)(iv) of the Rome Statute

The Rome Statute, which was adopted in 1998, established the International Criminal Court (ICC) and provided a broad framework for enforcing international humanitarian norms. It gives the court subject matter jurisdiction over four core crimes of genocide, crimes against humanity, war crimes, and the crime of aggression.[26] The destruction of the environment could arguably, in certain circumstances, be prosecuted under these categories of crimes, as examined below. While the Rome Statute is not an environmental criminal law document per se, it does provide some explicit protection for the environment in armed conflict, and since 2016, there has been a shift in the policy of the Prosecutor of the ICC to investigate crimes

---

[22] PROTOCOL ADDITIONAL TO THE GENEVA CONVENTIONS OF 12 AUGUST 1949, AND RELATING TO THE PROTECTION OF VICTIMS OF NON-INTERNATIONAL ARMED CONFLICTS (PROTOCOL II) art. 14, 1125 U.N.T.S (opened for signature June 8, 1977, entered into force Dec. 7, 1978).

[23] Carl E. Bruch, *The Environmental Law of War: All's Not Fair in (Civil) War: Criminal Liability for Environmental Damage in Internal Armed Conflict,* 25 VT. L. REV. 695, 722 (2001).

[24] AP II, *supra* note 22.

[25] See Australia, Statement at the Diplomatic Conference on the Reaffirmation and Development of International Humanitarian Law Applicable in Armed Conflicts (CDDH) (Geneva 1974–77), as cited in Matthew Gillett, *Eco-Struggles: Using International Criminal Law to Protect the Environment During and After Non-International Armed Conflict* in ENVIRONMENTAL PROTECTION AND TRANSITIONS FROM CONFLICT TO PEACE: CLARIFYING NORMS, PRINCIPLES, AND PRACTICES 240 (Carsten Stahn, Jens Iverson, and Jennifer S. Easterday 2017).

[26] ROME STATUTE art. 5, *supra* note 14.

relating to the "destruction of the environment," "exploitation of natural resources," and the "illegal dispossession" of land.[27] Article 8(2)(b)(iv) of the Rome Statute explicitly protects the natural environment in armed conflict by prohibiting the:

> Intentionally [launching of] an attack in the knowledge that such attack will cause incidental loss of life or injury to civilians or damage to civilian objects *or widespread, long-term and severe damage to the natural environment* which would be clearly excessive in relation to the concrete and direct overall military advantage anticipated. [28] [emphasis added].

According to Jessica Lawrence and Kevin Heller, the above provision represents a significant advancement for environmental protection in international law and, in theory, "could provide the nonhuman environment with previously unprecedented protection."[29] One of the reasons for this is that unlike earlier environmental provisions, individual criminal responsibility under Article 8(2)(b)(iv) for damage to the natural environment is not conditioned to injury to human beings. The use of the language "or" rather than "and" in the above provision implies that damage to the environment can be prosecuted in its own rights provided it is widespread, long-term, and severe, and equally disproportionate in relation to the anticipated military advantage.[30]

However, while Article 8(2)(b)(iv) has been recognized as the first "eco-centric" environmental war crime, the prospects for prosecuting this crime at the ICC has been hindered by several factors, including definitional issues for key terms of the Article, the strict requirement for intent, jurisdictional and other institutional limitations of the ICC. [31] Regarding definitional issues, for example, there was no definition for the key terms "widespread," "long-term

---

[27] INTERNATIONAL CRIMINAL COURT, *Policy Paper on Case Selection and Prioritisation* 14 (Sept. 15, 2016), https://www.icc-cpi.int/itemsDocuments/20160915_OTP-Policy_Case-Selection_Eng.pdf.

[28] ROME STATUTE, *supra* note 14, art 8(2)(b)(iv).

[29] Jessica C. Lawrence and Kevin Jon Heller, *THE FIRST ECOCENTRIC ENVIRONMENTAL WAR CRIME: THE LIMITS OF ARTICLE 8(2)(B)(IV) OF THE ROME STATUTE*, 20 GEO. INT'L ENVTL. L. REV. 61 (2007).

[30] One version of Article 8(2)(b)(iv) which was proposed during the negotiations for the Rome Statute criminalised damage to the environment without any proportionality qualifications to it. *See* Draft Statute for the International Criminal Court, p. 16, U.N. Doc. A/CONF.183/2/Add. 1 (1998).

[31] Lawrence and Heller, *supra* note 29, at 94-95.

and severe damage," or "natural environment." The principle of legality as a key principle of criminal law requires that the elements of crimes should be specific and that the objective elements of the crime and requisite *mens rea* are outlined clearly and in detail. It is difficult to predict what type of environmental damage would satisfy the requirement of "widespread long-term and severe."

One major barrier of Article 8(2)(b)(iv) to addressing environmental damage caused by armed conflicts within Africa is the jurisdictional limitation. This provision only applies to international armed conflicts making it almost certainly inapplicable to the serious conflicts within Africa, which have almost entirely been non-international, with no individual criminal accountability for damage to the natural environment. None of the twelve armed conflicts within Africa identified in the Rule of Law in Armed Conflicts (RULAC) database are international armed conflicts.[32] The lack of individual criminal responsibility for damage to the environment in the context of non-international armed conflict supports the call by many scholars for an amendment to the Rome Statute that would, at the very least, extend the application of Article 8(2)(b)(iv) to non-international armed conflict.[33] This sentiment was very much present during the negotiations for Additional Protocol II applicable to non-international armed conflicts. Australia had proposed that the destruction of the environment in the draft article should be prohibited both under international and non-international armed conflict, but this proposal was rejected.[34]

This chapter acknowledges that the Rome Statute does not provide direct environmental protection in the context of non-international armed conflict and re-echoes the need for reform to address this legal vacuum. However, the Rome Statute provides some indirect protection to the environment in the context of non-international armed conflict, and there is an opportunity for a broader or "greener" interpretation of the core crimes within the Rome Statute that could provide individual criminal accountability for damage to the environment during non-international armed conflict.

---

32 *See* RULE OF LAW IN ARMED CONFLICT (RULAC), *Conflicts,* available at http://www.rulac.org/browse/conflicts.

33 *See* Steven Freeland, *Addressing the Intentional Destruction of the Environment during Warfare under the Rome Statute of the International Criminal Court, Supranational Criminal Law* (2015); Lawrence and Heller, *supra* note 29 at 95.

34 Matthew Gillett, *supra* note 25 at 240.

2.3. Indirect Environmental Protections in the context of Non-International Armed Conflict

There are several conducts causing environmental damage in the context of non-international armed conflict that may attract individual criminal responsibility under the Rome Statute. Damage to the environment, depletion of natural resources and other crimes against the environment can arguably be prosecuted as part of war crimes, genocide or crimes against humanity. This section examines specific provisions and jurisprudence from the ICC that would provide the possibility for a broader interpretation of the above crimes to provide individual criminal accountability for environmental damage in the context of non-international armed conflict.

2.3.1. War Crimes

Article 8 of the Rome Statute defines a war crime as "grave breaches of the Geneva Conventions of 12 August 1949."[35] It is a criminal violation of the customary laws of war.[36] The relevant prohibitions applicable to non-international armed conflict include pillaging a town or place,[37] ordering the displacement of a civilian population for reasons related to the conflict,[38] and destroying or seizing the property of an adversary, subject to military necessity.[39] Pillaging, for example, is seen as an environmental-based crime[40] and has been used interchangeably with the words "spoliation", "plunder", and "looting" in the academic discourse. It is defined as the "forcible taking of private property by an invading or conquering army from the enemy's subjects"[41] for private or personal use.[42] In 2003, the UN Security Council condemned the plunder and illegal exploitation of the natural resources in

---

[35] ROME STATUTE, *supra* note 14, art 8.

[36] For a detailed discussion of the definition of a war crime, see Oona A. Hathaway et al., *What is a War Crime?* 43(1) YALE JOURNAL OF INTERNATIONAL LAW 53-113 (2019).

[37] ROME STATUTE, *supra* note 14, art 8(e)(v).

[38] *Id.* at art. 8(e)(viii).

[39] *Id.* at art. 8(e)(xii).

[40] See Olivia Radics and Carl Bruch, *The Law of Pillage, Conflict Resources, and Jus Post Bellum,* ENVIRONMENTAL PROTECTION AND TRANSITIONS FROM CONFLICT TO PEACE: CLARIFYING NORMS, PRINCIPLES, AND PRACTICES 145 (Carsten Stahn and Jens Iverson et al., eds.), (2017).

[41] BLACK'S LAW DICTIONARY (10th ed. 2015). This definition has also been adopted by the ICRC.

[42] *See* INTERNATIONAL CRIMINAL COURT, *Elements of Crimes,* art. 8(2)(b)(xvi), https://www.icc-cpi.int/NR/rdonlyres/336923D8-A6AD-40EC-AD7B-45BF9DE73D56/0/ElementsOfCrimesEng.pdf.

the Democratic Republic of Congo.[43] Jurisprudence from the Special Court for Sierra provides some precedence on how individuals can indirectly be prosecuted and held criminally accountable for damage to the environment in the context of non-international armed conflict as part of war crimes.

The tribunal, in the case of Charles Taylor,[44] made a good attempt to create a connection between war crimes and the pillage of a natural resource. Pillage was one of eleven counts with which Charles Taylor, former president of Liberia, was charged. In this case, the Trial Chamber noted that the crime of pillage includes instances of "'organized' and 'systematic' seizure of property from protected persons as well as to 'acts of looting committed by individual soldiers for their private gain.'"[45] As part of what was referred to as "Operation Pay Yourself," the tribunal found that there was looting of civilian property by soldiers in several districts in Sierra Leone on a large scale and in an indiscriminate manner.[46] Charles Taylor was convicted for aiding and abetting the crime of pillage by providing practical support, including weapons, military personnel, operational and moral support, which substantially led to the commission of the crime.[47] In the case of Prosecutor v. Sesay (Issa Hassan) and ors, the Trial Chamber held the accused persons responsible for a similar crime of pillage involving looting and destruction of civilian property, on the basis of joint criminal enterprise[48]. In determining the gravity of the criminal acts, the tribunal adopted an anthropocentric view focusing, among other things, on the number of victims, the impact of the pillage on victims and degree of suffering, and the considerable negative impact on the economy and development of the affected communities.[49] These cases demonstrate that it is possible to prosecute and convict the environmental crime of pillage in the context of a non-international armed conflict.

---

[43] S.C. Res. 1493, ¶ 28 U.N.Doc. S/RES/1493 (July 28, 2003).

[44] Prosecutor v. Charles Ghankay Taylor, Case No. SCSL-03-1-T, Judgment (May 18, 2012).

[45] AFRC Case, Prosecutor v. Brima (Alex Tamba) and ors, Case No SCSL-04-16-T, SCSL-04-16-T-613, Judgment, ¶¶ 750-57 (June 20, 2007).

[46] Prosecutor v. Taylor (Charles Ghankay), Case No. SCSL-03-1-T, Judgment, ¶¶ 533-46 (April 26, 2012).

[47] *Id.* ¶¶ 6921-37.

[48] Prosecutor v. Sesay (Issa Hassan) and ors, Case No. SCSL-04-15-T, Sentencing judgment, ¶¶ 173-78 (April 8, 2009); See also the case of Prosecutor v. Brima (Alex Tamba) and ors, the court found Alex Brima, Santigie Kanu, and Ibrahim Kamara guilty of pillage during the Sierra Leone civil war see AFRC Case, Prosecutor v. Brima (Alex Tamba) and ors, Case No. SCSL-04-16-T, Judgment, ¶ 2113 (June 20, 2007).

[49] Prosecutor v. Sesay (Issa Hassan) and ors, Case No. SCSL-04-15-T, Sentencing Judgment, ¶¶ 173-178 (April 8, 2009).

The natural resources of Sierra Leone, especially the diamond trade, played a vital role in fueling the civil war, and the term "blood diamond" is notably connected to the armed conflict in Sierra Leone. The report by the Panel of Experts appointed pursuant to UNSC Resolution 1306 concluded that there existed a link between illicit diamond trade and arms trade to the rebel forces in Sierra Leone.[50] Despite this finding, the SCSL construed the crime of pillaging more narrowly and did not charge any person for the pillaging of natural resources like diamonds as part of its war crime prosecution but rather focused exclusively on the pillaging of civilian property. A similar approach has been adopted by the ICC. In the case of Prosecutor v. Germain Katanga, the Trial Chamber found that, as a matter of fact, pillage was used in the conflict as a method of warfare and a form of "'pay,' 'booty,' or 'gain for the attackers.'"[51] Germain Katanga was found guilty of pillage, as part of war crime pursuant to Article 8(2)(e)(v) of the Rome Statute, for extensive destruction of civilian property, including houses, food, and animals.[52] However, the illegal exploitation of natural resources which provokes and sustains the conflict has not yet been addressed by the ICC. The prospects for prosecution for the looting of "blood diamonds" and pillaging of natural resources as part of war crimes committed in the Sierra Leone civil war became likely following the arrest of Michel Desaedeleer in 2015 in connection with a Belgian federal investigation.[53] Among other things, he was charged with war crimes for pillage involving the illicit trade of diamonds during the Sierra Leone civil war. However, the prospect for prosecution was lost when Desaedeleer died in Belgian custody while awaiting trial.

2.3.2. Crimes Against Humanity

According to Jessica Durney, crimes against humanity provide the broadest opportunity for the ICC to prosecute environmental crimes.[54] This reflects

---

[50] *Report of the Panel of Experts appointed Pursuant to UNSC Resolution 1306 (2000) Paragraph 19 in Relation to Sierra Leone* 150-151 (December 2000), https://mondediplo.com/IMG/pdf/un-report.pdf.

[51] Prosecutor v. Germain Katanga, Case No. ICC-01/04-01/07, Judgment pursuant to article 74 of the Statute, ¶ 519 (March 7, 2014).

[52] *Id.* ¶ 1691.

[53] Taegin Reisman, *Death of a Middleman Thwarts Blood Diamonds Case* (October 5, 2016), https://www.ijmonitor.org/2016/10/death-of-a-middleman-thwarts-blood-diamonds-case/.

[54] Jessica Durney, *Crafting a Standard: Environmental Crimes as Crimes Against Humanity Under the International Criminal Court* 24(2) HASTINGS ENVIRONMENTAL LAW JOURNAL 412-30 (2018).

some of the opinions in the 1985 Report by the UN Special Rapporteur for the Sub-Commission on Prevention of Discrimination and Protection that advocated for ecocide to be included as a crime against humanity.[55] Article 7 of the Rome Statute provides a list of specific actions that would constitute "crimes against humanity" if committed as part of a "widespread or systematic attack directed against any civilian population, with knowledge of the attack"[56] and "pursuant to or in furtherance of a State or organizational policy to commit such attack."[57]

There has been an increasing rise in the number of prosecutions for crimes against humanity in the ICC, including the Situation in the Republic of Kenya,[58] the Situation in Libya,[59] and the Situation in Cote d'Ivoire,[60] although these have not directly addressed environmental crimes. More so, grave human rights abuses committed by the Boko Haram Islamist group in Nigeria have been categorized as potential crimes against humanity by the ICC Prosecutor but were not investigated for any potential environmental crimes in the context of that conflict.[61]

There is philosophical justification for conceptualizing environmental crimes as crimes against humanity,[62] but this chapter's analysis is limited to the legal questions. While Article 7 does not explicitly mention the environment, three of the eleven acts constituting crimes against humanity ("extermination," "deportation or forcible transfer of population," and "other inhumane acts") provide possible avenues to address environmental harm,

---

[55] *Benjamin Whitaker (Special Rapporteur) Revised and Updated Report on the Question of the Prevention and Punishment of the Crime of Genocide* ¶ 33, UN ESCOR, Human Rights Sub Commission on the Prevention of Discrimination and Protection of Minorities, 38th Sess., UN Doc. E/CN.4/Sub.2/1985/6 (1985).

[56] ROME STATUTE, *supra* note 14, art. 7(1).

[57] *Id.*

[58] *See* The Prosecutor v. Uhuru Muigai Kenyatta, Case No. ICC-01/09-02/11-382-Red, Decision on the Confirmation of Charges Pursuant to Article 61(7)(a) and (b) of the Rome Statute (January 29, 2012).

[59] The Prosecutor v. Saif Al-Islam Gaddafi, Case No. ICC-01/11-01/11-2, Warrant of Arrest for Muammar Mohammed Abu Minyar Gaddafi (June 27, 2011).

[60] Situation in the Republic of Côte d'Ivoire, Case No. ICC-02/11-14-Corr, Corrigendum to "Decision Pursuant to Article 15 of the Rome Statute on the Authorisation of an Investigation into the Situation in the Republic of Côte d'Ivoire" (Nov. 15, 2011).

[61] INTERNATIONAL CRIMINAL COURT, *Report on Preliminary Examination Activities 2018* 216-228 (Dec. 5, 2018), https://www.icc-cpi.int/itemsDocuments/181205-rep-otp-PE-ENG.pdf.

[62] David N Otieno and Maureen Okoth, *Conceptualizing Environmental Crimes as Crimes Against Humanity: A Philosophical Justification* (2015), https://bit.ly/339uqbp.

although the anthropocentric nature of Article 7 presents a challenge to directly prosecuting environmental crimes as a crime against humanity.

i. Extermination

The destruction of the environment may be considered for prosecution under Article 7 of the Rome Statute, where it is used as an instrument to destroy a group of people. Extermination is defined as "the intentional infliction of conditions of life, inter alia the deprivation of access to food and medicine, calculated to bring about the destruction of part of a population."[63] It is possible that the burning of farmland, crops, towns, destruction of livestock and natural resources for the purpose of destroying part of a population can be prosecuted as a crime against humanity. There are several examples where indigenous and vulnerable populations have either been killed or have had their way of life destroyed because of damage to their natural habitat, which may have been of strategic value to the perpetrator, including profitable use. For example, the forest area inhabited by the Ache' Indians was destroyed with the intention to remove them from the land,[64] to the extent that the group is now believed to be extinct.[65] The scorched earth policy in the Darfur region in Sudan by former Sudanese president Omar Al Bashir, which was environmentally destructive, has been argued as constituting extermination as a crime against humanity.[66] In 2016, the ICC Prosecutor developed a new policy that gave special consideration to the prosecution of crimes within the Rome Statute "committed by means of, or that result in, inter alia, the destruction of the environment, the illegal exploitation of natural resources or the illegal dispossession of land."[67] Therefore, there is an increasing focus on prosecuting destruction to the environment as part of the crime against humanity pursuant to Article 7 of the Rome Statute. Durney has argued that

---

[63] Durney, *supra* note 54, at 412-30.

[64] M Munzel, *The Aché Indians: Genocide in Paraguay,* IWGIA Internal Document No. 11 (International Work Group for Indigenous Affairs, Copenhagen 1973).

[65] Sharp, *supra* note170, at 234-35. *See also* the case of the Marsh Arabs in Iraq where the state attempted to destroy the group by targeting and destroying the natural environment the group had relied on for their survival for millenia *see* Aaron Schwabach, *Ecocide and Genocide in Iraq: International Law, the Marsh Arabs, and Environmental Damage in Non-International Conflicts* 15 COLORADO J OF INT'L ENVIRONMENTAL L AND POL 1 (2004).

[66] *Situation in Darfur, Sudan: Prosecutor v. al Bashir,* Case No. ICC-02/05-01/09, Decision on the Prosecution's Application for a Warrant of Arrest against Omar Hassan Ahmad Al Bashir, ¶¶ 95-97 and 170 (March 4, 2009).

[67] ICC, *supra* note 27, ¶ 41.

this new policy can be applied to the systematic burning of farmland, crops, and villages of Rohingya Muslims and the widespread land grabbing in Cambodia as crimes against humanity.

Nevertheless, in each of these cases, the *mens rea* for the crime would need to be established. In the case of extermination under Article 7, what is required is intent with "knowledge" that the "perpetrator knew that the conduct was part of or intended the conduct to be part of a widespread or systematic attack directed against a civilian population."[68] This is less challenging than the *mens rea* for genocide which requires proving genocidal intent.

ii. Deportation or forcible transfer of population

Another opportunity for environmental damage to fall within the net of crimes against humanity is in relation to deportation or forcible transfer of population under article 7(1)(d) of the Rome Statute. This crime is defined as the "forced displacement of the persons concerned by expulsion or other coercive acts from the area in which they are lawfully present, without grounds permitted under international law."[69] According to the Internal Displacement Monitoring Centre (IDMC), Africa has experienced more conflict-related displacement than any other continent, with about 1.5 million people displaced in 2018 by conflict alone.[70] Drawing from the ICC Prosecutor's new policy on prioritizing cases, destruction of the environment, illegal exploitation of natural resources or the illegal dispossession of land can be prosecuted if they are the means by which the deportation or forcible transfer of population as a crime against humanity is committed. Land grabbing by foreign corporations is a major phenomenon in many parts of Africa, which often results in the displacement of indigenous communities.[71] In 2011, an Italian businessman in Senegal was handed over 20,000 hectares by the Senegalese government to grow sweet potatoes and sunflowers to produce biofuels for European cars despite the fact that the project would

---

68 *Elements of Crimes, supra* note 42, at art. 7(1)(b).

69 ROME STATUTE, *supra* note 14, art. 7(2)(d).

70 INTERNAL DISPLACEMENT MONITORING CENTRE (IDMC), *AFRICA REPORT ON INTERNAL DISPLACEMENT* 13 (IDMC 2019), https://www.internal-displacement.org/sites/default/files/publications/documents/201912-Africa-report.pdf.

71 Taiwo Ajala, *Examining the legal safeguards against the environmental impact of land grabbing in African countries: A critical review of Nigerian environmental law,* 20(1) ENVIRONMENTAL LAW REVIEW 3-15 (2018).

displace entire villages and destroy grazing lands for cattle.[72] In the context of Cambodia, Richard Rogers has argued that widespread land grabbing falls under this category of crimes against humanity, with 770,000 people adversely affected as a consequence, including by forcible displacement.[73]

When the means for survival, including land, cattle and other natural resources, are denied or destroyed during armed conflict, living conditions become unsustainable, resulting in displacement, which some have argued have resulted in more deaths than direct killings.[74] This massive displacement of people imposes a strain on the environment. For example, in Cameroon, a displacement camp reduced the grazing land that had previously been available to the local population.[75] In the Niger Delta region of Nigeria, where armed conflict is rife, oil spillage in the sea by Shell has deprived thousands of fishermen of their source of livelihood and clean water.[76] However, it is a requirement that the harm to the environment be part of a "widespread" or "systematic" attack against a civilian population. Isolated acts involving destruction to the natural environment, illegal exploitation of natural resources or dispossession of land would not meet this requirement. Luke Morfotte has criticized the ICC for failing to consider the economic motivations behind forced displacement in the context of the DRC and Uganda. He argues this was part of a plan or policy to remove neighboring clans from their natural environment for the purpose of acquiring their land and exploiting their natural resources.[77] In 2014, the Extraordinary Chamber in the Courts of Cambodia (ECCC), where the two accused persons were convicted for the forced transfer of at least 2 million people, thousands of whom died as a result of food shortage, lack of water and medical care.[78] There is a need for the ICC to address this form of forced displacement within

---

[72] Joan Martinez-Alier et al., *The many faces of land grabbing: Cases from Africa and Latin America,* 7 EJOLT REPORT NO. 10 (March 2014).

[73] GLOBAL DILIGENCE, *Communication Under Article 15 of the Rome Statute of the International Criminal Court The Commission of Crimes Against Humanity in Cambodia July 2002 to Present* 7 (Oct. 7, 2014).

[74] Luke Moffett, *Accountability for Forced Displacement in Democratic Republic of Congo and Uganda before the International Criminal Court,* 2 AFRICAN JOURNAL OF INTERNATIONAL CRIMINAL JUSTICE, 129, 130 (2015).

[75] AFRICA REPORT ON INTERNAL DISPLACEMENT, *supra* note 70, at 44.

[76] AMNESTY INTERNATIONAL, *Briefing: Shell Own up, Pay up, Clean Up* (December 2012), https://www.amnesty.org.uk/files/shell_briefing_2012_lores.pdf.

[77] Moffett, *supra* note 74, at 131.

[78] Prosecutor v. Nuon Chea and Khieu Samphan, Case No. 002/19-09-2017/ECCC/TC, Case 002/01 Judgement, ¶ 1053 (7 August 2014).

conflicts in Africa through a progressive interpretation of the crime against humanity in Article 7 of the Rome Statute. The 2016 policy by the ICC Prosecutor represents an important shift by seeking to prioritize cases involving environmental harm.

iii. Other Inhumane Acts

Furthermore, Article 7 of the Rome Statute can provide a basis for addressing environmental damage where such damage constitutes "other inhumane acts" subject to (i) the harm occurring as part of "a widespread or systematic attack directed against any civilian population" and (ii) the harm was "pursuant to or in furtherance of a state or organizational policy."[79] Several legal issues arise in applying this provision to prosecute environmental harm, including what specific acts are prohibited, the intent requirement, and what constitutes an "organization" when determining an organizational policy. The term "other inhumane acts" has been read broadly by the ICTR to include "acts or omissions that deliberately cause serious mental or physical suffering or injury or constitute a serious attack on human dignity."[80] This is consistent with some academic literature;[81] moreover, the ICC noted in the case of *Prosecutor v. Katanga* that this would cover serious violations of basic human rights drawn from principles of international human rights law and that the purpose of including "other inhumane acts" in the Rome Statute was to provide the flexibility to address serious violations of human rights.[82]

Widespread deforestation, destruction of crops, illegal exploitation of natural resources, and contamination of land and water are arguably all serious violations of basic human rights "of a similar character" to other conduct outlined in Article 7 -- and could amount to crimes against humanity. These are mostly violations of economic, social, and cultural rights, which Evelyn Schmid has argued may constitute crimes against humanity. She expresses the link between violations of ESC rights and crimes against humanity, arguing that devastating instances of preventing access to food and stealing of livestock could potentially be addressed under the umbrella of

---

[79] ROME STATUTE, *supra* note 14, art. 7(1)(k).

[80] Prosecutor v. Kayishema, Case No. ICTR-95-1-T, Judgement, ¶ 151 (May 21, 1999); Prosecutor v. Bagilishema, Case No. ICTR-95-1A-T, Judgement, ¶ 91 (June 7, 2001).

[81] Bernhard Kuschik, *Humaneness, Humankind and Crimes Against Humanity*, 2 GOETTINGEN J. INTL. L. 501, 502-10 (2010).

[82] Prosecutor v. Katanga, Case No. ICC-01/04-01/07, Decision on the Confirmation of Charges, ¶¶ 31-32, 446-449 (Sept. 30, 2008).

"other inhumane acts" pursuant to Article 7(1)(k).[83] They result in a serious attack upon human dignity and can cause serious physical or mental suffering to the affected population.[84] For example, deforestation and loss of biodiversity have a negative impact on the natural ecosystem with possible health consequences. The UN Committee on ESC Rights has stated that deforestation and the illicit trade of wood from the forest is a threat to the environment and that "environmental hygiene" is an element of the right to health under article 12 (2)(b) of the ICESCR.[85] In 2019, a joint report by the Institute for Health Policy Studies, Amazon Environmental Research Institute and Human Rights Watch found that deforestation-related fires had a significant negative impact on public health, including respiratory illnesses.[86] In addition, the Committee on ESC rights has stated that "impunity for human rights violations and the illegal exploitation of the country's natural resources … constitute major obstacles to the enjoyment of economic, social and cultural rights."[87] This would imply that damage to the environment which severely impacts on ESC rights, can potentially amount to crime against humanity; such would be the case in Southern Sudan, where the water supply of rural communities was targeted, prompting their displacement from the area, and allowing corporations to exploit the natural resources in the abandoned area.[88] In the AFRC case, the Appeals Chamber held that the prohibition against "other inhumane acts" should not be restrictively interpreted.[89] This opens up the possibility for widespread environmental damage resulting in serious human rights violations to be prosecuted.

---

[83] Evelyne Schmid, Taking Economic, Social and Cultural Rights Seriously in International Criminal Law, Cambridge, 160-162 (2015).

[84] Rome Statute, *supra* note 14, art. 7(1)(k).

[85] OFFICE OF THE HIGH COMMISSION FOR HUMAN RIGHTS, *Mapping Human Rights Obligations Relating to the Enjoyment of a Safe, Clean, Healthy and Sustainable Environment: Report No. 1* (December 2013) ¶¶ 12-16.

[86] Andre Albuquerque Sant Anna and Rudi Rocha, *Health Impacts of Deforestation-Related Fires in the Brazilian Amazon,* (2019) NOTA TÉCNICA n. 11, IEPS 1-10, https://www.hrw.org/sites/default/files/media_2020/08/Health%20Impacts%20of%20 Deforestation-Related%20Fires%20in%20the%20Amazon_EN_0.pdf.

[87] OFFICE OF THE HIGH COMMISSION FOR HUMAN RIGHTS, *Mapping Human Rights Obligations Relating to the Enjoyment of a Safe, Clean, Healthy and Sustainable Environment:* Report No. 1 (December 2013) ¶ 14.

[88] The Prosecutor v. Omar Hassan Ahmad Al Bashir, Case No. ICC-02/05-01/09-95, Second Warrant of Arrest for Omar Hassan Ahmad Al Bashir, ¶ 7 (July 12, 2010).

[89] AFRC Case, Prosecutor v. Brima (Alex Tamba) and ors, Case No. SCSL-2004-16-A, Appeal judgment, ¶ 185 (February 22, 2008).

Another legal issue to consider is the intent requirement. Article 7(1)(K) requires that the inhumane act be committed "intentionally." Actual or constructive knowledge to cause serious physical or mental suffering would meet this requirement, although the perpetrator is not required to possess knowledge of all the aspects of the attack and may indeed knowingly commit the act for ulterior motives.[90] When confirming the charges against Laurent Gbagbo, the Pre-Trial Chamber indicated that awareness of the consequences of the actions would be sufficient *mens rea* for "other inhumane acts."[91] While the motive for an operation may have been for profit, it may be a crime against humanity where the perpetrator was aware that their action would result in widespread damage and serious physical and mental suffering to the civilian population.

Continuous and knowing toxic waste dumping in many indigenous communities within Africa resulting in death, environmental and other significant health problems to a significant part of the population is certainly inhumane, and can potentially be prosecuted as a crime against humanity. For example, the dumping of radioactive and other toxic wastes on the shores of Somalia, which started in the 1980s and then continued and helped fuel the civil war in that country, had devastating health consequences and reflected a pattern of toxic colonialism and increased profitable illicit trade of toxic waste in Africa.[92] The UNEP, in its 2005 report on Somalia, concluded that "contamination from the waste deposits has thus caused health and environmental problems to the surrounding local fishing communities including contamination of groundwater…the health problems include acute respiratory infections, dry heavy coughing and mouth bleeding, abdominal [hemorrhages], unusual skin chemical reactions, and sudden death after inhaling toxic materials."[93] Dumping of the above toxic wastes in Somalia

---

90 UN Human Rights Council, *Report of the Detailed Findings of the Commission of Inquiry on Human Rights in the Democratic People's Republic of Korea* ¶ 1135, A/HRC/25/CRP.1 (7 February 2014).

91 Prosecutor v. Laurent Gbagbo, Case No. ICC-02/11-01/11, Decision on the Confirmation of Charges against Laurent Gbagbo, ¶¶ 235-236 (12 June 2014).

92 *See* Matiangai Sirleaf, *Prosecuting Dirty Dumping in Africa* in The African Court of Justice and Human and Peoples' Rights in Context: Development and Challenges, 553-589 (Charles Jalloh, Kamari Clarke, and Vincent Nmehielle 2019); Lassana Kone, *The Illicit Trade of Toxic Waste in Africa: The Human Rights Implications of the New Toxic Colonialism* (July 31, 2014), http://dx.doi.org/10.2139/ssrn.2474629.

93 United Nations Environmental Programme, *After the Tsunami: Rapid Environmental Assessment* 134 (Feb. 25, 2005), https://bit.ly/39FLpTK.

inflicted physical and mental suffering, and are serious violations of basic human rights "of a similar character" to others as outlined in Article 7.

In its ground-breaking ruling on The Social and Economic Rights Action Centre and the Centre for Economic and Social Rights v. Nigeria, the African Commission on Human and Peoples' Rights held that the Nigerian government had violated the rights of the Ogoni Indigenous peoples in the Niger Delta region of Nigeria, where there is an ongoing conflict.[94] The government had actively attacked the environment of the Ogoni people, using the Nigerian army to burn and destroy Ogoni villages as a response to their protests against environmental destruction by an oil company, which resulted in air pollution, exploitation of Ogoni land for oil, and disposal of toxic waste into Ogoni land and water.[95] Thousands of Ogoni people were rendered homeless as a result of the destruction carried out on their land by the Nigerian army. This decision provides an instructive guide for the ICC to prosecute environmental crimes given that the violations were massive and systematic similar to the ICC standard of "widespread" and "systematic."[96] Also, the violations imposed serious physical and mental suffering on the Ogoni people, given the finding that the "contamination of water, soil and air has had serious short and long-term health impacts, including skin infections, gastrointestinal and respiratory ailments, increased risk of cancers, and neurological and reproductive problems"[97] on the Ogoni people. This has been a major environmental concern to many Africa states to the extent that prosecuting illegal trade in hazardous waste is included as an international crime in the Malabo Protocol[98] establishing the African Court of Justice and Human and Peoples' Rights (ACJHR) with the jurisdiction of international crimes (discussed in detail in the last section of this chapter).

---

[94] The Social and Economic Rights Action Centre and the Centre for Economic and Social Rights v. Nigeria, African Commission on Human and Peoples' Rights, Comm. No. 155/96 (2001), https://www.escr-net.org/sites/default/files/serac.pdf [hereinafter "the Ogoni case"]; *See also* Centre for Minority Rights Development (Kenya) and Minority Rights Group International on behalf of Endorois Welfare Council v. Kenya, Case No. 276/2003, African Commission on Human and Peoples' Rights (February 4, 2010).

[95] The Ogoni Case, *supra* note 94, ¶¶ 2-6, 52.

[96] *See* Durney, *supra* note 54, at 420-21.

[97] The Social and Economic Rights Action Centre and the Centre for Economic and Social Rights v. Nigeria, African Commission on Human and Peoples' Rights, *supra* note 94, ¶ 2.

[98] African Union, PROTOCOL ON THE STATUTE OF THE AFRICAN COURT OF JUSTICE AND HUMAN RIGHTS, (July 1, 2008) [hereafter referred to as Malabo Protocol).

Lastly, for any environmental damage to be prosecuted as part of Article 7(1)(K), the damage must be "pursuant to or in furtherance of a State or organizational policy."[99] What kind of entity would constitute an "organization" for the purpose of this article has been the subject of academic debate.[100] One of the arguments against a broad interpretation of this provision is that it would extend the ICC's jurisdiction by bringing in possible new situations, and by so doing, undermine its mission as a court of last resort.[101] This narrow view limits the state or organizational policy requirement to entities that are states or "state-like" organizations. This view was amplified by Judge Kaul in his dissenting opinion in the Situation in the Republic of Kenya.[102] He opined that to be an "organization" for the purpose of Article 7 of the Rome Statute, the entity should "partake of some characteristics specific to the State."[103]

Based on the above view, it would be difficult to hold non-state actors like terrorist organizations, political parties, and corporations accountable under international criminal law for atrocities they commit, including widespread destruction of the environment. Advocates for a broader interpretation of state or organizational policy requirements argue that such a narrow interpretation would constrain the ability of international criminal law to respond to systematic or widespread attacks against civilians committed by non-state actors who do not possess a state-like characteristic.[104]

The ICC has adopted a progressive definition of the term to include "any organization that has the capability to perform acts that infringe on basic human values,"[105] taking into account the following:

---

[99] ROME STATUTE, *supra* note 14, art. 7(1)(k).

[100] Mathias Holvoet, *The State or Organisational Policy Requirement within the Definition of Crimes Against Humanity in the Rome Statute: An Appraisal of the Emerging Jurisprudence and the Implementation Practice by ICC States Parties*, 2 ICD BRIEF, 1-15 (2013).

[101] *Id.* at 9.

[102] Decision Pursuant to Article 15 of the Rome Statute on the Authorization of an Investigation into the Situation in the Republic of Kenya, Case No. ICC-01/09, Dissenting Opinion of Judge Hans-Peter Kaul, ¶ 51 (March 31, 2010).

[103] *Id.*

[104] *See* Marcello Di Filippo, *Terrorist Crimes and International Co-operation: Critical Remarks on the Definition and Inclusion of Terrorism in the Category of International Crimes*, EUROPEAN JOURNAL OF INTERNATIONAL LAW, 567 (2008); Matt Halling, *Push the Envelope –Watch It Bend: Removing the Policy Requirement and Extending Crimes Against Humanity*, 23 LEIDEN JOURNAL OF INTERNATIONAL LAW 827, 833 (2010).

[105] Decision Pursuant to Article 15 of the Rome Statute on the Authorization of an Investigation into the Situation in the Republic of Kenya, Case No. ICC-01/09, ¶¶ 90-93 (March 31, 2010).

i. whether the group is under a responsible command, or has an established hierarchy;

ii. whether the group possesses, in fact, the means to carry out a widespread or systematic against a civilian population;

iii. whether the group exercises control over part of the territory of a State;

iv. whether the group has criminal activities against the civilian population as a primary purpose;

v. whether the group articulates, explicitly or implicitly, an intention to attack a civilian population;

vi. whether the group is part of a larger group, which fulfills some or all of the abovementioned criteria.[106]

This broad definition was utilized by the ICC to prosecute crimes against humanity in three cases, namely *Situation in the Republic of Kenya,*[107] *Situation in Libya,*[108] and *the Situation in Cote d'Ivoire.*[109] This has also enabled investigations for crimes against humanity and the gross human rights abuses committed by *Boko Haram* and other non-state actors in Nigeria, DRC, Uganda, and the Central African Republic.[110] The above broad definition opens up the possibility that corporations having relevant institutional structure and capacity can qualify as an "organization" and be prosecuted for damage to the environment caused by their policies such as illegal exploitation of natural resources and illicit trade of toxic waste that result in serious physical or mental suffering.

---

[106] *Id.* ¶ 93; This interpretation was reinforced by the ICC in *Prosecutor* v. William Samoei Ruto, Henry Kiprono Kosgey and Joshua Arap Sang, Case No. ICC-01/09-01/11-373, Decision on the Confirmation of Charges Pursuant to Article 61(7)(a) and (b) of the Rome Statute, ¶ 33 (Jan. 23, 2012).

[107] *Id.*

[108] The Prosecutor v. Saif Al-Islam Gaddafi, Case No. ICC-01/11-01/11-2, Warrant of Arrest for Muammar Mohammed Abu Minyar Gaddafi (June 27, 2011).

[109] Situation in the Republic of Côte d'Ivoire, Case No. ICC-02/11-14-Corr, Corrigendum to Decision Pursuant to Article 15 of the Rome Statute on the Authorisation of an Investigation into the Situation in the Republic of Côte d'Ivoire (Nov. 15, 2011).

[110] *See* INTERNATIONAL CRIMINAL COURT, SITUATIONS UNDER INVESTIGATION at https://www.icc-cpi.int/pages/situation.aspx.

2.3.3. Genocide

The first codification of the Crime of Genocide under international law was in the Convention on the Prevention and Punishment of the Crime of Genocide (Genocide Convention) adopted in 1948 by the UNGA.[111] It embodies principles of customary international law[112] and has been ratified or acceded to by 152 states, including 135 African states (as of July 2020).[113] According to Article II of the Genocide Convention, the crime of genocide occurs when certain acts are committed with "intent to destroy, in whole or in part, a national, ethnical, racial or religious group."[114] The actions that would fall within this definition include:

a) Killing members of the group;

b) Causing serious bodily or mental harm to members of the group;

c) Deliberately inflicting on the group conditions of life calculated to bring about its physical destruction in whole or in part;

d) Imposing measures intended to prevent births within the group;

e) Forcibly transferring children of the group to another group.[115]

The above definition has been adopted verbatim by various international and hybrid tribunals, including the ICC,[116] ICTR,[117] and ICTY.[118] Article 1 of

---

111 CONVENTION ON THE PREVENTION AND PUNISHMENT OF THE CRIME OF GENOCIDE, 78 U.N.T.S. 277 (opened for signature Dec. 9, 1948, entered into force Jan. 12, 1951).

112 Application of the Convention on the Prevention and Punishment of the Crime of Genocide (Bosnia and Herzegovina v. Serbia and Montenegro), Separate Opinion of Judge Weeramantry, 640, 648 (July 11, 1996), https://www.icj-cij.org/files/case-related/91/091-19960711-JUD-01-05-EN.pdf.

113 UNITED NATION TREATY COLLECTION, CONVENTION ON THE PREVENTION AND PUNISHMENT OF THE CRIME OF GENOCIDE (as of July 30, 2020), https://treaties.un.org/Pages/ViewDetails.aspx?src=IND&mtdsg_no=IV-1&chapter=4&clang=_en.

114 CONVENTION ON THE PREVENTION AND PUNISHMENT OF THE CRIME OF GENOCIDE, *supra* note 111, art. 2.

115 *Id.*

116 ROME STATUTE, *supra* note 14, art. 6.

the Genocide Convention makes clear that Genocide can be committed during peacetime or wartime. For the purpose of prosecuting environmental damage, the most relevant action listed above will be (c) also captured by Article 6(c) of the Rome Statute to the effect that the deliberate infliction on a group "*conditions of life* calculated to bring about its physical destruction in whole or in part" [emphasis added] would amount to genocide.[119] The question here is whether damaging the environment with the deliberate intention of creating conditions of life that will bring about the physical destruction of a group could be prosecuted as genocide. The term "conditions of life" is defined to include the "deliberate deprivation of resources indispensable for survival, such as food or medical services, or systematic expulsion from homes."[120] Arguably, calculated and deliberate destruction of natural resources could be employed as a means of achieving the total or partial destruction of a national, ethnic, racial, or religious group. A 2020 report by the Commission on Human Rights in South Sudan found that starvation was deployed as a method of warfare in the conflict in South Sudan and that thousands of civilians were intentionally deprived of objects indispensable to their survival, including food.[121] The report found that both parties to the conflict deliberately and intentionally interfered with the capability of aid organizations to deliver vital foodstuffs to communities in need.[122]

One of the first attempts to explore using environmental damage as an underlying act for Genocide pursuant to Article 6 (c) of the Rome Statute was in the *Application for a Warrant of Arrest against President Omar Al-Bashir* (First Arrest Warrant),[123] former Sudanese President. Among other things, President Omar Al-Bashir was charged with genocide pursuant to Article 6(c) for deliberately inflicting on the Fur, Masalit, and Zaghawa ethnic groups conditions of life calculated to bring about their physical destruction.[124] To

---

[117] UN Security Council, STATUTE OF THE INTERNATIONAL CRIMINAL TRIBUNAL FOR RWANDA (as last amended on October 13, 2006*)*, November 8, 1994, art. 2.

[118] UN SECURITY COUNCIL, STATUTE OF THE INTERNATIONAL CRIMINAL TRIBUNAL FOR THE FORMER YUGOSLAVIA (as amended on 17 May 2002), May 25, 1993, art. 4.

[119] ROME STATUTE, *supra* note 14, art. 6 (c).

[120] ELEMENTS OF CRIMES, *Supra* note 42, at p. 3.

[121] HUMAN RIGHTS COUNCIL, "*There is nothing left for us*"*: starvation as a method of warfare in South Sudan*, UN Doc A/HRC/45/CRP.3 (5 October 2020), ¶ 11.

[122] *Id.*, ¶ 128.

[123] Situation in Darfur, Sudan: Prosecutor v. al Bashir, *supra* note 66.

[124] Prosecutor v. Omar Al-Bashir, Case No. ICC-02/05-01/09-3, Decision on the Prosecution's Application for a Warrant of Arrest against Omar Hassan Ahmad Al-Bashir, ¶ 93 (March 4, 2009).

establish the link between environmental damage and the crime of genocide, the Prosecutor argued that the perpetrators carried out severe environmental degradation and depletion of natural resources of the Fur, Masalit, and Zaghawa ethnic groups by destroying their means of survival, poisoning their water sources, and stealing livestock.[125] This, the Prosecutor argued, was a designed policy by the Government of Sudan (GoS) to deprive the targeted group of water needed for survival, with the goal that those not killed directly in the war would not be able to survive,[126] and resulted in the forcible displacement of a substantial part of groups targeted.[127] However, the Pre-Trial Chamber initially dismissed this charge of genocide, finding that "although there [were] reasonable grounds to believe that GoS forces at times contaminated the wells and water pumps of the towns and villages primarily inhabited by members of the Fur, Masalit, and Zaghawa groups that they attacked, there [were] no reasonable grounds to believe that such a contamination was a core feature of their attacks."[128]

In a Separate and Dissenting Opinion by Judge Anita Usacka, she observed that the charge of genocide had to be analyzed in "the context of Darfur's harsh terrain, in which water and food sources are naturally scarce, and shelter is of utmost importance."[129] She called for the recognition of the destruction of the "means of survival" as an important consideration and concluded that evidence of destruction of food supplies, food sources, water supplies, and water sources provided reasonable grounds to believe that the

---

125 Prosecutor v. Omar Al-Bashir, Case No. ICC-02/05-01/09-3, Decision on the Prosecution's Application for a Warrant of Arrest against Omar Hassan Ahmad Al-Bashir, ¶ 110 (March 4, 2009).

126 *Id.*

127 Situation in Darfur, ICC-02/05-157-AnxA, Public Redacted Version of the Prosecutor's Application under Article 58, 14 July 2008, ¶¶ 14 and 15, http://www.icc-cpi.int/iccdocs/doc/doc559999.pdf; in the case of the tribunal recognised that forcible transfer of population can be considered as a crime of Genocide where it materially leads to the physical and biological destruction of the population, resulting in the separation of the members of the population and the impossibility for them to reconstitute themselves as a group. *See* Prosecutor v. Blagojević (Vidoje) and Jokić (Dragan), Judgment, Case No IT-02-60-T, ICL 173 (ICTY 2005), ¶ 657.

128 Prosecutor v. Omar Al-Bashir, Case No. ICC-02/05-01/09-3, Decision on the Prosecution's Application for a Warrant of Arrest against Omar Hassan Ahmad Al-Bashir, ¶ 93 (March 4, 2009).

129 Prosecutor v. Omar Al-Bashir, Case No. ICC-02/05-01/09-3, Decision on the Prosecution's Application for a Warrant of Arrest against Omar Hassan Ahmad Al-Bashir, Separate and Partly Dissenting Opinion of Judge Anita Usacka, ¶¶ 98-102 (March 4, 2009).

means of survival of the ethnic groups had been systematically destroyed and that the groups were subjected to conditions calculated to bring about their destruction.[130] She found reasonable grounds to believe that Omar Al-Bashir had the required genocidal intent to be charged with genocide.[131] In the second ICC arrest warrant decision for Omar Al-Bashir, the Pre-Trial Chamber agreed with the above conclusion made by Judge Usacka, finding that:

> the acts of contamination of water pumps and forcible transfer coupled by resettlement by member of other tribes, were committed in furtherance of the genocidal policy and that the conditions of life inflicted on the Fur, Masalit and Zaghawa groups were calculated to bring about the physical destruction of a part of those ethnic groups.[132]

The above interpretation creates a scope for possible prosecution of environmental damage as an act underlying the crime of genocide, where the relevant action involves the deliberate destruction of natural resources, which are indispensable for human survival as a means of achieving the destruction of a specific population. However, while this may represent a progressive interpretation of the crime of genocide, it is still anthropocentric and falls short of recognizing "ecocide" as an act of genocide. Another challenge in prosecuting environmental damage as a crime of genocide is the high *mens rea* threshold required for conviction. Specific intent by the perpetrator to physically destroy, in whole or in part, a national, ethnic, racial, or religious group (genocidal intent) must be proven, and random actions targeting members of the protected group would not satisfy this requirement.[133] This poses a significant hurdle when attempting to prosecute transnational corporations. For example, while dumping of toxic wastes in the earlier examples of Nigeria and Somalia may severely impact the health of the indigenous communities and even kill the population, proving that the act was undertaken with that specific intent to destroy the group may be difficult. Also, the scope of application is limited to physical and biological destruction and does not apply to cultural genocide ("the destruction of both tangible (such as places of worship) as well as intangible (such as language) cultural

---

[130] *Id.*

[131] *Id.*, ¶¶ 98-99.

[132] The Prosecutor v. Omar Hassan Ahmad Al Bashir, Case No. ICC-02/05-01/09, Second Decision on the Prosecution's Application for a Warrant of Arrest, ¶¶ 38-39 (July 12, 2010).

[133] *Id.*, ¶ 1.

structures.")[134] In the case of *Prosecutor v. Vidoje Blagojević and Dragan Jokić*, the tribunal held that the term "destroy" in the definition of genocide does not include cultural genocide, stating that the "destruction in question is the material destruction of a group either by physical or by biological means, not the destruction of the national, linguistic, religious, cultural or other identity of a particular group."[135] This implies that it would be difficult to prosecute for genocide where the damage to the environment only results in the destruction of the cultural or religious identity of a group of people.

III. The Annex to the Malabo Protocol and the "African Criminal Court"

In June 2014, the African Union (AU) Assembly met in Malabo, capital of Equatorial Guinee, and adopted the Protocol on Amendments to the Protocol on the Statute of the African Court of Justice and Human Rights (the Malabo Protocol).[136] The Malabo Protocol merges the African Court of Justice and the African Court on Human and Peoples' Rights to create the African Court of Justice and Human and Peoples' Rights (ACJHR). According to the Statute of ACJHR, the Court will have three sections, namely a General Affairs Section, a Human Rights Section, and an International Criminal Law Section.[137] The introduction of an International Criminal Law Section of ACJHR represents a novel and significant step to create a Court with intra-African jurisdiction over international crimes, generally referred to as the "African Criminal Court." The Malabo Protocol and the Statute of the ACJHR annexed to it will come into force after ratification by fifteen AU member states. As of May 2019, fifteen states have signed the treaty, and it will only come into force after it has been ratified by fifteen member states. [138]

There are ongoing debates about the impact that such a court would have on international criminal justice. Some have argued the court would undermine the jurisdiction of the ICC and shield African Heads of States from

---

[134] See Leora Bilsky, Rachel Klagsbrun, The Return of Cultural Genocide?, 29(2) *EUROPEAN JOURNAL OF INTERNATIONAL LAW* 373, 374 (2018).

[135] Prosecutor v. Blagojević (Vidoje) and Jokić (Dragan), Case No IT-02-60-T, Judgment, ¶ 657 (Jan. 17, 2005).

[136] PROTOCOL ON THE STATUTE OF THE AFRICAN COURT OF JUSTICE AND HUMAN RIGHTS, supra note 98.

[137] PROTOCOL ON THE STATUTE OF THE AFRICAN COURT OF JUSTICE AND HUMAN RIGHTS (Annex), supra note 98, art. 16.

[138] African Union, *List of Countries which have Signed, Ratified/Acceded to the Protocol on Amendments to the Protocol on the Statute of the African Court of Justice and Human Rights*, https://bit.ly/39OhusH.

accountability for international crimes, whereas others argue it would complement the ICC and provide “African solutions to African problems.”[139] The perception of the ICC by African leaders as disproportionately targeting African states, especially following the indictments of Presidents Omar Al-Bashir and Uhuru Kenyatta, accelerated the adoption of the Malabo Protocol.[140] However, the Statute annexed to the Malabo Protocol represents a significant development for the protection of the environment. In addition to the four core crimes within the jurisdiction of the ICC, it incorporates within the criminal jurisdiction of the court two crimes damaging to the environment, namely the trafficking in hazardous wastes and the illicit exploitation of natural resources.[141] It also expands the definition of genocide, crimes against humanity, and war crimes provides for corporate criminal liability and addresses damage to natural resources, environmental or cultural heritage by terrorism. The analysis in this section will focus on the crimes in Articles 28G, 28L, and 28L*Bis* of the Statute of ACJHR and the extent to which they protect the environment.

3.1. Article 28G – Terrorism

According to Article 28G of the Statute of the ACJHR, terrorism means any unlawful act that “endangers the life, physical integrity or freedom of, or cause serious injury or death to…or causes or may cause damage to public or private property, natural resources, environmental or cultural heritage.”[142] An act would be unlawful for the purposes of Article 28(G) if it violates national criminal law, AU Law, or African regional economic community law, or international law.[143] The recognition of acts causing damage to natural resources, environmental or cultural heritage is a significant step in addressing environmental damage within African states. The mental elements

---

139 For some of this debate *see* Dire Tladi, *Immunities (Article 46Abis)* in THE AFRICAN COURT OF JUSTICE AND HUMAN AND PEOPLES' RIGHTS IN CONTEXT: DEVELOPMENT AND CHALLENGES 590-618 (Charles Jalloh, Kamari Clarke, and Vincent O. Nmehielle 2019).

140 Amnesty International, *Malabo Protocol: Legal and Institutional Implications of the Merged and Expanded African CourT* 8 (2016), http://ilawyerblog.com/wp-content/uploads/2016/05/Report-Malabo Protocol.pdf.

141 *See* PROTOCOL ON THE STATUTE OF THE AFRICAN COURT OF JUSTICE AND HUMAN RIGHTS (Annex), *supra* note 98, art. 28L and 28L*bis*; The African Criminal Court would also have jurisdiction to try the crime of unconstitutional change of government, piracy, terrorism, mercenaryism, corruption, money laundering, trafficking in persons, trafficking in drugs.

142 *See* PROTOCOL ON THE STATUTE OF THE AFRICAN COURT OF JUSTICE AND HUMAN RIGHTS (Annex), *supra* note 98, art. 28G (A).

143 *Id.*

of this crime include a special intent or motive by the perpetrator to (i) intimidate, put fear, coerce or induce a government, body, institution, public or (ii) disrupt public service, delivery of essential service or create a public emergency or (iii) create general insurrection in a state.[144]

The above definition is drawn almost verbatim from Article 1 of the 1999 OAU Convention on the Prevention and Combating of Terrorism, although the Malabo Protocol notes that Article 28(G) does not apply to struggles against colonialism, occupation, aggression, or domination by foreign forces.[145] This implies that damage to natural resources and environmental heritage within these contexts will have no accountability as terrorism within the African Criminal Court, even if particular conduct satisfies the physical and mental elements of the crime. More so, the scope of Article 28(G) is apparently limited to terrorism acts perpetuated outside the context of an armed conflict.[146] This arguably has the potential to address acts of terrorism damaging natural resources and environmental heritage committed during peacetime, whereas acts of terrorism committed during an international or non-international armed conflict may be prosecuted as part of war crimes. In addition, unlike other international criminal law provisions which require damage to be "severe," "widespread or systematic," or "serious,"[147] the Annex to the Malabo Protocol is broader and covers any "damage" to natural resources, the environment, or cultural heritage. The destruction of cultural heritage by terrorist organizations operating in Africa – including the landscape, archaeological sites, monuments, and other cultural objects -- could be prosecuted under this provision as acts of terrorism.

3.2. Article 28L – Trafficking in Hazardous Wastes

The dumping of hazardous waste in Africa by Western European companies has been a problem since the 1980s despite the lack of proper waste management systems in many states in Africa. While the nature of these toxic wastes in the past had included nuclear, pharmaceutical, and pesticides, in

---

[144] *See Protocol on the Statute of the African Court of Justice and Human Rights* (Annex), *supra* n 98, art. 28G (A) (1)-(3).

[145] *See Protocol on the Statute of the African Court of Justice and Human Rights* (Annex), *supra* n 98, art. 28G (C).

[146] *See* PROTOCOL ON THE STATUTE OF THE AFRICAN COURT OF JUSTICE AND HUMAN RIGHTS (Annex), *supra* note 98, art. 28G.

[147] *See* ROME STATUTE, *supra* note 14, arts. 7 and 8(2)(b)(iv); United Nations, *Draft comprehensive convention against international terrorism*, UN Doc A/59/894, https://www.ilsa.org/Jessup/Jessup08/basicmats/unterrorism.pdf.

recent years, there has been a "tsunami" of electronic wastes.[148] Trade in hazardous waste is noted to have become more profitable than trafficking in drugs, humans, and arms.[149] These have devasting environmental and health consequences. In 2006, in addition to pollution, twenty people were killed and thousands of others poisoned by an illegal dump of 500 tons of chemical muds in Abidjan, Cote d'Ivoire, by a Greek-owned tanker.[150] Similarly, the continuous dumping of radioactive and other toxic waste materials by Italian companies on the shores of Somalia resulted in significant pollution and health issues, including respiratory infections, heavy dry coughing, and mouth bleeding, abdominal hemorrhages, unusual skin chemical reactions, and sudden death after inhaling toxic materials.[151] Consequently, AU member States have made several attempts to criminalize trafficking in hazardous wastes, arguably more so in AU than in other regional mechanisms.

In May 1988, the Organisation for African Unity (Now AU) unanimously adopted a motion declaring that "the dumping of nuclear and industrial wastes in Africa is a crime against Africa and the African people."[152] On March 22, 1989, the Basel Convention on the Control of Transboundary Movements of Hazardous Wastes and their Disposal (Basel Convention) was adopted, making trafficking hazardous waste an offense with responsibility under public international law. Article 11 of the Basel Convention encouraged member states to enter regional arrangements to prohibit trafficking in hazardous wastes to less developed countries.[153] In response to this, the AU adopted the Bamako Convention on the Ban of the Import into Africa and the Control of Transboundary Movement and Management of Hazardous Wastes within Africa. It required State parties, among other things, to criminalize, within their jurisdiction, the importation of all hazardous waste into Africa and the dumping of hazardous wastes at sea, internal waters and waterways.[154]

---

148 *See* Kone, Lassana, *supra* note 92.

149 *Id.* at 1.

150 *Id.* at 5.

151 UNITED NATIONS ENVIRONMENTAL PROGRAMME, *supra* note 93, at 134.

152 OAU COUNCIL OF MINISTERS' RESOLUTION ON DUMPING OF NUCLEAR AND INDUSTRIAL WASTE IN AFRICA (1988), reproduced in C. Heyns' HUMAN RIGHTS LAW IN AFRICA 342 (2004).

153 BASEL CONVENTION ON THE CONTROL OF TRANSBOUNDARY MOVEMENTS OF HAZARDOUS WASTES AND THEIR DISPOSAL art. 11, opened for signature March 22, 1989, 1673 U.N.T.S 57 (entered into force May 5, 1992).

154 BAMAKO CONVENTION ON THE BAN OF THE IMPORT INTO AFRICA AND THE CONTROL OF TRANSBOUNDARY MOVEMENT AND MANAGEMENT OF HAZARDOUS WASTES WITHIN AFRICA art. 4, opened for signature Jan. 30, 1991, (entered into force April 22, 1998).

Article 28L(1) of the Statute of the ACHPR represents one of the first direct attempts to make trafficking in hazardous wastes a crime under international criminal law, assigning individual criminal responsibility. The crime of trafficking in hazardous waste is defined as:

> any import or failure to re-import, transboundary movement, or export of hazardous wastes proscribed by the Bamako Convention on the Ban of the Import into Africa and the Control of Transboundary Movement and Management of Hazardous Wastes within Africa, adopted in Bamako, Mali, in January 1991.[155]

What constitutes "hazardous wastes" for the purpose of Article 28L(1) is defined in Article 28L(2) and draws on the definition in the Bamako Convention and from the domestic legislation of State parties. Martin Heger considers reliance on domestic legislation for a definition of "hazardous waste" in the Statute of ACHPR to be problematic and may result in inconsistency in the definition of the crimes across different states.[156] Given the prevalence of illegal trafficking of hazardous wastes in Africa and the devastating environmental and health impact, the criminalization in Article 28L is, symbolically, an important step towards ensuring criminal accountability for environmental damage. There seems to be some connection between terrorism and trafficking in hazardous wastes. Not only have terrorists used trafficking in hazardous wastes to finance terrorist activities, exposing the public to hazardous or radioactive substances would satisfy the *actus reus* for the crime of terrorism under article 28G.[157]

3.3. Article 28L*Bis* – Illicit Exploitation of natural Resources

The illicit exploitation of natural resources has been a defining characteristic of many of the armed conflicts in Africa, including in Sierra Leone, Liberia, Angola, Central Africa Republic, and DRC. The impact on the environment can be severe, including the destruction of natural flora and fauna, increased health hazards, increased risk of natural disasters, ecological disturbances,

---

155 PROTOCOL ON THE STATUTE OF THE AFRICAN COURT OF JUSTICE AND HUMAN RIGHTS (Annex), *supra* n 98, art. 28L (1).

156 Martin Heger, *Trafficking in Hazardous Wastes (Article 28L) and Illicit Exploitation of Natural Resources (Article 28Lbis)* in THE AFRICAN CRIMINAL COURT: A COMMENTARY ON THE MALABO PROTOCOL 132 (G. Werle and M. Vormbaum 2017).

157 AFRICAN MODEL ANTI-TERRORISM LAW, (endorsed 30 June–1 July 2011).

and pollution of air, water, and land.[158] Natural resources have provided the motivation and means for many of the conflicts in Africa and also help sustain many of these conflicts. The abundance of natural resources in DRC – including diamonds, gold, copper, cobalt, timber, coffee, and oil – enabled the conflict and played a role in the commission of massive human rights violations. A 2010 report by the Office of the High Commissioner for Human Rights found that the military expenditures of Rwanda and Uganda between 1998 and 2002 were financed by the illegal exploitation of natural resources in DRC.[159] The gravity of such illegal exploitation of natural resources has led the UN Security Council, in numerous instances, to impose sanctions against individuals and entities involved in the trade of illicit natural resources – including in DRC and the Central Africa Republic, and in other instances, diamond sanctions against Sierra Leone, Angola, and Liberia.[160]

Article 28L*Bis* of the Statute of the ACJHR represents one of the first attempts to criminalize the illicit exploitation of natural resources at the international level. According to Article 28L*Bis*, the crime of "illegal exploitation of natural resources" is committed if certain actions "are of a serious nature affecting the stability of a state, region, or the Union."[161] The *actus reus* of the commission of the crime requires an agreement to exploit natural resources (a) in violation of the principle of peoples' sovereignty over their natural resources; (b) in violation of the legal and regulatory procedures of the State concerned; (c) through corrupt practices; (d) that is clearly one-sided; (e) without any agreement with the State concerned; (f) without complying with norms relating to the protection of the environment and the security of the people and the staff; and (g) in

---

[158] *See* Babagana Gutti et al, *Environmental Impact of Natural Resources Exploitation in Nigeria And the Way Forward* (2)(2) JOURNAL OF APPLIED TECHNOLOGY IN ENVIRONMENTAL SANITATION 95-102 (2012).

[159] Office of the High Commissioner for Human Rights, *Report of the Mapping Exercise documenting the most serious violations of human rights and international humanitarian law committed within the territory of the Democratic Republic of the Congo between March 1993 and June 2003* (August 2010) ¶ 768.

[160] *See* UNSC Resolution 2134 (2014), *Central Africa Republic* (28 January 2014) UN Doc S/RES/2134 (2014); UNSC Resolution 2136, *Democratic Republic of* Congo (30 January 2014) UN Doc S/RES/2136 (2014); UNSC resolution 1306 (2000) of 5 July 2000 (Sierra Leone); UNSC Resolution 1173, *The Situation in Angola* (12 June 1998); UNSC Resolution 1521, *The Situation in Liberia* (22 December 2003) UN Doc S/RES/1521; (Security Council Report, *UN Sanctions: Natural Resources* (November 2015).

[161] PROTOCOL ON THE STATUTE OF THE AFRICAN COURT OF JUSTICE AND HUMAN RIGHTS (ANNEX), *supra* n 98, art. 28L*bis*.

violation of the norms and standards established by the relevant natural resource certification mechanism.[162] There is some overlap between the war crime of pillage discussed earlier and the crime of illicit exploitation of natural resources. This overlap was captured in the 2016 ICC Prosecutor's policy on prioritizing cases, which seeks to give special consideration to the prosecution of crimes within the jurisdiction of the court committed by means of illegal exploitation of natural resources.[163]

However, there are some potentially problematic aspects of Article 28L*Bis*. For example, it seeks to criminalize violations of regulations or procedures on environmental governance which were not originally intended to be punished in criminal law. In addition, the provisions of Article 28L*Bis* have been criticized for being overly broad and for failing to define the mental elements required for the commission of the crime and other key terms used in defining the crime, including "serious nature" and "affecting the stability."[164] This has the potential to result in multiple interpretations of the same term and undermining the requirement of specificity in relation to crimes. Moreover, the modes of responsibility for crimes within the Statute of the court (as outlined in Article 28N) have been questioned to the extent that they apply to the environmental crimes within the Statute. The criminalization of preparatory acts, or the attempt to commit an environmental crime, is seen to be unnecessary at the international level[165] and technically problematic.[166]

In addition, Article 46A*Bis* exempts current Heads of States and other senior state officials from prosecution for crimes within the jurisdiction of the Court. This provision is inconsistent with the position in the Statutes of other

---

[162] *Id.*

[163] *See* also J.G. Stewart, *Corporate War Crimes: Prosecuting the Pillage of Natural Resources* (OPEN SOCIETY JUSTICE INITIATIVE PUBLICATION 2011).

[164] Daniëlla Dam and James G. Stewart, *Illicit Exploitation of Natural Resources - Art. 28L Bis of the Malabo Protocol* in THE AFRICAN COURT OF JUSTICE AND HUMAN AND PEOPLES' RIGHTS IN CONTEXT: DEVELOPMENT AND CHALLENGES 590-618 (Charles Jalloh, Kamari Clarke, and Vincent O. Nmehielle 2019).

[165] Martin Heger, *Trafficking in Hazardous Wastes (Article 28L) and Illicit Exploitation of Natural Resources (Article 28Lbis)* in THE AFRICAN CRIMINAL COURT: A COMMENTARY ON THE MALABO PROTOCOL 134-135 (G. Werle and M. Vormbaum 2017).

[166] *See* Ben Saul, *The Crime of Terrorism within the Jurisdiction of the African Court of Justice and Human and Peoples' Rights* in THE AFRICAN COURT OF JUSTICE AND HUMAN AND PEOPLES' RIGHTS IN CONTEXT: DEVELOPMENT AND CHALLENGES (Charles Jalloh, Kamari Clarke, and Vincent O. Nmehielle 2019).

international criminal tribunals[167] and risks allowing impunity on the environment by Heads of States and senior state officials to escape criminal accountability. Many scholars and practitioners have criticized this provision of the Statute of the ACJHR, although Dire Tladi argues that this is not inconsistent with customary international law.[168]

Nevertheless, Articles 28L and 28L*Bis* represent a significant milestone in enshrining an international crime that is eco-centric (as opposed to anthropocentric) by seeking to protect the environment in its own right rather than for its utilitarian survival benefits to human beings. Moreover, Article 46(C) of the Statute of the ACJHR enshrines corporate liability, making it possible to directly hold corporations criminally accountable for their involvement in the trafficking of hazardous wastes or the illicit exploitation of natural resources within Africa. However, there remain significant political, financial, and other practical challenges before the Statute can come into force and for the ACJHR to function effectively.[169]

IV. Conclusion

The 2016 policy by the ICC Prosecutor gave new momentum to the prosecution of environmental damage by the ICC. As argued in this chapter, while the ICC's ability to directly prosecute environmental damage is limited by its subject matter jurisdiction, there are avenues for a progressive interpretation of its core crimes. However, these possibilities to address environmental damage within the subject matter jurisdiction of the ICC is dependent on an anthropocentric interpretation of the core crimes. Attempts to include the crime of mass destruction of ecosystems (ecocide), geocide, or environmental degradation within the scope of the ICC's jurisdiction were

---

[167] *See* STATUTE OF THE INTERNATIONAL CRIMINAL TRIBUNAL FOR RWANDA, *supra*, note 117, art. 6; ROME STATUTE, *supra* note 14, art. 27; STATUTE OF THE INTERNATIONAL CRIMINAL TRIBUNAL FOR THE FORMER YUGOSLAVIA, *supra* note 118, art. 7.

[168] Dire Tladi, *Immunities (Article 46Abis)* in THE AFRICAN COURT OF JUSTICE AND HUMAN AND PEOPLES' RIGHTS IN CONTEXT: DEVELOPMENT AND CHALLENGES 590-618 (Charles Jalloh, Kamari Clarke, and Vincent O. Nmehielle 2019).

[169] For details on these challenges Matiangai Sirleaf, *supra* note 92, at 553-589.

rejected by the framers and have, to date, been unsuccessful.[170] International criminal law can and needs to respond more to addressing damage to the environment. The Malabo Protocol represents a significant attempt to directly address environmental damage within Africa by enshrining trafficking in hazardous wastes and the illicit exploitation of natural resources as an international crime attracting individual criminal responsibility. These crimes have, in many instances, provided the means and motivation for many of the sustaining conflicts in Africa. Despite the practical challenges for the Malabo Protocol coming into force and the potential interpretive problems concerning environmental crimes, it represents an important development for the protection of the environment and corporate criminal responsibility under international law.

Bibliography

AFRICAN CENTRE FOR THE STUDIES AND RESEARCH ON TERRORISM, *African Model Anti-Terrorism Law, Final Draft as Endorsed By the 17th Ordinary Session of the Assembly of the Union (endorsed June 30, 2011 – July 1, 2011)*, African Union Common Repository, https://archives.au.int/handle/123456789/8313

AFRICAN CONVENTION ON THE CONSERVATION OF NATURE AND NATURAL RESOURCES (REVISED), African Union, (March 7, 2017), https://au.int/en/treaties/african-convention-conservation-nature-and-natural-resources-revised-version.

AFRICAN UNION, *List of Countries Which Have Signed, Ratified/Acceded To the Protocol On Amendments To the Protocol On the Statute of the African Court of Justice and Human Rights*, https://au.int/sites/default/files/treaties/36398-sl-PROTOCOL%20ON%20AMENDMENTS%20TO%20THE%20PROTOCOL%20ON%20THE%20STATUTE%20OF%20THE%20AFRICAN%20COURT%20OF%20JUSTICE%20AND%20HUMAN%20RIGHTS.pdf.

Taiwo Ajala, *Examining the Legal Safeguards Against the Environmental Impact of Land Grabbing in African Countries: A Critical Review of Nigerian Environmental Law*, 20 (1) ENVIRONMENTAL LAW REVIEW 20 (2018).

---

170 Anastacia Greene, *THE CAMPAIGN TO MAKE ECOCIDE AN INTERNATIONAL CRIME: QUIXOTIC QUEST OR MORAL IMPERATIVE?*, 30(3) Fordham Environmental Law Review 1 (2019); Christopher H. Lytton, *ENVIRONMENTAL HUMAN RIGHTS: EMERGING TRENDS IN INTERNATIONAL LAW AND ECOCIDE*, 13 Environmental Claims Journal 73 (2000); Peter Sharp, *PROSPECTS FOR ENVIRONMENTAL LIABILITY IN THE INTERNATIONAL CRIMINAL COURT*, 18 VA. Envtl. LJ 217 (1999); Mohammed Saif-Alden Wattad, *ROME STATUTE AND CAPTAIN PLANET: WHAT LIES BETWEEN CRIME AGAINST HUMANITY AND THE NATURAL ENVIRONMENT*, 19 Fordham Environmental Law Review 266 (2009); Frédéric Mégret, *THE CASE FOR A GENERAL INTERNATIONAL CRIME AGAINST THE ENVIRONMENT*, in SUSTAINABLE DEVELOPMENT, INTERNATIONAL CRIMINAL JUSTICE, AND TREATY IMPLEMENTATION 50-70 (Sébastien Jodoin and Marie-Claire Cordonier Segger 2013).

AMNESTY INTERNATIONAL, *Briefing: Shell Own Up, Pay Up, Clean Up* (December 2012), https://www.amnesty.org.uk/files/shell_briefing_2012_lores.pdf.

AMNESTY INTERNATIONAL, *Malabo Protocol: Legal and Institutional Implications of the Merged and Expanded African Court,* (May 2016), http://ilawyerblog.com/wp-content/uploads/2016/05/Report-Malabo Protocol.pdf.

Application of the Convention on the Prevention and Punishment of the Crime of Genocide (Bosnia and Herzegovina v. Serbia and Montenegro), Separate Opinion of Judge Weeramantry, 996 I.C.J. 640, 648, (July 11, 1996), https://www.icj-cij.org/files/case-related/91/091-19960711-JUD-01-05-EN.pdf.

Statement on behalf of Australia at the Diplomatic Conference on the Reaffirmation and Development of International Humanitarian Law Applicable in Armed Conflicts ("CDDH") (Geneva 1974–77), as cited in Matthew Gillett, *Eco-Struggles: Using International Criminal Law to Protect the Environment During and After Non-International Armed Conflict in Environmental Protection and Transitions* from CONFLICT TO PEACE: CLARIFYING NORMS, PRINCIPLES, AND PRACTICES 240 (Carsten Stahn, Jens Iverson, and Jennifer S. Easterday, 2017).

Kevin Bales, BLOOD AND EARTH: MODERN SLAVERY, ECOCIDE, AND THE SECRET TO SAVING THE WORLD (2016).

BAMAKO CONVENTION ON THE BAN OF THE IMPORT INTO AFRICA AND THE CONTROL OF TRANSBOUNDARY MOVEMENT AND MANAGEMENT OF HAZARDOUS WASTES WITHIN AFRICA (opened for signature Jan. 30, 1991, entered into force April 22, 1998), Art. 4, African Union, https://au.int/sites/default/files/treaties/7774-treaty-0015_-_bamako_convention_on_hazardous_wastes_e.pdf.

BASEL CONVENTION ON THE CONTROL OF TRANSBOUNDARY MOVEMENTS OF HAZARDOUS WASTES AND THEIR DISPOSAL (opened for signature March 22, 1989, entered into force May 5, 1992), Art. 11, 1673 U.N.T.S 57.

Nadia Bernaz, *Enhancing Corporate Accountability For Human Rights Violations: Is Extraterritoriality the Magic Potion?* J. BUS. ETHICS 117 (2013).

Ulrich Beyerlin and Thilo Marauhn, INTERNATIONAL ENVIRONMENTAL LAW (1st ed. 2011).

Rene L. Beyers et al., *Resource Wars And Conflict Ivory: The Impact of Civil Conflict on Elephants in The Democratic Republic of Congo - The Case of the Okapi Reserve,* 6 (11) PLOS ONE (2011).

Leora Bilsky and Rachel Klagsbrun, *The Return of Cultural Genocide?,* 29 (2) EUROPEAN JOURNAL OF INTERNATIONAL LAW 373 (2018).

Patricia Birnie and Allan Boyle, INTERNATIONAL LAW AND THE ENVIRONMENT (2002).

BLACK'S LAW DICTIONARY (10th ed. 2015).

Carl E. Bruch, *The Environmental Law of War: All's Not Fair in (Civil) War: Criminal Liability For Environmental Damage in Internal Armed Conflict,* 25 VT. L. REV. 695, 722 (2001).

Centre for Minority Rights Development (Kenya) and Minority Rights Group International on behalf of Endorois Welfare Council v. Kenya, Case No. 276/2003, African Commission on Human and Peoples' Rights (Feb. 4, 2010).

CONVENTION ON CIVIL LIABILITY FOR DAMAGE RESULTING FROM ACTIVITIES DANGEROUS TO THE ENVIRONMENT, ETS No.150 (opened for signature June 21, 1993).

CONVENTION ON THE PREVENTION AND PUNISHMENT OF THE CRIME OF GENOCIDE, 78 U.N.T.S. 277 (entered into force Jan. 12, 1951).

Daniëlla Dam and James G. Stewart, ILLICIT EXPLOITATION OF NATURAL RESOURCES - ART. 28LBIS OF THE MALABO PROTOCOL IN THE AFRICAN COURT OF JUSTICE AND HUMAN AND PEOPLES' RIGHTS IN CONTEXT: DEVELOPMENT AND CHALLENGES (2019).

Decision Pursuant to Article 15 of the Rome Statute on the Authorization of an Investigation into the Situation in the Republic of Kenya, International Criminal Court, Case No. ICC-01/09 (March 31, 2010).

Decision Pursuant to Article 15 of the Rome Statute on the Authorization of an Investigation into the Situation in the Republic of Kenya, International Criminal Court, Case No. ICC-01/09, Dissenting Opinion of Judge Hans-Peter Kaul (March 31, 2010).

Marcello Di Filippo, *Terrorist Crimes and International Co-Operation: Critical Remarks on the Definition and Inclusion of Terrorism in the Category of International Crimes*, EUROPEAN JOURNAL OF INTERNATIONAL LAW (2008).

DRAFT STATUTE FOR THE INTERNATIONAL CRIMINAL COURT 16, U.N. Doc. A/CONF.183/2/Add. 1 (1998).

Jessica Durney, *Crafting a Standard: Environmental Crimes as Crimes Against Humanity Under the International Criminal Court*, 24 (2) HASTINGS ENVIRONMENTAL LAW JOURNAL (2018).

Steven Freeland, *Addressing the Intentional Destruction of the Environment During Warfare Under the Rome Statute of the International Criminal Court*, SUPRANATIONAL CRIMINAL LAW (2015).

GLOBAL DILIGENCE, COMMUNICATION UNDER ARTICLE 15 OF THE ROME STATUTE OF THE INTERNATIONAL CRIMINAL COURT: THE COMMISSION OF CRIMES AGAINST HUMANITY IN CAMBODIA JULY 2002 TO PRESENT (Oct. 7, 2014).

Anastacia Greene, *The Campaign to Make Ecocide an International Crime: Quixotic Quest or Moral Imperative?*, 30 (3) FORDHAM ENVIRONMENTAL LAW REVIEW 1 (2019).

Babagana Gutti et al., *Environmental Impact of Natural Resources Exploitation in Nigeria and the Way Forward*, JOURNAL OF APPLIED TECHNOLOGY IN ENVIRONMENTAL SANITATION (2012).

Matt Halling, *Push the Envelope – Watch it Bend: Removing the Policy Requirement and Extending Crimes Against Humanity*, 23 LEIDEN JOURNAL OF INTERNATIONAL LAW 827 (2010).

Oona A. Hathaway et al., *What is a War Crime?* 43 (1) YALE JOURNAL OF INTERNATIONAL LAW (2019).

Martin Heger, TRAFFICKING IN HAZARDOUS WASTES (ARTICLE 28L) AND ILLICIT EXPLOITATION OF NATURAL RESOURCES (ARTICLE 28LBIS) IN THE AFRICAN CRIMINAL COURT: A COMMENTARY ON THE MALABO PROTOCOL (G. Werle and M. Vormbaum, eds., 2017).

Mathias Holvoet, *The State or Organizational Policy Requirement Within The Definition of Crimes Against Humanity in the Rome Statute: An Appraisal of the Emerging Jurisprudence and the Implementation Practice by ICC States Parties*, 2 ICD BRIEF (2013).

HUMAN RIGHTS COUNCIL, *"There is nothing left for us": Starvation As a Method of Warfare in South Sudan*, UN Doc A/HRC/45/CRP.3 (October 5, 2020).

INTERNAL DISPLACEMENT MONITORING CENTRE (IDMC), AFRICA REPORT ON INTERNAL DISPLACEMENT (2019), https://www.internal-displacement.org/sites/default/files/publications/documents/201912-Africa-report.pdf.

INTERNATIONAL CRIMINAL COURT, ELEMENTS OF CRIMES Art. 8(2)(b)(xvi), https://www.icc-cpi.int/NR/rdonlyres/336923D8-A6AD-40EC-AD7B-45BF9DE73D56/0/ElementsOfCrimesEng.pdf.

INTERNATIONAL CRIMINAL COURT, *Policy Paper on Case Selection and Prioritisation* (Sept. 15, 2016), https://www.icc-cpi.int/itemsDocuments/20160915_OTP-Policy_Case-Selection_Eng.pdf.

INTERNATIONAL CRIMINAL COURT, *Report on Preliminary Examination Activities 2018* (Dec. 5, 2018), https://www.icc-cpi.int/itemsDocuments/181205-rep-otp-PE-ENG.pdf.

INTERNATIONAL CRIMINAL COURT, SITUATIONS UNDER INVESTIGATION at https://www.icc-cpi.int/pages/situation.aspx.

Černič Jernej, CORPORATE ACCOUNTABILITY FOR HUMAN RIGHTS IN THE BUSINESS AND HUMAN RIGHTS LANDSCAPE: MOVING FORWARD, LOOKING BACK (Jena Martin and Karen Bravo, eds., 2015).

Lassana Kone, THE ILLICIT TRADE OF TOXIC WASTE IN AFRICA: THE HUMAN RIGHTS IMPLICATIONS OF THE NEW TOXIC COLONIALISM (July 31, 2014), http://dx.doi.org/10.2139/ssrn.2474629

Louis J. Kotzé and Duncan French, *The Anthropocentric Ontology of International Environmental Law and the Sustainable Development Goals: Towards an Ecocentric Rule of Law in the Anthropocene*, 7 GLOBAL JOURNAL OF COMPARATIVE LAW 5 (2018).

Bernhard Kuschik, *Humaneness, Humankind and Crimes Against Humanity*, 2 GOETTINGEN J. INTL. L. 501 (2010).

Jessica C. Lawrence and Kevin Jon Heller, *The First Ecocentric Environmental War Crime: The Limits of Article 8(2)(B)(Iv) of the Rome Statute*, 20 GEO. INT'L ENVTL. L. REV. 61 (2007).

Michael J. Lawrence et al., *The Effects of Modern War and Military Activities on Biodiversity and the Environment*, 23 (4) ENVIRONMENTAL REVIEWS 443 (2015).

LEGALLY BINDING INSTRUMENT TO REGULATE, IN INTERNATIONAL HUMAN RIGHTS LAW, THE ACTIVITIES OF TRANSNATIONAL CORPORATIONS AND OTHER BUSINESS ENTERPRISES (OEIGWG CHAIRMANSHIP REVISED DRAFT 2019), https://www.ohchr.org/Documents/HRBodies/HRCouncil/WGTransCorp/OEIGWG_RevisedDraft_LBI.pdf.

Christopher H. Lytton, *Environmental Human Rights: Emerging Trends in International Law and Ecocide*, 13 ENVIRONMENTAL CLAIMS JOURNAL 73 (2000).

Linus Nnabuike Malu, THE INTERNATIONAL CRIMINAL COURT AND PEACE PROCESSES: CÔTE D'IVOIRE, KENYA AND UGANDA (2019).

Joan Martinez-Alier, et al., *The Many Faces of Land Grabbing: Cases from Africa and Latin America* 7, EJOLT REPORT No. 10 (March 2014).

Frédéric Mégret, *The Case For a General International Crime Against the Environment*, in SUSTAINABLE DEVELOPMENT, INTERNATIONAL CRIMINAL JUSTICE, AND TREATY IMPLEMENTATION (Sébastien Jodoin and Marie-Claire Cordonier Segger, 2013).

Frédéric Mégret, *The Challenge of an International Environmental Criminal Law* (April 5, 2010), https://papers.ssrn.com/sol3/Delivery.cfm/SSRN_ID 1583610_code372721.pdf?abstractid=1583610&mirid=1

Luke Moffett, *Accountability For Forced Displacement in Democratic Republic of Congo and Uganda Before the International Criminal Court,* 2 AFRICAN JOURNAL OF INTERNATIONAL CRIMINAL JUSTICE, 129, 130 (2015).

M. Munzel, *The Aché Indians: Genocide in Paraguay,* IWGIA INTERNAL DOCUMENT NO. 11 (International Work Group for Indigenous Affairs, Copenhagen 1973).

Rosemary Mwanza, *Enhancing Accountability for Environmental Damage Under International Law: Ecocide as a Legal Fulfilment for Ecological Integrity,* 19 (2) MELBOURNE JOURNAL OF INTERNATIONAL LAW (2018).

Janet Nackoney, et al., *Impacts of Civil Conflict on Primary Forest Habitat in Northern Democratic Republic of the Congo 1990–2010,* BIOL. CONSERV. (2014), https://langint.pri.kyoto-u.ac.jp/ai/intra_data/JanetNackoney/Nack oneyJ2014-BC.pdf.

Mark Notaras, *Should Ecocide Be Deemed a Crime Against Peace?,* OUR WORLD (3 May 2010), https://ourworld.unu.edu/en/should-ecocide-be-deemed-a-crime-against-peace.

OAU COUNCIL OF MINISTERS' RESOLUTION ON DUMPING OF NUCLEAR AND INDUSTRIAL WASTE IN AFRICA (1988), reproduced in C. Heyns, *Human Rights Law in Africa* (2004).

David N. Otieno, and Maureen Okoth, CONCEPTUALIZING ENVIRONMENTAL CRIMES AS CRIMES AGAINST HUMANITY: A PHILOSOPHICAL JUSTIFICATION (2015), https://pa pers.ssrn.com/sol3/papers.cfm?abstract_id=2674065.

Prosecutor v. Omar Al-Bashir, Case No. ICC-02/05-01/09-3, Decision on the Prosecution's Application for a Warrant of Arrest against Omar Hassan Ahmad Al-Bashir (March 4, 2009).

Prosecutor v. Omar Al-Bashir, Case No. ICC-02/05-01/09-3, Decision on the Prosecution's Application for a Warrant of Arrest against Omar Hassan Ahmad Al-Bashir, Separate and Partly Dissenting Opinion of Judge Anita Usacka (March 4, 2009).

Prosecutor v. Omar Hassan Ahmad Al Bashir, Case No. ICC-02/05-01/09-95, Second Warrant of Arrest for Omar Hassan Ahmad Al Bashir (July 12, 2010).

Prosecutor v. Blagojević (Vidoje) and Jokić (Dragan), Case No IT-02-60-T, Judgment (Jan. 17, 2005).

Prosecutor v. Alex Tamba Brima, Brima Bazzy Kamara and Santigie Borbor Kanu (the AFRC Accused), SCSL-04-16-T, Judgment (Special Court for Sierra Leone, Jun. 20, 2007).

Prosecutor v. Alex Tamba Brima, Brima Bazzy Kamara and Santigie Borbor Kanu (the AFRC Accused), SCSL-04-16-A, Appeal judgment (Special Court for Sierra Leone, February 22, 2008).

Prosecutor v. Nuon Chea and Khieu Samphan, Case No. 002/19-09-2017/ECCC/TC, Case 002/01 Judgement (7 August 2014).

Prosecutor v. Thomas Lubanga Dyilo, Case No. ICC- 01/04-01-06-2842, Judgment Pursuant to Article 74 of the Statute (March 14, 2012).

Prosecutor v. Saif Al-Islam Gaddafi, Case No. ICC-01/11-01/11-2, Warrant of Arrest for Muammar Mohammed Abu Minyar Gaddafi (June 27, 2011).

Prosecutor v. Laurent Gbagbo, Case No. ICC-02/11-01/11, Decision on the Confirmation of Charges against Laurent Gbagbo (12 June 2014).

Prosecutor v. Taylor (Charles Ghankay), Case No. SCSL-03-1-T, Judgment (April 26, 2012).

Prosecutor v. Charles Ghankay Taylor, Case No. SCSL-03-1-T, Judgment (May 18, 2012).

Prosecutor v. Germain Katanga, Case No. ICC-01/04-01/07, Judgment pursuant to article 74 of the Statute (March 7, 2014).

Prosecutor v. Katanga, Case No. ICC-01/04-01/07, Decision on the Confirmation of Charges (Sept. 30, 2008).

Prosecutor v. Kayishema, Case No. ICTR-95-1-T, Judgement (May 21, 1999).

Prosecutor v. Ferdinand Nahimana, Case No. ICTR- 99- 52- T, Judgment (Dec. 3, 2003).

Prosecutor v. Uhuru Muigai Kenyatta, Case No. ICC-01/09-02/11-382-Red, Decision on the Confirmation of Charges Pursuant to Article 61(7)(a) and (b) of the Rome Statute (January 29, 2012).

Prosecutor v. William Samoei Ruto, Henry Kiprono Kosgey and Joshua Arap Sang, Case No. ICC-01/09-01/11-373, Decision on the Confirmation of Charges Pursuant to Article 61(7)(a) and (b) of the Rome Statute (Jan. 23, 2012).

Prosecutor v. Sesay (Issa Hassan) and ors, Case No. SCSL-04-15-T, Sentencing Judgment (April 8, 2009).

Prosecutor v. Issa Hassan Sesay et al, Case No. SCSL-04-15-T, Judgment (Mar. 2, 2009).

PROTOCOL ADDITIONAL TO THE GENEVA CONVENTIONS OF 12 AUGUST 1949, AND RELATING TO THE PROTECTION OF VICTIMS OF INTERNATIONAL ARMED CONFLICTS (PROTOCOL I) Art. 35, (opened for signature June 8, 1977, entered into force Dec. 7, 1978), 1125 U.N.T.S.

PROTOCOL ADDITIONAL TO THE GENEVA CONVENTIONS OF 12 AUGUST 1949, AND RELATING TO THE PROTECTION OF VICTIMS OF NON-INTERNATIONAL ARMED CONFLICTS (PROTOCOL II), (opened for signature June 8, 1977, entered into force Dec. 7, 1978), 1125 U.N.T.S.

PROTOCOL OF 1978 RELATING TO THE INTERNATIONAL CONVENTION FOR THE PREVENTION OF POLLUTION FROM SHIPS, (entered into force Oct. 2, 1983), 1340 U.N.T.S.

PROTOCOL ON THE STATUTE OF THE AFRICAN COURT OF JUSTICE AND HUMAN RIGHTS (MALABO PROTOCOL), African Union (July 1, 2008).

Olivia Radics and Carl Bruch, THE LAW OF PILLAGE, CONFLICT RESOURCES, AND JUS POST BELLUM IN ENVIRONMENTAL PROTECTION AND TRANSITIONS FROM CONFLICT TO PEACE: CLARIFYING NORMS, PRINCIPLES, AND PRACTICES (Carsten Stahn, Jens Iverson et al., eds.) (2017).

Taegin Reisman, *Death Of a Middleman Thwarts Blood Diamonds Case,* INTERNATIONAL JUSTICE MONITOR, (October 5, 2016), https://www.ijmonitor.org/2016/10/death-of-a-middleman-thwarts-blood-diamonds-case/

Report of The Detailed Findings of The Commission Of Inquiry On Human Rights In The Democratic People's Republic Of Korea, UN HUMAN RIGHTS COUNCIL, A/HRC/25/CRP.1 (Feb. 7, 2014).

Report of the Panel of Experts appointed Pursuant to UNSC Resolution 1306 (2000) Paragraph 19 in Relation to Sierra Leone 150-151 (December 2000), https://mondediplo.com/IMG/pdf/un-report.pdf.

ROME STATUTE OF THE INTERNATIONAL CRIMINAL COURT (last amended 2010) Art. 8(2)(b)(iv), July 17, 1998, 2187 U.N.T.S. (entered into force on July 1, 2002).

RULE OF LAW IN ARMED CONFLICT (RULAC), *Conflicts*, available at http://www.rulac.org/browse/conflicts.

Albuquerque Sant'Anna and Rudi Rocha, *Health Impacts of Deforestation-Related Fires in the Brazilian Amazon* (2019) NOTA TÉCNICA n. 11, IEPS 1-10, https://www.hrw.org/sites/default/files/media_2020/08/Health%20Impacts%20of%20Deforestation-Related%20Fires%20in%20the%20Amazon_EN_0.pdf.

Ben Saul, THE CRIME OF TERRORISM WITHIN THE JURISDICTION OF THE AFRICAN COURT OF JUSTICE AND HUMAN AND PEOPLES' RIGHTS IN THE AFRICAN COURT OF JUSTICE AND HUMAN AND PEOPLES' RIGHTS IN CONTEXT: DEVELOPMENT AND CHALLENGES (Charles Jalloh, Kamari Clarke, and Vincent O. Nmehielle, eds., 2019).

Evelyne Schmid, TAKING ECONOMIC, SOCIAL AND CULTURAL RIGHTS SERIOUSLY IN INTERNATIONAL CRIMINAL LAW (2015).

Aaron Schwabach, *Ecocide and Genocide in Iraq: International Law, the Marsh Arabs, and Environmental Damage in Non-International Conflicts*, 15 COLORADO JOURNAL OF INT'L ENVIRONMENTAL LAW AND POLICY 1 (2004).

Peter Sharp, *Prospects For Environmental Liability in The International Criminal Court*, 18 VA. ENVTL. LJ 217 (1999).

Matiangai Sirleaf, PROSECUTING DIRTY DUMPING IN AFRICA IN THE AFRICAN COURT OF JUSTICE AND HUMAN AND PEOPLES' RIGHTS IN CONTEXT: DEVELOPMENT AND CHALLENGES (Charles Jalloh, Kamari Clarke, and Vincent Nmehielle, eds., 2019).

Situation in Darfur, ICC-02/05-157-AnxA, Public Redacted Version of the Prosecutor's Application under Article 58, 14 July 2008, paragraphs 14 and 15, http://www.icc-cpi.int/iccdocs/doc/doc559999.pdf.

Situation in Darfur, Sudan: Prosecutor v. al Bashir, Case No. ICC-02/05-01/09, Decision on the Prosecution's Application for a Warrant of Arrest against Omar Hassan Ahmad Al Bashir (March 4, 2009).

Situation in the Republic of Côte d'Ivoire, Case No. ICC-02/11-14-Corr, Corrigendum to "Decision Pursuant to Article 15 of the Rome Statute on the Authorisation of an Investigation into the Situation in the Republic of Côte d'Ivoire" (Nov. 15, 2011).

The Social and Economic Rights Action Centre and the Centre for Economic and Social Rights v. Nigeria, AFRICAN COMMISSION ON HUMAN AND PEOPLES' RIGHTS, Comm. No. 155/96 (2001), https://www.escr-net.org/sites/default/files/serac.pdf.

Negasi Solomon et al., *Environmental Impacts and Causes of Conflict in the Horn of Africa: a Review*, 177 EARTH-SCIENCE REVIEW (2018).

J.G. Stewart, *Corporate War Crimes: Prosecuting the Pillage of Natural Resources*, OPEN SOCIETY JUSTICE INITIATIVE (2011).

Dire Tladi, IMMUNITIES (ARTICLE 46ABIS) IN THE AFRICAN COURT OF JUSTICE AND HUMAN AND PEOPLES' RIGHTS IN CONTEXT: DEVELOPMENT AND CHALLENGES (Charles Jalloh, Kamari Clarke, and Vincent O. Nmehielle, eds., 2019).

U. C. JHA, ARMED CONFLICT AND ENVIRONMENTAL DAMAGE (2nd ed. 2014).

U.N. CONVENTION ON THE LAW OF THE SEA, (opened for signature Dec. 10, 1982, entered into force Nov. 16, 1994), 1833 U.N.T.S. 397.

UNESCO website, at http://whc.unesco.org/en/danger/, accessed July 4, 2020.

UNITED NATIONS, DRAFT COMPREHENSIVE CONVENTION AGAINST INTERNATIONAL TERRORISM, UN Doc A/59/894, https://www.ilsa.org/Jessup/Jessup08/basicmats/unterrorism.pdf.

UNITED NATIONS ENVIRONMENTAL PROGRAMME, AFTER THE TSUNAMI: RAPID ENVIRONMENTAL ASSESSMENT (Feb. 25, 2005), https://wedocs.unep.org/handle/20.500.11822/8372.

UNITED NATIONS ENVIRONMENTAL PROGRAMME, PROTECTING THE ENVIRONMENT DURING ARMED CONFLICT: AN INVENTORY AND ANALYSIS OF INTERNATIONAL LAW (2009).

UNITED NATIONS OFFICE OF THE HIGH COMMISSIONER FOR HUMAN RIGHTS, MAPPING HUMAN RIGHTS OBLIGATIONS RELATING TO THE ENJOYMENT OF A SAFE, CLEAN, HEALTHY AND SUSTAINABLE ENVIRONMENT REPORT NO. 1, (A/HRC/25/53), (December 2013).

UNITED NATIONS OFFICE OF THE HIGH COMMISSIONER FOR HUMAN RIGHTS, REPORT OF THE MAPPING EXERCISE DOCUMENTING THE MOST SERIOUS VIOLATIONS OF HUMAN RIGHTS AND INTERNATIONAL HUMANITARIAN LAW COMMITTED WITHIN THE TERRITORY OF THE DEMOCRATIC REPUBLIC OF THE CONGO BETWEEN MARCH 1993 AND JUNE 2003 (AUGUST 2010), https://www.ohchr.org/en/countries/africaregion/pages/rdcprojetmapping.aspx

UNSC RESOLUTION 1173, THE SITUATION IN ANGOLA, (June 12, 1998).

UNSC RESOLUTION 1306: SIERRA LEONE, (July 5, 2000).

UNSC RESOLUTION 1521: THE SITUATION IN LIBERIA, UN Doc S/RES/1521, (December 22, 2003).

UNSC RESOLUTION 2134: CENTRAL AFRICA REPUBLIC, UN Doc S/RES/2134, (January 28, 2014).

UNSC RESOLUTION 2136: DEMOCRATIC REPUBLIC OF CONGO, UN Doc S/RES/2136, (January 30, 2014).

UN SECURITY COUNCIL, STATUTE OF THE INTERNATIONAL CRIMINAL TRIBUNAL FOR RWANDA (AS LAST AMENDED ON 13 OCTOBER 2006), November 8, 1994.

UN SECURITY COUNCIL, STATUTE OF THE INTERNATIONAL CRIMINAL TRIBUNAL FOR THE FORMER YUGOSLAVIA (AS AMENDED ON MAY 17, 2002), May 25, 1993.

UNITED NATIONS SECURITY COUNCIL RESOLUTION 1493, U.N.Doc. S/RES/1493 (July 28, 2003).

UNITED NATIONS SECURITY COUNCIL RESOLUTION 2136: DEMOCRATIC REPUBLIC OF CONGO (January 30, 2014), UN Doc S/RES/2136 (2014).

Mohammed Saif-Alden Wattad, *Rome Statute and Captain Planet: What Lies Between Crime Against Humanity and the Natural Environment*, 19 FORDHAM ENVIRONMENTAL LAW REVIEW (2009).

Benjamin Whitaker (Special Rapporteur), *Revised and Updated Report on the Question of the Prevention and Punishment of the Crime of Genocide* ¶ 33, UNITED NATIONS HUMAN RIGHTS SUBCOMMISSION ON THE PREVENTION OF DISCRIMINATION AND PROTECTION OF MINORITIES, 38th Sess., UN Doc. E/CN.4/Sub.2/1985/6 (1985).

Chapter 4

Legal challenges to the inclusion of a crime of ecocide in the Rome Statute of the International Criminal Court

Beatrice L. Hamilton

Rolin-Jaequemyns International Law Institute Ghent and Edinburgh Centre for Global and International Law

Abstract: If proof that ecocide exists is needed, at least in its cumulative form, one needs only look to global warming. The inclusion of an environmental crime in the international criminal code has already been considered, provisionally adopted, debated and omitted by decision, yet, efforts to establish an even more elaborate crime, the crime of ecocide, continue. The initiative to bring about criminal charges for severe environmental damage is, for its most part, motivated by the ambition to prevent States and corporations from causing such damage. It is envisaged that the crime of ecocide would be a strict liability crime that arises where extensive damage is caused disregard of the cause. This chapter will engage with the legal challenges associated with the insertion of the crime of ecocide in the current criminal code: the Rome Statute of the International Criminal Court. The first part of the chapter will engage with the development of environmental crimes. The second part of the chapter will examine the current legal status of environmental crimes and challenges thereof, and the third part will question whether the inclusion of the crime of ecocide as it is understood today in the current Criminal Code is feasible.

Keywords: ecocide, genocide, crimes against humanity, International Criminal Court, Rome Statute, Polly Higgins, codification of environmental crime law, state liability, corporate criminal liability, International Law Commission.

***

I. Introduction

Popular use of the term "ecocide" is said to have originated with Professor Arthur Galston (the scientist who identified the defoliant effects of the chemical later developed into Agent Orange) during the Conference on War Crimes and the American Conscience in Washington D.C. in 1970.[1] During his address, Galston condemned Operation Ranch Hand and called for an international agreement to ban ecocide.[2] The term "ecocide" was again referred to during the 1972 United Nations Stockholm Conference on the Human Environment,[3] where Mr. Olof Palme, the then Prime Minister of Sweden, labeled the Vietnam War an "ecocide" during his opening speech.[4] The term "ecocide" (also sometimes referred to as "geocide") itself is not universally defined; however, it is generally understood to mean extensive damage to the environment or its destruction.[5] The act of ecocide in itself is not a new phenomenon, and the causing of severe damage to the environment and its destruction extend back to times where primitive societies destroyed areas of the environment by over-grazing and the use of fire, leading to soil erosion[6] and later to the industrial era where waste dumping and pollution were commonplace. Today ecocide is viewed by the collective magnitude of the damage caused to the environment by human

---

[1] There are, however, some accounts that suggest that the term "ecocide" was already in use in as early as the 1960s. *See e.g.*, ROB WHITE AND DIANE HECKENBERG, GREEN CRIMINOLOGY: AN INTRODUCTION TO THE STUDY OF ENVIRONMENTAL HARM 54 (2014).

[2] Richard Falk, *Environmental Warfare and Ecocide: Facts, Appraisals and Proposals*, 4 BULLETIN OF PEACE PROPOSALS (1973) cited in Gwynn MacCarrick, *International Monsanto Tribunal In The Hague Terms of Reference 6: Could the Past and Present Activities of Monsanto Constitute a Crime of Ecocide, Understood as Causing Serious Damage or Destroying the Environment, So as to Significantly and Durably Alter the Global Commons or Ecosystem Services Upon Which Certain Human Groups Rely?* (2016) 52; Damien Short, THE ECOCIDE-GENOCIDE NEXUS IN REDEFINING GENOCIDE: SETTLER COLONIALISM, SOCIAL DEATH AND ECOCIDE 40 (2016); Ricardo Pereira, *After the ICC Office of the Prosecutor's 2016 Policy Paper on the Case Selection and Prioritisations: Towards an International Crime of Ecocide?*, CRIMINAL LAW FORUM 180 (2020).

[3] UN CONFERENCE ON THE HUMAN ENVIRONMENT, UNGA Res. 2581 (XXIV), UN Doc. A/Conf.48/14/Rev.1., (Jan. 8, 1969).

[4] Tork Björk, (1996), *The emergence of popular participation in world politics: United Nations Conference on Human Environment* 1972 (unpublished MA dissertation, University of Stockholm), 15 cited in Short, *supra* note 2, 41.

[5] MacCarrick, *supra* note 2 at 60.

[6] Ludwik A. Teclaff, *Beyond Restoration - The Case of Ecocide*, 34 (4) NATURAL RESOURCES JOURNAL 935 (1991).

activities[7], with the common measure and most significant concern being global warming. Over the last decade, there have been strong indications that public opinion that a crime of ecocide should be instituted is strengthening. Among the more significant are the 2011 mock trial in the Supreme Court in the UK, the 2012 European Citizens attempt to form a joint EU position on the crime of ecocide and the 2016 mock international tribunal of Monsanto at the Hague.[8] At their core, these initiatives aim to prevent environmental damage as committed mainly by States and corporations through the institution of criminal liability for the act of ecocide. As understood today, the intention is that what is commonly referred to as the "crime of ecocide" would be a strict liability crime that arises when mass environmental damage is caused, in disregard of the cause.[9] The purpose of this chapter is to explore the legal challenges that are associated with the insertion of the crime of ecocide in the current international criminal code. The first part of the chapter will offer insights into the legal environment that led to the provisional inclusion of an environmental crime in the 1991 Draft Code of Crimes Against the Peace and Security of Mankind and the omission of the crime from the 1996 version. The second part of the chapter will examine the current legal status of environmental crimes and challenges thereof, and the third part will question whether the inclusion of the crime of ecocide in the current international criminal code is feasible in view of the jurisprudential development of what is described as the crime of ecocide to date and the object that the crime should be that of strict liability.

II. The Legal Development of Environmental Crimes

A. The origin of concept

The idea that environmental damage of magnitude or the destruction of the environment should be criminalized was born out of efforts to develop what is known today as the crime of genocide and can be traced back to Raphael Lemkin, who in an address at the International Conference for Unification of Criminal Law in Madrid in 1933 urged the international community to recognize that the destruction of a nation or an ethnic group could be achieved through cultural destruction and not only through physical killing.[10]

---

[7] *Id.* at 934.
[8] Pereira, *supra* note 2 at 180.
[9] Teclaff, *supra* note 7 at 934; Polly Higgins, Damien Short et al., *Protecting the planet: A proposal for a law of ecocide, Crime,* 59(1) LAW AND SOCIAL CHANGE, 15 (2013).
[10] Short, *supra* note 2 at 40.

Lemkin's concept was that a law that prohibits the deliberate destruction of a nation or an ethnic group by either physical genocide (which Lemkin associated with the concept of barbarity) or by undermining its way of life (which Lemkin associated with the concept of vandalism) was needed.[11] The term "genocide" itself is composed of the Greek word "genos," meaning tribe or race, and the Latin word "cide," meaning destruction,[12] and although at the time Lemkin's work focused on the "genos," it was Lemkin's work that identified that the destruction of a people could be achieved by means other than killing.[13] The concept of genocide by means other than killing was later developed further by Professor Richard Falk, who established a direct link between genocide and the environment. According to Falk (1973), the crime of genocide as appeared in the 1954 Draft Code of Crimes Against the Peace and Security of Mankind did account for killing. However, did not account for the effects of environmental damage as a means to bring about genocide.[14] In response, Falk submitted a draft convention on the crime of ecocide and called for new international documents that address ecological crimes, and in particular, an international convention on the crime of ecocide and a draft protocol on environmental warfare.[15] Despite the fact that, at the time, Falk's Draft convention focused on ecocide as an element of war crimes of intent and did not address peacetime environmental damage,[16] Falk's work contributed to the development of the understanding of ecocide as a crime.

B. The provisional inclusion of Article 26 in the 1991 Draft Code of Crimes against the Peace and Security of Mankind[17]

The first effort to codify an autonomous environmental crime was pursued by the ILC through the attempted inclusion of the crime in the Draft Code of Crimes Against the Peace and Security of Mankind, which was originally

---

[11] Oksana Grechenkova, *Certain problems of fighting ecocide*, Vol. VIII, Iss. 3(25) JOURNAL OF ADVANCED RESEARCH IN LAW AND ECONOMICS 824 (2017); Polly Higgins et al, *supra* note 9.

[12] *Id.*

[13] Dirk Moses, *Empire, colony, genocide: keywords and the philosophy of history* in Dirk Moses (Ed.), EMPIRE, COLONY, GENOCIDE: CONQUEST, OCCUPATION, AND SUBALTERN RESISTANCE IN WORLD HISTORY, 12-13 (2010) cited in Higgins, Short and South, *supra* note 8, 11; *Id.*

[14] Short, *supra* note 2 at 42.

[15] Pereira, *supra* note 2 at 184.

[16] Short, *supra* note 2 at 42.

[17] For the text of the draft articles provisionally adopted by the Commission at its forty-third session, see UN (1994), YEARBOOK OF THE INTERNATIONAL LAW COMMISSION 1991, VOL. II, PART II, UN, New York, https://doi.org/10.18356/bdf8c8ed-en, 94–107.

drafted in 1954,[18] revised in 1991[19] and eventually adopted by the ILC during its Forty-Eighth Session in 1996[20].[21] The first Draft Code (which came into effect in 1954) did not engage with the protection of the environment, which according to Christian Tomuschat (member in 1996), considering that, as late as the 1950's, awareness of the necessity of protecting the environment did not exist, is understandable. [22] The 1954 Draft Code strongly reflected the Nuremberg principles, which at the time was consistent with the ILC's 1947 mandate to formulate principles of international law as derived from the Nuremberg principles,[23] and to prepare a Draft Code of Offenses Against the Peace and Security of Mankind that "clearly indicates the place to be accorded to these principles."[24] The Nuremberg Charter assigned individual criminal responsibility for three categories of crimes: crimes against peace,[25] crimes against humanity[26] and war crimes.[27] The Nuremberg judgment clarified the concept of individual criminal liability, which is prevalent in international

---

[18] DRAFT CODE OF OFFENCES AGAINST THE PEACE AND SECURITY OF MANKIND, YEARBOOK OF THE INTERNATIONAL LAW COMMISSION 1954, VOL. II, PART II, UN, NewYork, https://legal.un.org/ilc/texts/instruments/english/draft_articles/7_3_1954.pdf.

[19] DRAFT CODE OF CRIMES AGAINST THE PEACE AND SECURITY OF MANKIND, YEARBOOK OF THE INTERNATIONAL LAW COMMISSION 1991, VOL. II, PART II, UN, New York, https://doi.org/10.18356/bdf8c8ed-en.

[20] DRAFT ARTICLES ON INTERNATIONAL LIABILITY FOR THE INJURIOUS CONSEQUENCES OF ACTS NOT PROHIBITED BY INTERNATIONAL LAW, UN (2000), YEARBOOK OF THE INTERNATIONAL LAW COMMISSION 1996, VOL. II, PART II, UN, NewYork, https://doi.org/10.18356/8782fa60-en.

[21] Short, *supra* note 2 at 44.

[22] Document ILD (XLVIII)/DC/CRD.3 Document on crimes again the environment, prepared by Mr Christian Tomuschat, member of the International Law Commission, Tomuschat, 1996, 17 ¶ 4.

[23] PRINCIPLES OF INTERNATIONAL LAW RECOGNIZED IN THE CHARTER OF THE NÜRNBERG TRIBUNAL AND IN THE JUDGMENT OF THE TRIBUNAL, WITH COMMENTARIES, UN (1950), YEARBOOK OF THE INTERNATIONAL LAW COMMISSION 1950, VOL. II, UN, New York, https://doi.org/10.18356/cc800c08-en.

[24] FORMULATION OF THE PRINCIPLES RECOGNIZED IN THE CHARTER OF THE NURNBERG TRIBUNAL AND IN THE JUDGMENT OF THE TRIBUNAL [1947] UNGA 76; A/RES/177 (II) (November 21, 1947); Short, *supra* note 2 at 44.

[25] CHARTER OF THE INTERNATIONAL MILITARY TRIBUNAL – ANNEX TO AGREEMENT FOR THE PROSECUTION AND PUNISHMENT OF THE MAJOR WAR CRIMINALS OF THE EUROPEAN AXIS (1945) 82 U.N.T.S. 279.

[26] *Id.*

[27] *Id.*

criminal law to date: *...that... Crimes against international law are committed by men, not by abstract entities.*[28]

The 1991 Draft Code, which was provisionally adopted by the ILC on 12 July 1991,[29] included Article 26, which was the first provision capable of imposing individual criminal liability for environmental damage whether caused in peace or wartime.[30] Article 26 of the 1991 Draft Code, titled "Wilful and severe damage to the environment," provided that "An individual who wilfully causes or orders the causing of widespread, long-term and severe damage to the natural environment shall, on conviction thereof, be sentenced ...". In its commentary to Article 26, the ILC explained that while Article 26 was based on Article 55(1) of Additional Protocol I to the Geneva Conventions 1949,[31] unlike Article 55(1), the scope *ratione materiae* of Article 26 of the 1991 Draft Code was wider than that of Article 55(1) of Additional Protocol I since the operation of Article 26 was not limited to damage caused during armed conflicts only.[32]

The inclusion of Article 26 in the 1991 Draft Code appears to have been strongly connected to and potentially the result of the ILC's work on the Draft Articles on the Responsibility of States for Internationally Wrongful Acts[33] in 1980. Article 19(3)(d) of the 1980 Draft Articles on the Responsibility of States specifically stated that a serious breach of an international obligation of essential importance for the safeguarding and preservation of the human environment such as massive pollution of the atmosphere and the high seas could constitute an international crime. The concept of responsibility for the global commons itself arose in the 1970s following the *Barcelona Traction*

---

28 TRIAL OF THE MAJOR WAR CRIMINALS BEFORE THE INTERNATIONAL MILITARY TRIBUNAL, VOL. I, Nürnberg 1947 at 223.

29 YEARBOOK OF THE INTERNATIONAL LAW COMMISSION 2011, Vol. II, Part II, UN, New York, https://legal.un.org/ilc/publications/yearbooks/english/ilc_2011_v2_p2.pdf, 94, ¶ 176.

30 COMMENTARY TO ARTICLE 26, DRAFT CODE OF CRIMES AGAINST THE PEACE AND SECURITY OF MANKIND, YEARBOOK OF THE INTERNATIONAL LAW COMMISSION 1991, VOL. II, PART II, UN, New York, https://doi.org/10.18356/bdf8c8ed-en, at 107, ¶ 2.

31 PROTOCOL ADDITIONAL TO THE GENEVA CONVENTIONS OF 12 AUGUST 1949, AND RELATING TO THE PROTECTION OF VICTIMS OF INTERNATIONAL ARMED CONFLICTS (PROTOCOL I), June 8, 1977, 1125 U.N.T.S. 3.

32 COMMENTARY TO ARTICLE 26, DRAFT CODE OF CRIMES AGAINST THE PEACE AND SECURITY OF MANKIND, YEARBOOK OF THE INTERNATIONAL LAW COMMISSION 1991, VOL. II, PART II, UN, New York, https://doi.org/10.18356/bdf8c8ed-en, at 107, ¶ 2.

33 ARTICLE 19 DRAFT ARTICLE ON STATE RESPONSIBILITY, adopted on first reading, *see* YEARBOOK 1980, VOL. II (PART II) at 32.

Case.[34] In 1986 the Special Rapporteur himself proposed that a provision making breaches of International Law for the protection of the environment a punishable act should be inserted in the list of crimes against humanity. The Special Rapporteur's proposed draft article 12 (Acts constituting crimes against humanity) read as follows:

> The following constitute crimes against humanity: severely and perhaps even irreparably prejudiced by certain human activities.
>
> The following constitute crimes against humanity:
>
> ...
>
> Any serious breach of an international obligation of essential importance for the safeguarding and preservation of the human environment.[35]

In his commentary, the Special Rapporteur stressed that within the framework of its project on state responsibility, the Commission had in the meantime included serious breaches of obligations regarding the safeguarding and preservation of the environment in the group of international crimes. Thus, it seemed, to him, obvious that the Draft Code had to follow the example set by the Commission itself. In a brief comment, the Special Rapporteur stated that "It is not necessary to emphasize the growing importance of environmental problems today. The need to protect the environment would justify the inclusion of a specific provision in the draft code."[36] The ILC itself was also of the view that Article 26 of the Draft Code was consistent with Article 19(3)(d) of its 1980 Draft Articles on the Responsibility of States:

> The Commission's concern regarding harm to the environment has already been reflected in the adoption on first reading of draft article 19, on State responsibility. Under paragraph 3 (d) of the article, "the

---

[34] Case Concerning the Barcelona Traction, Light and Power Co., Ltd (Belgium v. Spain), Second Phase [1970] ICJ Rep 3.

[35] UN, YEARBOOK OF THE INTERNATIONAL LAW COMMISSION 1986, VOL. II, PART I, UN, New York, https://legal.un.org/ilc/publications/yearbooks/english/ilc_1986_v2_p1.pdf, 85-86.

[36] Cited in Document ILD (XLVIII)/DC/CRD.3 *Document on crimes again the environment*, prepared by Mr Christian Tomuschat, member of the International Law Commission, Tomuschat, 1996, 17 ¶ 5.

> safeguarding and preservation of the human environment" is already regarded as one of the fundamental interests of the international community and a breach of an obligation of essential importance for the safeguarding and preservation of the human environment has been defined as an international crime. In considering the draft code, the Commission also took the view that protection of the environment was of such importance that some particularly serious attacks against this fundamental interest of mankind should come under the Code and the perpetrators should incur international criminal responsibility.[37]

The 1991 Draft Code itself could be considered remarkable since although Article 26 was a crime of intent and therefore did not address reckless or negligent conduct as envisaged for the crime of ecocide and was limited to individuals only as well as appear to have been conditional that the environmental crime must occur within the framework of the Draft Code being crimes against the peace and security of mankind (including war crimes),[38] the Draft Code not only recognized of environmental concerns but was also the first and only Draft Code to list the willful causing of extensive environmental damage as an autonomous crime independent of the core crimes: crimes against peace, crimes against humanity and war crimes. Environmental damage caused during armed conflict was addressed in a separate provision, being Article 22 of the Draft Code, which provided that:

> 1. An individual who commits or orders the commission of an exceptionally serious war crime shall, on conviction thereof, be sentenced [to ...].
>
> 2. For the purposes of this Code, an exceptionally serious war crime is an exceptionally serious violation of principles and rules of international law applicable in armed conflict consisting of any of the following acts:
>
> ...

---

[37] *Draft Code of Crimes against the Peace and Security of Mankind*, YEARBOOK OF THE INTERNATIONAL LAW COMMISSION 1991, VOL. II, PART 2, UN, New York, https://doi.org/10.18356/bdf8c8ed-en, Commentary to Article 26, 107 at 1.

[38] Mark Allan Gray, *The International Crime of Ecocide*, 26 (26.2) CALIFORNIA WESTERN INTERNATIONAL LAW, 53. (1996).

(d) employing methods or means of warfare which are intended or may be expected to cause widespread, long-term and severe damage to the natural environment;

The inclusion of Article 26 in the 1991 Draft code, however, was not without debate. Of main concern was the element of "wilful damage," that is, the requirement that the crime must be that of intent. Some States argued that Article 26 was inconsistent with Article 22(2)(d), which addressed environmental damage in wartime. Pursuant to Article 22(2)(d), it was a war crime not only to employ methods or means of warfare that are intended to cause widespread, long-term and severe damage to the environment but also to employ methods and means of warfare that *may be expected* to cause such damage, which meant that employing methods and means of warfare that may be expected to cause such damage was a crime even where the purpose of employing such methods or means was other than to cause damage to the environment.[39] Australia, for example, argued that the inconsistency between Article 26 and Article 22 could lead to deliberate violations of International Law for the protection of the environment since if the damage is not caused with the intent to damage the environment, but rather for the purpose of economic gain, the conduct would escape the provision,[40] and that the requisite *mens rea* in Article 26 - *wilfully causing or ordering the causing of widespread, long-term and severe damage to the natural environment* – should be lowered so as to be consistent with article 22.[41] Belgium also argued that the *mens rea* of Article 26 should be amended to conform with the concept of damage in Article 22(2)(d) since the concept of willful damage alone is too restrictive.[42] Uruguay went further and proposed that given the nature of the consequences of the conduct, being widespread, long-term and severe damage to the natural environment, the requirement of willfulness should be widened from instances of willfully caused damage (willful wrongs) so as to also include damage that is caused through negligence or lack of precaution (culpable wrongs).[43] Austria took a different approach and argued that since

---

39 *Draft Code of Crimes against the Peace and Security of Mankind*, Yearbook of the International Law Commission 1991, Vol. II, Part 2, UN, New York, https://doi.org/10.18356/bdf8c8ed-en, *Commentary to Article 26* at 107, ¶ 6.

40 Document ILD (XLVIII)/DC/CRD.3 *Document on crimes again the environment*, prepared by Mr. Christian Tomuschat, member of the International Law Commission, Tomuschat, 1996 at18, ¶ 50.

41 *Id.* at 18 ¶ 9.

42 *Id.* at 18, ¶ 27.

43 *Id.* at 19, ¶ 9.

perpetrators usually act for want of commercial profits, intent should not be a requirement at all.[44]

The final result of the debate was the complete removal of Article 26 from the final Draft Code, which was adopted in 1996. Although during its forty-seventh session in 1995, the Commission decided to establish a working group that would meet at the beginning of the forty-eighth session in order to examine the inclusion of the crime and expressed its intention to complete the second reading during that session,[45] the Special Rapporteur, Mr. Doudou, expressed doubts as to whether it was advisable at this point in time to exceed the boundaries of the framework of the Nuremberg Charter,[46] and suggested that given the lack of State support, the time was not yet ripe for a provision of the nature of Article 26, and that before making a decision the Commission deemed it useful to hold a discussion in a small working group to be convened during the forty-eighth session.[47] The proposal of the Special Rapporteur to delete Article 26 was extensively discussed by the General Assembly during its fiftieth session in October 1995; however, eventually, Article 26 was removed from the Draft Code. The only two provisions relevant to the crime of ecocide in the 1996 Draft Code were Article 17(c) on the crime of genocide and the new Article 20(g) on war crimes, which on the recommendation of the Special Rapporteur amended Article 22(2)(d) of the 1991 Draft Code. Article 17 on the crime of genocide provided that:

> A crime of genocide means any of the following acts committed with intent to destroy, in whole or in part, a national, ethnic, racial or religious group, *such as*:
>
> ...
>
> (c) Deliberately inflicting on the group conditions of life calculated to bring about its physical destruction in whole or in part. (Emphasis added)

Article 20 on damage to the environment during armed conflicts provided that:

---

[44] *Id.* at 18, ¶30.

[45] *Id.* at 16 ¶ 1 and 17 ¶ 2; UN (1995), YEARBOOK OF THE INTERNATIONAL LAW COMMISSION 1992, VOL. II, PART 2, UN, New York, https://doi.org/10.18356/46a5b0b6-en, 32 ¶141.

[46] *Id.* at 16 ¶ 1 and 17 ¶ 2.

[47] *Id.*

> Any of the following war crimes constitutes a crime against the peace and security of mankind when committed in a systematic manner or on a large scale:
>
> ...
>
> (g) In the case of armed conflict, using methods or means of warfare not justified by military necessity with the intent to cause widespread, long-term and severe damage to the natural environment and thereby gravely prejudice the health or survival of the population and such damage occurs.

The amendment of Article 22(2)(d) of the 1991 Draft Code into Article 20(g) of the 1996 Draft Code was significant since although the new provision, Article 20(g), disposed of the subject of debate - *employing methods or means of warfare which... may be expected to cause widespread, long-term and severe damage to the natural environment* – the removal of the element "may be expected to cause..." also meant that Article 20(g) was limited to wilful damage only. Article 20(g) also narrowed the crime to use of methods and means of warfare that are not justified by military necessity only, thereby accommodating the necessities of war over environmental considerations, as well as imposed a higher threshold for the *mens rea* by limiting the crime to circumstances where the crime must have been intended to gravely prejudice the health or survival of the population, which meant that any damage to the environment per se was not a crime unless the intention of the damage was to gravely prejudice the health or survival of the population. An added condition is that the damage must have occurred, which meant that, in the first-place, intention, per se, was insufficient.

III. The Legal Status of the Crime of Ecocide – The Current Position

A. Criminal liability for environmental damage under Article 8(2)(b)(iv) of the Rome Statute

The Draft Code of Crimes Against the Peace and Security of Mankind eventually became the Rome Statute of the ICC,[48] which was adopted in 1998, entered into force on 1 July 2002 and is the current international criminal code. Pursuant to Article 5 of the Rome Statute, the ICC has jurisdiction to hear cases that relate to

---

[48] ROME STATUTE OF THE INTERNATIONAL CRIMINAL COURT, July 17, 1998, 2187 U.N.T.S. 90 [hereinafter 'Rome Statute'].

four categories of crimes only, being: the crime of genocide, crimes against humanity, war crimes and the crime of aggression. The only provision that directly refers to environmental damage as an element of a crime under the Rome Statute is Article 8(2)(b)(iv), which is listed under the heading 'War Crimes'. Pursuant to Article 8(2)(b)(iv), the crime entails the:

> Intentionally launching an attack in the knowledge that such an attack will cause incidental loss of life or injury to civilians or damage to civilian objects, or widespread, long-term and severe damage to the natural environment that would be clearly excessive in relation to the concrete and direct overall military advantage anticipated.

Article 8(2)(b) lists other crimes that are relevant to the environment; however, these crimes are predominantly anthropocentric in nature and grant protection to the environment only to the extent that the environment is part of the subject matter addressed in these provisions, for example, to the extent of its role as a civilian object.[49]

Whether Article 8(2)(b)(iv) is more useful for the purpose of criminalizing ecocide in the context of war than its predecessor, Article 20(g) of the 1996 Draft Code, is debatable.

The difference between Article 8(2)(b)(iv) and Article 20(g) of the 1996 Draft Code is significant since Article 8(2)(b)(iv) omits the defense of military necessity, is more outcome orientated due to its focus on excessive damage as well as disposes of the anthropocentric focus that the damage must prejudice the health or survival of the population. At the same time, however, the omission of the requirement that the damage must have occurred in combination with the requirement of intention and knowledge renders the crime a crime of intent, which narrows the scope of the crime. Knowledge in itself is more difficult to prove since it is a subjective matter. Compared to

---

49 Other war crimes relevant to the protection of the environment under the Rome Statute include: the extensive destruction and appropriation of property, not justified by military necessity and carried out unlawfully and wantonly (a grave breach), Article 8(2)(a)(iv); Intentionally directing attacks against civilian objects, Article 8(2)(b)(ii); Attacking or bombarding, by whatever means, towns, villages, dwellings or buildings which are undefended and which are not military objectives, Article 8(2)(b)(v); Destroying or seizing the enemy's property unless such destruction or seizure be imperatively demanded by the necessities of war, Article 8(2)(b)(xiii); Pillaging a town or place, even when taken by assault, Article 8(2)(b)(xvi); Employing poison or poisonous weapons, Article 8(2)(b)(xvii); Employing asphyxiating, poisonous or other gases, and all analogous liquids, materials or devices, Article 8(2)(b)(xviii).

Article 22(2)(d) of the 1991 Draft Code, Article 8(2)(b)(iv) is much narrower since it does not include damage that 'may' occur, requires knowledge of the consequences of the attack and is limited to the act of launching an attack rather than to any use of methods and means of warfare whether in attack of defense as well as to excessive damage which is measured relative to the military advantage gained rather than to any widespread, long-term and severe damage.

B. Criminal liability at the national level

Despite the removal of Article 26 from the 1996 Draft Code and the Commission's agenda, several States decided to incorporate an environmental crime in their domestic legislation. The incorporation of an environmental crime into national legislation has both positive and negative aspects. The positive aspects are the recognition by States that ecocide ought to be criminalized (at least at the national level) and the strong deterrent power that is associated with criminal charges. The incorporation of the crime into national law systems, however, also raises concerns. In the first place, the incorporation of the crime into the law of any one State is jurisdictional and does not in itself prohibit damage in other jurisdictions, with the most likely commodity being forum shopping. The quality of law, its implementation and its enforcement also strongly depend on the quality of governance prevalent in each jurisdiction and the capacities and circumstances of each individual State, which more often than not is likely to lead to inconsistent findings.

An even more complex outcome that could arise from the incorporation of an environmental crime in national codes is that the incorporation of criminal charges in domestic legislation is capable of preventing the prosecution of individuals at the international level since the jurisdiction of the ICC is complementary to national law.[50] The ICC does not have jurisdiction to hear a case where the case is being investigated or prosecuted by the State which has jurisdiction over the case, unless the State is either unwilling or unable genuinely to carry out the investigation or prosecution,[51] where the State decided not to prosecute the person concerned, unless the decision resulted from the unwillingness or inability of the State genuinely to

---

[50] ROME STATUTE, art. 17.

[51] *Id.* art. 17(1)(a); The Preamble to the Rome Statute also emphasizes that that the International Criminal Court established under this Statute shall be complementary to national criminal jurisdictions.

prosecute,[52] where the person has already been tried by the relevant State,[53] or where the case is not of sufficient gravity to justify further action by the Court.[54] This, however, is offset by the fact that a situation may arise where national law may be the only means through which a perpetrator may be brought to justice since the jurisdiction of the ICC is also voluntary, and unless a case is referred to the ICC by the UNSC, for the ICC to have jurisdiction, the concerned State must be either a signatory to the Rome Statute or voluntarily accept to the jurisdiction of the Court.[55]

As a separate issue, the voluntary and complementary systems of the ICC should also be borne in mind in any proposal for the establishment of a forum other than the ICC, for example, an independent criminal environmental court, since while a new forum may overcome difficulties for the inclusion of the crime of ecocide in the Rome Statute, it is highly unlikely that States would be willing to forgo sovereignty rights or for that matter agree to grant compulsory jurisdiction to any international forum.

C. Criminal liability for other than individuals – Challenges to establishing criminal liability for States and multinational corporations

1. Challenges to establishing criminal liability for States

Can a State be held criminally liable for ecocide? There are some circumstances that appear to justify that a State as a whole should be held criminally liable, for example, where ecocide is committed on behalf of a State by one of its organs (for example, in warfare), or where the act of ecocide could be considered that of the State as a whole, for example, in the case of serious emissions. As mentioned earlier, the international criminal law system

---

[52] *Id.* art. 17(1)(b); Article 17(2) of the Rome Statute states that: *In order to determine unwillingness in a particular case, the Court shall consider, having regard to the principles of due process recognized by international law, whether one or more of the following exist, as applicable: (a) The proceedings were or are being undertaken or the national decision was made for the purpose of shielding the person concerned from criminal responsibility for crimes within the jurisdiction of the Court referred to in Article 5; (b) There has been an unjustified delay in the proceedings which in the circumstances is inconsistent with an intent to bring the person concerned to justice; (c) The proceedings were not or are not being conducted independently or impartially, and they were or are being conducted in a manner which, in the circumstances, is inconsistent with an intent to bring the person concerned to justice.*

[53] *Id.* art. 17(1)((c).

[54] *Id.* at art. 17(1)(d).

[55] *Id.* art. 12 and art. 13.

rests on the liability of individuals only, and although individual liability is additional to the liability of the State, States cannot be held liable under the Criminal Code. In as early as 1951, during discussions on the Statute of the Criminal Court, the Committee on Criminal Justice determined that the responsibility of states for actions constituting international crimes is of a political character and that the court cannot solve such issue.[56] Article 4 of the first Draft Code, the 1954 version, also clarified that "responsibility of certain persons for crimes against mankind, envisaged in this Code, does not influence the responsibility of States according to international law."

Following the renewed interest in the Draft Code, in 1983, the ILC presented UNGA with the question of whether, given the political character of the international responsibility of States, States were subject to criminal liability; however, in 1984, the ILC arrived at the decision to continue with the development of the Criminal Code on the basis of individual criminal liability for the time being.[57] The distinction between individual criminal liability and State responsibility and the focus of the criminal code on criminal liability for individuals only, continues to date. Article 25(1) of the current Code, the Rome Statute, clearly provides that the jurisdiction of the Court is limited to persons. Article 25(4) of the Rome Statute also clarifies the separation between State responsibility and individual criminal liability "no provision in this Statute relating to individual criminal responsibility shall affect the responsibility of States under international law." Conceptually then, if criminal liability for States is a political rather than a legal matter, a situation could arise where States can commit crimes at international law, however, cannot be held criminally responsible for these crimes since criminal responsibility for States exists only as a doctrine.[58] It has been argued, however, that the political responsibility of a State can be realized through the particular responsibilities that the State voluntarily assumes[59] Under current International Law, the responsibility of States is determined in accordance with the specific sanctions that are prescribed by the relevant provisions of the conventions

---

[56] Grechenkova, *supra* note 11, at 824.

[57] *Id. at* 824.

[58] *Id.* at 825.

[59] Teclaff argues that the absence in conventions spelling out State liability for damage to the environment does not mean that such liability does not exist. Rather it means that State liability and its scope must be sought in the cumulative effect of obligations assumed directly or indirectly by States, Teclaff, *supra* note 6 at 945.

that the State is a signatory to, or in the lack of, according to the principles of State responsibility,[60] with the prescribed remedy being reparation.[61]

Article 58 of the 2001 Articles on the Responsibility of States,[62] which was adopted by the ILC in its fifty-third session in November 2001, also supports and recognizes that State responsibility is separate from individual criminal liability: "these articles are without prejudice to any question of the individual responsibility under international law of any person acting on behalf of a State." This, however, does not necessarily mean that States cannot be held criminally liable since pursuant to Article 40(1) of the Articles on the Responsibility of States, which provides that a State may be criminally liable for a serious breach of an obligation arising under a peremptory norm of general international law. A breach is considered serious if it involves a gross or systematic failure by the responsible State to fulfill the obligation.[63] In addition, Article 41 of the Articles on the Responsibility of States provides that a serious breach of an obligation arising under a peremptory norm of general international law by a State could lead to obligations and consequences for other States as well. Pursuant to Article 41, other States are under obligation to cooperate to bring to an end through lawful means any serious breach within the meaning of article 40, and to not recognize as lawful a situation created by a serious breach within the meaning of article 40, nor render aid or assistance in maintaining that situation.

In terms of scope, however, Article 40 is narrower than Article 19(3)(d) on international crimes and international delicts of the 1980 Draft Articles on the Responsibility of States, which is said to have motivated the inclusion of Article 26 in the 1991 draft Code. Article 19 listed as an international crime the serious breach by a State of an obligation essential for the protection of fundamental worlds interests, including peace and security, human rights and the safeguarding and preservation of the human environment. Subparagraph 19(3)(d) specifically identified as criminal a serious breach of an international obligation of essential importance for the safeguarding and preservation of the human environment, such as those prohibiting massive pollution of the atmosphere or the seas. In contrast to Article 19(3)(d) of the 1980 Draft Articles, Article 40(1) of the 2001 version does not make any reference to the human environment or offers examples of the damage referred to, and the

---

60 International Law Commission, *Articles on the Responsibility of States for Internationally Wrongful Acts*, G.A. Res 56/83 annex, U.N. Doc. A/Res/56/83 (Dec. 12, 2001).

61 *Id.* art. 31(1).

62 *Id.*

63 *Id.* art. 40(2).

reference made to obligations that arise from the breach of the peremptory norms of general International Law is of a general nature. Teclaff argued that while Article 19(3)(d) was not free of ambiguity, the essence of the examples that were listed in Article 19(3)(d) was that where international crimes were committed by massive pollution to the atmosphere or the sea, it was not necessary to articulate clearly accepted obligations.[64] According to Teclaff, under Article 19(3)(d), it was the massiveness of the damage that transformed pollution into a crime, where substantial damage was considered a delict and any damage that exceeded this level was considered an international crime.[65] On the positive, however, since Article 40(1) is open-ended, its content could be argued in accordance with timely developments in customary International Law. Whether criminal liability for States under Article 40 (and 41) would be a useful mechanism for holding States criminally liable for ecocide, however, is uncertain since: (1) liability under the principle of State responsibility is based on fault[66] (a serious breach of an obligation arising under a peremptory norm of general International Law), which is inconsistent with the object that the crime of ecocide should be a strict liability provision that arises upon the occurrence of the damage or destruction, and (2) since pursuant to Article 40(1) the elements for establishing liability demand that the breach would be a breach of a peremptory norm as well as that the breach would be gross and systematic, the requirements result in a high threshold, which is less likely to occur.

2. Challenges to establishing multinational corporate criminal liability

Timely notions hold that while multinational corporations are the main contributors to environmental damage, they generally escape liability at both the international and national levels. Bosselmann, for example, argues that failure to hold corporations responsible for environmental damage under international environmental law is a function of economic rationality.[67] For example, the international order developed rules that confer and consolidate certain privileges for the corporate entities, such as the replacement of the

---

[64] Teclaff, *supra* note 6 at 953.
[65] *Id.* at 953.
[66] *Id.* at 949-50.
[67] Klaus Bosselmann, *Losing the Forest for the Trees: Environmental Reductionism in the Law, Sustainability, 2430 (2010); Jose E. Alvarez, Are Corporations "Subjects" of International Law?*, 9 (1) SANTA CLARA JOURNAL OF INTERNATIONAL LAW 1, 12- 15 (2011); Rosemary Mwanza, *Enhancing accountability for environmental damage under International Law: Ecocide as a legal fulfilment of ecological integrity*, MELBOURNE JOURNAL OF INTERNATIONAL LAW, 593 (2018).

espousal system, which allows home states to bring a claim on behalf of a corporation whose interest injured by the conduct of the host state, with a system of international investor-state arbitration regime that grants corporations the right to bring claims directly.[68] According to Bosselmann, the consolidation of corporate privilege through International Law can explain the reluctance of the International Law order to expose corporations to direct accountability for environmental harm and human rights violations.[69] It has been suggested that criminal liability for multinational corporations could be acknowledged at the international level based on causal connection and guilt.[70] The logic behind this proposition is that since organizations delegate the tasks of preparing and executing strategic and operational decisions, behavior that is based on these decisions should be taken to be that of the organization since the decisions are made by decision-makers and other parties that control the entity and therefore could be taken to be the *alter ego* of that entity.[71] Establishing criminal liability on the basis of the *alter ego* approach, however, would be impossible under the current state of the international legal system since unless Article 25 of the Rome statute would be amended to extend the jurisdiction of the Court, under the current version of the Rome Statute, the ICC does not have jurisdiction over corporations - not being natural persons. Even if Article 25 would be amended so as to extend the jurisdiction of the ICC to multinational corporations, the crimes currently listed in the Rome Statute do not include the crime of ecocide, which means that corporate liability for environmental damage would be limited to the specific circumstances encompassed by the core crimes.

National law systems also do not prove an effective mechanism for holding multinational corporations criminally liable for environmental damage. Although several States (including the U.S. and France) implemented a domestic regime under which corporations can be held criminally liable,[72] as a general rule, the number of convictions of multinational corporations for environmental damage at the domestic level is relatively low.[73] One of the challenges to holding multinational corporations criminally liable for environmental damage at the national level is that by their nature, multinational corporations generally operate across jurisdictions, each which may or may not have a criminal code, and with the added complexity of the

---

[68] *Id.* at 593 (Mwanza).

[69] *Id.*

[70] Grechenkova, *supra* note 11, at 824.

[71] *Id.*

[72] *Id.*

[73] *Id.*

operation of the corporate veil. Combatting this situation would require not only that national criminal law would be present in all jurisdictions where multinational corporations operate, but also that national law must be consistent across the board and that an international regime to combat the effects of the corporate veil would be developed by collaboration. Whether such a restructure is feasible across jurisdictions is debatable, particularly in view of corporate contributions to economies. One of the greater disconnects of the time is not necessarily the disconnect between environmental protection and the law, but rather it is the disconnect between the prevalent economic model and the environment. Global warming forced the international community to address environmental concerns, yet, the realities of the economy are difficult to ignore, and at least those realities that mankind is accustomed to. The relationship, therefore, could be viewed as three-sided: the environment, the economy and the law.

Can States be held criminally liable for ecocide committed by multinational corporations? It is now accepted that States have an obligation to prevent significant transboundary harm to other States and the global commons.[74] Article 5(1) of the Draft Articles on International Liability for the Injurious Consequences of Acts not Prohibited by International Law[75] confirms that a breach of the obligation to prevent significant transboundary harm leads to the responsibility of States:

> The present articles are concerned with activities that are not prohibited in international law, either intrinsically or as to their effects. That being so, there can—as it were by definition—be no question that the occurrence of significant transboundary harm would give rise to a case of State responsibility, which is concerned with acts which in one respect or another are prohibited by international law, that is, by unlawful acts.

The Draft Articles apply to activities that are not prohibited by international law; however, they involve a risk of causing significant transboundary harm[76] and to activities that are not prohibited by international law that do not involve a risk of causing significant transboundary harm, but none the less cause such

---

[74] *Trail Smelter* Arbitration (*United States v. Canada*) (1941) 3 RIAA 1911 (*Trail Smelter Case*).
[75] *Draft Articles on International Liability for the Injurious Consequences of Acts not Prohibited by International Law*, UN (2000), YEARBOOK OF THE INTERNATIONAL LAW COMMISSION 1996, VOL. II, PART 2, UN, New York, https://doi.org/10.18356/8782fa60-en.
[76] *Id.* at art. 1(a).

harm through their physical consequences.[77] The "risk of causing significant transboundary harm" ranges from a high probability of causing significant transboundary harm to a low probability of causing disastrous harm. [78]

The obligation of States to prevent significant transboundary harm means that States could be held responsible for significant transboundary harm to other States and/or to the global commons that is caused by corporations that operate in territories under their jurisdiction or control. The main shortcoming in terms of criminalizing ecocide is that suits for "upstream – downstream" States are civil suits, which are heard before the ICJ, with the most common remedy being compensation or other relief as negotiated between the parties.[79] Factors that are taken into account in determining the responsibility of States for significant transboundary harm include: the extent to which the State complied with its obligations to prevent the harm,[80] the extent to which the State exercised due diligence in preventing or minimizing the damage,[81] the extent to which the State knew or had means of knowing that an activity is occurring or about to be carried out,[82] the extent to which the State benefits from the activity,[83] the extent to which the affected State shares in the benefit[84] the extent to which assistance to either State is either available or has been provided by third States or international organizations,[85] the extent to which compensation is reasonably available or has already been provided to injured persons,[86] the extent to which the law of the injured State provides for compensation or other relief for the same harm,[87] the standards of protection applied in relation to a comparable activity by the affected State and in regional and international practice[88] and the extent to which the State causing the harm has taken measures to assist the affected State in minimizing the harm.[89]

---

77 *Id.*

78 *Id.* at art. 2(a).

79 *Id.* at art. 21.

80 *Id.* at art. 22(a).

81 *Id.* at art. 22(b).

82 *Id.* at art. e 22(c).

83 *Id.* at art. 22(d).

84 *Id.* at art. 22(e).

85 *Id.* at art. 22(f).

86 *Id.* at art. 22(g).

87 *Id.* at art. 22(h).

88 *Id.* at art. 22(i).

89 *Id.* at art. 22(j).

3. The Poly Higgins proposal

In April 2010, Polly Higgins, a U.K. lawyer and activist, submitted a proposal to the United Nations for an amendment to the Rome Statute so as to include the crime of ecocide. In her proposal, Higgins suggested that the principle of superior responsibility, which appears in Article 28 of the Rome Statute, should be applied to both States and corporations.[90] Article 28 is titled: "Responsibility of commanders and other superiors In addition to other grounds of criminal responsibility under this Statute for crimes within the jurisdiction of the Court." Article 28(a) deals with the responsibility of commanders for crimes committed by forces under his/her effective command and control, and Article 28(b) provides for the responsibility of superiors for crimes committed by subordinates under his/her effective control. Pursuant to Article 28(b), a superior shall be criminally responsible for crimes committed by subordinates under his or her effective authority and control as a result of his or her failure to exercise control properly over such subordinates where: (i) The superior either knew or consciously disregarded information, which clearly indicated that the subordinates were committing or about to commit such crimes,[91] (ii) the crimes committed concerned activities that were within the effective responsibility and control of the superior,[92] and (iii) the superior failed to take all necessary and reasonable measures within his or her power to prevent or repress the commission of the crimes or to submit the matter to the competent authorities for investigation and prosecution. [93] What stems from Article 28 is that since the responsibility of the supervisor arises from his/her "failure to exercise control properly over such subordinates," the provision lowers the threshold from intention to failure, which better corresponds with the object of the crime of ecocide.

Whether the superior responsibility regime would be effective, however, would greatly depend on the degree of difficulty or ease associated with establishing effective control in the corporate context, and even more significantly, that States would consent to the comprehensive obligations that arise from Higgins' proposal. In her proposal, Higgins defined ecocide as follows: *Ecocide is the extensive damage to, destruction of or loss of ecosystem(s) of a given territory, whether by human agency or by other causes, to such an extent that peaceful enjoyment by the inhabitants of that territory has been severely diminished.* In her proposal, Higgins also suggested that the reference

---

[90] Higgins et al., *supra* note 9.

[91] Rome Statute, art. 28(b)(i).

[92] Rome Statute, art. 28(b)(ii).

[93] *Id.* art. 28(b)(ii).

to "whether by human agency or by other causes" would apply as follows: that naturally occurring ecocide, whether related to climate change or not, would become the responsibility of governments and that ecocide caused by human activities would become the responsibility of governments and businesses and that those who are policymakers, directors and those responsible for funding investments would become legally responsible for ensuring that any business practice that causes mass damage, destruction or loss of ecosystems would be terminated.[94] The extended obligations proposed are particularly ambitious considering that the idea of criminal liability for States in the first place is already subject to opposition.[95] In fact, it has been suggested that such opposition may be lessened if ecocide would be considered an aggravated tort or delict, and only some extreme acts would be labeled a crime. According to Teclaff, an aggravated tort would still constitute an offense *erga omnes,* and States would still be able to bring charges, as well as take peaceful countermeasures.[96]

IV. Can Ecocide Be Considered an International Crime under Current International Law?

Any discussion on the criminalization of ecocide must first ask whether the crime of ecocide as understood today could be included in the Rome Statute in the first place. Four main considerations come to mind. The first is whether the crime of ecocide is considered sufficiently serious to warrant its inclusion in the Criminal code. The second is the question of whether, in the lack of an autonomous environmental provision for what is commonly referred to as the crime of ecocide, criminal charges for the act of ecocide are sufficiently supported by law. The third is the question of whether in the lack of such autonomous provision whether the crime of ecocide could be included in the Rome Statute as an element of one or more of the core crimes, and the fourth pertains to challenges that arise from the elements of the crime of ecocide as envisaged today and the connections made between the crime of ecocide and global warming, namely, the requirement of *mens rea* and causation.

---

[94] Higgins et al., *supra* note 9.
[95] Teclaff, *supra* note 6 at 953-54.
[96] *Id.*

A. Is the "crime of ecocide" sufficiently serious to be considered the fifth crime under the Rome Statute?

Article 22(1) of the Rome Statute, on the *Nullum crimen sine lege* principle (included in Part 3 on the general principles of criminal law) states that a person shall not be criminally responsible under the Statute unless the conduct in question constitutes, at the time it takes place, a crime within the jurisdiction of the Court. One of the limitations placed on the jurisdiction of the Court is that the jurisdiction of the ICC is limited to the most serious crimes of concern to the international community as a whole,[97] which means that in order for the crime of ecocide to be considered the fifth crime under the Rome Statute (and for the Rome Statute to be amended accordingly), the crime would need to be considered of the utmost seriousness. Considering the advent of global warming and the growing awareness of the importance of the environment for the survival of mankind, it is reasonable to assume that serious environmental damage would be viewed as a matter of concern to the international community as a whole.

The ICC OTP Policy Paper, issued on September 15, 2016, which sets out the considerations that guide the exercise of prosecutorial discretion in the selection and prioritization of cases for investigation and prosecution,[98] also supports that the gravity of the offense is a determinant factor. The Policy Paper is an internal document that reflects on the weight that is afforded to the seriousness of the crime and, as such, does not give rise to legal rights.[99] The paper is based on, *inter alia*, the Rome Statute, the Rules of Procedure and Evidence, the Regulations of the Court, the Regulations of the Office, the prosecutorial strategy and other policy documents of the Office as well as the experience of the Office over its first decade of activities. It also draws from the jurisprudence of the ICC and international and national practice in this field.[100] According to the Policy Paper, the OTP will select cases for investigation and prosecution in light of the gravity of the crimes, the degree of responsibility of the alleged perpetrators and the potential charges. The weight given to each criterion will depend on the facts and circumstances of each case and each situation, and the stage of development of the case hypothesis and investigation.[101] The OTP's assessment of gravity includes

---

[97] ROME STATUTE, art. 1.

[98] ICC, Office of the Prosecutor, *Policy Paper on Case Selection and Prioritisation*, September 15, 2016, 3 ¶ 1.

[99] *Id.* at 3 ¶ 2.

[100] *Id.* at 3 ¶ 35.

[101] *Id.* at 12 ¶ 34.

both quantitative and qualitative considerations. As stipulated in regulation 29(2) of the Regulations of the Office, the factors that guide the Office's assessment include the scale, nature, manner of commission, and impact of the crimes.[102] The scale of the crimes may be assessed in light of inter alia, the number of direct and indirect victims, the extent of the damage caused by the crimes, particularly the bodily or psychological harm caused to the victims and their families, their geographical or temporal spread. [103] The manner of commission of the crimes may be assessed in light of, inter alia, the means employed to execute the crime, the extent to which the crimes were systematic or resulted from a plan or organized policy or otherwise resulted from the abuse of power or official capacity...or resulting in, the destruction of the environment or protected object.[104] The impact of the crimes may be assessed in light of, inter alia, the increased vulnerability of victims, the terror subsequently instilled, or the social, economic and environmental damage inflicted on the affected communities. In this context, the Office will give particular consideration to prosecuting Rome Statute crimes that are committed by means of, or that result in, inter alia, the destruction of the environment, the illegal exploitation of natural resources or the illegal dispossession of land.[105]

Whether the crime of ecocide could be considered serious enough so as to justify its inclusion in the Criminal Code would depend on the approach of the international community, which could be based on the seriousness attached to environmental damage on a stand-alone basis, relative to the seriousness of the core crimes already included in the Rome Statute or a combination thereof, and on the definition of the term itself, since it is unlikely that criminal charges would be brought for minor environmental damage. The crime of ecocide is defined by the magnitude of the damage caused, that is, severe damage or destruction; however, while the crime deals with environmental damage of magnitude, there is no universal definition for the crime and the elements of the crime, and the thresholds vary among the different definitions. Gray often mentioned a definition of ecocide; for example, it is proposed that to be legally described as ecocide, the ecological damage must be serious, as well as extensive or lasting, and result in international consequences.[106] On the other hand, Higgins described ecocide as the extensive loss or damage to the

[102] *Id.* at 13 ¶ 37.
[103] *Id.* at 13 ¶ 38.
[104] *Id.* at 13-14 ¶ 40.
[105] *Id.* at 14 ¶ 41.
[106] Gray, *supra* note 38 at 215-16.

ecosystem(s) in a given territory. As also mentioned earlier, the ICC OTP's assessment of gravity includes both quantitative and qualitative considerations, which according to regulation 29(2) of the Regulations of the Office, include the scale, nature, manner of commission, and impact of the crimes. If one looks, for example, at Article 8(2)(b)(iv) on environmental damage during armed conflicts, the provision itself does not offer a definition for the terms "widespread, long-term and severe" damage, which means that not only it would be difficult to prove *mens rea,* but the *actus reus* is also uncertain. Considering that pursuant to Article 22(2) of the Rome Statute, the definition of the crime must be strictly construed, and in case of ambiguity, the definition of the crime would be interpreted in favor of the person being investigated, prosecuted or convicted, the likelihood of succeeding in a claim on the basis of what could be considered a vague *actus rea* could be considered low. The situation is even more nuanced for the crime of ecocide since while Article 8(2)(b)(iv) focuses on the use of methods and means of warfare that may cause the said damage, the crime of ecocide is defined solely by the magnitude of the damage, which means that the parameters of what such damage entails must be clearly defined. Whether the international community would view the crime of ecocide as sufficiently serious to warrant its inclusion as an autonomous crime in the Rome Statute on equal foot to the core crimes already included is in itself uncertain, particularly considering that Article 8(2)(b)(iv) is not only listed as an element of war crimes but is also listed under the heading 'Other serious violations of the laws and customs applicable in international armed conflict, within the established framework of international law…' rather than under the heading for grave breaches. Whether the crime of ecocide would exceed the status of Article 8(2)(b)(iv) would depend on the weight that the international community would assign to environmental concerns. It may be that at the time of its inclusion, Article 8(2)(b)(iv) was not conceived as warranting a stronger position relative to the other war crimes listed.

The requirement of seriousness in itself could impose significant limitations on what is envisaged as the crime of ecocide. Even if the crime were accepted and included in the Rome Statute, since the jurisdiction of the Courts extends to the most serious crimes only, any environmental crime that falls under the threshold of outmost serious would fall outside the jurisdiction of the Court, and only extreme environmental damage, such as occurred as a result of Chernobyl nuclear accident, the Fukushima disaster, the Torrey Canyon oil spill, the Amoco Cadiz spill, the Exxon Valdez oil spill and the Bhopal disaster in India[107], would be caught by the provision. Whether this is sufficient to

[107] Pereira, *supra* note 2 at 197 (2020).

meet the object of the crime as envisaged is debatable. As Mr. Christian Tomuschat of the ILC Committee pointed out: It does not appear that any voice has questioned the wisdom of qualifying damage to the environment by criteria that clearly indicate that only harm of exceptional dimensions shall be taken into account.[108]

B. Is the "crime of ecocide" sufficiently supported by international law?

A situation exists where on the one hand, there is growing recognition that environmental crimes cannot be ignored any longer and must be both prevented and punished (criminal charges considered of high deterrent power), while on the other, criminal liability is not arbitrary and must be justified by law. Article 21(1) of the Rome Statute states that the applicable law for cases before the Court is:

> In the first place, this Statute, Elements of Crimes and its Rules of Procedure and Evidence;
>
> In the second place, where appropriate, applicable treaties and the principles and rules of international law, including the established principles of the international law of armed conflict;
>
> Failing that, general principles of law derived by the Court from national laws of legal systems of the world including, as appropriate, the national laws of States that would normally exercise jurisdiction over the crime, provided that those principles are not inconsistent with this Statute and with international law and internationally recognized norms and standards.

Arises from this that in the lack of a clear statement of the crime in the Rome Statute (or even as a complementary source of law where appropriate), the law must exist to support criminalization.

1. Applicable treaties and the principles and rules of international law

If war crimes were used as an example, the relevant law upon which the Court has jurisdiction to hear a case and criminal liability could be established is clearly specified. Pursuant to Article 5(c) of the Rome Statute, the ICC has jurisdiction to try war crimes for grave breaches of the 1949 Geneva

---

[108] Tomuschat, *supra* note 22 at 24.

Conventions[109] and their 1977 Protocols[110] and serious violations of the laws and customs applicable in international armed conflicts. Showing that the crime of ecocide is sufficiently supported by law may prove more difficult since, in the first place, the term "ecocide" did not develop its jurisprudence in international conventions, and even more significantly, there is no International Law to date that supports the criminalization of ecocide (notwithstanding regional agreements that criminalize environmental crimes). International Environmental Law generally tends to impose "soft" obligations. Some conventions define certain activities crimes. However, these conventions are generally subject matter specific, and therefore would require a definition capable of addressing ecocide relative to a particular activity.

Reliance on national criminal systems (even if they arise from international instruments) is not likely to be an effective tool. The issue of national law as a basis for criminalization at the international level was discussed as early as the debates on the question of whether Article 26 should be included in the Draft Code. According to Mr. Pellet, the inclusion of Article 26 had no legal basis:

> ...the working group had attempted a quadruple back flip: it adopted the basic assumption that an offence under national law was a crime and concluded from that alleged crime under national law that an offence was established under international law; it assimilated that offence to a crime, without any kind of basis, and without proving that there was any *opinio juris* whatsoever to that effect in the international

---

109 GENEVA CONVENTION FOR THE AMELIORATION OF THE CONDITION OF THE WOUNDED AND SICK IN ARMED FORCES IN THE FIELD, Aug. 12, 1949, 75 U.N.T.S. 31 (hereinafter Geneva Convention I); GENEVA CONVENTION FOR THE AMELIORATION OF THE CONDITION OF WOUNDED, SICK AND SHIPWRECKED MEMBERS OF ARMED FORCES AT SEA, Aug. 12, 1949, 75 U.N.T.S. 85 (hereinafter Geneva Convention II); GENEVA CONVENTION RELATIVE TO THE TREATMENT OF PRISONERS OF WAR, Aug. 12, 1949, 75 U.N.T.S. 135 (hereinafter Geneva Convention III); GENEVA CONVENTION RELATIVE TO THE PROTECTION OF CIVILIAN PERSONS IN TIME OF WAR, Aug. 12, 1949, 75 U.N.T.S. 287 [hereinafter Geneva Convention IV].

110 PROTOCOL ADDITIONAL TO THE GENEVA CONVENTIONS OF 12 AUGUST 1949, AND RELATING TO THE PROTECTION OF VICTIMS OF INTERNATIONAL ARMED CONFLICTS, 8 JUNE, 1977, 1125 U.N.T.S. 3, PROTOCOL ADDITIONAL TO THE GENEVA CONVENTIONS OF 12 AUGUST 1949, AND RELATING TO THE PROTECTION OF VICTIMS OF NON-INTERNATIONAL ARMED CONFLICTS (PROTOCOL II), 8 JUNE 1977, 1125 U.N.T.S. 609.

community; and it transformed an international crime into a crime against the peace and security of mankind.[111]

2. *"General principles of law derived by the Court from national laws of legal systems of the world"*

Another argument presented by Mr. Fellet was that under the national legislation of States, serious offenses against the environment were not treated as a crime or even as a serious offense, although there is a move in that direction.[112] Considering that some States did institute criminal codes, the question would be if this is sufficient to demonstrate sufficient State practice to support that customary law to that effect exists or even a principle of law (at both the international and national levels) since it is unlikely that the rules of criminal liability would be ignored, relaxed or amended.[113]

C. Alternative methods for criminalizing ecocide under the Rome Statute

An alternative method for holding a person criminally liable for environmental damage under the Rome Statute would be through the inclusion of the crime of ecocide as an element of one (or possibly more) of the four core crimes already listed in the Rome Statute. Such inclusion, however, would limit the crime to the particular context of each core crime.

1. *Ecocide as an element of genocide*

Pursuant to Article 6 of the Rome Statute, "genocide" means: "...any of the following acts committed with intent to destroy, in whole or in part, a national, ethnical, racial or religious group." Pursuant to Article 6(c): "Deliberately inflicting on the group conditions of life calculated to bring about its physical destruction in whole or in part." A limitation to the inclusion of the crime as an element of the crime of genocide is that the environmental damage must be committed with the intent to destroy a particular group.

---

[111] UN (1999), YEARBOOK OF THE INTERNATIONAL LAW COMMISSION 1996, Vol. I, https://doi.org/10.18356/f51db988-en, 8 ¶ 16.

[112] *Id.*

[113] UN (1999), YEARBOOK OF THE INTERNATIONAL LAW COMMISSION 1996, Vol. I, UN, New York, https://doi.org/10.18356/f51db988-en, 8 ¶ 16.

2. Inclusion as an element of crimes against humanity

Inclusion under crimes against humanity also presents challenges. To be considered a crime against humanity, the crime must be executed as part of a widespread or systematic attack against the civilian population,[114] which means that many environmental crimes that do not meet these conditions would fall outside the ambit of the provision.

3. Ecocide as an element of the crime of aggression

Inclusion as an element of the crime of aggression could prove the most challenging. Pursuant to Article 8 *bis (2)* of the Rome Statute, an act of aggression means the use of armed force by a State against the sovereignty, territorial integrity or political independence of another State, or in any other manner inconsistent with the Charter of the United Nations. For extreme environmental damage to fall within the ambit of the crime, the damage must be committed through the use of aggressive means, which constitutes a very high threshold. It is doubtful that even the conduct of nuclear experiments that interfere with a State's territorial integrity could be classified as an armed force.

4. Ecocide as an element of war crimes

Inclusion of the crime of ecocide under the heading "war crimes" means that the only condition where criminal charges could be brought for environmental damage is where the damage occurred during armed conflict. Peacetime ecocide is excluded. The inclusion of ecocide as an element of war crimes also raises the question of whether the parallel application of Article 8(2)(b)(iv) and the crime of ecocide during armed conflicts would be effective.

D. Challenges arising from the elements of the crime

Two main difficulties arise from the elements of the crime of ecocide as envisaged that may strongly affect the inclusion of the crime in the Rome Statute as well as the capacity to prove that the crime was indeed committed.

1. The question of **mens rea**

The main point of debate throughout the history of the crime of ecocide (and a contributing factor to the removal of Article 26 from the 1996 Draft Code) is the question of whether the crime of ecocide should be a crime of intention or a strict liability crime. The proposition that the crime of ecocide should be a

---

114 ROME STATUTE, art. 7.

strict liability crime is an attractive one since a strict liability provision would not only mean that if the requirement of intent is disposed of, the onus of proof for intent is also dismissed and the only requirement remaining is proof that the damage had in-fact occurred, but also that unintentional damage would also be captured by the provision. Gray argued that a strict liability provision is also likely to advance the precautionary principle as well as the polluter pay principle.[115] Under the current Code, however, the insertion of strict liability is not feasible since, in order to be heard before the ICC, the crime must be a crime of intent. Article 30 of the Rome Statute clearly states this term: *a person shall be criminally responsible and liable for punishment for a crime within the jurisdiction of the Court only if the material elements are committed with intent and knowledge.*

2. Causation

Showing causation for extreme significant damage could be challenging. Although certain damage could be directly linked to causing, much of the environmental damage today, particularly related to global warming, is not identifiable and could be described as the joint and accumulated consequence of many activities. As Mr. Christian Tomuschat explained:

> Everybody who lives in modern industrialized societies contributes his or her share to of modern technology is inevitably tied to the use of energy, the biggest part of which is precisely produced by burning fossil fuels. In the last analysis, furthermore, nobody can evade the necessities of life and survival. Even persons living far away from centres of modern life are simply compelled to rely on fire to satisfy their basic needs. From the very outset, it would appear to be clear beyond any reasonable doubt that this general phenomenon does not fall within the scope ratione materiae of the draft Code. The draft Code cannot possibly deal with harm to the environment by accumulation, where an infinite multitude of separate actions cause damage not individually, but conjunctively in their combination. It would be absurd to postulate that humankind constitutes nothing more than a society of criminals. It may well be that it is on a dangerous path. However, criminal law can hardly be used as an instrument to call into question the generally accepted order.[116]

---

[115] Gray, *supra* note 104 at 4.

[116] Tomuschat, *supra* note 22 at 26 ¶ 45

V. Conclusions

There appear to be three main causes of disconnect between contemporary environmental concerns and the current state of international law that impact the prospect for the successful incorporation of criminal liability for ecocide. The first is the applicability of criminal law to individual perpetrators only and, as a result, the omission of criminal liability for States and multinational corporations. The second is the fact that any amendments to the criminal law system are subject to State approval, as was already demonstrated by the Article 26 experience, and the third is the enabling of corporate structures that accommodate avoidance of legal consequences. Proposals for establishing the crime of ecocide are ambitious; yet, the jurisprudence of the crime is not necessarily sufficiently developed to support inclusion in the current instrument regulating international criminal conduct, the Rome Statute.

Of primary importance is developing a coherent and widely accepted definition that clarifies the elements of the crime and its thresholds, which could potentially elaborate on such thresholds through the provision of a non-exhaustive list of examples.

The second issue of utmost importance for the successful inclusion of the crime in the Rome Statute is the amendment of Article 25, to enable the inclusion of States and corporations. Considering the current global environment, with the outmost environmental concern being global warming, there is a strong likelihood that the time may indeed be ripe for such a provision, and there are good prospects that the inclusion of the crime in the Rome Statute crime may be considered, providing that the crime would be limited to the most serious environmental crimes of concern to the international community as a whole. The main challenge under this scenario would be the topic of strict liability since the jurisdiction of the ICC is limited to crimes of intent. Whether this is a sufficient ground to forgo inclusion even under this term is debatable.

Bibliography

Jose E. Alvarez, *Are Corporations "Subjects" of International Law*, 9 (1) SANTA CLARA JOURNAL OF INTERNATIONAL LAW 1 (2011).

Klaus Bosselmann, LOSING THE FOREST FOR THE TREES: ENVIRONMENTAL REDUCTIONISM IN THE LAW, SUSTAINABILITY (2010).

Case Concerning the Barcelona Traction, Light and Power Co., Ltd. (Belgium v. Spain), Second Phase (1970), ICJ Rep. 3.

CHARTER OF THE INTERNATIONAL MILITARY TRIBUNAL – ANNEX TO AGREEMENT FOR THE PROSECUTION AND PUNISHMENT OF THE MAJOR WAR CRIMINALS OF THE EUROPEAN AXIS (1945), 82 UNTS 279.

COMMENTARY TO ARTICLE 26, DRAFT CODE OF CRIMES AGAINST THE PEACE AND SECURITY OF MANKIND, YEARBOOK OF THE INTERNATIONAL LAW COMMISSION 1991, Vol. II, Part 2, UN, New York, https://doi.org/10.18356/bdf8c8ed-en.

DOCUMENT ILD (XLVIII)/DC/CRD.3 DOCUMENT ON CRIMES AGAIN THE ENVIRONMENT, prepared by Mr Christian Tomuschat, member of the International Law Commission, Tomuschat, 1996.

DRAFT ARTICLES ON INTERNATIONAL LIABILITY FOR THE INJURIOUS CONSEQUENCES OF ACTS NOT PROHIBITED BY INTERNATIONAL LAW, UN (2000), YEARBOOK OF THE INTERNATIONAL LAW COMMISSION 1996, Vol. II, Part 2, UN, New York, https://doi.org/10.18356/8782fa60-en.

DRAFT CODE OF CRIMES AGAINST THE PEACE AND SECURITY OF MANKIND, YEARBOOK OF THE INTERNATIONAL LAW COMMISSION 1991, Vol. II, Part 2, UN, New York, https://doi.org/10.18356/bdf8c8ed-en.

DRAFT CODE OF OFFENCES AGAINST THE PEACE AND SECURITY OF MANKIND, YEARBOOK OF THE INTERNATIONAL LAW COMMISSION 1954, Vol. II, Part 2, UN, New York, https://legal.un.org/ilc/texts/instruments/english/draft_articles/7_3_1954.pdf.

Richard Falk, *Environmental Warfare and Ecocide: Facts, Appraisals and Proposals*, 4 BULLETIN OF PEACE PROPOSALS (1973).

FORMULATION OF THE PRINCIPLES RECOGNIZED IN THE CHARTER OF THE NURNBERG TRIBUNAL AND IN THE JUDGMENT OF THE TRIBUNAL (1947) UNGA 76; A/RES/177 (II) (21 November 1947).

GENEVA CONVENTION FOR THE AMELIORATION OF THE CONDITION OF THE WOUNDED AND SICK IN ARMED FORCES IN THE FIELD, 75 U.N.T.S. 31, (Aug. 12, 1949).

GENEVA CONVENTION FOR THE AMELIORATION OF THE CONDITION OF WOUNDED, SICK AND SHIPWRECKED MEMBERS OF ARMED FORCES AT SEA, 75 U.N.T.S. 85, (Aug. 12, 1949).

GENEVA CONVENTION RELATIVE TO THE TREATMENT OF PRISONERS OF WAR, 75 U.N.T.S. 135, (Aug. 12, 1949).

GENEVA CONVENTION RELATIVE TO THE PROTECTION OF CIVILIAN PERSONS IN TIME OF WAR, 75 U.N.T.S. 287, (Aug. 12, 1949).

Mark Allan Gray, *The International Crime of Ecocide*, 26.2 CALIFORNIA WESTERN INTERNATIONAL LAW, (1996).

Oksana Grechenkova, *Certain problems of fighting ecocide*, JOURNAL OF ADVANCED RESEARCH IN LAW AND ECONOMICS Vol. VIII, Iss. 3 (25), (2017).

Polly Higgins, Damien Short et al., *Protecting the planet: A proposal for a law of ecocide, Crime,* 59 (1) LAW AND SOCIAL CHANGE, (2013).

INTERNATIONAL LAW COMMISSION, ARTICLES ON THE RESPONSIBILITY OF STATES FOR INTERNATIONALLY WRONGFUL ACTS, G.A. Res 56/83 annex, UN Doc. A/Res/56/83 (Dec. 12, 2001).

Gwynn MacCarrick, *International Monsanto Tribunal in the Hague Terms of Reference 6: Could the past and present activities of Monsanto constitute a crime of ecocide, understood as causing serious damage or destroying the environment, so as to significantly and durably alter the global commons or ecosystem services upon which certain human groups rely?* (2016).

Dirk Moses, *Empire, colony, genocide: keywords and the philosophy of history*, Dirk Moses (Ed.), EMPIRE, COLONY, GENOCIDE: CONQUEST, OCCUPATION, AND SUBALTERN RESISTANCE IN WORLD HISTORY, (2010).

Rosemary Mwanza, *Enhancing accountability for environmental damage under International Law: Ecocide as a legal fulfilment of ecological integrity*, MELBOURNE JOURNAL OF INTERNATIONAL LAW, (2018).

Ricardo Pereira, *After the ICC Office of the Prosecutor's 2016 Policy Paper on the Case Selection and Prioritisations: Towards an International Crime of Ecocide?*, CRIMINAL LAW FORUM (2020).

PRINCIPLES OF INTERNATIONAL LAW RECOGNIZED IN THE CHARTER OF THE NÜRNBERG TRIBUNAL AND IN THE JUDGMENT OF THE TRIBUNAL, WITH COMMENTARIES, YEARBOOK OF THE INTERNATIONAL LAW COMMISSION 1950, Vol. II, UN, New York, (1950), https://doi.org/10.18356/cc800c08-en.

PROTOCOL ADDITIONAL TO THE GENEVA CONVENTIONS OF 12 AUGUST 1949, AND RELATING TO THE PROTECTION OF VICTIMS OF INTERNATIONAL ARMED CONFLICTS (PROTOCOL I), 1125 U.N.T.S. 3, (June 8, 1977).

PROTOCOL ADDITIONAL TO THE GENEVA CONVENTIONS OF 12 AUGUST 1949, AND RELATING TO THE PROTECTION OF VICTIMS OF NON-INTERNATIONAL ARMED CONFLICTS (PROTOCOL II), 1125 U.N.T.S. 609, (June 8, 1977).

ROME STATUTE OF THE INTERNATIONAL CRIMINAL COURT, 2187 U.N.T.S. 90, *Trail Smelter* Arbitration (United States v. Canada), (1941), 3 RIAA 1911, (July 17, 1998).

Damien Short, THE ECOCIDE-GENOCIDE NEXUS IN REDEFINING GENOCIDE: SETTLER COLONIALISM, SOCIAL DEATH AND ECOCIDE (2016).

Ludwik A. Teclaff, *Beyond Restoration - The Case of Ecocide*, 34 (4) NATURAL RESOURCES JOURNAL 935 (1991).

UN CONFERENCE ON THE HUMAN ENVIRONMENT, UNGA Res. 2581 (XXIV), UN Doc. A/Conf.48/14/Rev.1., (Jan. 8, 1969).

Rob White and Diane Heckenberg, GREEN CRIMINOLOGY: AN INTRODUCTION TO THE STUDY OF ENVIRONMENTAL HARM 54 (2014).

YEARBOOK OF THE INTERNATIONAL LAW COMMISSION 2011, Vol. II, Part II, UN, New York, https://legal.un.org/ilc/publications/yearbooks/english/ilc_2011_v2_p2.pdf.

YEARBOOK OF THE INTERNATIONAL LAW COMMISSION 1996, Vol. I, UN, New York, https://doi.org/10.18356/f51db988-en.

YEARBOOK OF THE INTERNATIONAL LAW COMMISSION 1991, Vol. II, Part II, UN, New York, https://doi.org/10.18356/bdf8c8ed-en.

YEARBOOK OF THE INTERNATIONAL LAW COMMISSION 1986, Vol. II, Part I, UN, New York, https://legal.un.org/ilc/publications/yearbooks/english/ilc_1986_v2_p1.pdf, 85-86.

YEARBOOK OF THE INTERNATIONAL LAW COMMISSION 1992, Vol. II, Part II, UN, New York, https://doi.org/10.18356/46a5b0b6-en, 32.

Chapter 5

The International Court for the Environment – Could the International Court for the Environment offer a solution for the problem of international environmental crimes?*

David Krott, LL.M.

Vrije Universiteit Brussels

Abstract: This chapter promotes the creation of an International Court for the Environment and puts forward a definition of international environmental crimes to clarify the jurisdiction of the court regarding criminal misconduct. The globalized world needs an International Court for the Environment, not only to adjudicate all environmentally related cases, but in particular, to handle international environmental crimes on the international level. International courts and dispute settlement institutions have established a broad network for judicial decisions based on international law. They govern disputes between states, between corporations and states, as well as between individuals and states. Within this network, an institution regarding the governing of the global environment is missing, disregarding the extraordinary importance of the natural environment as the basis for humanity. I argue for an International Court for the Environment as a welcome addition to fill the existing gap. Not only for cases regarding the general handling of the natural environment on the international level but also regarding potentially criminal acts harming the environment on a wide scale.

Keywords: International Court for the Environment, International Court of the Environment Foundation, International Court for the Environment

Coalition, defining international environmental crimes, global commons, National Green Tribunal, Environment Court of New Zealand, International Court of Justice.

***

I. Introduction

From time-to-time international law needs new stimuli for further development. Just as the establishment of the World Trade Organisation (WTO) and the ICC set new benchmarks in international law, the creation of new international bodies addressing environmental challenges could open a new chapter for global environmental governance and preservation. Bodies established to address global challenges more appropriately, or to promote international law in general, can provide these stimuli. Major environmental threats on a global scale present international challenges and those craving for effective multilateral action. This is especially true for environmental harm resulting from potentially criminal acts – international environmental crimes or green crimes. The Napalm bombardment of the Vietnamese jungle during the Vietnam War, the Deepwater Horizon oil spill in the Gulf of Mexico, ivory trade between Africa and Asia, the worldwide trade in ozone-depleting substances, or smuggling of genetically engineered plants present historic, current and potential future repercussions with the potential to qualify for international environmental crimes.[1] Their common ground is that these harmful acts are not in any way properly addressed on an international level. Therefore, the International Court for the Environment (ICE) might just be the "missing link" in the sphere of international legal institutions to finally have a common judicial ground regarding environmental issues.

The following chapter explores the idea of the foundation of an ICE and whether such an international environmental court would be a useful

---

* This chapter is inspired by the author's master thesis titled "*Guilty or not guilty – The call for international environmental criminal law*", written at the University of Otago in Dunedin, New Zealand in 2017.

[1] Banks et al., ENVIRONMENTAL CRIME – A THREAT TO OUR FUTURE 19 (2008); Polly Higgins, ERADICATING ECOCIDE X (*2010*); Armin Rosencranz and Siddharth Johar, *Illegal Smuggling of Ozone-depleting Substances,* 45(2) Environmental Policy and Law 73, 76 (2015); Sam Cowie, Seeking Answers to Catastrophic Brazil Mine Disaster, https://www.aljazeera.com/indepth/features/2015/12/seeking-answers-catastrophic-brazil-disaster-151224071626923.html (02 January 2016); Nigel South, *A Green Field for Criminology: A Proposal for a Perspective,* 2(2) Theoretical Criminology 211, 219 (1998).

addition to the existing international institutions to help to contain international environmental degradation. This analysis specifically focuses on the handling of international environmental crimes in front of the suggested environmental court. In this light, it evaluates the possibilities of creating an overarching definition for international environmental crimes in the vicinity of the ICE to end the dilemma regarding the existing debate on the interpretation of international environmental crime.

The chapter starts with a general explanation of what an ICE entails, where the idea comes from, its core competencies, and its advantages. Following this introductory part, the chapter then focuses on the development of a definition for international environmental crimes under the ICE statute. The chapter finishes with a discussion on some of the many challenges of such a new court.

II. The International Court for the Environment as criminal judicial tribunal for green crimes?

In 1920, the ICJ was founded, mainly in reaction to the tragedy of World War I and following the realization that an increasingly globalized world needs international courts as an anchor. The ICJ was intended to work as a guardian of international relations to ensure peaceful coexistence. Since then, new international jurisdictional organs have been formed to stabilize international relations. In an ever more globalized world, the global problem of worldwide environmental degradation through international environmental harm is apparent. In many ways, the situation today driving demand to set up a new specialized environmental court does not seem to be much different from that which drove the establishment of the ICJ in 1920. Global environmental problems are increasingly obvious and multifaceted today. Not only have they led to a high rate of environmental degradation, but these problems trigger an even higher rate of human suffering.

Many international efforts to tackle environmental degradation or crime are often eclipsed by issues seeming to be more pressing or simply attracting more media attention. Since the attacks on the World Trade Centre in 2001, terrorism is the highest-ranking threat in many states. Due to disproportionate media attention, terror appears as the by far most pressing issue in international relations. Of course, terrorism cannot be denied as a critical problem, but the overall international environmental damage, might in a long-term view, be responsible for more harm than all terror attacks combined. In addition, environmental harm does a fair share in financing terror groups globally: in 2014, the Islamic State's largest form of income was derived from illegally trading oil, and the Revolutionary Armed Forces of Colombia are involved in illegal mining activities.[2]

The idea for an international environmental court is not entirely new. In 1992, the International Court of the Environment Foundation (ICEF) was established to promote the establishment of an ICE.[3] Only one year later, the final statement of the first ICEF Conference set out the need for general international jurisdiction for global environmental problems.[4] In the following years, the ICEF campaigned in support of the idea in a number of fora and to several states, with the International Court for the Environment Coalition (ICE Coalition) joining ICEFs cause after 2008.[5] In 2002 more than 120 senior judges from more than 60 countries concluded within the context of the Johannesburg World Summit on Sustainable Development:

> By promoting the establishment of a judicial body such as an International Court for the Environment, the international community would effectively respond to the challenge – and also exciting opportunity – of how States and non-state actors can actively partake in ensuring compliance to globally agreed commitments on sustainable development.[6]

---

[2] United Nations Security Council, *The Islamic State in Iraq and the Levant and the Al-Nusrah Front for the People of the Levant: Report and Recommendations Submitted Pursuant to Resolution*, 2170 (2014); Johan Bergenas and Ariella Knight, *Green terror: Environmental crime and illicit financing*, 35(1) School of Advanced International Studies Review 119, 119 (2015).

[3] ICEF is a non-profit NGO which promotes the creation of an International Court of the Environment; Ole W. Pedersen, *An International Environmental Court and International Legalism*, 24(3) JOURNAL OF ENVIRONMENTAL LAW 547, 548 (2012).

[4] Deirdre E. Pirro, Project for an international court of the environment - Origins and development, https://www.biopolitics.gr/biowp/wp-content/uploads/2013/04/Pirro.pdf (last visited 30 July 2020).

[5] The ICE Coalition represents a number of environmental, legal, business, academic and NGO stakeholders who are in favour of an International Court for the Environment; Pirro, *supra* note 4; Pedersen, *supra* note 3 at 548.

[6] ICE COALITION, *Environmental Institutions for the 21st Century: An International Court for the Environment* STAKEHOLDER FORUM'S PROGRAMME ON SUSTAINABLE DEVELOPMENT 4 (2011) at 12.

To this day, many scholars promote this idea and demand political and law-making action.[7] In 2010 the Faculty of Architecture of the University of Pennsylvania and the ICE Coalition launched a project to create a building suitable to host the ICE. This project led to several astonishing architectural conceptions of the building for a potential new international court.[8] Of course, the construction of the building is not of significant legal relevance, but it underlines the seriousness of the idea.

Despite this promotion of the idea of an ICE, many experts see only a small chance of an ICE actually being created.[9] The establishment of an international court is a difficult task and requires strong negotiations. One objection to the foundation of an ICE in the near future is made on the basis that no environmental dispute is solely international.[10] Therefore the existing domestic courts dealing with environmental crimes are sufficient for appropriate litigation. In contrast to this point, no environmental problem is wholly domestic and national courts have to work within strict boundaries. In an increasingly globalized world, an ICE could handle legal questions with a vast international reach more appropriately. Pedersen expressed his skepticism with the idea of an ICE in 2012 with the remark that, if it is not possible to persuade state parties to agree upon a continuation of the Kyoto Protocol because of their fears for their economies, then it is unlikely that there will be support for a powerful ICE.[11] During the discussions leading up to a climate change agreement, a justified question was raised: How are humans to agree on enforcing a climate change agreement with an international institution when they cannot create an effective climate change treaty beforehand? As it turns out, a new climate change agreement was

---

[7] Philip Riches and Stuart A. Bruce Brief 7: *Building an International Court for the Environment: A Conceptual Framework*, 7 GOVERNANCE AND SUSTAINABILITY ISSUE BRIEF SERIES 1 at 2 (2013); Stephen Hockman, *The Case for an International Court for the Environment*, 3(1) JOURNAL OF COURT INNOVATION 215, 229 (2010); Amedeo Postiglione, *A More Efficient International Law on the Environment and Setting up an International Court for the Environment within the United Nations*, 20 ENVIRONMENTAL LAW 321, 323 (1990).

[8] ICE Coalition and University of Pennsylvania, PENN DESIGN PROJECT, http://www.ice coalition.org/penn-design-project (last visited 30 July 2020).

[9] Riches and Bruce, *supra* note 7 at 5.

[10] Philippe Sands, *Litigating Environmental Disputes: Courts, Tribunals and the Progressive Development of International Environmental Law*, 8 GLOBAL FORUM ON INTERNATIONAL INVESTMENT 1, 6-7 (2008).

[11] Postiglione, *supra* note 7 at 556.

agreed-upon in 2015.[12] Whether this agreement is sufficient and effective remains to be seen, but its mere existence shows that there is a lot of movement in this area, and things can change fast.[13] The idea of an ICE might seem idealistic, but the same was said about the UN and the ICC before these institutions were founded.[14] Yet today, the UN occupies the center-stage in the international community, and the ICC is widely recognized as a legitimate international court. Admittedly the chances of states signing on to a project like an ICE are not very high. Nevertheless, it might be worth a try to protect the environment. Big projects often start with a low chance of success.

The ICE is meant to be the primary court dealing with all sorts of international environmental matters.[15] At this stage, it is needed to state that the proposed court was not intended to be a specific international criminal court but to be a general entity operating on the international level to solve international environmental problems. Of course, international environmental crimes would not be the only concern for the ICE. The list of overall environmental problems stretches long. That is why it is not called an "International Criminal Court for the Environment". However, international environmental crimes do play a central role on an international level, and they could or should therefore be a part of the jurisdictional powers of the potential ICE.

It also has to be noted that there is not one common agreed idea for an ICE, but one idea with a lot of different facets.

1. The core competencies of the International Court for the Environment

As mentioned at the beginning of this chapter, international environmental crimes are not the only environmental problem on the international level by far. An increase in the global human population, general trans-border pollution, dumping hazardous waste at sea, ozone layer destruction, the greenhouse effect, desertification or the disastrous impacts due to the policies of industrialized states towards countries of the global south are only part of all international environmental challenges.[16] The idea behind the creation of the ICE would be to have one common forum to deal with this whole variety of international environmental matters.[17] The ICE would

---

12 PARIS AGREEMENT – UNITED NATIONS FRAMEWORK CONVENTION ON CLIMATE Change (open for signature 16 February 2016, entered into force 4 November 2016).

13 Hockman, *supra* note 7 at 226.

14 *Id.* at 230.

15 ICE Coalition, *supra* note 6.

16 Postiglione, *supra* note 7 at 323.

17 ICE Coalition, *supra* note 6 at 4.

be the court of final resort for the most serious environmental cases on our planet.[18] And in particular, the ICE should be dealing with potential criminal acts harming the environment.

The rapid growth of multilateral environmental agreements (MEAs), statutes, and national constitutions concerning the environment is in desperate need of specialized interpretation.[19] The ICE could bundle all these and provide a steady, internationally harmonized solution. A new ICE could enforce general international environmental law and decide on disputes arising from treaties or out of international customary law.[20] For domestic courts, the ICE could provide assistance and further guidance for questions with international relevance, for example, via a system of prejudicial questions. Furthermore, the ICE could work as a last resort. Domestic environmental cases could proceed up to the ICE, for example, by appeal or on request of the judges. The ICE could also function as a review body for other international bodies' decisions related to the environment, such as the Kyoto enforcement branch.[21] Through its work, the ICE could also affect the business world. The court could, for example, set out environmental guidelines, develop risk management programs and improve practices for globally active corporations to reduce environmental catastrophes.[22]

Environmental issues most often raise disputed scientific claims, which result in the co-existence of various scientific views.[23] Lack of knowledge is one of the main concerns regarding the existing international courts and was even pilloried by Judges Bruno Simma and Awn Al-Khasawneh in the *Pulp Mills Case* in 2006.[24] That is why specialists, who not only have expertise in legal questions but also environmental science, are needed. To ensure that scientific aspects are considered carefully, the judges could hear evidence from experts in the relevant fields and decide whose is most compelling. Another option would be to provide the ICE with its own scientific committee to give additional – independent – environmental background knowledge and make profound recommendations to the judges for a final decision.[25] The

---

[18] Hockman, *supra* note 7 at 229.

[19] ICE Coalition, *supra* note 6 at 12.

[20] Hockman, *supra* note 7 at 228.

[21] *Id.* at 229; The Kyoto enforcement branch is part of the Compliance Committee of the Kyoto Protocol from 2005. It has the responsibility to determine consequences for parties not meeting their commitments under the Kyoto Protocol.

[22] Hockman, *supra* note 7 at 224.

[23] Sands, *supra* note 10 at 4.

[24] Riches and Bruce, *supra* note 7 at 1.

[25] Hockman, *supra* note 7 at 223.

creation of special panels, dealing for example, solely with pollution or deforestation matters, would be another possibility.[26] These panels could help the judges develop maximum expertise in one particular field on a legal and scientific basis, allowing them to adequately deal with complex cases. However, this would probably require a longer development. In terms of the judges, a mixed composition of specialized environmental judges and judges with a more general background would be desirable to absorb all the different contexts international environmental law involves.[27] In criminal matters, experts on international criminal law would be an asset. There are a number of possibilities to ensure the ICE decides its cases with maximum expertise, and a mixture of all these possibilities could be the preferable one. An internal scientific committee helps the ICE prepare the cases, and external specialists provide further information to the judges to reach a balanced verdict.

However, this court would not primarily be a criminal court. But this would be a prerequisite to deal with international environmental crimes. Lately, every court fulfills its own obligation on an international level, similar to national criminal courts or national constitutional courts on the national level. The ICJ primarily handles the relationships between states. The ICC looks after the most heinous international crimes, and the Special Court for Sierra Leone, for example, only looks after what happened in this particular conflict in Sierra Leone. An environmental court could be, in that sense, a welcome enrichment to the pool of international courts because in addition to the ICJ and the ICC, the ICE would handle the relationship between humans and the environment. As this human-environment relationship involves potential criminal behaviors, it would be conceivable that the ICE handles these particular crimes as well.

2. Draft Statutes for the International Court for the Environment

The ICE Foundation has drafted a concept plan for the potential ICE.[28] The only step missing so far is the political will and an international decision to set up such an environmental court. Despite this missing political will, certain activist groups have worked on draft statutes for an ICE. Article 10 of the ICE Coalition drafts states that an ICE shall "protect the environment as a fundamental human right in the name of the international community."[29]

---

[26] *Id.* at 229.

[27] Philippe Sands, *supra* note 10 at 4.

[28] ICE Foundation, *Draft articles for an International Court for the Environment,* http://www.icefcourtpress.org/statute.html (last visited 30 July 2020).

[29] *Id.*

This is similar to the idea of the global commons.[30] The global natural environment is – confined under national jurisdiction or not – lastly, a "good" that should be managed under an international regime. In a sense, this is comparable to the existing legal paradigms in Antarctica or Outer Space.

The idea regarding the ICE includes giving a court jurisdiction over any environmental dispute involving state responsibility to the international community and disputes concerning environmental damage caused by private or public parties, including states, where it is presumed that, due to its size, characteristics and kind, this damage affects interests that are fundamental for safeguarding and protecting the human environment on Earth.[31]

The ICEF Draft Statute is ambitious and clearly indicates a wide perception of environmental harm. Arguably, this wide scope is the very reason why the proposal did not get much backing within the international community of states.[32]

Philip Riches and Stuart A. Bruce summarise the five purposes for a potential ICE as followed:

1. clarify and ascertain environmental legal obligations;
2. facilitate harmonization of and complement existing legislative and judicial systems;
3. provide access to justice to a broad range of actors through open standing rules;
4. provide workable solutions to modern environmental concerns;
5. build trust among the international community.[33]

---

30 "Gobal commons" refer to areas and natural resources that are not subject to any national jurisdiction, but are shared by a number of states, if not the international community of states as a whole. They are comprised by the High Seas, Antarctica, Outer Space and the atmosphere; *see* Garett Hardin, *The Tragedy of the Commons*, 162(3859) SCIENCE 1243 (1968).

31 ICE Foundation, *supra* note 28.

32 Pedersen, *supra* note 3 at 549.

33 Riches and Bruce, *supra* note 7 at 3.

The responsibilities of the court are listed by Stephen Hockman:

1. adjudicating significant environmental disputes involving the responsibility of members of the international community;

2. adjudicating disputes between private and public parties with an appreciable magnitude (at the discretion of the president of the court);

3. ordering emergency, injunctive and preventative measures as necessary;

4. mediating and arbitrating environmental disputes;

5. instituting investigations, where necessary, to address environmental problems of international significance.[34]

Interestingly, international environmental crimes are not even mentioned in the listed purposes or responsibilities. In addition to the listed schemes, neither the Draft Statutes of the ICEF nor the ICE Coalition refers directly to international environmental crimes. Both lists show that the primary task of the ICE is a more general one. The ICE shall take over the general supervision of the world's environment. That means that the purposes and responsibilities of the ICE are defined quite broadly to allow the court to engage in lots of different environmental matters.

Stephen Hockman further suggests the implementation of a right to a healthy environment into the work of the court.[35] This right would allow for broad coverage and could ensure access to legal aid through an international court for private parties and NGOs, next to the regular state parties in international law.[36] The other main international courts do not allow standing for non-state actors.[37] The growing environmental awareness means that the court could be open for various actors, especially non-state actors.[38]

---

[34] Hockman, *supra* note 7 at 223.
[35] *Id.* at 223.
[36] *Id.* at 223.
[37] Pedersen, *supra* note 3 at 550.
[38] ICE Coalition, *supra* note 6 at 7.

Klaus Bosselmann puts into play the idea of the ICE being able to issue advisory opinions, similar to those that can be issued by the ICJ.[39] While not technically binding, ICJ advisory opinions usually are quite powerful because ignoring them would cause an international moral disgrace.[40] The ICJ's advisory opinions steer the development of international law, and so could the ICE influence the international environmental law regime as well.

The specifics of the concrete functioning of the ICE are beyond the scope of this contribution which focuses on the general idea and the purpose of the ICE as an international court for international environmental crimes. Questions regarding the number of chambers, the selection process of the judges and the specifics of the functionality of the court are lastly a decision of secondary importance. This does not counteract the general idea of a judicial environmental entity. Of importance is that the court itself comes to life with a wide enough mandate to make a change in the legal handling of the environment.

3. What would be the advantages of a new International Court for the Environment?

The central argument in favor of an ICE is that the world is facing a number of serious environmental problems, and there is a need for international attention and legal interpretation of all global environmental issues. Currently, existing international institutions are not equipped to handle this plethora of challenges.[41] A guiding court could manifest itself as a stable anchor in highly disputed and controversial questions regarding the global environment. This legal guidance by a court is comparable to the decisions of national constitutional courts as the highest institution on the national level, such as the United States Supreme Court or the "Bundesverfassungsgericht" (Federal Constitutional Court) in Germany.

The problem of environmental destruction increasingly attracts the public's attention to the point that it is becoming one of the main concerns of our times.[42] It cannot be denied that human activity is bringing harm to the natural environment. Especially the discussion on climate change and its drivers has put environmental preservation high up on the list of public discussion as well as on the agendas of high-ranking politicians. The so-

---

39 Klaus Bosselmann EARTH GOVERNANCE: TRUSTEESHIP OF THE GLOBAL COMMONS 216 (2015).

40 *Id.* at 216.

41 Pedersen, *supra* note 3 at 550.

42 Hockman, *supra* note 7 at 224; ICE Coalition, *supra* note 6 at 4.

called “Fridays for future” demonstrations have drawn thousands of people in numerous countries out on the streets to protest for immediate climate action. Therefore, the time has never been better to promote the idea of an international environmental court. An ICE could, even more, sharpen public awareness and add credibility to the international law regime.[43] From a criminal law perspective, the ICE could ensure widespread international environmental protection even within national state boundaries, whose domestic courts and/or governments fail to sanction international environmental crimes.[44]

The numbers of non-state actors on both sides of environmental crimes – both perpetrators and conservationists trying to protect the environment – are growing.[45] The outdated practice of banning non-state actors from appearing before international courts goes against wider developments in supranational jurisdiction, which can be proven by the 1998 Convention on Access to Information, Public Participation in Decision-making and Access to Justice in Environmental Matters (Aarhus Convention) or the procedures in front of the courts of the EU. The Aarhus Convention simplifies the access to environmental information and ensures transparency of public authorities towards the public in environmental matters.[46] The constitutive treaties of the European Union allow, for example, domestic courts to refer cases to the European Court of Justice and natural persons to directly sue European authorities for mistreatment before the aforementioned court.[47] This is why an ICE should be a legal forum for state and non-state parties.[48] In a criminal case, the ICE would need jurisdiction over individuals to prosecute the potential perpetrators. It is also worth considering the provision of access to

---

43 Pedersen, *supra* note 3 at 550.

44 Mark A. Drumbl, *Waging war against the world: The need to move from war crimes to environmental crimes*, 22(1) FORDHAM INTERNATIONAL LAW JOURNAL 122, 148 (1998).

45 Riches and Bruce, *supra* note 7 at 2.

46 CONVENTION ON ACCESS TO INFORMATION, PUBLIC PARTICIPATION IN DECISION-MAKING AND ACCESS TO JUSTICE IN ENVIRONMENTAL MATTERS 2161 UNTS 447 (opened for signature 25 June 1998, entered into force 30 October 2001), art 4(1).

47 CONSOLIDATED VERSION OF THE TREATY OF THE EUROPEAN UNION C 326/13 (26 October 2012), art 19(3)(1); CONSOLIDATED VERSION OF THE TREATY OF THE FUNCTIONING OF THE EUROPEAN UNION C 115/47 (13 December 2007), art 265, 267.

48 Riches and Bruce, *supra* note 7 at 2; Hockman, *supra* note 7 at 223.

the ICE for environmental refugees[49] fleeing because of a destructed environment due to, for example, the effects of climate change or impacts resulting from large-scale environmental crimes. The same can be said about the problems of indigenous tribes resulting from anthropogenic environmental degradation. It is in many cases true that the people most affected by environmental degradation are the poor and powerless.[50] Often their home states do not offer a sufficient judicial system, and there is no independent national or international environmental institution they could turn to. An open ICE could strengthen their rights and would generally be a large step to ensure environmental justice for all.[51] In many ways, the ECHR, with its 47-member states, has set a positive example in this regard.[52] The Convention established the ECtHR situated in Strasbourg. This court has not only decided on several ground-breaking cases in the sphere of human rights[53] but ruled in cases with environmental elements.[54] Just as the ECtHR has made a difference in the field of human rights, the ICE could make a difference in the field of international environmental law and, more specifically, in international environmental criminal law.

Some countries have established specialized environmental courts adjudicating environmental cases: examples are the Environment Court of New Zealand or the National Green Tribunal in India. Thus, both of these institutions are worth a closer look. The Indian parliament created the

---

[49] The term "environmental refugee" refers to "*people who have been forced to leave their traditional habitat, temporarily or permanently, because of a marked environmental disruption (natural and/or triggered by people) that jeopardizes their existence and/or seriously effects the quality of their life*" Often people not only flee because of environmental reasons, but for various reasons. Nevertheless, a degraded environment is often at least a part of the decision. For the definition see Diane C. Bates, Environmental Refugees? Classifying Human Migrations Caused by Environmental Change, 23(5) POPULATION AND ENVIRONMENT 465 (2002).

[50] ICE Coalition, *supra* note 6 at 12.

[51] *Id.*

[52] The European Convention of Human Rights was signed in November 1950 and entered into effect in September 1953. The Convention established the European Court of Human Rights, which takes "cases by any person who feels their rights have been violated under the Convention by a state party".

[53] *See* for example *Salduz v. Turkey* App no 36391/02 (ECtHR, 27 November 2008) or *Görgülü v. Germany* App no 74969/01 (ECtHR, 26 Mai 2004).

[54] *See* for example *Tatar v. Romania* App no 657021/01 (ECtHR, 27 January 2009) or *Giacomelli v. Italy* App no 59909/00, (ECtHR, 02 November 2006).

environmental tribunal via the National Green Tribunal Act in 2010.[55] This parliamentary decision was influenced by article 21 of India's constitution, which assures the citizens of the subcontinent the right to a healthy environment under the protection of life and personal liberty.[56] The National Green Tribunal Act of 2010 describes the act as "an act to provide for the establishment of a National Green Tribunal for the effective and expeditious disposal of cases relating to environmental protection and conservation of forests and other natural resources including enforcement of any legal right relating to the environment and giving relief and compensation for damages to persons and property and for matters connected therewith or incidental thereto."[57] § 17 and § 20 of the National Green Tribunal Act allow the tribunal to issue compensation in specific cases or penalties for non-compliance with its decisions. The act sets out that "where any offence under this Act has been committed by a company, every person who, at the time the offence was committed, was directly in charge of, and was responsible to the company for the conduct of the business of the company, as well as the company, shall be deemed to be guilty of the offence and shall be liable [...]".[58] This strict civil liability would be desirable in a criminal sense. Additionally, the tribunal does not have jurisdictional powers in terms of potential environmental crimes.[59] The National Green Tribunal of India remains a civil court.

In contrast, the Environment Court of New Zealand evolved from the former Planning Tribunal under the Resource Management Amendment Act in 1996.[60] It is the jurisdictional entity for plans, resource consents and environmental issues.[61] The court deals mainly with questions arising under the Resource Management Act, for example, considering the future effects of polluting emissions. The environmental court holds the same powers as a New Zealand District Court.[62] In addition to this, the Environment Court of New Zealand does not have any jurisdiction over environmental crimes.

Few countries have incorporated these forms of specialized environmental courts in their national jurisdiction. Yet, these judicial entities do not have

---

[55] National Green Tribunal Act of 2010, No 19 (2010). Dr. Dayana Maliyekkal discusses the NGT further in her chapter on India and the Kole Wetlands.

[56] Constitution of India Part III, art. 21; Gitanjali Nain Gill ENVIRONMENTAL JUSTICE IN INDIA: THE NATIONAL GREEN TRIBUNAL 73 (2017).

[57] National Green Tribunal Act of 2010, No 19 (2010), preamble.

[58] *Id.* § 27.

[59] *Id.* § 17, 20.

[60] Resource Management Amendment Act of 1996, No 160 (1996), § 6.

[61] *Id.* § 6.

[62] *Id.* § 278.

criminal jurisdiction and are not entitled to decide on matters of environmental harm through a potentially criminal act.[63] Nevertheless, they can be seen as welcome examples of highly specialized environmental courts. Most cases involving the environment are of a multi-disciplinary nature. Therefore, they are better addressed in a specialized forum. Their very existence underlines the high value the environment should have in legal procedures in general and thus a fortiori in criminal law. This is true on both the national and the international level. Therefore, these national examples could be a model for the international level.

4. Judicialization

Judicialization means "the transfer of decision-making rights from legislature, the cabinet or the civil service to the courts."[64] Judicialization is germane to this discussion because if an ICE is established, it would be a court that is only bound to the interests and the laws of the international community and not to the legislature or executive of any sovereign state. The judges working at the ICE would deliver a verdict "in the name of humanity" and judicialize violations of primary and conventional norms concerning the environment.[65]

This socio-legal approach could empower international environmental criminal law to develop on its own. The ICE could further influence and form the sphere of international environmental law. Weak enforcement, lack of legitimacy, and slow and lax implementation could be improved.[66] This would counteract against some of the most criticized points in international law. This development to a centralized and internationalized approach of environmental governance could overcome developments in some countries

---

[63] According to § 14 of the National Green Tribunal Act of 2010, the Tribunal has jurisdiction over "all civil cases were a substantial question relating to the environment (including enforcement of any legal right relating to the environment), is involved". The Act itself refers to specific environment-related enactments, such as the Air Act of 1981 or the Biological Diversity Act of 2002, which are the base for the tribunal's decisions; The Environment Court of New Zealand is an appellate court. The basis for decisions of the Environment Court of New Zealand is the Resource Management Act of 1991, whit most of the cases coming from appeals brought against decisions of local authorities. Next to this main act the court has jurisdiction e.g. under the Forests Act of 1949, the Biosecurity Act of 1993 or the Crown Minerals Act of 1991.

[64] Torbjorn Vallinder, *When the Courts Go Marching In,* in Neal Tate and Torbjorn Vallinder (ed) THE GLOBAL EXPANSION OF JUDICIAL POWER 13 (1995).

[65] Postiglione, *supra* note 7 at 323.

[66] Pedersen, *supra* note 3 at 556.

to draw back on environmental protection. A climate change denier as head of state or a national environmental agency would lose some of its dread.

This form of law-making is often demanded by interest groups when political decisions are not in their interest.[67] It is even seen as a form of "world government approach without the government."[68] Strict environmental governance lastly helps states, businesses and civil society altogether.[69] While the stylization of a world government might be a bit over the top, this form has a chance of influencing the faith of humanity from an angle of community instead of limited nation-state views. This is especially necessary for environmental matters. As said many times throughout this chapter, international environmental crimes pose a global threat and need a fast and stringent answer. The task of the ICE is to judge and not to mediate.

III. The International Court for the Environment as a "fresh start" for a definition of international environmental crimes – The freedom of definition

As mentioned above, the ICE was not meant to be a primary court for international environmental crimes. However, with the environmental expertise in place, it might be the institution of first choice regarding environmental problems of criminal nature.

The question regarding a universal definition of international environmental crimes has long been a dilemma. To this point, there is no agreed-upon definition for this critical term.[70] Several approaches and suggestions for a definition for the conducts in question exist, but they are highly debated, differ in wording and scope and are not in the least universally accepted. Admittedly it is very hard to find a solution in the light of the complexity of international environmental harm. This dilemma blocks an international response to the problem and contributes to the existing toothless fight against the issue.

A definition is the starting point of every legal activity to set out a clear framework for the matters in question. This is especially true for criminal law. The ICE could come up with a solution for this problem. An entirely new court could, within the process of its foundation, create a definition of international

---

[67] Neal Tate, *Why the Expansion of Judicial Power,* in Neal Tate and Torbjorn Vallinder (ed) THE GLOBAL EXPANSION OF JUDICIAL POWER 29 (1995).
[68] Eric Posner, THE PERILS OF GLOBAL LEGALISM 24 (1995).
[69] Riches and Bruce, *supra* note 7 at 3.
[70] Philippe Sands, PRINCIPLES OF INTERNATIONAL ENVIRONMENTAL LAW 894 (2003); Christian Nellemann et al, *The rise of environmental crime* (UNEP, Nairobi, 2016) at 17.

environmental crimes to ensure their legal handling without being bound by currently existing restrictive definitions of criminal acts on the international level. The establishing (fictional) "Convention of an International Environmental Criminal Court" should therefore start off with a definition. Due to further development of the definition through case law and other international law advancements and science, the chosen universal definition could sink in.

Nonetheless, there needs to be a definition to have a starting point. The dilemma of a lacking definition could be observed in the development process of the Rome Statute. The definition of "crimes of aggression" was omitted during the Rome Conference in 1998 due to the fact that the state parties could not agree upon a uniform definition.[71] This left a colorless term without much actual jurisdictional use, and the crime of aggression was referred to as "crime in waiting."[72] In 2010 a definition was added during the Kampala Conference to overcome those obstacles, which is seen as a significant step forward for international criminal law.[73] This, again, underlines the importance of a definition.

To tackle international environmental crimes properly, it has to be thought about, what is meant by "international," what constitutes a "crime" against the environment, what is the scope of "environmental" in this regard? Then the question has to be raised how can we combine these terms to an appropriate and precise definition? This freedom of definition could be a unique characteristic and demarcate the ICE from the ICC. Within the ICC, a potential environmental crime provision would only be possible within the boundaries of the existing definitions of the ICC crimes. In fact, in many ways, genocide, crimes against humanity, war crimes as well as the crime of aggression contain environmental aspects, which might entitle the ICC to look closer into international environmental misconducts. However, these environmental links are subject to a wide interpretation of the descriptions of

---

71 Anouk T. Boas, *The definition of the crime of aggression and its relevance for contemporary armed conflict*, http://www.internationalcrimesdatabase.org/upload/documents/20141020T170547-ICD%20Brief%201%20-%20Boas.pdf (last visited 30 July 2020).

72 ROME STATUTE OF THE INTERNATIONAL CRIMINAL Court 2187 UNTS 3 (opened for signature 17 July 1998, entered into force 1 July 2002), art 5(2); Matthias Schuster, *The Rome Statute and the Crime of Aggression: A Gordion Knot in regard to this Solution*, 14 CRIMINAL LAW FORUM 1, 17(2003); Mohammed M Gomaa, *The definition of the crime of aggression and the ICC jurisdiction over that crime*, in Mauro Politi and Giuseppe Nesi (ed) *The International Criminal Court and the crime of aggression* 56 (2005).

73 Alexander G Willis, *The Crime of aggression and the resort to force against entities in statu nascendi*, 10(1) JOURNAL OF INTERNATIONAL CRIMINAL JUSTICE 83, 83 (2012).

the potential crimes. They do not state a clear link. A criminal conviction on this basis does therefore seem unlikely.

1. What is the opportunity of a new definition in this context?

The sphere of international environmental crimes involves a lot of environmental harm, which could be seen as "criminal." For an effective approach against these acts, it is very important that the international community is on the same page about what should be tackled to ensure a consistent approach. From a criminal law point of view, a definition of a crime is of utmost importance. Without a proper description of what action is deemed a crime, there cannot be a criminal conviction, which is manifested within the principle of *nullum crimen sine lege.*

A newly set definition offers the chance to implement all the acts causing significant environmental harm as crimes: the wider the definition, the greater the potential environmental benefit of actually having a legal regime for international environmental crimes in place. It needs, nevertheless, to be so clear that a conviction on its basis is possible. The creation of a new court could be the perfect environment and starting point to implement this new definition. In the course of the creation of the ICE, there would be the most freedom to newly define international environmental crimes. A new definition offers the chance to empower the ICE with the widest possible competency.

In contrast to the greening of the ICC, a new definition within the sphere of the ICE would not be bound and restricted by already existing definitions. The international environmental criminal law regime could start off with a clean slate. Therefore, a coherent definition of the term is a prime opportunity to implement strong environmental protection via international criminal law within the ICE.

Definition in general means to create an exact description of the nature, scope and meaning of a term.[74] Figuratively speaking, that is comparable to storing only specific objects inside a box. Opening the box means there are only these specific gadgets in there. A definition, therefore, creates a box containing all the aspects of a certain term. Whenever the term is needed, the box can be opened, showing the true meaning of the term.

In the case of international environmental crimes, the definition has to incorporate the whole complexity of the topic: the wide range of stakeholders involved, the general internationality of environmental crimes, the many

---

[74] Oxford Dictionary, "Definition", www.oxforddictionaries.com (last visited 30 July 2020).

drivers of these crimes, the vast impacts on numerous fields, and the entanglement with other areas of organized crime. All these different aspects and facets of international environmental crime have to be taken into account to formulate a definition.[75] A definition covering as much environmental harm as possible comprises the most potential for environmental protection. International environmental crimes should not represent one intrinsic act but should include a wide range of environmentally harmful activities. Next to international environmental crimes, environmental offenses should be formulated to cover international situations as well.[76] The term international environmental crime has to be kept broad to contain all the different areas of international environmental crimes and allow room for new development in this sector. At the same time, the definition has to be specific enough to ensure international judicial action is possible and a distinction from other crimes can be made. Especially in criminal law, a determination between what is lawful and unlawful has to be precise. This definition, therefore, has to be broad and strict in equal measure. It is vital to find this balance to ensure effectiveness in usage. If the description is too broad, it functions as a gateway for speculation and misuse, and if it is too strict, it cannot cover the wide topic of international environmental crimes. Furthermore, there is a risk that a wide definition will not be applied in practice as it remains too general. It has to be kept in mind that each international environmental crime itself has its own definition and that the term refers to an umbrella term encompassing all the acts against the environment deemed to be unlawful.

Returning to the aforementioned example, regarding a definition as a box containing all the aspects, the specific acts would be boxes inside this box with their own contents. International environmental crimes are a crucible of all circumventions of environmental legislation and environmental harm in general. Ecocide,[77] a most heinous international environmental crime, would, in the light of the abovementioned metaphor, for example, be a "box within

---

[75] Michael J. Lynch and Paul B. Stretesky, GREEN CRIMINOLOGY 3 (2012).

[76] United Nations Economic and Social Council, *The Role of Criminal Law in the Protection of the Environment* Res/1994/15 (1994).

[77] Higgins defines ecocide (or genocide) as "extensive destruction, damage or loss of ecosystems of a given territory, whether by human agency or other causes, to such extent that peaceful enjoyment by the inhabitants of that territory has been severely diminished" (Higgins, *supra* note 1 at 62). In the general sphere of international environmental crimes "ecocide" takes the top of the crime pyramid, similar to genocide within the ICC-crimes; in many ways ecocide illustrates the environmental counterpart of genocide. It has to be noted, however, that international environmental crimes stretch further than "ecocide".

the box." Given the complexity and breadth of the topic, definitional decisions have to be made very carefully.

2. How should international environmental crimes be defined under the International Court for the Environment?

Unencumbered by the scope and nature of an existing jurisdiction, a new ICE could be given a new definition of international environmental crimes to work with and apply. To achieve the most for the environment, this definition should be broad but will also need to achieve some compromises between the relevant stakeholders and not set unrealistically high or low thresholds. It shall draw a line between simply "using" the environment and "criminally" exploiting it. There has to be a strict separation between lawful use of the environment and unlawful destruction. Defining certain environmental harm as a crime might be a vital component in helping slow down the overall environmental degradation. This would strengthen general prevention as a principle in international criminal law and act as a strong deterrent against potential perpetrators.

Given that international environmental crime consists of three different terms, this text will first point out the meaning of every single component of international environmental crimes independently. However, since the determination of the single parts of "international environmental crimes" obviously cannot happen without establishing some form of connection, in the end, the three elements will be combined to produce a new definition of the term international environmental crime as a whole.

a. Definition of "international"

International environmental crimes are linked to the international community in a special sense. In a way, all criminal environmental harm creates a global impact, as all ecosystems are interconnected; lastly, the earth represents one big ecosystem. The word "international" determines between the application of national law or international law. It indicates that in this discussion, international law is the spotlight.

At first sight, the definition of the word "international" appears to be quite clear and plain. In general, the term is used to describe the involvement of two or more states in any matter. This is due to the historic usage of the word relating to the regulations of the interactions of states.[78] However, international law does not only create obligations and rules for states but affects individuals,

---

[78] Larry May, CRIMES AGAINST HUMANITY, 5 (2015).

people, generations, animals, and nature itself.[79] Environmental affairs especially do not only create disputes between states, but they also threaten the global environment as the basis of human life.[80] A remarkable feature of international environmental crimes is that they offer the chance to go beyond states with the power of public international law. Many of the potential criminal conduct results from corporate behavior and not directly from state actions. This can be seen in the examples of the Bhopal catastrophe, the Bento Rodriguez dam collapse, or the Deepwater Horizon oil spill.[81] Therefore, it is of high importance that the definition is not limited to state action but also includes acts committed through stakeholders, such as international corporations or private actors when determining international scope.

The proliferation of the impacts of environmental wrongdoing tends not to be localized. They result in international, even global, impacts with little regard to the actual site of the cause.[82] In fact, environmental crimes are transboundary crimes by their very nature with global reach, albeit of varying intensity.[83] Most acts that occur within the sphere of international environmental crimes cannot be constrained to the soil of the perpetrator.[84] Even if the act occurs on one state's soil, the impacts are likely to spread across state borders. This is where national law hits a wall.

The focus for the term international must lie in the impacts. It has to be considered that some impacts are deferred. This is why the impacts have to be seen in a long-term perspective of the general state of health of the Earth. Crimes on the local level can evolve to national, regional, and global levels over the years. Environmental harm can move across borders, which can be observed, for example, in the international trade in hazardous waste.[85] Environmental crimes should be awarded the status of international crimes in

---

[79] Cynthia Giagnocavo and Howard Goldstein, *Law Reform or World Re-form: The Problem of Environmental Rights*, 35(2) McGILL LAW JOURNAL 345, 347 (1990).

[80] Wilfried Erbguth and Sabine Schlacke, UMWELTRECHT 152 (2019) (Ger.).

[81] Stuart Diamond, *The Bhopal Disaster: How it happened*, https://www.nytimes.com/1985/01/28/world/the-bhopal-disaster-how-it-happened.html (28 January 1985); Cowie, *supra* note 1; Alejandra Borunda, We still don't know the full impacts of the BP oil spill, 10 years later, https://www.nationalgeographic.com/science/2020/04/bp-oil-spill-still-dont-know-effects-decade-later/ (20 April 2020).

[82] Banks et al., *supra* note 1 at 3.

[83] Johan Bergenas and Ariella Knight, *Green terror: Environmental crime and illicit financing*, 35(1) SCHOOL OF ADVANCED INTERNATIONAL STUDIES REVIEW 119, 120 (2015).

[84] Erbguth and Schlacke, *supra* note 80 at 152.

[85] Rob White, TRANSNATIONAL ENVIRONMENTAL CRIME: TOWARD AN ECO-GLOBAL CRIMINOLOGY 14 (2011).

general because they affect the global human society.[86] Crimes regarding genocide are always limited to a specific region or specific ethnicities, whereby international environmental crimes affect the whole international community. Philippe Sands states:

> It is a trite observation that environmental problems, although they closely affect municipal laws, are essentially international; and that the main structure of control can therefore be no other than that of international law. [87]

Rob White describes this worldwide interconnectedness with the effects of the commonly known "butterfly effect":

> The fluttering of butterfly wings in the southern hemisphere can translate into hurricane force winds in the northern part of the world.[88]

Every act in one place of the world, without regard to scope or triviality, will impact another part of the world.[89] Local can be global as well as global can be local in the interconnected networks – such as the ecosystems – of the world.

Trading in ozone-depleting substances (ODS) is a prime example in this regard. Trade taking place in one state will lead to the usage of the banned chemicals somewhere else, which then ultimately enter the atmosphere and unfold their chemical properties attacking the ozone layer. This attack on the ozone layer will not be right above the spot of the point of trade or the area of usage, but anywhere in the world. The first hole in the ozone layer was discovered in Antarctica, where no ODS-industry or industry is located. The Montreal Protocol[90] has clearly addressed the ODS-problem as one of the global community of states. This example underlines the internationality of the topic. This proliferation of the harm of international environmental crimes from national damage to international mischief can also be observed in the radioactive downfall of the Chernobyl catastrophe. The dangers of

---

[86] Steven Freeland, ADDRESSING THE INTERNATIONAL DESTRUCTION OF THE ENVIRONMENT DURING WARFARE UNDER THE ROME STATUTE OF THE INTERNATIONAL CRIMINAL COURT 245 (2015).

[87] Sands, *supra* note 70 at 1.

[88] White, *supra* note 85 at 1.

[89] *Id.*

[90] MONTREAL PROTOCOL ON SUBSTANCES THAT DEPLETE THE OZONE LAYER 1522 UNTS 3 (opened for signature16 September 1987, entered into force 01 January 1989).

space pollution might also fall under this category, as Tamara Blagojevic explains in her chapter regarding environmental damage in Outer Space.

b. Definition of "environmental"

What is meant by the term "environmental" and by the "environment"? There is no fixed definition of "the environment." It can refer to the vicinity, meaning the surroundings in which a human being lives, or it can be defined as the whole (or part) of the natural world. However, there is a difference between the human environment and the natural environment. The first refers to cities, villages and human infrastructure. In this context, general environmental law on a domestic level includes neighbors' noise or handling of dog mess.[91] In contrast, the natural environment is the basis of all life on Earth.[92] It surrounds all living species and provides them with a system that allows life.

The domination of the human race has led to a certain arrogance of humans when it comes to the environment.[93] Humans see themselves as a separate entity because human life is flourishing despite the degradation of the surrounding environment.[94] However, this "flourishing" is only possible to a specific turning or tipping point. Figuratively speaking, it is like a ship steering into an ice field. As long as the icecap is fragile and not too thick, the ship will not have any problems, but after some time, even a modern, highly developed icebreaker reaches the point where the ship is not able to continue to break through the ice. It will get stuck, or it will sink.

Nevertheless, states see the environment within their borders as their territory where they can do what they want, including any form of degradation. Principle 21 of the 1972 Stockholm Declaration[95] underpins this perception, but it also states that countries should "not cause damage to the environment of other states or of areas beyond the limits of national jurisdiction."[96] This view can be compared to private ownership of land. On the one hand, the owner has the freedom to use his private land. On the other hand, there are certain rules

---

91 Melanie Wellsmith, *Wildlife Crime: The Problem of Enforcement*, 17 EUROPEAN JOURNAL ON CRIMINAL POLICY AND RESEARCH 125, 127 (2011).

92 Onelica Andrade, *Environmental crime summit*, 42(3) ENVIRONMENTAL POLICY AND LAW 159, 164 (2012); Higgins, *supra* note 1 at 61.

93 Cormac Cullinan, WILD LAW: A MANIFEST FOR EARTH JUSTICE 44 (2003).

94 *Id.*

95 STOCKHOLM DECLARATION OF THE UNITED NATIONS CONFERENCE ON THE HUMAN ENVIRONMENT, UN Doc. A/CONF. 48/14 (16 June 1972).

96 UNITED NATIONS CONFERENCE ON THE HUMAN ENVIRONMENT GA Res 2994, XXVII (1972) principle 21.

governing what the owner is allowed to do and what not. This is to protect neighbors and the community in general. National law forbids certain acts harming small privately-owned parts of the environment. Today the no-harm rule can be considered as customary international law.[97] It becomes clear that states cannot do everything that they want to do. There are certain international rules to obey to prevent injuries in or on the territory of another state or of the properties or persons therein.[98]

The 1976 Environmental Modification Convention[99] includes in its article II the following definition of environmental modification techniques: "natural processes, the dynamics, composition or structure of Earth, including its biota, lithosphere and atmosphere or of outer space."[100] This shows the broadness of the term "environmental." It includes outer space, the atmosphere, Antarctica, the high seas, but it does not state that the environment is a precondition of human society. In the Draft Articles for an ICE, the ICE Coalition describes the environment as the "common preserve of mankind."[101] And that is basically what it is: the natural human habitat.

The term "environment" is not limited to a natural approach. The destruction of the environment through international environmental crimes also comprises "cultural ecocide", especially on indigenous nations, who are highly dependent on a functioning habitat.[102] This cultural side of environmental harm should therefore be included within the term of international environmental crimes.

---

97 Jorge E. Vinuales, *The contribution of the International Court of Justice to the development of international environmental law: A contemporary assessment,* 32 FORDHAM INTERNATIONAL LAW JOURNAL 232, 237, 253 (2008).

98 *Trail Smelter Arbitration* (United States v. Canada) (Arbitration) [1941].

99 Former CONVENTION ON THE PROHIBITION OF MILITARY OR ANY OTHER HOSTILE USE OF ENVIRONMENTAL MODIFICATION TECHNIQUES.

100 CONVENTION ON THE PROHIBITION OF MILITARY OR ANY OTHER HOSTILE USE OF ENVIRONMENTAL MODIFICATION TECHNIQUES 1108 UNTS 151 (open for signature 18 March 1977, entered into force 5 October 1978) art. 2.

101 ICE Coalition, *ICE Coalition Draft Articles for an International Court of the Environment,* https://static1.squarespace.com/static/56c0ae80ab48de4417bd17fa/t/56d33d594c2f85dc2df9ef37/1456684377825/Draft+Protocol+for+an+ICE.pdf (last visited 30 July 2020), art. 1.

102 Tim Boekhout van Solinge, *Deforestation Crimes and Conflicts in the Amazon,* 18(4) CRITICAL CRIMINOLOGY 263, 264 (2010); Leo Mukosi's chapter on the Dakota Access Pipeline analyzes the crime of cultural genocide. However, the DAPL would also meet the definition of cultural ecocide.

c. Definition of "crime"

What is a "crime", and what is an "international crime"? These questions have been on the agenda of criminologists for a long time. As the topic "crime" itself is such a wide subject, the primary direction of this text has to be kept in mind. In the scope of this article, the more precise question is: "What is an international crime in relation to the environment"?

In order to develop a suitable description of the term "crime" in this particular area, the following part is trying to introduce the difference between crime and international crime. It then focuses on the victims and the potential perpetrators of international environmental harm. Following this, the *actus reus* and the *mens rea* of potential international environmental crimes are touched upon. To round up the question of what an international crime is in relation to the environment, the concept of ecocentrism will be introduced and applied.[103]

i. Crime and international crime

A crime is definitely something that has to be handled carefully, especially when newly criminalizing previously non-criminal conduct is at stake. It is described in different ways. Broadly, a crime is a "socially harmful act or omission that breaches the values protected by a state" and represents an "event prohibited by law, one which can be followed by prosecution in criminal proceedings and, thereafter, by punishment on conviction."[104] In contrast to this, the German Criminal Code defines crimes in § 12 I StGB as "illegal acts which are imposing a minimum of a one-year prison sentence." The central player in criminalization is the state.[105] Therefore, the central player in international criminalization should be the community of states. The understanding of a crime developed throughout history and contains cultural reasons, social developments, moral thoughts, public opinions and the general understanding that committing a crime is something wrong.[106]

When a border-crossing element comes into play, and more jurisdictions are involved with the criminal act, a clear conviction becomes more challenging.[107]

---

[103] In addition to the following part, Dr. Zoi Aliozi explored green criminology from a legal as well as philosophical way in her chapter.

[104] Andrew P. Simester and George R. Sullivan, CRIMINAL LAW-THEORY AND DOCTIRNE 1 (2007).

[105] White, *supra* note 85 at 4.

[106] Irina Marchuk, THE FUNDAMENTAL CONCEPT OF CRIME IN INTERNATIONAL CRIMINAL LAW 69 (2014).

[107] *Id.*

The Rome Statute, however, constitutes in its article 5(1)(a)-(d) the major international crimes: genocide, crimes against humanity, war crimes and the crime of aggression. However, the general understanding of international crimes is wider. It includes all violations of criminal norms derived out of an international agreement or customary law and encompasses, for example, drug trafficking or human trafficking. International criminal law encompasses inherently all norms which directly justify, preclude or regulate culpability in any way.

ii. Victims and perpetrators of international environmental crimes

The consideration of the victims of international environmental crimes is important to get the full picture. Environmental crime cannot easily be compared to street crime. Unlike classic crimes, environmental crimes comprise, for example, industrial pollution, corporate criminality and the impact and legacy of military operations on landscapes, water supply and air quality.[108] A feature of environmental crimes is the dual victimization of people and the environment.[109] Sometimes, the human and natural population of an entire region is affected by an international environmental harmful act and, at times, even confronted with irreversible effects. Street crime is usually limited to only one victim or at least a limited group of people.[110] This perspective leaves the social impact of crimes out, but both street crimes and environmental crimes comprise this social influence in equal shares.

Another point of view sees international environmental crimes as frequently victimless.[111] However, there cannot be a crime without a victim. Even if victims are aware of environmental harms, crimes go unreported because those affected do not consider themselves as direct victims or even as victims at all.[112] The fact that, next to humans, non-human entities can be considered as victims is one of the reasons that governments, enforcement agencies and criminal law in general struggle with appropriate responses to international

---

108 Polly Higgins, Damien Short and Nigel South, *Protecting the Planet: a Proposal for a Law of Ecocide*, 59(3) CRIME, LAW AND SOCIAL CHANGE 251, 251 (2013).

109 Yingyi Situ and David Emmons, ENVIRONMENTAL CRIME: THE CRIMINAL JUSTICE SYSTEM'S ROLE IN PROTECTING THE ENVIRONMENT 5 (2000); Lynch and Stretesky, *supra* note 75 at 4.

110 *Id.*

111 Samantha Bricknell, *Environmental crime in Australia*, 109 Research and Public Policy Series 1, 2 (2010).

112 Elaine Barclay and Robyn Bartel, *Defining environmental crime: The perspective of farmers*, 39 JOURNAL OF RURAL STUDIES 188, 189 (2015).

environmental crimes.[113] Granting personhood to the environment or environmental entities might dissolve the issue of non-human victims. New Zealand, for example, showed the possibility to grant certain rights to natural bodies. In 2018 the island nation declared the Whanganui River as a person in legal matters.[114] The reader has already been introduced to this idea by Prayank Jain in his chapter on environmental personhood.

Opposite of the victim, there is the perpetrator. Environmental offenders can be considered criminals. At first sight, it might seem strange to see someone harming the environment as on a par with a mass murderer, but the scale of international environmental crimes requires a different conclusion.

iii. Actus reus

The principle of personal culpability says that punishment is always directed to personal guilt.[115] It is not suitable to work with collective punishment.[116] Each individual has to bear the responsibility for their own actions themselves. As a crime is always a mix of objective and subjective elements, there needs to be conduct and a form of intent, recklessness or negligence.

The question which should be raised in this regard is whether the actus reus of environmental crimes refers to the harm of the environment, humans, or both? Crime also defines itself by a specific seriousness of harm to differ from offenses.[117] The aforementioned distinction between a strict legalist and a socio-legal approach comes into play here. Is the conduct of violating existing international legal rules regarding international environmental law a crime, or is it the harm done itself? The strict legalist approach seems an "easy" and straightforward way of defining something as an international environmental crime, and from a criminologists' point of view, the strict legalist theory seems appealing at first sight. Crime is whatever the criminal law defines it as.[118] Thus crime is a behavior prohibited by a criminal code, and a criminal would be the person behind this behavior.[119] Most of the usual definitions of "crime" tend to follow this approach. This basically means, if a treaty or any other international obligation forbids a specific act or sets out rules for a certain

---

[113] *Id.*

[114] Te Awa Tupua (Whanganui River Claims Settlement) Act of 2017, No 17 (2017), § 14.

[115] Gerhard Werle, VOELKERSTRAFRECHT 116 (2012) (Ger.).

[116] *Id.*

[117] White, *supra* note 85 at 5.

[118] Situ and Emmons, *supra* note 108 at 2.

[119] *Id.*

type of conduct in environmental matters, and someone contravenes the stated prohibition or rules, this results in committing a crime.

In contrast to this strict concept, the socio-legal approach centers on morality and values. This theory focuses on the actual harm done to the environment. Rob White points out, in this regard, that transnational environmental harm constitutes a crime.[120] Human behavior, no matter if collective or individual, is in general considered as a major source of environmental harm.[121] Not all acts "contravening environmental protection or offending notions of green mortality are crimes."[122] The harm done, for example, by illegally cutting down a single tree is negligible, but environmental crimes occur on a massive scale and are usually done by big and well-organized transnational syndicates, corporations, states or terror networks. To differentiate between harmful and harmless acts, a definition is necessary. The potential of environmental harm is much higher than the criminal impact on individual victims.[123] Serious environmental damage which is not part of an international treaty should still be treated as an international environmental crime.

iv. Mens rea

A definition of a crime has to encompass both the element of actus reus and the element of mens rea. *Mens rea* ranges from intent, through reckless, to negligent.[124] The question is, which intensity of *mens rea* is appropriate for international environmental crimes?[125] It would be quite a difficult task to prove the requirement of intention in relation to international environmental crimes.[126] Article 8(2)(b)(iv) of the Rome statute is the only provision within the Rome Statute directed to environmental harm. Following this provision, a war crime might inter alia be an act that includes:

---

[120] White, *supra* note 85 at 1.

[121] Angus Nurse, *Linking the green and the mainstream*, in Angus Nurse (ed) CRITICAL PERSPECTIVE ON GREEN CRIMINOLOGY 109 (2014).

[122] Angus Nurse, *Introduction*, in Angus Nurse (ed) CRITICAL PERSPECTIVE ON GREEN CRIMINOLOGY 6 (2014).

[123] *Id.* at 3.

[124] UNITED NATIONS ECONOMIC AND SOCIAL COUNCIL "DRAFT DECLARATION OF PRINCIPLES ON HUMAN RIGHTS AND THE ENVIRONMENT" UN Doc E/CN 4/Sub 2/1994/9 (1994).

[125] Marchuk, *supra* note 105 at 69; Werle, *supra* note 114 at 116.

[126] Drumbl, *supra* note 44 at 143.

> ...intentionally launching an attack in the knowledge that such attack will cause incidental loss of life or injury to civilians or damage to civilian objects or widespread, long-term and severe damage to the natural environment which would be clearly excessive in relation to the concrete and direct overall military advantage anticipated.[127]

One of the main problems of article 8(2)(b)(iv) of the Rome Statute is the incredibly high *mens rea*, which is almost impossible to prove. Claiming to misunderstand the provision could already be enough for exculpation.[128] To date, the ICC has never prosecuted anyone for committing an international environmental crime, which outlines the difficulties of the article once more.

It is common knowledge that acts intervening in nature cause environmental harm. Any serious damage to the natural environment done by humans constitutes a breach of duty of care, and this breach consists in tortious conduct when attempted with intention, recklessness or negligence.[129] Besides this, environmental crimes are linked with other forms of serious international crimes, including organized criminal movements.[130] Therefore, international environmental crimes should work with a wide mens rea, including intention, recklessness and negligence, to be able to encapsulate all those harmful acts.

v. Ecocentrism as an anchor

The term "harm" is not used equally around international environmental crimes.[131] There are three different perceptions: the anthropocentric, the biocentric, and the ecocentric approach.[132] Anthropocentrism separates humans from the general world's ecosystem and sees the human race as superior over all living and non-living things (human-centered).[133] Everything that is "non-human" is instrumentalized to serve humans.[134] Economic or profit interests always go first, and environmental protection is only done for the sake of resource management. Therefore, the criminalization of

---

127 ROME STATUTE, art 8(2)(b)(iv).

128 Jessica C. Lawrence and Kevin J. Heller, *The First Ecocentric Environmental War Crime: The Limits of Article 8(2)(b)(iv) of the Rome Statute*, 20 GEORGETOWN INTERNATIONAL ENVIRONMENTAL LAW REVIEW 1, 79 (2007).

129 Drumbl, *supra* note 44 at 143.

130 Nurse, *supra* note 120 at 3.

131 Barclay and Bartel, *supra* note 111 at 189.

132 Rob White, *Environmental crime in global context: exploring the theoretical and empirical complexities*, 16(3) CURRENT ISSUES IN CRIMINAL JUSTICE 271, 274 (2005).

133 *Id.*

134 *Id.*

environmental harm serves solely to protect humans, and environmental protection is only secondary.

In contrast to this human-centered approach, biocentrism is centered on the environment itself (species-centered).[135] It promotes equality between humans and non-human species, meaning that human beings have the exact same moral worth as other species.[136] Decisions based on this conception should be made according to which outcomes are most likely to foster the widest possible human and non-human diversity of life.[137] The third approach in this row is called ecocentrism. Following the concept of ecocentrism, humans are a part of complex ecosystems that should be preserved for their own sake via the notion of rights and the environment (socio-ecological centered).[138] The interconnectedness of all life on Earth is central to this approach. That implies that humans have the power to conduct acts with global consequences, and therefore they have a responsibility not to exceed the limits of the planet's ecosystems.

Whether the anthropocentric, biocentric, or ecocentric theory is followed, the direction of the socio-legal approach stays the same. Environmental harm in any way contains criminal energy. Nevertheless, the distinction is important because the theories depict the role of humans and predetermine an approach to the issue. All these approaches generate different views on the handling of international environmental crimes. Due to these various angles, a definition of international environmental crime is definitely controversial as well as ambiguous.[139] History shows that not only the anthropocentric view has been applied in international conventions and treaties, as seen in the 1972 World Heritage Convention or the Convention on Biological Diversity (CBD).[140] These agreements do serve humans, but not exclusively.[141]

The vast majority of existing definitions require the strict violation of existing international environmental regulation, as outlined by the definition of Yingyi Situ and David Emmons or Fajardo del Castillo.[142] Gavin Hayman

---

[135] *Id.*

[136] White, *supra* note 132.

[137] *Id.*

[138] *Id.*

[139] White, *supra* note 85 at 1.

[140] Patricia Birnie and Alan Boyle, INTERNATIONAL LAW AND THE ENVIRONMENT 257 (2002).

[141] *Id.*

[142] Situ and Emmons, *supra* note 95 at 3; Teresa Fajardo del Castillo, *International environmental law and environmental crime: An introduction,* EUROPEAN UNION ACTION TO FIGHT ENVIRONMENTAL CRIME 7 (2015).

and Duncan Brack use the same approach, but they extend it with the premise that the perpetrator needs to pursue a financial benefit of some sort.[143] But as explained above, this linkage to financial ties does not seem especially helpful for a strong development for environmental protection. The definition proposed by Mary Clifford and Terry Edwards, which describes international environmental crimes as "act committed with the intent to harm or with a potential to cause harm to ecological and/or biological systems and for the purpose of securing business or personal advantage,"[144] refers to environmental harm as starting point. But it also links international environmental crimes strictly to financial benefits, which again ignores the fact that environmental harm can also occur without a direct financial pursuit. The United Nations Environment Protocol (UNEP) and INTERPOL deliver an interesting description. They speak of a

> collective term describing any illegal activity carried out by a criminal entity to generate profits, which results in harm to our ecosystem, by damaging environmental quality, hastening biodiversity loss, and depleting natural resources.[145]

This is accurate because of the many different directions international environmental crimes can take. Their approach, however, also implies a benefit to individuals, companies or groups, but that does not have to be a financial one, which differs in this approach from the aforementioned definitions.

As outlined above, the anthropocentric approach centering solely on the human race is not expedient. It is simply not effective in such a complex topic to focus on one aspect, respectively, on one species, and it does not describe ecological reality and biodiversity.[146] Biocentrism, which prioritizes the environment, is the extreme opposite, centering not on humans but also the environment.[147] Ecocentrism sees humans as a part of one overarching interacting ecosystem.[148] International environmental criminal law shall do its share on the way to a healthy environment as a habitat for humans. Normally environmental entities do not possess their own rights, and they

---

[143] Gavin Hayman and Duncan Brack, *International Environmental Crime – The Nature and Control of Environmental Black Markets* (2009).

[144] Mary Clifford and Terry D. Edwards ENVIRONMENTAL CRIME 113 (2011).

[145] INTERPOL-UN, *Strategic Report: Environment, Peace and Security,* available at www.unep.org (2016).

[146] Birnie and Boyle, *supra* note 141 at 257.

[147] Kloepfer and Heger, *supra* note 135 at 18.

[148] White, *supra* note 133.

cannot be legally harmed through environmental damage.[149] In the last decades, the legal status of the environment is growing exponentially, as seen, for example, in the development of environmental laws within nation states and on the international level in the 2015 Paris Agreement on Climate Change, which clearly states the coherences between ecology and humans. There are simply no (logical) reasons why significant environmental harms should be excluded from any criminological system.[150]

d. Definition of "international environmental crimes"

As seen above, the words "international", "environmental", and "crime" each have a meaning and a definition of their own. Henceforth it is time to combine the outcome of those three elements to form a specific definition for "international environmental crime." This newly crafted definition shall ensure that the jurisdiction of the ICE covers as many environmentally harmful acts as possible. Through this new definition of international environmental crimes, the ICE would be independent of existing limitations on that matter: the ICE would not be bound by other treaties or other jurisdictions. The ICE could rather start off with a clean slate and implement its own legal interpretations. Thus, the ICE could have the greatest influence in environmental criminal matters on an international level and develop into a significant institution within the international law regime.

The Rome Statute defines its crimes primarily through listing more or less specific acts committed under particular circumstances. This limits the scope of the Rome Statute crimes to these listed specific acts and often hinders further development of the provisions of the Rome Statute. To avoid this type of limitation, the definition, therefore, needs to be a broader one at this stage. This would help the court to establish a strong standing within international jurisdiction. Of course, this "raw" definition needs further specification to lead to a clear prosecution. The elements of the crime of the Rome Statute could be an example of how this specification could be achieved.[151] Also, this "raw" definition enables the court to establish its own boundaries and limitations in the course of its development and its judgments. Again, this is comparable to the aforementioned metaphor of a box within a box. In this case, the sub-boxes each represent a particular act of a crime under the Rome Statute. While the big box stands for international crimes in general.

---

149 Kloepfer and Heger, *supra* note 135 at 18.

150 Lynch and Stretesky, *supra* note 75 at 3.

151 ROME STATUTE, art 9.

As a result of the aforesaid, international environmental crimes shall be defined as:

> An international environmental crime is an intended, reckless or negligent precipitated act causing harm or potential harm with possible international significance for nature as basis of life for humankind and all other species on Earth affecting the human community across state borders.

This definition eschews a referral to existing international agreements to allow the ICE to focus on environmental harm as the main fact and eventually encompasses all parts of the term "international environmental law." Undeniably, the parts of the definition above do have to be interpreted in a detailed manner to create an enforceable crime.

The first part introduces the criminal facet and clarifies that environmental harm, as well as only potential harm, is subject to criminal investigation. It furthermore implies that not only intended but also reckless and negligent acts can be considered as international environmental crime. The middle part imports the environmental aspect and clarifies that the environment is a vital part of human existence. It has to be preserved for the sake of the environment itself and to ensure an appropriately human life within this environment. This middle part also introduces a threshold to the definition. Only environmental harm with potential international significance is to be considered an international environmental crime. The third part refers to the internationality and vast scope of international environmental crimes. The link to the human community recognizes that humans suffer when their environment is harmed in any way. As mentioned above, this definition is, on the one hand, broad to honor the value as a collective term, but on the other hand, specific enough to target environmental crimes directly.

In light of a newly founded ICE, this definition could help ensure that the problem of international environmental crimes can be properly addressed on the international level.

IV. What would be the challenges of establishing a new International Court for the Environment?

Despite the opportunity an ICE represents, it is still highly controversial.[152] A frequently raised question is: why should there be a case for an ICE when there

---

[152] Pedersen, *supra* note 3 at 552.

was never one for the former ICJ chamber for environmental matters?[153] When the unsuccessful ICJ chamber for environmental matters was dissolved in 2006, then-President Rosalyn Higgins stated in front of the UN General Assembly that "states do prefer environmental law not to be compartmentalized, but to find its place within international law as a whole."[154] This and the chamber's history of no referrals reduces the chances of a strong standing for an ICE.[155] Furthermore, key challenges here are the reluctance of states, the fact that cases are often not solely environmental matters, competence problems, political differences regarding environmental issues, funding mechanisms and the location of the court.

States are, in general, hesitant about referring international environmental disputes to international adjudication.[156] This is even truer for today's development to shrink the focus on national states. Another example for this reluctance can be seen in the work of the International Court of Environmental Arbitration and Conciliation (ICEAC), which was set up in 1994 in Mexico by several lawyers.[157] It was created to hold court over all environmental disputes, but no state has ever accepted a petition for conciliation.[158] Nevertheless, it can be argued that in today's time, the environment receives more and more attention and that, therefore, the possibility of environmental cases is growing further. The view that the natural environment is a global "resource" worth protecting is gaining popularity. Therefore, the argument for including international environmental issues within the general sphere of international law is losing its power. The global environment is a central problem and not only an annex to a different international argument.

---

[153] The ICJ chamber for environmental matters was set up in 1993 following the developments of the Rio Convention in 1992, but was dissolved in 2006, due to the fact that it was not used as intended. One of the chambers major flaws was that it was set to cover "*any environmental case*" without further definition; *see* Basile Cartier, *Chamber for Environmental Matters: International Court of Justice*, in Helene Ruiz Fabri (ed.), Max Planck Encyclopedias of International Procedural Law (2008).

[154] ICJ ANNUAL REPORT 2006-2007, 2007, 299.

[155] Pedersen, *supra* note 3 at 553.

[156] Sands, *supra* note 10 at 4.

[157] Eckard Rehbinder and Demetrio Loperena, *Legal Protection of Environmental Rights: The Role and Experience of the International Court of Environmental Arbitration and Conciliation*, 31 ENVIRONMENTAL POLICY AND LAW 280, 282 (2001); Pedersen, *supra* note 3 at 552.

[158] Rehbinder and Loperena, *supra* note 158 at 282.

As a matter of fact, it is often difficult for existing international courts to distinguish between the international law regimes primarily governing a case. The *Gabcikovo-Nagymaros Case*[159] and the *Pulp Mills Case*,[160] which are often used as examples for ICJ cases with environmental elements, can, in this regard, be used as an argument against an ICE because the crucial point of these cases were treaty obligations, which fall within the scope of the ICJ.[161] Even in the "old" or "classic" examples for environmental cases in front of international judicial organs, such as the *Pacific Fur Seal Arbitration*[162] in 1893, *Trail Smelter Arbitration*[163] in 1941 or *Lac Lanoux Case*[164] in 1957, primarily show a conflict between economic and ecological interests and not one of environmental concern.[165] A solely environmental case is difficult to imagine due to the explained complexity of international environmental crimes and international environmental issues in general. In contrast to this argument, it should be kept in mind that as the well-being of the natural environment rises into one of the main goals of the international community of states, it will be more likely to create cases with an environmental core question.

To ensure a controlled environment for the international courts, there have to be strict boundaries between their areas of responsibility. This clear distinction between the courts can be found in domestic legal systems, where, for example, criminal courts, civil courts and administrative courts handle their specific field of law. The distinction is even clearer in countries where specialized environmental courts have been set up, such as the abovementioned National Green Tribunal in India or the Environment Court of New Zealand. On an international level, the ICJ handles general questions of international law, and the ICC deals with criminal cases. An ICE handling parts of both could likely lead to competence problems. The same problem applies to the creation of several regional environmental courts. Regional institutions might be a little bit closer to the actual environmental problem, but this response could potentially cause overlap problems with other regional multilateral institutions. Though, a coherent mandate for the ICE could prevent these potential issues in the delimitation of competencies. Both of the aforementioned national judicial entities in India and New Zealand

---

159 *See Gabcikovo-Nagymaros Project* (Hungary v. Slovakia) (Judgement) [1997] ICJ Report 7.

160 *See Pulp Mills on the River Uruguay* (Argentina v. Uruguay) (Judgement) [2019], ICJ Report 14.

161 Pedersen, *supra* note 3 at 551.

162 *See Bering Sea Arbitration* (United States v. United Kingdom) (Arbitration) [1893].

163 *See Trail Smelter Arbitration* (United States v. Canada) (Arbitration) [1941].

164 *See Lac Lanoux Arbitration* (France v. Spain) (Arbitration) [1957].

165 Sands, *supra* note 10 at 3.

provide specialized jurisdiction for specific national environmental codes.[166] They cannot be regarded as criminal courts. Nevertheless, does their example show that a distinction of jurisdictional powers is possible? Therefore, these courts can be seen as an example, also for setting up a specialized court within the criminal law regime for environmental crimes.

The general approach of creating a new jurisdiction for every slightly new issue in international law cannot be a way for the future. This landscape of numerous courts brings competence and jurisdictional problems due to overlapping jurisdiction, which is inefficient. Furthermore, it might lead to confusion and probably result in a complete loss of belief in a functioning system of international adjudication. International legal governance needs consistent and strong institutions and not a distracting number of entities dealing with different issues. This slows down legal development on an international level and blocks effective solution building.

On the other hand, however, the importance of the natural environment as the habitat for humanity is prone to special jurisdiction in international law. To govern the global environment effectively, this area should not be left within a general institution. In contrast to the point above, an international environmental court might bring back faith in international cooperation. In fact, the ICE might be a missing harmonizing factor within the current fragmentation of MEA's and the general handling of environmental problems on the international level.

Another problem for an ICE is the fact that there is no common international agenda on how to deal with the environment within the state community yet.[167] There are big differences between the states, especially between developed states and non-developed countries.[168] Developed states also have differing opinions on environmental topics, as seen in the controversial discussion between the US and the EU regarding genetic engineering or climate change.[169]

---

166 The National Green Tribunal in India decides on the basis of the National Green Tribunal Act of 2010, as well as some explicitly listed enactments, such as the Forest (Conservation) Act of 1980 or the Public Liability Insurance Act of 1991; The Environment Court of New Zealand bases its verdicts primarily on the Resource Management Act of 1991, but also has some powers regarding other specifically listed acts, e.g. the Biosecurity Act of 1993.

167 *Id.* at 4.

168 *Id.*

169 *Id;* Frankfurter Allgemeine Zeitung, Trump verkuendet Amerikas Rueckzug aus Klimaabkommen, https://www.faz.net/aktuell/donald-trump-verkuendet-ausstieg-aus-pariser-klimaabkommen-15043428.html (01 Juni 2017).

An ICE-Convention could even out the countering opinions and serve as a guideline on dealing with the natural environment on a global level. This opportunity, however, does not overcome the fact that political negotiations for an environmental court on an international level would be a challenging task, given the current global political tensions and disagreements, particularly regarding environmental matters.

Funding of the ICE is another politically sensitive issue. Philip Riches and Stuart A. Bruce suggest an approach to funding by either state parties or by fees issued by the court.[170] As a third option, they suggest financing by corporations in the form of long-term contributions in return for access to the international institution.[171] All three options are accompanied by hurdles. Funding through states may deter states from signing the agreement in the first place, and fees associated with submitting a case may be unattractive to parties due to the potential costs. Grants by corporations may threaten the ICE's integrity and independence of the court.

Next to all the political, financial and legal questions, even the mundane debate about the location of the new International Court for the Environment raises difficult issues. The UN has offices around the world, UNEP headquarters are based in Nairobi, and the existing "world-courts" are located in The Hague. A connection between the ICE, the ICJ, and the ICC in The Hague would seem like the easiest way. The Hague is already the "world's capital of international courts" and provides the needed infrastructure. But to locate the ICE in countries with a high percentage of environmental challenges, in general, would create an even stronger message. The idea of strengthening the countries of the Global South has to be kept in mind. Placing an internationally respected court in a developing country is a risk, but one with a statement. It would send a clear message to those involved in criminal actions around the world's precious environment, stating: that the global community is no longer willing to tolerate international environmental crime and the overall environmental degradation, especially in the Global South.

V. Conclusion

The ICE could play a vital role in the future of international law and international relations. There is simply no major international court with deep enough experience and specialization in environmental matters yet in

---

[170] Riches and Bruce, *supra* note 7 at 4.

[171] *Id.*

existence.[172] Furthermore, a criminal provision within the court's statute giving a clear definition of international environmental crimes and granting the ICE jurisdiction on these matters would be a wide step towards an effective international environmental regime.

The foundation of the ICE would provide this needed specialized experience. The other advantages of an ICE include a centralized system for a number of stakeholders, the freedom of definition for environmental crimes, enhancement of the body of law regarding international environmental issues, newly grown consistency in judicial resolutions of international environmental disputes, increased focus on preventative measures, global environmental standards of care and stricter enforcement of international environmental treaties.[173] Some say that only an ICE-like institution can effectively address global issues and disputes in the environmental sphere.[174] In the light of the aforesaid, the ICE has the general potential to be the right forum for international environmental crimes, even with the ICC and the ICJ in existence. In addition to the existing international jurisprudence, an ICE could blend in to uphold the concerns of the environment. However, the many challenges in this regard have to be kept in mind.

The foundation of such an international court is not only a question of the legal requirements but mainly one of international politics. In recent years the world has seen a frightening amount of nationalism in key states. The tactic of closing up borders and putting more border barriers in place does not pay off in environmental matters. Climate change cannot be stopped by a border wall, desertification will not be blocked by a border official, and polluted water does not respect maritime borders drawn on a map. Nevertheless, the national states do still play a vital role in combatting international environmental crime. Border controls work well in detecting illegally traded ivory, rhino horn, or timber. However, the balance between control of national states on the one hand and international cooperation, on the other hand, has to be well-rounded.

A weakened version of an ICE definitely has a chance of being born, but it might then be another addendum to the generally weak international

---

[172] ICE Coalition, *supra* note 6 at 8; Riches and Bruce, *supra* note 7 at 2.

[173] Hockman, *supra* note 6 at 223-224.

[174] Kenneth F. McCallion and Rajan Sharma, *Environmental Justice without Borders: The Need for an International Court of the Environment to Protect Fundamental Environmental Rights*, 32(3) THE GEORGE WASHINGTON JOURNAL OF INTERNATIONAL LAW AND ECONOMICS 351, 365 (2000).

enforcement in environmental issues.[175] To simplify the introduction of an ICE, a first step might be the introduction of an ad hoc tribunal on international environmental issues.[176] In light of the current politics, this could be an achievable option. Despite its "compromise-status," this ad hoc institution could be a cornerstone of the future ICE and provide declaratory clarification and adjudication and a general dispute resolution forum for urgent matters for those who submit to its jurisdiction.[177] Regarding environmental crimes, a new international environmental crime convention with an ad hoc court and the possibility of a later permanent court might be the easier way than setting up a fully functional international court in the first place. The ICC took similar steps in its development, with the Tokyo and Nuremberg Trials being the first step and the foundation of the ad-hoc tribunals (ICTY and ICTR) being the middle step before the ICC was introduced in 2001.[178] In fact, an environmental ad-hoc tribunal for particular trans- or international environmental disasters could be a first step in the direction of an ICE.

Even though the ICE will not abolish environmental crime on the international level or magically help heal the relationship between humanity and nature, an institution is indeed needed to govern the environment worldwide, especially from a criminal perspective. These criminal acts – under the aforementioned definition – have proven to be a threat to the international community of states and, lastly, to humanity. Green crimes have to be taken on by the community of states as a whole: a solo action is welcome, but – sadly – not more than a drop in the bucket. Strengthening international collaboration is therefore not an option; it is the only solution to combat threats originating from international environmental crimes. Therefore, the International Court for the Environment can become a new cornerstone to the path to an environmental regime on international law, especially in the sphere of green crimes.

---

175 Joost Pauwelyn, *Judicial Mechanisms: Is there a Need for a World Environment Court?*, in Bradnee Chambers and Jessica F. Green (ed) REFORMING INTERNATIONAL ENVIRONMENTAL GOVERNANCE: FROM INSTITUTIONAL LIMITS TO INNOVATIVE REFORMS 150, 159 (2005).

176 Hockman, *supra* note 7 at 226; Riches and Bruce, *supra* note 6 at 5.

177 Hockman, *supra* note 7 at 226.

178 Kai Ambos INTERNATIONALES STRAFRECHT 113 (2018).

Bibliography

Kai Ambos, INTERNATIONALES STRAFRECHT, München, C.H.Beck (2018).

Onelica Andrade, *Environmental Crime Summit*, 42 ENVIRONMENTAL POLICY AND LAW no. 3 at 59 (2012).

Banks et. al., ENVIRONMENTAL CRIME - A THREAT TO OUR FUTURE, London, EIA (2008).

Elaine Barclay and Robyn Bartel, *Defining Environmental Crime: The Perspective of Farmers*, 39 JOURNAL OF RURAL STUDIES 188 (2015).

Diane C. Bates, *Environmental Refugees? Classifying Human Migrations Caused by Environmental Change*, 24 POPULATION AND ENVIRONMENT, no. 5 at 465 (2002).

Johan Bergenas and Ariella Knight, *Green Terror: Environmental Crime and Illicit Financing*, 35(1) SCHOOL OF ADVANCED INTERNATIONAL STUDIES REVIEW 119 (2015).

Patricia Birnie and Alan Boyle, INTERNATIONAL LAW AND THE ENVIRONMENT, Oxford University Press (2002).

Anouk Boas, *The definition of the crime of aggression and its relevance for contemporary armed conflict*, INTERNATIONAL CRIMES DATABASE (June 1, 2013), http://www.internationalcrimesdatabase.org/upload/documents/20141020T170547-ICD%20Brief%201%20-%20Boas.pdf.

Tim van Solinge Boekhout, *Deforestation Crimes and Conflicts in the Amazon*, CRITICAL CRIMINOLOGY 18, no. 4 at 263 (2010).

Klaus Bosselmann, EARTH GOVERNANCE: TRUSTEESHIP OF THE GLOBAL COMMONS, Elgar (2015).

Samantha Bricknell, *Environmental crime in Australia*, 109 RESEARCH AND PUBLIC POLICY SERIES (2010).

Basile Cartier, *Chamber for Environmental Matters: International Court of Justice*, in Helene Ruiz Fabri (ed.), MAX PLANCK ENCYCLOPEDIAS OF INTERNATIONAL PROCEDURAL LAW, Oxford University Press (2008).

Mary Clifford and Terry D Edwards, *Environmental Crime*, Jones and Barlett Learning (2011).

Sam Cowie, *Seeking Answers to Catastrophic Brazil Mine Disaster*, AL JAZEERA (Jan. 3, 2016), https://www.aljazeera.com/indepth/features/2015/12/seeking-answers-catastrophic-brazil-disaster-151224071626923.html.

CORMAC CULLINAN, WILD LAW: A MANIFESTO FOR EARTH JUSTICE, Green Books (2003).

Mark Drumbl, *Waging war against the world: The need to move from war crimes to environmental crimes*, FORDHAM INTERNATIONAL LAW JOURNAL 22, no. 1 at 122 (1998).

Wilfried Erbguth and Sabine Schlacke, UMWELTRECHT, Nomos (2010).

Teresa Fajardo del Castillo, *International environmental law and environmental crime: An introduction*, EUROPEAN UNION ACTION TO FIGHT ENVIRONMENTAL CRIME (2015).

STEVEN FREELAND, ADDRESSING THE INTERNATIONAL DESTRUCTION OF THE ENVIRONMENT DURING WARFARE UNDER THE ROME STATUTE OF THE INTERNATIONAL CRIMINAL COURT, Intersentia (2015).

Cynthia Giagnocavo and Howard Goldstein, *Law Reform or World Re-form: The Problem of Environmental Rights*, McGILL LAW JOURNAL 35, no. 2 at 345 (1990).

Gitanjali Nain Gill, ENVIRONMENTAL JUSTICE IN INDIA: THE NATIONAL GREEN TRIBUNAL, Routledge (2017).

Mohammad Gomaa, *The definition of the crime of aggression and the ICC jurisdiction over that crime* in Mauro Politi and Giuseppe Nesi (eds.), THE INTERNATIONAL CRIMINAL COURT AND THE CRIME OF AGGRESSION, Ashgate (2005).

Garett Hardin, *The Tragedy of the Commons*, SCIENCE 162, no. 3859 at 1243 (1968).

Gavin Hayman and Duncan Brack, *International Environmental Crime – The Nature and Control of Environmental Black Markets,* ROYAL INSTITUTE OF INTERNATIONAL AFFAIRS (2009).

Polly Higgins, ERADICATING ECOCIDE, Shepheard-Walwyn (2010).

Polly Higgins, Damien Short et al., *Protecting the Planet: a Proposal for a Law of Ecocide,* CRIME, LAW AND SOCIAL CHANGE 59, no. 3 at 251 (2013).

Stephen Hockman, *The Case for an International Court for the Environment,* JOURNAL OF COURT INNOVATION 3, no. 1 (2010): 215.

ICE Coalition, *Environmental Institutions for the 21st Century: An International Court for the Environment,* STAKEHOLDER FORUM'S PROGRAMME ON SUSTAINABLE DEVELOPMENT, 2011.

ICE Foundation, *Draft articles for an International Court for the Environment,* http://www.icefcourtpress.org/statute.html (last visited 30 July 2020).

Michael Kloepfer and Martin Heger, UMWELTSTRAFRECHT, C. H. Beck (2014).

Jessica C. Lawrence and Kevin J. Heller, *The First Ecocentric Environmental War Crime: The Limits of Article 8(2)(b)(iv) of the Rome Statute,* GEORGETOWN INTERNATIONAL ENVIRONMENTAL LAW REVIEW 20, no. 1 (2007).

Michael Lynch and Paul B Stretesky, GREEN CRIMINOLOGY, Oxford University Press (2012).

Irina Marchuk, THE FUNDAMENTAL CONCEPT OF CRIME IN INTERNATIONAL CRIMINAL LAW, Springer-Verlag (2014).

Larry May, CRIMES AGAINST HUMANITY, Cambridge University Press (2005).

Kenneth McCallion and Rajan Sharma, *Environmental Justice without Borders: The Need for an International Court of the Environment to Protect Fundamental Environmental Rights,* THE GEORGE WASHINGTON JOURNAL OF INTERNATIONAL LAW AND ECONOMICS 32, no. 3 at 351 (2000).

Christian Nellemann et al., THE RISE OF ENVIRONMENTAL CRIME, UNEP (2016).

Angus Nurse, *Linking the green and the mainstream,* in Angus Nurse (ed.), *Critical Perspective on Green Criminology,* INTERNET JOURNAL OF CRIMINOLOGY (2014).

Joost Pauwelyn, *Judicial Mechanisms: Is there a Need for a World Environment Court?,* in Bradnee Chambers and Jessica F Green (eds.), REFORMING INTERNATIONAL ENVIRONMENTAL GOVERNANCE: FROM INSTITUTIONAL LIMITS TO INNOVATIVE REFORMS, United Nations University Press, 2005.

Ole Pedersen, *An International Environmental Court and International Legalism,* 24(3) JOURNAL OF ENVIRONMENTAL LAW 24, no. 3 at 547 (2012).

Deirdre Pirro, *Project for an international court of the environment - Origins and development,* BIOPOLITICS, (2002), http://www.biopolitics.gr.

Amedeo Postiglione, *A More Efficient International Law on the Environment and Setting up an International Court for the Environment within the United Nations*, 20 ENVIRONMENTAL LAW at 321 (1990).

Eckhard Rehbinder and Demetrio Loperena, *Legal Protection of Environmental Rights: The Role and Experience of the International Court of Environmental Arbitration and Conciliation*, ENVIRONMENTAL POLICY AND LAW 31 at 280 (2001).

Philip Riches and Stuart A. Bruce, *Brief 7: Building an International Court for the Environment: A Conceptual Framework*, GOVERNANCE AND SUSTAINABILITY ISSUE BRIEF SERIES 7 (2013).

Armin Rosencranz and Siddharth Johar. Illegal Smuggling of Ozone-depleting Substances, ENVIRONMENTAL POLICY AND LAW 45, no. 2 at 73 (2015).

Philippe Sands, *Principles of International Environmental Law*, Cambridge University Press (2003).

Philippe Sands, *Litigating Environmental Disputes: Courts, Tribunals and the Progressive Development of International Environmental Law*, GLOBAL FORUM ON INTERNATIONAL INVESTMENT 8 (2008).

Matthias Schuster, *The Rome Statute and the Crime of Aggression: A Gordion Knot in regard to this Solution*, CRIMINAL LAW FORUM 14 (2013).

Andrew Simester and George R Sullivan, CRIMINAL LAW THEORY AND DOCTRINE, Hart Publishing, (2007).

Yingyi Situ and David Emmons, ENVIRONMENTAL CRIME: THE CRIMINAL JUSTICE SYSTEM'S ROLE IN PROTECTING THE ENVIRONMENT, SAGE Publications (2000).

Nigel South, *A Green Field for Criminology: A Proposal for a Perspective*, THEORETICAL CRIMINOLOGY 2, no. 2 at 211 (1998).

Neal Tate, *Why the Expansion of Judicial Power*, in Neal Tate and Torbjorn Vallinder (eds.), THE GLOBAL EXPANSION OF JUDICIAL POWER, New York University Press (1995).

Torbjorn Vallinder, *When the Courts Go Marching In*, in Neal Tate and Torbjjorn Vallinder (eds.), THE GLOBAL EXPANSION OF JUDICIAL POWER, New York University Press, (1995).

Jorge Vinuales, *The contribution of the International Court of Justice to the development of international environmental law: A contemporary assessment*, FORDHAM INTERNATIONAL LAW JOURNAL 32 at 232 (2008).

Melanie Wellsmith, *Wildlife Crime: The Problem of Enforcement*, EUROPEAN JOURNAL ON CRIMINAL POLICY AND RESEARCH 17 at 125 (2011).

Gerhard Werle, VOELKERSTRAFRECHT, Mohr Siebeck (2012).

Rob White, TRANSNATIONAL ENVIRONMENTAL CRIME: TOWARD AND ECO-GLOBAL CRIMINOLOGY, Willan Publishing (2011).

Rob White, *Environmental crime in global context: exploring the theoretical and empirical complexities*, CURRENT ISSUES IN CRIMINAL JUSTICE 16(3) at 271 (2005).

Alexander Willis, *The Crime of aggression and the resort to force against entities in statu nascendi*, 10(1) JOURNAL OF INTERNATIONAL CRIMINAL JUSTICE 10, no. 1 at 83 (2012).

Frankfurter Allgemeine Zeitung, *Trump verkuendet Amerikas Rueckzug aus Klimaabkommen* (June 1, 2017), https://www.faz.net/aktuell/donald-trump-verkuendet-ausstieg-aus-pariser-klimaabkommen-15043428.html.

Chapter 6

Dakota Access Pipeline a Case of Cultural Genocide? Through an Indigenous Data Sovereignty Lens

Leo Mukosi

James E Rogers College of Law (Indigenous Peoples Law and Policy)
University of Arizona

Abstract: Green crimes, especially those that happen as a result of developmental projects that are carried out without proper consultation and consideration of Indigenous Peoples cultural perspectives, arguably amount to the crime of genocide against the Indigenous Peoples involved. This is particularly true in cases where developmental projects not only threaten the environment but also Indigenous Peoples' cultures and lifeways through the destruction of sacred and religious sites. Indigenous data sovereignty denotes Indigenous Peoples' right to determine the means of collection, access, analysis, interpretation, management, dissemination, and reuse of data pertaining to Indigenous Peoples from whom it has been derived or whom it relates.[1] Historically, the lack of participation of Indigenous Peoples in their data processes pertaining to developmental projects that affect their lives is not only inimical to tribal self-determination but also threatens the very existence of the Indigenous groups. When data about Indigenous Peoples is collected by federal or state agencies or other non-indigenous entities, such data are used for the priorities of those agencies.[2] In this chapter, I use the

---

[1] Tahu Kukutai and John Taylor, DATA SOVEREIGNTY FOR INDIGENOUS PEOPLES: CURRENT PRACTICE AND FUTURE NEEDS IN INDIGENOUS DATA SOVEREIGNTY: TOWARD AN AGENDA 1,7, Kau Kukutai and John Taylor eds., (2016).

[2] Rebecca Tsosie, *Governance and Informational Privacy: Constructing "Indigenous Data Sovereignty"*, 80 MONT. L. REV. 229 (2019) at 242.

Dakota Access Pipeline (DAPL) to illustrate how lack of adequate indigenous participation harms Indigenous culture. This chapter is divided into three parts: the first part provides a synopsis of the laws on tribal consultation in the USA. The second part establishes the causal link between the lack of adequate indigenous participation in the collection or application of data through consultation, and cultural genocide, as exemplified by the DAPL. The final part provides recommendations based on principles drawn from Indigenous data sovereignty that can be applied during and after the consultation process to safeguard indigenous cultures.

Keywords: Indigenous data sovereignty, Dakota Access Pipeline, Standing Rock Sioux Tribe, Standing Rock Reservation, United States, UNDRIP, Indigenous Peoples, cultural genocide, tribal consultation, self-determination, CARE principles.

***

I. The Dakota Access Pipeline: Background

The DAPL stretches for 1,172-miles underground, transporting light sweet crude oil by pipelines up to 30 inches in diameter from the Bakken/Three Forks production area in North Dakota to Patoka, Illinois.[3] The DAPL crosses federally regulated waters of the United States under the Corps' jurisdiction at least 204 times and also crosses the Missouri River in two locations upstream of the Standing Rock Reservation inhabited by members of the Standing Rock Sioux Tribe.[4] Other tribes whose treaty rights were affected by the DAPL are the Cheyenne River, Yankton, and Oglala Sioux tribes that subsequently opposed the construction of the DAPL.[5]

The DAPL runs through the territory that Standing Rock retained after their ancestral land was significantly trimmed as a result of the Fort Laramie Treaties of 1851 and 1868,[6] as well as subsequent statutes enacted by

---

[3] *Moving America's Energy: The Dakota Access Pipeline*, https://daplpipelinefacts.com/ (last visited June 21, 2020).

[4] Walter E. Stern, *"Black Snakes" Or Essential Infrastructure: Dakota Access Pipeline, Standing Rock Sioux Tribe V. U. S. Army Corps of Engineers, The Federal Government's Tribal Consultation Obligations, and Why This Matters*, MODRALL SPERLING (2018).

[5] Carla F. Fredericks and Jesse D. Heibel, *Standing Rock, the Sioux Treaties, and the Limits of the Supremacy Clause*, 89 U. COLO. L. REV. 477 (2018).

[6] Treaty of Fort Laramie with Sioux, Etc., Sept. 17, 1851, 11 Stat. 749.

congress.[7] Accordingly, the main argument advanced by the Standing Rock Tribe in opposition of the DAPL is that the pipeline violates Article II of the Fort Laramie Treaty, which guarantees the "undisturbed use and occupation" of reservation lands surrounding the proposed location of the pipeline.[8]

The dominant narrative of DAPL protests has placed the environmental protection movement at the center of the protests while sidelining Indigenous religion and culture. In reality, the adverse effects of the pipeline range from the environmental impacts to water sources near the pipeline to the destruction of indigenous cultural heritage.[9] Precisely, the effects of the pipeline on the tribes include; destruction and damage to burial grounds and sites of religious and cultural worship, and disturbance of the tribe's relationship with water sources, such as the Missouri River and Lake Oahe in North and South Dakota, which are "sacred to the [Standing Rock Sioux Tribe] and are central to the Tribe's practice of religion."[10]

The Great Sioux Nation retains long-standing cultural affiliations with wide swaths of the north-central United States, as well as the off-reservation rights reserved by treaties. The DAPL runs through treaty lands that were never ceded.[11] The Standing Rock's religious practices predate Judaism, Christianity, and Islam by centuries.[12] The tribe attaches respect to land water and living organisms; thus, subsistence activities are ineluctably tied to culture.[13]

a. The Corps Jurisdiction over the DAPL

The US Army Corps of Engineers (the Corps) has three main mission areas, namely (1) engineer regiment, (2) military construction, and (3) civil works.[14] Through their regulatory program, the Corps is responsible for authorizing activities that could affect federally regulated waters and wetlands. They

---

[7] Act of Mar. 2, 1889, ch. 405, 25 Stat. 888.

[8] *Id.*

[9] Haydee J. Djikstal, *The Dakota Access Pipeline and the Destruction of Cultural Heritage: Apply the Crime Against Humanity of Persecution Before the ICC*, Minnesota Journal of International Law. 277 (2019).

[10] *Id.*

[11] Stern, *supra* note 4.

[12] *The Standing Rock Sioux tribe Impacts of an Oil Spill from the Dakota Access Pipeline on the Standing Rock Sioux Tribe.* A report was prepared under the direction of Mike Faith, Jr., Chairman of the standing rock tribe. (February 21 2018).

[13] *Id.*

[14] CONGRESSIONAL RESEARCH SERVICE, *Oil and Natural Gas Pipelines: Role of US Army Corps of Engineers*, (June 21-28, 2017).

approve activities that cross or affect Corps lands and projects through the Civil Works program.[15] The DAPL transports crude oil pipeline from North Dakota to Illinois, crossing the Corps' jurisdictional waters, thus falling under the Permit Program.[16] Section 404 of the Clean Water Act (CWA) sets forth the Corps authority over the discharge of dredged or fill material into waters of the United States, including wetlands.[17] Similarly, section 10 of the Rivers and Harbors Act authorizes the Corps to regulate the structures and/or work affecting the course, condition, or capacity of navigable waters.[18]

Further, the Corps' jurisdiction over DAPL flows from the CWA. The CWA requires the Secretary of the Army, acting through the Chief of Engineers, to issue permits, after notice and opportunity for public hearings for the discharge of dredged or fill material into the navigable waters at specified disposal sites.[19] Further, the Corps then determines whether the multiple DAPL crossings fall within the Corps' Nationwide Permit 12 (NWP 12), which only allows pipeline crossings of regulated waters if the activity disturbs no more than a half-acre of waters of the United States.[20] Section 14 of the Rivers and Harbors Act of 1899 which authorizes the Corps to grant permission for the alteration or permanent occupation or use of any of the [specified] public works when in the judgment of the [Corps] such occupation or use will not be injurious to the public interest and will not impair the usefulness of such work also determines the Corps jurisdiction over the DAPL.[21] Additionally, Section 28 of the Mineral Leasing Act of 1920 establishes the jurisdiction of the Corps to authorize the DAPL through the granting of easement flows.[22] Additionally, the Corps jurisdiction emanates from Section 28 of the Mineral Leasing Act of 1920, which authorizes the Secretary of the Interior or appropriate head agency to grant the right of way through any Federal lands for the construction of pipelines.[23]

---

[15] *Id.*

[16] *Id.*

[17] 33 U.S.C. §1344.

[18] 33 U.S.C. §403.

[19] *Id.* The Secretary may issue permits, after notice and opportunity for public hearings for the discharge of dredged or fill material into the navigable waters at specified disposal sites. Not later than the fifteenth day after the date an applicant submits all the information required to complete an application for a permit under this subsection, the Secretary shall publish the notice required by this subsection.

[20] Stern, *supra* note 4.

[21] *Id.*

[22] 30 U.S.C. § 185.

[23] *Id.*

b. Tribal Consultation in the US

In the United States, the framework of agency consultation with tribal governments is fragmented across executive orders, statutes, or regulations that require agencies to consult with tribal governments about federal projects that impact tribal interests.[24] There is currently no single unified policy that works across all agencies and departments to provide a government-wide standard for meaningful consultation.[25] In the section that follows, I lay out the sources from which the obligation to consult with Indian tribes emanates, describe the inadequacies and flaws thereof, and finally argue that said inadequacies affected the DAPL consultation process.

i. Executive Orders and Tribal Consultation

An Executive Order (EO) is a published directive from the President of the United States that has the force of law regulating Federal government operations relating to a particular matter.[26] There are many EOs that relate to the Federal government's relationship with Indian tribes, particularly with regard to cultural resource consultation.[27] However, it is worth pointing out that the relations between Native Americans and the Federal government were and are in many respects still mainly characterized by the abuse and domination of the former by the latter.[28] Accordingly, Federal policy toward Native Americans was designed to disband them and sell their land.[29]

During the Nixon era, "a new and balanced relationship between the United States government and the Native Americans was introduced."[30] President Nixon, who was often referred to as a "Champion for Native Americans," enacted policies intended to end over two centuries of federal actions

---

[24] M. Eitner, *Meaningful Consultation with Tribal Governments: A uniform standard to guarantee that federal agencies properly consider their concerns.* UNIVERSITY OF COLORADO LAW REVIEW 85:867–901 (2014).

[25] *Id.*

[26] AMERICAN BAR ASSOCIATION, *What is an Executive* Order? https://www.americanbar.org/groups/public_education/publications/teaching-legal-docs/what-is-an-executive-order-/ (last visited July 5, 2020).

[27] *Id.*

[28] RICHARD NIXON FOUNDATION, *President Nixon: Champion for Native Americans*, https://www.thoughtco.com/richard-nixons-influence-american-indian-affairs-4082465 (last visited November 18 2020).

[29] NATIVE VOICES, *Congress seeks to abolish tribes, relocate Indian Americans*, https://www.nlm.nih.gov/nativevoices/timeline/488.html (last visited November 18, 2020).

[30] *Special Message to Congress on Indian Affairs*, 213 PUB. PAPERS 564 (July 8, 1970).

designed to destroy Indigenous Peoples' self-determination. This introduced a new era of federal policy that aligned with Native Americans' rights to control their own destiny. President Nixon's actions paved the way for several executive orders, which were codified by subsequent administrations to shape the unique relationship of the United States with Native Americans on different subject matters.[31]

President Bill Clinton further fostered the intergovernmental relationship between Native Americans and the Federal government. In 1994 he issued a Memorandum on Government-to-Government Relations with Native American Tribal Governments.[32] Regarding the consultation of tribal governments by agencies, the memorandum stated that ... "[a]ll such consultations are to be open and candid so that all interested parties may evaluate for themselves the potential impact of relevant proposals."[33]

Further, President Clinton issued EO 13007 of 1996, which required as part of its implementation process, the consultation with appropriate Indian tribes and religious leaders, and the expeditious resolution of disputes relating to agency action on Federal lands that may adversely affect access to the ceremonial use of, or the physical integrity of sacred sites.[34] President Clinton also issued EO 13175 in 2000 – Consultation and Coordination with Tribal Government. Section 5 of EO 13175 provided a comprehensive procedural framework for agencies to follow when consulting with Indian tribes as follows:

> a) Each agency shall have an accountable process to ensure meaningful and timely input by tribal officials in the development of regulatory policies that have tribal implications. Within 30 days after the effective date of this order, the head of each agency shall designate an official with principal responsibility for the agency's implementation of this order. Within 60 days of the effective date of this order, the designated official shall submit to the Office of Management and Budget (OMB) a description of the agency's consultation process.

---

[31] RICHARD NIXON FOUNDATION *supra*, note, 28.

[32] *Memorandum on Government-to-Government Relations with Native American Tribal Governments*, 30 WEEKLY COMP. PRES. DOC. 936 (May 2, 1994). Two years later, president Clinton issued Executive Order in 1996, directed federal agencies to accommodate access to and ceremonial use of Native American sacred sites by Native American religious practitioners, as well as avoid adversely affecting the physical integrity of such sacred sites.

[33] *Id.* at 936-37.

[34] Exec Order No 13007, 61 C. F.R 26771 (May 1996).

b) To the extent practicable and permitted by law, no agency shall promulgate any regulation that has tribal implications, that imposes substantial direct compliance costs on Indian tribal governments, and that is not required by statute, unless the agency consulted with tribal officials early in the process of developing the proposed regulation.[35]

Likewise, President Barack Obama was regarded as a champion for Indian Country. He took steps to strengthen relations between the Federal government and Native Americans that included institutionalizing an annual White House Tribal Nations summit and appointed Native Americans to strategic government positions.[36] In 2009, President Barack Obama further issued a Presidential Memorandum directing each agency to submit a detailed plan of action describing how the agency will implement the policies and directives of EO 13175.[37] Through the memorandum, President Obama pledged his administration's commitment to regular and meaningful consultation and collaboration with tribal officials in policy decisions that have tribal implications, including as an initial step through the complete and consistent implementation of Executive Order 13175.[38]

As a way to consolidate the EO 13175 passed in 2000 by President Clinton, President Obama in 2013 passed EO 13647 to coordinate a more effective and efficient process for executive departments, agencies, and offices to honor the United States commitment to tribal consultation as set forth in EO 13175 of November 6, 2000.[39]

The above EOs guide agencies in creating and revising their tribal consultation policies and action plans.[40] Agencies like the Department of Agriculture (USDA), the Health and Human Services (HHS), the Department of Homeland Security (DHS) and the Bureau of Land Management (BLM) have designed policies on tribal consultation based on EOs.[41] Policies enacted

---

[35] Exec Order No 13175, 65 FR 67249 (2000).

[36] Rob Capriccioso, *Barack Obama and Richard Nixon Among Best Presidents for Indian Country* INDIAN COUNTRY TODAY, https://indiancountrytoday.com/archive/barack-obama-and-richard-nixon-among-best-presidents-for-indian-country-bJnChvj2_EKI5u8jISt1Hw (last visited November 10th 2020).

[37] Tribal Consultation, 74 Fed. Reg. 57,881 (Nov. 5, 2009).

[38] Eitner, *supra* note 24 at 878.

[39] Exec Order 13647 C.F.R. 39539.

[40] UNITED STATES GOVERNMENT ACCOUNTABILITY OFFICE (GAO) *Tribal Consultation, Additional Actions Needed for Infrastructure Projects* GAO-19-22 (March 2019).

[41] *Id.*

by agencies share a common shortcoming: they do not create a right of action for tribes seeking redress for a failure to follow proper consultation procedure. This renders the consultation process only a ceremonial procedure that neither precludes agencies from proceeding with actions detrimental to the tribe nor provides any recourse thereafter.[42]

ii. Statutory Provisions Requiring Consultation

In addition to EOs, the consultation of tribes in the US is also affirmed in the legislation, as shown in Table 1 below.

Table 1. Tribal Consultation.

LEGISLATION	TRIBAL CONSULTATION PROVISION
American Indian Religious Freedom Act	Requires consultation with tribes to ensure access to religious sites so American Indians may practice their traditional religions
Archeological Resources Protection Act	Requires any agency to consult with tribal governments before permitting excavations on tribal land
National Historic Preservation Act	Requires that all agencies consult with Indian tribes or Native Hawaiian organizations "that attach religious and cultural significance" to particular properties
Native American Graves Protection and Repatriation Act	Requires agency consultation not only with tribal governments, but also with traditional religious leaders and lineal descendants about the "treatment and disposition of specific kinds of human remains, funerary objects, sacred objects, and other items."
Indian Self-Determination and Education Assistance Act	Mandates consultation for specific actions taken by the Department of the Interior (DOI) and the Indian Health Service, which is part of HHS

iii. The Court on DAPL Consultation

The granting of a Nationwide Permit (NWP) by the Corps allowing the DAPL construction triggered a series of legal proceedings initiated by tribes that were affected by the decision. In 2016, the Standing Rock filed a motion for preliminary injunction in the U.S. District Court for the District of Columbia, which alleged that "the Corps flouted its duty to engage in tribal consultations

---

[42] *Id.*

under the National Historic Preservation Act (NHPA) and that irreparable harm will ensue."[43]

A NWP 12 is a general permit under the CWA that authorizes discharges associated with the construction, maintenance, repair, and removal of utility lines and associated facilities, including oil and gas pipelines.[44] A NWP is subject to General Conditions with which approved actions must comply.[45] General Condition 20 does not allow an activity to be authorized in cases where the district engineer determines that it may affect properties listed, or eligible for listing, in the National Register of Historic Places, until the requirements of Section 106 of the NHPA have been satisfied. Meanwhile, Section 106 of the NHPA says:

> The head of any Federal agency having direct or indirect jurisdiction over a proposed Federal or federally assisted undertaking in any State and the head of any Federal department or independent agency having authority to license any undertaking shall, prior to the approval of the expenditure of any Federal funds on the undertaking or prior to the issuance of any license, as the case may be, take into account the effect of the undertaking on any district, site, building, structure, or object that is included in or eligible for inclusion in the National Register. The head of any such Federal agency shall afford the Advisory Council on Historic Preservation established under Title II of this Act a reasonable opportunity to comment with regard to such undertaking.[46]

The Corps approved DAPL activities under NWP 12 along federally regulated waters at hundreds of discrete places along a nearly 1,200-mile route.[47] The Standing Rock and Cheyenne River Sioux tribes argued that in granting the permit, the Corps did not fully comply with their required responsibility to first engage tribal consultations required by the NHPA.[48]

While the Corps had agreeably conducted a Section 106 process prior to granting the NWP, the Standing Rock tribe alleged that the consultation was

---

[43] *Standing Rock Sioux Tribe v. U.S. Army Corps of Eng'rs*, No. 16-1534 (JEB) (D.D.C. Aug. 4, 2016) [Hereinafter *Standing Rock* 2016].

[44] JDSUPRA USACE, *Nationwide Permit 12 Vacated: What You Need to Know*, https://www.jdsupra.com/legalnews/usace-nationwide-permit-12-vacated-what-17066/ (Last visited 18 November 2020).

[45] *Id.*

[46] National Historic Preservation Act Section 106.

[47] *Standing Rock* 2016, *supra* note 43, ¶ 61.

[48] *Id* at 62.

too narrow and did not include historical properties along the entire pipeline route.[49] Accordingly, the tribes argued that the Corps failed to offer them a reasonable opportunity to participate in the Section 106 process as to the narrow scope of the construction activity that the Corps did consider to be an effect of the permitted waterway activities.[50]

The court rejected the tribes' argument regarding the insufficiency of the Corps' consultation, recognizing that the Corps made multiple attempts to engage the Standing Rock in consultations to identify historical resources at Lake Ohe, but the tribes refused to engage in these consultations. On that basis, the court said that the Corps exceeded its NHPA obligation; for example, the Corps took numerous trips to Lake Oahe with members of the Tribe to identify sites of cultural significance.[51] The court further rejected the tribe's claim that the Corps was required to consult them on the impact to cultural resources along the entire pipeline route as the tribes did not have an absolute right to participate in cultural surveying at every permitted undertaking.[52] Therefore, the court did not grant the injunctive order because the tribe had not shown that it was likely to succeed on the merits of its claims that the Corps violated the NHPA.[53]

Immediately after the 2016 district court judgment, the Department of the Army (Army), U.S. Department of Justice (DOJ), and U.S. Department of the Interior (DOI) issued a joint statement considering the potential improvements to the federal government's consultation obligations.[54] Subsequently, the Corps announced its intention to suspend the construction of DAPL, subject to the Corps' reconsideration of its statutory obligations under the National Environmental Policy Act (NEPA)[55] However, following President Donald Trump's assumption of office in January 2017, he signed a Presidential Memorandum ordering the Secretary of the Army to expedite the approval of the DAPL.[56] In addition, during the same month, President Trump issued an EO expediting the environmental review and approval process required by the NEPA for high-priority infrastructure projects like DAPL.[57] Subsequent to these

[49] *Id.*
[50] *Id* at 76.
[51] *Id.*
[52] *Id.*
[53] *Standing Rock* 2016, *supra* note 43.
[54] Secretarial Order No. 3342.
[55] *Id.*
[56] *Presidential Memorandum Regarding Construction of the Dakota Access Pipeline* (Jan 24, 2017).
[57] Executive Order 13766.

actions by the executive, on February 27, 2017, the US Army of Corps granted easement allowing the DAPL to cross under the Missouri River at Lake Oahe, north of the Standing Rock Sioux Reservation.

As the Cheyenne River Sioux and the Standing Rock Sioux tribes had been unsuccessful in their attempts to seek preliminary injunctions under the NHPA,[58] the tribes later shifted their focus to the NEPA, arguing that the Corps was supposed to prepare an Environmental Impact Statement (EIS).[59] The court stated that even though it had not prepared an EIS, the Corps had complied with NEPA for the most part, save for the failure to adequately consider: 1) whether the project's effects were likely to be "highly controversial"; (2) the impact of a hypothetical oil spill on the [Plaintiff] tribe's fishing and hunting rights; and (3) the "environmental-justice effects of the project."[60] In light of the Corps' non-compliance with NEPA, the court remanded these inadequacies to the Corps.[61] However, the court did not vacate the decision to grant an easement as there was a 'serious possibility' that the Corps would be able to substantiate its prior conclusions.[62]

Following the Corps' failure to rectify the aforementioned three defects, the District Court issued an order on July 6, 2020, which vacated the easement of the DAPL and required that the pipeline be shut down and drained of oil within 30 days.[63] The court's decision to shut down the DAPL pending the Corps' curing a defect of non-compliance with NEPA represents a jurisprudential shift toward the recognition of the Indigenous Peoples' rights to conservation, protection of the environment, and self-determination. However, the perpetual disregard for Native Americans' cultural heritage reflected by the court's failure to consider the Tribes' NHPA[64] claims throughout the DAPL litigation and also in the case under discussion cannot be ignored.

---

[58] *Standing Rock Sioux Tribe v. Army Corps* ¶ 62. The court concluded that the Tribe is unlikely to succeed on the merits of its NHPA claim — and because the Tribe has failed to show that any harm will befall it in the absence of an injunction.

[59] *Standing Rock Sioux Tribe v. United States Army Corps of Eng'rs*, 440 F. Supp. 3d 1, ¶ 13. (D.D C. 2020) [Hereinafter, *Standing Rock* 2020].

[60] *Standing Rock Sioux Tribe v. U.S. Army Corps of Eng'rs, Civil Action* No. 16-1534 (JEB), (2017).

[61] *Id.*

[62] *Standing Rock* 2020, *supra* note 59.

[63] *Id.*

[64] National Historic Preservation Act, 54 U.S.C. §§ 300101-307108 (1966).

Native American tribes in the U.S. have historically invoked the NEPA, which courts often refer to as a "stop, look and listen" provision[65] to challenge the agencies' approval of actions that affect the environment. When a federal agency develops a proposal to take a major federal action, the NEPA requires an environmental review to be carried out.[66] The environmental review under NEPA may involve three different levels of analysis, namely: (1) Categorical Exclusion Determination (CARTEX),[67] (2) Environmental Assessment (EA),[68] and (3) Environmental Impact Statement (EIS).[69]

An EIS is required in situations where the proposed major federal activity is determined to have a significant environmental impact.[70] An action with a "significant environmental impact" requires considerations of both *context*[71]

---

[65] *Narragansett Indian Tribe v. Warwick Sewer Auth.*, 334 F.3d 161, 166 (1st Cir.2003).

[66] United States Environmental Protection Agency; *National Environmental Policy Act Review Process,* https://www.epa.gov/nepa/national-environmental-policy-act-review-process (last visited on October 23, 2020) [hereinafter, *US EPA, NEPA, Review Process*].

[67] 40 C.F.R § 1508. A federal action may be *categorically excluded* from a detailed environmental analysis when the federal action normally does not have a significant effect on the human environment.

[68] *Id.* If a categorical exclusion does not apply to the proposed federal action, an Environmental Assessment determining whether or not a federal action has the potential to cause significant environmental effects is prepared Following an Environmental Assessment, either of the following happen, (1) If the agency determines that the action will not have significant environmental impacts, the agency will issue a Finding of No Significant Impact (FONSI). A FONSI is a document that presents the reasons why the agency has concluded that there are no significant environmental impacts projected to occur upon implementation of the action, (2) If the EA determines that the environmental impacts of a proposed Federal action will be significant, an Environmental Impact Statement is prepared.

[69] *US EPA, NEPA, Review Process, supra* note 5.

[70] *Id.*

[71] 40 C.F.R § 1508.27(b). Context refers to that the significance of an action must be analyzed in several contexts such as society as a whole (human, national), the affected region, the affected interests, and the locality. Significance varies with the setting of the proposed action. For instance, in the case of a site-specific action, significance would usually depend upon the effects in the locale rather than in the world as a whole. Both short- and long-term effects are relevant.

and *intensity.*[72] As stated in *National Parks Conservation Ass'n v. Semonite,*[73] implicating any one of the ten factors (considered when evaluating intensity) may be sufficient to require the development of an EIS. [74]

A review of precedent shows that courts in the US have historically given agencies time to 'cure' a defect in situations when the agency did not prepare an EIS where it is later proven to be required.[75] More often than not, courts vacate the Corps action while remanding the action to the agency for preparation of an EIS.[76] In deciding whether or not to vacate a deficient agency's action, the court looks at two factors, namely: (1) the seriousness of the order's deficiencies and (2) the disruptive consequences of an interim change that may itself be changed.[77] These factors were enacted in the case of

---

[72] *Id.* Intensity refers to the severity of impact. Responsible officials must bear in mind that more than one agency may make decisions about partial aspects of a major action. (1) Impacts that may be both beneficial and adverse. A significant effect may exist even if the Federal agency believes that on balance the effect will be beneficial. (2) The degree to which the proposed action affects public health or safety. (3) Unique characteristics of the geographic area such as proximity to historic or cultural resources, park lands, prime farmlands, wetlands, wild and scenic rivers, or ecologically critical areas. (4) The degree to which the effects on the quality of the human environment are likely to be highly controversial. (5) The degree to which the possible effects on the human environment are highly uncertain or involve unique or unknown risks. (6) The degree to which the action may establish a precedent for future actions with significant effects or represents a decision in principle about a future consideration. (7) Whether the action is related to other actions with individually insignificant but cumulatively significant impacts. Significance exists if it is reasonable to anticipate a cumulatively significant impact on the environment. Significance cannot be avoided by terming an action temporary or by breaking it down into small component parts. (8) The degree to which the action may adversely affect districts, sites, highways, structures, or objects listed in or eligible for listing in the National Register of Historic Places or may cause loss or destruction of significant scientific, cultural, or historical resources. (9) The degree to which the action may adversely affect an endangered or threatened species or its habitat that has been determined to be critical under the Endangered Species Act of 1973. (10) Whether the action threatens a violation of Federal, State, or local law or requirements imposed for the protection of the environment.

[73] *National Parks Conservation Ass'n v. Semonite,* 916 F.3d 1075, 1082 (D.C. Cir. 2019).

[74] *See supra* note 8.

[75] *Williston Basin Interstate Pipeline Co. v. FERC,* 519 F.3d 497, 504 (D.C. Cir. 2008).

[76] *Id.*

[77] *Id.*

Allied-Signal v. United States Nuclear Regulatory Commission, where the court vacated the easement based on the first factor.[78]

Courts usually vacate agencies' orders where deficiencies are deemed to be serious.[79] Very rarely, however, have courts in the US vacated an agency's action pending an EIS, based solely on critiques issued by tribal experts, to the effect that the agency's proposed action has adverse effects on the environment that tribes depend on or indigenous culture.[80] Where the agencies' deficiency is in relation to a major economic project like DAPL, courts seldom suspend the agencies' action to avoid "potentially dire economic consequences of vacatur" even in cases addressing environmental harm.[81]

In the case of *Sierra Club v. FERC,* the court vacated the decision of the Federal Energy Regulatory Commission to approve the construction and operation of three new interstate natural-gas pipelines in the southeastern U.S., based on the critiques raised by non-Indigenous environmental groups.[82] Similarly, the court, in the case of *Wild Horse Preservation Campaign v. Perdue,* vacated the decision of the United States Forest Service to eliminate 23, 000 hectares of wild horse territory after a non-Indigenous plaintiff, the American Wild Horse Preservation Campaign, critiqued the agency's decision.[83] Notably, this decision is arguably one of the few, if not the first, where the court set aside an agency's action based solely on environmental justice concerns raised by Native American environmental experts.[84] Signaling a departure from the norm, the court ordered the shutdown of an economically significant project, the DAPL, while acknowledging two of the most important rights of Indigenous People: the right to sovereignty and the right to the conservation and protection of the environment.[85] The court rejected the Corps' attempt to disregard the critiques raised by the tribal experts in their comments regarding the former's decision to grant easement to DAPL.[86] According to the court, tribes are not akin to the

---

[78] *Allied-Signal, Inc. v. U.S. Nuclear Regulatory Comm'n,* 988 F.2d 146, 150-51, 300 U.S. App. D.C. 198 (D.C. Cir. 1993).

[79] *Id.*

[80] *See Standing Rock Sioux Tribe* v. *U.S. Army Corps of Eng'rs* (Standing Rock IV), 282 F. Supp. 3d 91, 109 (D.D.C. 2017).

[81] *Id.* ¶ 103-06; *see also Am. Water Works Ass'n v. EPA,* 40 F.3d 1266, 1273 (D.C. Cir. 1994); *Friends of the Capital Crescent Trail v. Fed. Transit Admin.,* 218 F.Supp.3d 53, 60 (D.D.C. 2016); *California Cmtys. Against Toxics v. U.S. EPA,* 688 F.3d 989, 993–94 (9th Cir. 2012).

[82] *Sierra Club v. FERC,* 867 F.3d 1357, 1379 (D.C. Cir. 2017).

[83] *Wild Horse Preservation Campaign v. Perdue,* 873 F.3d 914, 932 (D.C. Cir. 2017).

[84] *Id.*

[85] *Id.* ¶ 17-25.

[86] *Id.*

non-governmental organizations but are… "domestic dependent nations that exercise inherent sovereign authority over their members and territories"…these sovereign nations prepared expert comments with the help of not only third-party consultants but also their own relevant governmental departments.[87]

Tribal experts raised points of scientific controversy regarding DAPL, and the Corps did not adequately address these questions during remand.[88] The court found that Corps did not adequately respond to the Tribal experts' critiques as expressed in the comments regarding the leak detection system,[89] the highly questionable operator's safety history, the lack of a contingency plan to deal with a hypothetical spill occurring during under harsh North Dakota winter conditions and the worst case discharge.[90]

Indigenous Peoples' rights to the conservation and protection of the environment, as well as the right to self-determination, are recognized at the UN level in treaties and declarations.[91] The court's decision to shut down DAPL based on tribal concerns, specifically relying on the evidence given by tribal experts, can be interpreted as a court-driven initiative towards the conservation and protection of Indigenous Peoples environment and self-determination, in line with international human rights law.

The UNDRIP is currently the most comprehensive international human rights instrument affirming the inherent rights of Indigenous Peoples, and it recognizes the Indigenous rights to the protection and conservation of the environment.

---

87 *Id.*

88 *Id.*

89 *Id* ¶ 17. Tribal experts had expressed concerns in their comments regarding the low detection rate of the leak detection system used at DAPL stating that it was weak and inefficient as the system was not even designed to detect leaks that constituted 1% or less of the pipe's flow rate. This meant that, considering the rate of the oil flow about 25,200 gallons — "could be released continuously, over a long period of time, without detection.

90 *Id.* The pipeline's maximum release time in hours, plus the maximum shutdown response time in hours (based on historic discharge data or in the absence of such historic data, the operator's best estimate), multiplied by the maximum flow rate expressed in barrels per hour (based on the maximum daily capacity of the pipeline), plus the largest line drainage volume after shutdown of the line section(s) in the response zone expressed in barrels (cubic meters).

91 *See* G.A. Res. 61/295, United Nations Declaration on the Rights of Indigenous Peoples art. 26 (Sept. 13, 2007).

> Indigenous peoples have the right to the conservation and protection of the environment and the productive capacity of their lands or territories and resources. States shall establish and implement assistance programs for indigenous peoples for such conservation and protection, without discrimination.[92]

Moreover, the UNDRIP affirms Indigenous Peoples right to self-determination when it says the following:

> Indigenous peoples, in exercising their right to self-determination, have the right to autonomy or self-government in matters relating to their internal and local affairs, as well as ways and means for financing their autonomous functions.[93]

It would be remiss to conclude an analysis of the July 6 ruling without mentioning that in the same ruling, the court still rejected the Tribe's claims based on the NHPA.[94] The Corps did not consider the Tribal Historical Preservation Officer's findings which revealed that the corridor through which the DAPL ran carried 27 graves and 82 cultural features, including significant stone features of the Standing Rock peoples' spiritual ways.[95] As a result, the construction of the DAPL inflicted damage to the said tribal historical sites.[96] The failure of the court to consider the Tribes NHPA claims throughout the DAPL litigation highlights the flagrant disregard for Indigenous Peoples cultural heritage by State and private actors.

An agency under NEPA is obligated to prepare a detailed, "comprehensive EIS if its proposal constitutes a major Federal action significantly affecting the quality of the human environment.[97] No matter how detailed the EA[98] submitted is, it can never substitute for an EIS; therefore, the submission of an

---

[92] *Id.* at art 29.

[93] *Id.* at art 4 *see also* art 3, and 5.

[94] National Historic Preservation Act, Section 6 requiring a federal agency to consider the effect of its "undertakings" on property of historical significance, which includes property of cultural or religious significance to Indian tribe.

[95] Chip Colwell, *How the archaeological review behind the Dakota Access Pipeline went wrong?* THE CONVERSATION, https://theconversation.com/how-the-archaeological-review-behind-the-dakota-access-pipeline-went-wrong-67815 (last visited 06/28/2020).

[96] *Standing Rock*, 2020.

[97] *Taxpayers of Mich. Against Casinos v. Norton*, 433 F.3d 852 (D.C. Cir. 2006).

[98] *See supra* note 68.

EA did not exempt the Corps from the obligation to prepare an EIS.[99] Therefore, the Corps' failure to prepare an EIS for the pipeline was a "serious" violation of NEPA because it allowed the Corps to make a significant decision without legally required procedures designed to ensure informed decision-making and public accountability.[100]

In November 2015, Dakota Access LLC prepared a 983 paged Environmental Assessment for the Corps. The EA included a section of 'Affected Environment and Potential Impacts of the Proposed Action and No Action Alternative.[101] Most of what was covered under this section is beyond the scope of this chapter. For the purposes of this discussion, the focus will be on the Corps' assessment of Cultural and Historic Resources and Native American Consultations under the said section. Class II/Class III cultural resource inventory of the proposed Project Area was carried out on the flowage easement and federally-owned lands traversed by the Project Area.[102] The background studies determined that only one previously recorded site is mapped within the portion of the 400-ft survey corridor that traverses the flowage easements.[103] The identified site, also known as the Buford-Trenton Irrigation System (BTIS), is a National Register nominated cultural resource consisting of a pumping plant, main canal, and associated irrigation components.[104] The prepared EA indicated that the DAPL project intersects with only one irrigation canal of the BTIS, and impacts to the feature would be avoided via Horizontal Directional Drilling (HDD) to ensure the integrity of construction design for these historic-age features is preserved.[105] Eight other cultural resources were identified based on a previous cultural resource survey; these were reported to be entirely avoided as the proposed HDD workspace would be positioned beyond the mapped boundaries of these sites.[106]

---

99 *Anderson v. Evans*, 371 F. 3d. 475, 494 (9th Cir 2004).

100 Standing Rock Sioux Tribe v. U.S. Army Corps of Engineers Amended Consolidated Brief of Standing Rock Sioux tribe, Cheyenne River Sioux Tribe, Oglala Sioux Tribe, and Yankton Sioux Tribe Regarding Remedy.

101 DAKOTA ACCESS LLC, *Draft Environmental Assessment Dakota Access Pipeline Project Crossings of Flowage Easements and Federal Lands*, (2015), https://usace.contentdm.oclc.org/digital/collection/p16021coll7/id/2426./

102 *Id.* at 57.

103 *Id.* at 56.

104 *Id.*

105 *Id.*

106 *Id.*

A Class II/Class III Archaeological Survey was also conducted within a 400-foot environmental survey and resulted in the documentation of one new archaeological site, a singular lithic flake in isolated contexts and is not eligible for listing in the National Register of Historic Places.[107] According to the prepared EA, there were no other previously or newly recorded historic properties identified on or near the flowage easements that are crossed by the Project.[108] It is important not to ignore that consultation with federally-recognized tribal entities for the portions of the Project area defined for the EA has not been concluded.

Archeologists view the world through the lens of science and history while they lack the expertise and knowledge to identify traditional properties which are grounded in identity, culture, spirituality.[109] As a result, archeological reviews rarely consider how Indigenous Peoples view their own heritage unless they sincerely seek tribal input through consultation.[110] The NHPA requires federal lead agencies to assess the effects of permitted actions on historic properties.[111] Historic properties are defined in the NHPA as prehistoric and historic archaeological sites, standing structures, or other historic resources listed in or eligible for listing in the National Register of Historic Places.[112] Regrettably, some of the tribal cultural sites are not registered in the Register of Historic Places.

Not only did the Archeologists and agents who carried out the DAPL EA fail to seriously consider input or consultation with the tribes, but they did not even indicate the presence of the Standing Rock reservation, which is a half-

---

[107] *Id.*

[108] *Id.*

[109] Colwell, *supra* note 95.

[110] *Id.*

[111] Section 106 of the National Historic Preservation Act; The head of any Federal agency having direct or indirect jurisdiction over a proposed Federal or federally assisted undertaking in any State and the head of any Federal department or independent agency having authority to license any undertaking shall, prior to the approval of the expenditure of any Federal funds on the undertaking or prior to the issuance of any license, as the case may be, take into account the effect of the undertaking on any district, site, building, structure, or object that is included in or eligible for inclusion in the National Register. The head of any such Federal agency shall afford the Advisory Council on Historic Preservation established under Title II of this Act a reasonable opportunity to comment with regard to such undertaking.

[112] *Id.*

mile away, despite numerous letters written to the Corps about the tribes' concerns with the project.[113]

An independent archeological review was conducted by Mentz-Wilson Consultants, LLC, a company run by Mr. Tim Mentz Sr., a member of the Hunkpapa and Pa Baksa (Cuthead Dakota) bands of the Standing Rock Sioux Tribe.[114] Mentz Wilson Consultants primarily focuses on conducting archaeological and/or Tribal identification survey work within North and South Dakota, Minnesota, and Iowa.[115] Mr. Mentz was the first certified Tribal Historic Preservation Officer (THPO) for the Standing Rock Sioux Tribe for twelve years and had worked for the Standing Rock Tribe in different capacities, totaling the number of his years working with the tribe to 39.[116] The Mentz Wilson Consultants' archeological review revealed that the corridor through which the DAPL runs carries 27 graves and 82 cultural features, including significant stone features of the Standing Rock peoples' spiritual ways.[117] The Class II/III archeological review, conducted by the DAPL consultants, did not identify these religious and cultural sites that would be affected by the DAPL construction because the archeologists lacked a connection that the Standing Rock tribe has to its spiritual walk of life.[118]

Table 2 below shows sites of significant cultural and historic value to the Standing Rock and other tribes that were ignored by the archeologists who carried out the archeological review.[119] Even though some of the sites listed on the table below are not immediately in the pipeline's corridor, expert evidence shows that they are still susceptible to the destructive effects of the DAPL construction activities, which include but are not limited to the movement of heavy equipment, moving and stringing of pipe.

---

113 Declaration of Dave Archambault II in Support of Motion for Preliminary Injunction, *Standing Rock Sioux Tribe v. U.S. Army Corps of Eng'rs,* No. 16-1534 (JEB) (D.D.C. Aug. 4, 2016) [hereinafter Archambault Declaration of Aug. 3, 2016.

114 *Standing Rock Sioux Tribe v.* U.S. *Army Corps of Engineers,* Case No. 1:16-cv-1534-JEB: Declaration of Tim Mentz Support of Motion for Injunction. [Hereinafter Mentz].

115 Stern, *supra* note 4.

116 *Id.*

117 Colwell, *supra* note 95.

118 *Id.*

119 Mentz, *supra* note 114.

Table 2. Cultural and Historical Standing Rock Sites.

CULTURAL SITE	SIGNIFICANCE	DISTANCE FROM PIPELINE	RISK OF DESTRUCTION
Iyokaptan Tanka	One of the most important and rare archeological finds in North Dakota Used as measuring stick for leadership, who fasted or vision quested in the "cup" of the Big Dipper to make the ultimate commitment to the people.	75 feet	High
Chante Tinza Wapaha	This site indicates that a pledge was made between two Strong Heart members sharing their vision quest that had a similar purpose to be sealed with prayer when using the coup stick in battle (also contains a grave).	Extends into the pipeline corridor	Very High
Mato Wapiya	This was the Bear Medicine man's presence or fasting area connected to the Strong Heart society. This is an extra-ordinary site where the Bear Medicine Man received his gift of healing.	A few feet from the pipeline corridor	Very High
Itancha	This is a site that brought chiefs and the society leaders together to fast together for unifying their bands or bringing a consolidation of people for protection and making of relatives. There is oral history to this site still remembered by members of the Standing Rock Sioux Tribe.	About 1 Foot	Very High
Grave and Stone Arc	The Arc represents the handle of the Iyokaptan Tanka or Big Dipper. This is a very important site to the Standing Rock Sioux Tribe.	Within the DAPL pipeline	Very High

The Standing Rock Sioux and the Cheyenne River Sioux Tribes have persistently expressed opposition to the pipeline construction, citing the prospect of irreparable damage to cultural sites that would likely result from the construction.[120] Over half a million gallons of oil are pumped through the Missouri and Lake Oahe rivers river a day, risking the water that is central to

[120] Archambault Declaration of Aug. 3, 2016.

the tribes' survival and practice of religious and cultural exercises to contamination in the event of a pipeline leakage.[121]

Despite the fact that tribal members do not have access to all the sites of cultural and historic significance mentioned above (some of these are located on land that is now privately owned), their existence is still very important to the tribes as it forms part of their cultural heritage. When such sites are destroyed, the cultural connection will also be interrupted.[122] Since the commencement of the pipeline, some cultural sites have already been irreparably destroyed after a stretch of land was graded by the DAPL, notwithstanding the protests and opposition to the granting of construction permits and a request for injunctive relief by the tribes.[123]

The other destruction, which was mostly referred to in the legal submissions made to the court, was the religious and cultural heritage of the Standing Rock Sioux Tribe and Cheyenne River Sioux Tribe near Cannon Ball, North Dakota.[124] Precisely, the submissions indicated that the burial grounds, sacred sites, and historically significant areas on either side of Lake Oahe were at a high risk of irreparable destruction from the construction as they lay either in the direct path of the pipeline or in close vicinity.[125] The affected cultural and religious sites are significant, not only to the Standing Rock Sioux and the Cheyenne River Sioux Tribes, but also to the Mandan and the Arikara tribes.[126] The submission by the tribes further stated that gravesites and burial grounds were located in areas that would be disturbed by construction both during the preparatory stages of construction on the ground surface and once the pipeline was constructed below the ground.[127] These gravesites and burial lands are of heightened cultural and religious significance to the tribes.[128]

II. The Destruction of Tribal Cultural Property is Cultural Genocide

In her chapter, Beatrice Hamilton noted that when Raphael Lemkin invented the term "genocide," he envisaged safeguarding against much more than just the destruction of a nation owing to coordinated plans to carry out mass

---

[121] *Id.*
[122] Haydee J, *supra* note 9 at 166.
[123] *Id.*
[124] *Id.*
[125] *Id.*
[126] *Standing Rock, supra* note, 12.
[127] *Id.*
[128] *Id.*

destruction or killing of a nation's members.[129] The intentional destruction of a nations' culture is one of the factors that Lemkin anticipated would fall under the purview of the crime of genocide.[130]

The inclusion of a collectively shared aspect: culture, as an element of an international crime, seemed like a departure from the narrative that defines state-based domestic and international law, based on the premise that human rights violations are adjudged as distinct encroachment on individual liberties and rights.[131] Ana Vrdoljak argues that the prevailing internationally recognized definition of genocide undermines the reasoning that the destruction of collective identity is the fundamental driving force behind genocidal activities aimed at destroying the group as reflected in the Convention on the Prevention and Punishment of the Crime of Genocide (Genocide Convention).[132]

The final draft of the Genocide Convention in 1948 adopted a state-based international law crime that did not encompass the intentional destruction of a nation's culture.[133] The Genocide Convention limits the scope of the features of Genocide to biological and physical aspects.

> ...acts committed with intent to destroy, in whole or in part, a national, ethnical, racial or religious group, as such:
>
> a) Killing members of the group;
>
> b) Causing serious bodily or mental harm to members of the group;
>
> c) Deliberately inflicting on the group conditions of life calculated to bring about its physical destruction in whole or in part;
>
> d) Imposing measures intended to prevent births within the group;
>
> e) Forcibly transferring children of the group to another group.

---

[129] Dr Rudolf C Ryser, Amelia Marchand, and Deborah Presentation, *Cultural Genocide CLE*, WORLD PEACE THROUGH LAW SECTION OF THE WASHINGTON STATE BAR ASSOCIATION, (April 3 2020). https://search.informit.com.au/documentSummary;dn=273886063150734;res=IELIAC;type=pdf.

[130] *Id.*

[131] *Id.*

[132] Ana Filipa Vrdojak *Human Rights and Genocide: The Work Lauterpacht and Lemkim in Morden International Law* 20 EJIL 1163-94. 4 (2009).

[133] UN GENERAL ASSEMBLY, Convention on the Prevention and Punishment of the Crime of Genocide, 9 December 1948, United Nations, Treaty Series, VOL. 78, P. 277.

The above definition does not include the destruction of culture and its attributes, as suggested in Lemkin's initial conceptualization of the crime of genocide. Up to this date, there is widespread speculation among scholars as to why Lemkin, who was involved in the drafting of the Genocide Convention, abandoned his commitment to the cultural dimension of the crime, an aspect which seemed to have immensely influenced his original view on genocide.[134] One prominent argument made is that the Genocide Convention was an expression of political forces; the framers did not want to criminalize their own behavior, and hence they were not comfortable with including cultural genocide in the same category akin to the Holocaust. For example, the Soviet Union was opposed to the inclusion of political groups in light of the absence of consensus on what constituted a group and its destruction.[135]

Various scholarly attempts have been made to define cultural genocide, stemming from the insight provided by Lemkin's conceptualization of the crime of genocide; Dr. Rudolf Ryser, an eminent Indigenous Rights scholar, defines cultural genocide as follows:

> The intentional and coordinated effort to eradicate the foundations of life for nations with the aim of annihilating the groups themselves primarily by substituting the dominating influence of a controlling power.[136]

Comparably, Lawrence Davison defines cultural genocide as "the purposeful weakening and ultimate destruction of cultural values and practices of feared out-groups."[137] While the current international human rights law framework does not define cultural genocide, the same body of law recognizes the intrinsic value culture has to a people, and has thus incorporated this right in various instruments. The Universal Declaration of Human Rights[138] and the

---

[134] Leora Bilsky and Rachael Klagsbrun, *The return of Cultural Genocide*? EUROPEAN JOURNAL OF INTERNATIONAL LAW, Volume 29, Issue 2, at 373–96 (May 2018).

[135] Lindsay Kingston, *The Destruction of Identity, Cultural Genocide and Indigenous Peoples* JOURNAL OF HUMAN RIGHTS 14 (1) (2015).

[136] Ryser, *supra* note 129.

[137] Lawrence Davison, CULTURAL GENOCIDE, New Brunswick, NJ: Rutgers University Press (2012).

[138] UN GENERAL ASSEMBLY, Universal Declaration of Human Rights, 10 DECEMBER 1948, 217 A (III) ART 27(1). says "everyone has the right freely to participate in the cultural life of the community, to enjoy the arts and to share in scientific advancement and its benefits".

ICESCR[139] recognize everyone's right to freely participate in the cultural life of the community. The latter further enjoins State Parties to take steps to achieve the full realization of the right to culture, such steps being necessary for the conservation, development, and diffusion of culture.[140]

The United Nations Educational, Scientific and Cultural Organization (UNESCO) adopted a convention to protect Intangible Cultural Heritage, which includes the practices, representations, and expressions, knowledge, skills –as well as the instruments, objectives and spaces associated therewith.[141] For Indigenous Peoples, intangible cultural heritage is usually in the form of traditional knowledge, which is gained as a result of their association with the environment.

The UNDRIP recognizes the right of Indigenous peoples to cultural practices as follows:

> Indigenous peoples have the right to practice and revitalize their cultural traditions and customs. This includes the right to maintain, protect and develop the past, present and future manifestations of their cultures, such as archaeological and historical sites, artifacts, designs, ceremonies, technologies and visual and performing arts and literature.[142]

The UNDRIP further requires States to provide redress through effective mechanisms, which may include restitution, developed in conjunction with indigenous peoples, with respect to their cultural, intellectual, religious, and spiritual property taken without their free, prior and informed consent or in violation of their laws, traditions and customs.[143] The scope and elements of the principle of free, prior and informed consent shall be discussed in the final part of this chapter.

---

[139] UN General Assembly, International Covenant on Economic, Social and Cultural Rights, 16 December 1966, United Nations, Treaty Series, vol. 993, p. 3, Art 15.
[140] *Id.* at Art 15 (2).
[141] The United Nations Educational, Scientific and Cultural Organization (UNESCO) Basic Texts of the 2003 Convention for the Safeguarding of the Intangible Cultural Heritage.
[142] UN General Assembly, United Nations Declaration on the Rights of Indigenous Peoples: resolution / adopted by the General Assembly, 2 October 2007, A/RES/61, Article 11.
[143] Art 11 (2).

During the International NGO Conference on Discrimination Against Indigenous Populations convened in Geneva, Switzerland in 1977, Indigenous leaders expressed their wish to have the crime of genocide include the intentional and systematic destruction of societies.[144] This line of thinking resurfaced 30 years later, during the negotiations for the draft UNDRIP, where provision on cultural genocide and genocide was suggested.[145] The draft construed cultural genocide as the elimination of a group culture as a whole, as a collective and individual right not to be subjected to ethnocide and cultural genocide. The absence of an internationally recognized legal definition of cultural genocide makes it difficult to prevent and punish acts of violence directed at indigenous cultures. However, some scholars have expressed optimism over the current lack of codification to cultural genocide as it may provide sufficient space to reshape and adapt it to the task of cultural protection, in view of all the suggestions made over the years regarding this topic.[146]

While the value that Indigenous Peoples attach to their culture cannot be overemphasized, the ulterior goal of cultural violence is the disappearance of Indigenous communities.[147]

Indigenous peoples derive their existence from the land and all its diversity. The relentless opposition to the DAPL by the Standing Rock Sioux and Cheyenne River Sioux Tribes is testimony to the protective relationship between Indigenous peoples and the land. When functional ecological systems in Indigenous societies are disrupted or broken, their health and culture are also impacted, causing ripple effects that may affect cultural and socio-economic stability.[148]

According to Tinker, cultural genocide destroys the cultural structures of existence that give Indigenous people a sense of holistic, communal integrity.[149] Cultural genocide diminishes the freedom of Indigenous Peoples

---

144 INTERNATIONAL NGO CONFERENCE ON DISCRIMINATION AGAINST INDIGENOUS POPULATIONS IN THE AMERICAS, Geneva, Switzerland, (1977).

145 *Elisa Novic,* From 'Genocide' to 'Persecution': 'Cultural Genocide' and Contemporary International Criminal Law in Cultural Rights as Collective Rights, *STUDIES IN INTERCULTURAL HUMAN RIGHTS,* (2016).

146 Edward C Luck, *Cultural Genocide and the Protection of Cultural Heritage,* J. PAUL GETTY TRUST OCCASIONAL PAPERS IN CULTURAL HERITAGE POLICY 2 (2018).

147 Ryser, *supra* note 129.

148 *Id.*

149 George Tinker E, MISSIONARY CONQUEST: THE GOSPEL AND NATIVE AMERICAN CULTURAL GENOCIDE, Fortress Press, (1993).

to practice cultural traditions and live out their lives in culturally appropriate patterns. It effectively destroys a people by eroding both their self-esteem and the relationships that bind them together as a community.[150] While cultural genocide is often a direct result of physical genocide, systematic and structural practices, not always consciously designed to cause destruction of culture, can also result in cultural genocide.[151] Indeed, conscious intent remains an important element; however, cultural genocide can still occur at a systematic level and is largely subliminal.[152] Accordingly, cultural genocide proponents argue that proof of intent should not be used as a litmus test for determining whether cultural genocide occurred since the consequences of structural violence on Indigenous Peoples' culture can still be severe, regardless of direct intention.[153]

As demonstrated earlier in this chapter, allowing the Dakota Access Pipeline to transport oil under Lake Oahe did not only affect the tribe's fishing rights or hunting rights under the Treaty of 1851, it also adversely impacted the fundamental practices, emotional experiences, and identity of a culture.[154] Kingston suggests the following three issues to be reconsidered as part of a serious discussion to address the threat that indigenous cultures continue to face;

1) International recognition of cultural genocide,

2) framing and advocacy approaches, and

3) renewing indigenous self-determination.

This section will focus only on the third aspect: renewing Indigenous self-determination, particularly when decisions are made regarding developmental projects which may destroy Indigenous peoples' cultures. The focus is on ways of renewing Indigenous self-determination whenever there is a project like DAPL so that the risk of cultural genocide can be minimized on tribes. I further explore the notion of tribal consultation as an internationally recognized right; its essential components, namely, free and prior informed consent, participation, and Indigenous data sovereignty.

---

150 *Id.*

151 Kingston, *supra* note 135.

152 *Id.*

153 *Id.*

154 TREATY OF FORT LARAMIE 1851.

Over the years, international law has evolved to respond to the increasing conflict arising from resource extraction and large-scale development projects on lands occupied by Indigenous peoples.[155] Consultation of Indigenous Peoples in decision-making processes that affect them, especially on matters relating to land and natural resources, is a strongly emerging and widely recognized right.[156]

Indigenous Peoples globally are known to have a deep connection to their lands which plays a central cultural, social, and economic role within their communities. The two main international human rights instruments guaranteeing the rights of Indigenous Peoples currently are the International Labor Organization Convention 169, and the UNDRIP prescribes a framework of consultation and participation of Indigenous Peoples. Article 19 of the UNDRIP states:

> States shall consult and cooperate in good faith with the indigenous peoples concerned through their own representative institutions in order to obtain their free, prior and informed consent before adopting and implementing legislative or administrative measures that may affect them.[157]

While using different wording, ILO Convention 169 enshrines a consultation and participation framework that is considered complementary to that of the UNDRIP. A comprehensive framework for consultation and participation of Indigenous Peoples is laid down in Article 6 of the ILO Convention 169, which says:

> a) consult the peoples concerned, through appropriate procedures and in particular through their representative institutions, whenever consideration is being given to legislative or administrative measures which may affect them directly;

---

155 S.J Rombouts, HAVING A SAY: INDIGENOUS PEOPLES, INTERNATIONAL LAW AND FREE, PRIOR AND INFORMED CONSENT, Wolf Legal Publishers, 414-15 (2014). Bas Rombouts, *The Evolution of Indigenous Peoples' Consultation Rights Under the ILO and UN Regimes: A Comparative Assessment of Participation, Consultation, and Consent Norms Incorporated in ILO Convention No. 169 and the UN Declaration on the Rights of Indigenous Peoples and Their Application by the Inter-American Court of Human Rights in the Saramaka and Sarayaku Judgments.* 53 STAN. J. INT'L L. 169,197-200 (2017).

156 *Id.*

157 *Id.* art 19.

b) establish means by which these peoples can freely participate, to at least the same extent as other sectors of the population, at all levels of decision-making in elective institutions and administrative and other bodies responsible for policies and programs which concern them;

c) establish means for the full development of these peoples' own institutions and initiatives, and in appropriate cases, provide the resources necessary for this purpose.

d) consultations carried out in application of this Convention shall be undertaken, in good faith and a form appropriate to the circumstances, with the objective of achieving agreement or consent to the proposed measures.

The ILO Convention 169 is dedicated to restoring and maintaining Indigenous Peoples' identities which were interrupted by assimilationist colonial policies. To achieve this goal, the ILO Convention 169 promotes the participation of Indigenous Peoples in decision-making processes that affect them. The consultation framework is further explained in Article 7, paragraph 1:

> The peoples concerned shall have the right to decide their own priorities for the process of development as it affects their lives, beliefs, institutions and spiritual well-being and the lands they occupy or otherwise use, and to exercise control, to the extent possible, over their own economic, social and cultural development. In addition, they shall participate in the formulation, implementation and evaluation of plans and programs for national and regional development, which may affect them directly.

Since its adoption, only twenty-three countries have ratified the ILO Convention 196. The US is among the countries that have pledged to protect the human rights of their large indigenous populations but are yet to sign the Convention.[158] Comparably, even though the US, along with Australia, New Zealand, Canada, initially refused to sign the UNDRIP, fearing that the autonomy it recognized for Indigenous Peoples was problematic and would undermine the sovereignty of their own states, these states later supported the UNDRIP.

---

[158] UNDRIP, *supra* note 142.

In addition to laying down the general Indigenous Peoples consultation norms, the ILO Convention 169 enshrines targeted consultation provisions. Of relevance to this is Part II of the ILO Convention 169, which extensively acknowledges Indigenous Peoples' collective rights to land and resources rights and the importance of the national legal system recognizing and protecting these.[159] Article 15 provides:

> The rights of the peoples concerned to the natural resources pertaining to their lands shall be specially safeguarded. These rights include the right of these peoples to participate in the use, management and conservation of these resources.

Both the UNDRIP and the ILO Convention 169 have affirmed the right to participation and consultation as well as the rights to land resources and resources.[160] The ILO Convention 169 is legally binding, yet the US did not sign it, making the UNDRIP the instrument from which the USA's international obligation to consult can be derived, and because it is not legally binding, arguably the US commitment to the principles enshrined in it remains minimal.[161]

III. Indigenous Data Sovereignty in the context of Indigenous Peoples Consultation

A fast-emerging international law norm, Indigenous Peoples Data Sovereignty, refers to "the right of a nation to govern the collection, ownership, and application of its own data."[162] Due to its multidimensional nature, Indigenous data sovereignty addresses several issues pertinent to Indigenous Peoples where data use, collection and application are involved.[163] Indigenous data encompasses information, knowledge and data (about their peoples, resources and environments, and collective cultural knowledge and belongings) that is collected by governments, institutions and external

---

159 Rombouts *supra* note 155.
160 For example, the frequency of terms like "aspirational" and "non-binding" by the US governments' officials in reference to the UNDRIP is cited as an attempt to exempt itself from any legal responsibility to the UNDRIP.
161 *Id.*
162 D. Rodriguez-Lonebear and S.C. Rainie S.C, *US Indigenous Data Sovereignty founding documents*, (2016), http://usindigenousdata.arizona.edu/about-us-.
163 Kukutai, *supra* note 1.

individuals.[164] Such data are intrinsic to Indigenous Peoples' capacity and capability to advance their human rights and responsibilities to all of creation.[165]

For the purpose of the present chapter, Indigenous data sovereignty shall be presented as a strategic framework to advance Indigenous self-determination, particularly in cultural heritage issues.[166] As an advocacy movement, Indigenous data sovereignty strengthens the capacity of Indigenous Peoples to exercise their political right to self-determination in an era where government policy is "data-driven."[167] In this section, I argue that Indigenous data sovereignty advances the right to self-determination, particularly in situations involving the consultation of Indigenous Peoples prior to the commencement of the so-called high-priority infrastructure projects.

The right to self-determination is a moral right inherent to individuals and collective groups who constitute a people. All peoples have a political right to govern themselves autonomously and to freely consent to political arrangements with other governments.[168] Various international law instruments recognize the right to self-determination as a fundamental principle, including the Charter of the United Nations,[169] the ICCPR,[170] and the ICESCR.[171]

---

[164] *Care Principles for Indigenous Data Governance.* The increasing convergence of technology infrastructure and digital connectivity has raised the value of data across the globe. https://static1.squarespace.com/static/5d3799de845604000199cd24/t/5d79c383e904c741c9e9cd86/1568260995760/CARE+Principles+for+Indigenous+Data+Governance_FINAL_Sept+06+2019.pdf (last visited November 26 2020).

[165] *Id.*

[166] *Id.*

[167] *Id.*

[168] Frank Przetacznik, *The Basic Collective Human Right to Self Determination of Peoples and Nations as a Prerequisite for Peace*, 8 NYLS JOURNAL OF HUMAN RIGHTS: 1 (1990).

[169] UN GENERAL ASSEMBLY, International Covenant on Civil and Political Rights, 16 December 1966, United Nations, Treaty Series, vol. 999, 171, ART 1, "All people have the right of self-determination. By virtue of that they freely determine their political status and freely determine their political status and freely pursue their economic, social and cultural development."

[170] *Id.*

[171] UN GENERAL ASSEMBLY, International Covenant on Economic, Social and Cultural Rights, 16 December 1966, United Nations, Treaty Series, vol. 993, 3, The right of self-determination has also been recognized in other international and regional human rights instruments such as Part VII of the Helsinki Final Act 1975 and Article 20 of the African Charter on Human and Peoples' Rights as well as the Declaration on the Granting of Independence to Colonial Territories and Peoples. It has been endorsed by

The international expression of self-determination did not include Indigenous Peoples as it was only reserved for internationally recognized nation-states.[172] Many Indigenous Peoples are sub-groups within these nation-states but without international recognition.[173] The scope and meaning of Indigenous Peoples' self-determination remain a hotly contested topic among scholars.

The UNDRIP is the first international human rights instrument that expressly recognizes the right of the Indigenous Peoples to self-determination;

> "Indigenous peoples have the right to self-determination. By virtue of that right they freely determine their political status and freely pursue their economic, social and cultural development." Self-determination for Indigenous Peoples is generally perceived as a right to self-governance within the framework of the state in addition to a right to participate effectively in that framework.[174]

The positivist statist centered approach to self-determination argues that Indigenous Peoples do not have their separate status under international law but are subordinate to local surrounding nation-states.[175] Conversely, the people-centered approach to self-determination represents the view that Indigenous Peoples as a new locus of subjectivity in international law.[176] The UNDRIP arguably supports the positivist approach to self-determination as it closes with a chapter that requires Indigenous Peoples to give way to the rights of the State in the exercise of their rights envisaged in the declaration:

---

the International Court of Justice. Furthermore, the scope and content of the right of self-determination has been elaborated upon by the United Nations Human Rights Committee and Committee on the Elimination of Racial Discrimination as well as international jurists and human rights experts.

[172] INDIAN COUNTRY TODAY, *What Is Indigenous Self Determination and When Does It Apply?*, https://indiancountrytoday.com/archive/what-is-indigenous-self-determination-and-when-does-it-apply-xmO_BGShT0mVMpLh7IC-c (last visited July 25,2020).

[173] *Id.*

[174] *See* S James Anaya, INDIGENOUS PEOPLES IN INTERNATIONAL LAW (2004), 104–06 (distinguishing between constitutive and ongoing self-determination).

[175] Fransesca Panzironi, *Indigenous Peoples Right to Self Determination and Development Policy* (Thesis submitted to fulfil the requirements for the award of Doctor of Philosophy Faculty University of Sydney).

[176] *Id.*

> Nothing in this Declaration may be interpreted as implying for any State, people, group or person any right to engage in any activity or to perform any act contrary to the Charter of the United Nations or construed as authorizing or encouraging any action which would dismember or impair, totally or in part, the territorial integrity or political unity of sovereign and independent States.

Comparably, the ILO Convention 169 does not separate the use of the term 'peoples' with reference to Indigenous Peoples;

> The use of the term peoples in this Convention shall not be construed as having any implications as regards the rights which may attach to the term under international law.

In light of the persistent controversy and absence of consensus regarding the admissibility and legitimacy of the right to self-determination of Indigenous Peoples, it is important to adopt an approach to self-determination that shapes and maintains the relationships between Indigenous People and the state. A relational approach to self-determination was proposed by Benedict Kingsbury.[177] It aims to reconstruct the norm within the realm of international law and facilitate an agreement on the political-legal formulation of the indigenous right to self-determination.[178] Francesca Panzironi proposes the acknowledgment and integration of indigenous knowledge systems as well as the adoption of the principle of FPIC within the design, implementation and evaluation of development policies.[179] This approach constitutes the 'fundamental elements for the implementation of a freedom-oriented understanding of self-determined development policies.'[180] Panzironi's approach is in line with the principle of Indigenous data sovereignty, which advocates for culturally sensitive data collection and processing system while requiring that Indigenous Peoples be consulted in situations when data about them is collected.[181] In the United States, consultation requirement stems from the Federal government's trust responsibility and is reflected in various EO's and statutory provisions mentioned above.[182]

---

[177] *Id.*
[178] *Id.*
[179] Panzironi, *supra* note 102.
[180] *Id.*
[181] *Id*
[182] *Id.*

Through promoting the consultation of Indigenous People and application of their knowledge, Indigenous data sovereignty is consistent with a model of self-determination that facilitates the reconstruction of the terms and dynamics of the relational interactions between the state and Indigenous People.[183] More so, data sovereignty fosters the development of legal principles that regulate enduring relations between indigenous peoples and states.[184] Indigenous data sovereignty provides for a process of relational engagement between the affected tribes and the developmental practitioners so that Indigenous cultural perspectives can be incorporated in the archeological review and also their consent be obtained before the commencement of the pipeline.

This relational approach to self-determination is also enshrined in the UNDRIP, particularly when it comes to the development or use of their lands or territories and other resources by introducing the principle of free prior and informed consent.

> States shall consult and cooperate in good faith with the indigenous peoples concerned through their own representative institutions in order to obtain their free and informed consent prior to the approval of any project affecting their lands or territories and other resources, particularly in connection with the development, utilization or exploitation of mineral, water or other resources.[185]

The UNDRIP further enjoins States to take appropriate measures to mitigate the adverse environmental, economic, social and cultural, or spiritual impact.[186] In situations where the Indigenous Peoples' religious and spiritual property is taken without their free, prior, and informed consent in violation of their laws, traditions and customs, the UNDRIP requires States to provide effective mechanisms of compensation.[187]

The principle of Indigenous data sovereignty responds to the historical lack of participation of Indigenous Peoples in their data processes that subsequently threaten tribal self-determination.[188] When data about Indigenous Peoples is collected and stored by non-indigenous parties such as

---

[183] Tsosie, *supra* note 2.

[184] *Id.*

[185] *Id.* Art 33(2).

[186] *Id.* Art 32 (3).

[187] *Id.* Art 11 (2).

[188] *Id.*

researchers, federal or state agencies, such data are used for the priorities of those parties, and access is determined by the rules of those governments or institutions.[189]

As a remedy, indigenous data sovereignty is designed to enable Indigenous Peoples to reclaim control of their data[190] In the context of DAPL, the first step towards realizing Indigenous Peoples' data sovereignty would be through consultation with Indigenous Peoples prior to the commencement of projects. A proper consultation process would identify and place the relevant Indigenous leaders (for example, Tribal Historical Preservation Officer) at the forefront in collecting information regarding their cultural heritage, religious beliefs, traditional practices, and the legal rights, which could be affected by the construction of the pipeline.[191] The affected Indigenous Peoples would participate in the decision-making process to decide the route of the pipeline that would leave their cultural heritage uninterrupted. Indigenous People would finally maintain geographic jurisdiction over digitized data pertaining to the entire process.[192]

IV. Recommendations

1. Implementing the Principles of Data Sovereignty in Consultation to safeguard Indigenous Cultural Heritage

In this section, I will make recommendations prescribing the integration of the principles of Indigenous data sovereignty to create harmony between high priority infrastructure projects and Indigenous Peoples cultures. First, I present the principle of FPIC as a procedural right element of data sovereignty as it deals mainly with the administrative process that agencies consulting Indigenous Peoples should follow.[193] Further, I argue that there is a substantive right element of data sovereignty in the form of the CARE principles, which define the scope of the rights of Indigenous People in relation to their data and the corresponding obligations of external entities or

---

[189] Tsosie *supra*, note 2.

[190] Stephanie Russo, Carroll, *Indigenous Data Governance: Strategies from United States Native Nations*. DATA SCIENCE JOURNAL, 18(1) (2019).

[191] US DEPARTMENT OF THE INTERIOR BUREAU OF LAND MANAGEMENT TRIBAL CONSULTATION https://www.blm.gov/services/tribal-consultation (last visited December 13, 2020).

[192] ICELANDIC HUMAN RIGHTS CENTER, *supra* note 190.

[193] FOOD AND AGRICULTURE ORGANIZATION OF THE UNITED NATIONS (FAO), *Free and Prior Informed Consent, an Indigenous Peoples Right and a good Practice for Local Communities: Manual for Project Practitioners*, (2016) http://www.fao.org/3/a-i6190e.pdf.

individuals when handling such data.[194] CARE entails collective benefit, authority to control, responsibility, and ethics.[195] The procedural and substantive elements of data sovereignty are interrelated because the CARE principles can be adequately realized only if the steps for implementing FPIC are properly followed.[196]

a. Free and Prior Informed Consent

FPIC has become a widely recognized principle protected by international human rights standards and is embedded in the Indigenous Peoples right to self-determination, which allows them to freely pursue their economic, social, and cultural development.[197] In situations where large-scale development projects pose a significant threat to Indigenous Peoples, it is becoming a recognized international law norm that FPIC is a mandatory requirement.[198] FPIC enhances the effective participation of indigenous people in decisions that affect their lives while protecting Indigenous Peoples' right to self-determination.[199] The United Nations Permanent Forum on Indigenous Issues (UNPFII), the UN Food and Agriculture Organization (FAO), and the Working Group on Indigenous Peoples have provided guidance on the elements of FPIC and how it should be implemented.[200]

FPIC requires consent to be given voluntarily and without coercion, intimidation or manipulation; therefore, it is free.[201] Consent usually ceases to

---

194 Substantive law refers to the body of rules that determine the rights and obligations of individuals and collective bodies.

195 Stephanie Russo Carroll and Jane Anderson, *Working with the CARE Principles: Operationalizing Indigenous Data Governance, https://www.adalovelaceinstitute.org/operationalising-indigenous-data-governance/* (last visited November 29, 2020).

196 ICELANDIC HUMAN RIGHTS CENTER, *Substantive Human Rights,* https://www.humanrights.is/en/human-rights-education-project/human-rights-concepts-ideas-and-fora/substantive-human-rights (last visited December 15, 2020).

197 *Id.* Art 11 (2).

198 Rombouts, *supra* note 155.

199 *Id.*

200 FOOD AND AGRICULTURE ORGANIZATION OF THE UNITED *NATIONS* (FAO), *Free and Prior Informed Consent, an Indigenous Peoples Right and a good Practice for Local Communities: Manual for Project Practitioners,* 2016 http://www.fao.org/3/a-i6190e.pdf (last visited November 29, 2020).

201 UNPFII, *Rep. of the International Workshop on Methodologies Regarding Free, Prior and Informed Consent and Indigenous Peoples,* U.N. Doc. E/C.19/2005/3 (Feb. 17, 2005) (presented at the fourth session of the United Nations Permanent Forum on Indigenous Issues in New York on May 16–27, 2005).

be free when offers, pleas, or bids do turn into forms of more "hostile" coercion like very subtle forms of bribery.[202] Indigenous communities from whom the consent is sought need to be the ones in charge of the consent process, free from any conditions imposed by outsiders.[203] As the right holders, Indigenous Peoples are the ones to determine the process, timeline, location, and decision-making structure.[204] The practitioners need to offer information about the project transparently and objectively at the request of Indigenous people.[205]

The element of prior means that consent has to be obtained before the authorization or commencement of the project at the very early stages.[206] Ample time needs to be provided for the Indigenous community concerned to understand, access, and analyze information on the proposed activity. The decision-making process of the Indigenous peoples will determine the amount of time needed. The information should be provided before the initiation of the activity, at the beginning or initiation of an activity, process or phase of implementation. If the Indigenous people propose a decision-making timeframe, it has to be respected as it reflects the time needed to understand and evaluate the activity under consideration.[207]

Informed applies to the nature of engagement and type of information the Indigenous people should be furnished with in order to decide on whether to give consent or not. The information provided to the Indigenous Peoples needs to consistent, accurate, and transparent. Information also needs to be delivered in a culturally appropriate format, including a language that the Indigenous People understand.[208]

Informed consent also needs to include both negative and positive aspects of the proposed activity after a preliminary assessment of the possible economic, social, cultural, and environmental impacts. Additionally, informed consent needs to be complete by way of giving full details about the proposed project, its reversibility, purpose and scope, and this information has to be accessible by all groups and communities to be potentially affected. It has to be delivered in a

---

202 Rombouts, *supra* note 155.

203 FAO, *supra* note 206.

204 *Id.*

205 *Id.*

206 *Id.*

207 *Id.*

208 *Id.*

culturally sensitive manner.[209] Finally, the Indigenous Peoples concerned need to be informed on an ongoing basis.[210]

b. The CARE Principles

A very significant component of Indigenous Data Sovereignty are the CARE principles: a set of global principles for the governance of Indigenous data.[211] The CARE principles are designed to guide the inclusion of Indigenous Peoples in data governance across contemporary data ecosystems.[212] The CARE principles can be viewed as a substantive right that "empowers Indigenous Peoples by shifting the focus of data governance from solely regulated consultation to value-based relationships that position data approaches within Indigenous cultures and knowledge systems to the benefit of Indigenous Peoples."[213]

The current open data and open science movement's existing principles, FAIR (findable, accessible, interoperable, reusable), place focus primarily on facilitating increased data sharing among entities.[214] Meanwhile, the newly emerging CARE principles countervail the major limitation within the open data and open science movement, namely, the failure to address power differentials and historical contexts.[215] Over the years, the persistent advancement of Indigenous self-determination has awakened aspirations beyond merely procedural data sharing within Indigenous Peoples, hence the assertion of greater control over the application and use of Indigenous data and Indigenous knowledge for collective benefit.[216]

The development of the CARE principles is still a work in progress. As such, the creation of a comprehensive set of guidelines and standards that prescribes how the CARE principles should be implemented in various

---

209 *Id.*

210 *Id.*

211 Stephanie Russo, *et al The CARE Principles for Indigenous Data Governance*, DATA SCIENCE JOURNAL, 19(1), at 43 (2020).

212 *Id.*

213 *Id.*

214 *Id.*

215 *Id.*

216 RDA, INTERNATIONAL INDIGENOUS DATA SOVEREIGNTY INTEREST GROUP, *CARE Principles for Indigenous Data Governance*, (September 2019). https://static1.squarespace.com/static/5d3799de845604000199cd24/t/5d79c383e904c741c9e9cd86/1568260995760/CARE+Principles+for+Indigenous+Data+Governance_FINAL_Sept+06+2019.pdf (last visited November 26, 2020).

contexts or sectors is currently underway. The Global Indigenous Data Alliance (GIDA), the main proponent and working group for the CARE principles, is spearheading the development of guidelines for implementing the CARE principles in the form of the 'Recommended Practice for the Provenance of Indigenous Data'.[217] The anticipated date for the completion of the project is July 2023.[218]

The envisaged objectives for the upcoming Recommended Practice/ guidelines for the implementation of the CARE principles are:

1) To provide the rules by which the provenance of Indigenous Peoples' data should be described and recorded.

2) To outline the core parameters for providing and digitally embedding provenance information for Indigenous Peoples' data.

3) To establish the common descriptors and controlled vocabulary for provenance, including recommendations for metadata fields that can be used across industry sectors, including machine learning (ML) and artificial intelligence (AI) contexts, biodiversity and genomic science innovation and other associated databases.

4) To support proper and appropriate disclosure of originating data information.

5) To support the long-term identification of Indigenous Peoples' data for future use, connecting data to people and place, and when appropriate, supporting future benefit sharing options.[219]

Due to the current absence of guidelines for implementation, there is yet to be a case study that exemplifies the efficacy of implementing the CARE principles in the consultation of Indigenous Peoples in the context of developmental projects like the DAPL. Nonetheless, the CARE principles have thus far been successfully explored in the contexts of scientific

---

[217] INDIGENOUS DATA WORKING GROUP, *Recommended Practice for Provenance of Indigenous Peoples' Data* https://development.standards.ieee.org/myproject-web/public/view.html#pardetail/8382 (last visited November 30, 2020).

[218] *Id.*

[219] *Id.*

data,[220]collections environments, government environments and, most recently, in the development of COVID 19 guidelines.[221]

In order to formulate recommendations that are inspired by the 'CARE principles, I draw on the approach adopted by the GIDA in implementing the CARE principles in developing guidelines for sharing COVID-19 data in June 2020.[222] The COVID-19 data sharing guidelines were designed to advance the Indigenous Peoples' 'authority to control' by recommending that Indigenous People be placed at the forefront to lead and/or participate in designing data systems that involve the collection, analysis, and sharing of Indigenous data.[223]

Applying the above approach in the DAPL context, this chapter recommends the re-conceptualization or re-alignment of the existing laws, regulations, and policies regarding Indigenous Peoples consultation with the CARE principles, namely, collective benefit, authority to control, responsibility, and ethics.[224] Indigenous Peoples need to be included in the process of crafting land development policies so that their religious and cultural beliefs can be included.[225]

As the GIDA highlights, 'Indigenous Peoples' participation in and contribution to the data revolution is dependent on addressing impoverished or absent data and metadata.'[226] In the DAPL context, the archeological review is an example of a set of data that excluded Indigenous Peoples' perspectives which were presented by the Tribal Historical Preservation Officer.[227] The participation of Indigenous Peoples in the data revolution can be enhanced by consulting the affected tribes to understand their cultural

---

220 Carroll, *supra* note 195.

221 RDA COVID-19 INDIGENOUS DATA WG, *Data sharing respecting Indigenous data sovereignty.* In RDA COVID-19 Working Group (2020). Recommendations and guidelines on data sharing. RESEARCH DATA ALLIANCE. https://doi.org/10.15497/rda00052 (Last visited November 30, 2020). The GIDA and RDA created COVID-19 Guidelines for Data Sharing Respecting Indigenous Data Sovereignty. The guidelines promote external investments in Indigenous community-controlled data infrastructures and bidirectional capacity enhancement for information sharing among Indigenous and non-Indigenous entities.

222 *Id.*

223 *Id.*

224 *Id.*

225 Jack F, *Existing Federal Law and the Protection of Sacred Sites Possibilities and Limitations* CULTURAL SURVIVAL QUARTERLY MAGAZINE, https://www.culturalsurvival.org/publications/cultural-survival-quarterly/existing-federal-law-and-protection-sacred-sites (last visited December 1, 2020).

226 INDIGENOUS DATA WORKING GROUP, *supra* note 233.

227 *Id.*

values, religious beliefs, traditional practices, and legal rights, which could be affected by the pipeline.

Until 2023, when the Recommended Practice for Provenance of Indigenous Peoples' Data is finalized to provide a consistent way of implementing the CARE principles, consultation of Indigenous Peoples should be carried out in ways that promote collective benefit, authority to control, responsibility, ethics.

c. Recommendations

The FAO published a manual for project practitioners to follow when implementing FPIC. In the situation of the DAPL construction, the collection and analysis of data were important procedural steps to be taken in view of how the project posed a potential threat to sites religiously and historically important to the Standing Rock Sioux and Cheyenne River Sioux Tribes. The implementation of FPIC varies depending on the specific local context in which a project is to be developed and the nature of the project. If implemented properly, FPIC can be an umbrella principle embodying all the essential elements of consultation: participation, self-determination, and Indigenous data sovereignty. I now outline a five-stage process of implementing FPIC, based on the Manual for Project Practitioners issued by the FAO.

Step 1: Identify Indigenous People Concerned and their Representatives

It was important for the DAPL project proponents to take extensive efforts to identify the Indigenous groups that could be affected by the pipeline project. Information regarding affected groups may be located using the assistance of Indigenous Peoples' self-governance entities; community-based organizations; national or regional confederations, councils and organizations; universities and research institutions; non-profit organizations.[228] Once the affected Indigenous community had been identified, it is important to understand their language, customs, and rights regarding the area to be affected by the pipeline, as well as identify the representatives of these groups. This preliminary identification step process was not adequately followed since there was no mention of the existence of tribes in the EA report.

Step 2: Document Geographic and Demographic Information through Participatory Mapping

The mapping process is designed to identify and record the land usage, natural resources, communication channels, and customary rights of the

---

[228] Food and Agriculture Organization of the United Nations, *supra* note 200.

identified Indigenous groups. Participation of the affected tribes in this process is important. For instance, if the DAPL included the relevant tribes during this process, they would have identified the "non-negotiables" – the sacred, spiritual and cultural sites of the tribes. This stage would also require the project practitioner to identify the relevant legal frameworks or a tribal attorney who would facilitate the engagement of the tribe with outsiders on this issue. In the case of DAPL, a Historical Preservation Officer who understands the history and culture of the tribes would have been the right person for providing guidance.[229]

Step 3: Designing a Participatory Communication Plan and Carry out Iterative Discussions Through Which Project Information will be disclosed in a Transparent Way

To do this, the project practitioners would need to understand the diverse levels of literacy of the affected tribes in order to assess if they can understand the technical aspects of the project. A participatory communication plan would also need to be arranged to provide effective communication. A time and place most convenient for tribes should be picked for meetings. Tribes need to be aware of their rights to accept, partially accept, reject, or choose not to give an opinion on the proposal.[230] The practitioners for the DAPL project did not establish any formal channels of communication with the tribes.

Step 4: Consent, Document Indigenous Peoples' Needs need to be included in the Project, and agree on a Feedback and Complaints Mechanism

This stage requires mutual agreements to be reached by both sides, cognizant of the customary modes of decision making and consensus seeking that work for each tribe. The process also needs to be documented using languages accessible to the tribal members. If there are any additional needs identified during the discussions, they need to be included, including the possible negative effects. Where tribes withhold their consent, the conditions that need to be met for them to give their consent need to be recognized as well if in the event that tribes refuse renegotiation, as we saw during the DAPL, their right to refuse must be respected.[231] Consent of the tribes affected by DAPL was never obtained by the agencies as the tribes refused to participate in a

[229] *Id.*
[230] *Id.*
[231] *Id.*

purported consultation process that did not include historical properties along the entire pipeline route.[232]

Step 5: Conduct Participatory Monitoring and Evaluation of the Agreement

This stage highlights the principle that FPIC is an ongoing process. Communities affected by the project need to be informed on a regular basis about its progress and any new risks discovered. This process also needs to provide the Indigenous Peoples with opportunities to ask questions, raise concerns, and inspect the activities on their land. An effective monitoring process can be ensured by using independent monitors, including the voices of diverse parties affected, providing mechanisms for feedback, and maintaining anonymity where input is requested.[233]

V. Conclusion

The successful implementation of the rights of Indigenous Peoples to prior consultation safeguards their cultural heritage. In the United States, there are EOs, statutes, and precedent from court cases that guide agencies on how to consult with tribal governments prior to approving federal projects that impact Native American cultural heritage. The approval of the DAPL and the subsequent contentious litigation challenging it exemplifies perfectly how Indigenous cultural heritage suffers when the principles of Indigenous consultation are not effectively implemented. Not following proper consultation procedures is one example of the systematic and structural practices that weaken and ultimately destroy the Indigenous cultural values and practices, hence arguably amounts to what scholars refer to as cultural genocide. Indigenous data sovereignty is a rapidly emerging theory that gives Indigenous Peoples the right to govern the collection and ownership of their own data. The principles of data sovereignty can be interpreted as procedural and substantive right elements that can be invoked during and after the process consultation process prior to the commencement of developmental projects like the DAPL to harmonize such projects with Indigenous Peoples cultures.

---

232 *Id.*

233 *Id.*

Bibliography

33 U.S.C. §1344.

33 U.S.C. §403.

30 U.S.C. § 185.

40 C.F.R § 1508.

40 C.F.R § 1508.27(b).

Act of Mar. 2, 1889, ch. 405, 25 Stat. 888.

Allied-Signal, Inc. v. U.S. Nuclear Regulatory Comm'n, 988 F.2d 146, 150-51, 300 U.S. App. D.C. 198 (D.C. Cir. 1993).

The American Bar Association, *What is an Executive Order?* https://www.americanbar.org/groups/public_education/publications/teaching-legal-docs/what-is-an-executive-order-/ (last visited July 5, 2020).

Am. Water Works Ass'n v. EPA, 40 F.3d 1266, 1273 (D.C. Cir. 1994).

S James Anaya, Indigenous Peoples in International Law, 104–06 (2004).

Anderson v. Evans, 371 F. 3d. 475, 494 (9th Cir 2004).

Archambault Declaration of Aug. 3, 2016.

Leora Bilsky and Rachael Klagsbrun, *The return of Cultural Genocide?* European Journal of International Law, Volume 29, Issue 2, at 373–96 (May 2018).

California Cmtys. Against Toxics v. U.S. EPA, 688 F.3d 989, 993–94 (9th Cir. 2012).

Rob Capriccioso, *Barack Obama and Richard Nixon Among Best Presidents for Indian Country* Indian Country Today, https://indiancountrytoday.com/archive/barack-obama-and-richard-nixon-among-best-presidents-for-indian-country-bJnChvj2_EKI5u8jISt1Hw (last visited November 10th 2020).

Care Principles for Indigenous Data Governance. The increasing convergence of technology infrastructure and digital connectivity has raised the value of data across the globe. https://static1.squarespace.com/static/5d3799de845604000199cd24/t/5d79c383e904c741c9e9cd86/1568260995760/CARE+Principles+for+Indigenous+Data+Governance_FINAL_Sept+06+2019.pdf (last visited November 26 2020).

Chip Colwell, *How the archaeological review behind the Dakota Access Pipeline went wrong?* The Conversation, https://theconversation.com/how-the-archaeological-review-behind-the-dakota-access-pipeline-went-wrong-67815 (last visited 06/28/2020).

Congressional Research Service, *Oil and Natural Gas Pipelines: Role of US Army Corps of Engineers*, (June 21-28, 2017).

Dakota Access LLC, *Draft Environmental Assessment Dakota Access Pipeline Project Crossings of Flowage Easements and Federal Lands*, (2015), https://usace.contentdm.oclc.org/digital/collection/p16021coll7/id/2426./

Lawrence Davison, CULTURAL Genocide, New Brunswick, NJ: Rutgers University Press (2012).

Declaration of Dave Archambault II in Support of Motion for Preliminary Injunction, *Standing Rock Sioux Tribe v. U.S. Army Corps of Eng'rs*, No. 16-1534 (JEB) (D.D.C. Aug. 4, 2016).

Haydee J. Dijkstal, *The Dakota Access Pipeline and the Destruction of Cultural Heritage: Apply the Crime Against Humanity of Persecution Before the ICC,* Minnesota Journal of International Law. 277 (2019).

M. Eitner, *Meaningful Consultation with Tribal Governments: A uniform standard to guarantee that federal agencies properly consider their concerns.* University of Colorado Law Review 85:867–901 (2014).

Executive Order No 13007, 61 C. F.R 26771 May 1996.

Executive Order No 13175, 65 FR 67249 2000.

Executive Order 13647 C. F.R. 39539.

Executive Order 13766.

Jack F, *Existing Federal Law and the Protection of Sacred Sites Possibilities and Limitations* Cultural Survival Quarterly Magazine, https://www.culturalsurvival.org/publications/cultural-survival-quarterly/existing-federal-law-and-protection-sacred-sites (last visited December 1, 2020).

Food and Agriculture Organization of the United *Nations* (FAO), *Free and Prior Informed Consent, an Indigenous Peoples Right and a good Practice for Local Communities: Manual for Project Practitioners,* (2016) http://www.fao.org/3/a-i6190e.pdf.

Carla F. Fredericks and Jesse D. Heibel, *Standing Rock, the Sioux Treaties, and the Limits of the Supremacy Clause,* 89 U. Colo. L. Rev. 477 (2018).

Friends of the Capital Crescent Trail v. Fed. Transit Admin., 218 F.Supp.3d 53, 60 (D.D.C. 2016).

Richard Nixon Foundation, *President Nixon: Champion for Native Americans*, https://www.thoughtco.com/richard-nixons-influence-american-indian-affairs-4082465 (last visited November 18 2020).

G.A. Res. 61/295, United Nations Declaration on the Rights of Indigenous Peoples art. 26 (Sept. 13, 2007).

Icelandic Human Rights Center, *Substantive Human Rights* https://www.humanrights.is/en/human-rights-education-project/human-rights-concepts-ideas-and-fora/substantive-human-rights (last visited December 15, 2020).

Indian Country Today, *What Is Indigenous Self Determination and When Does It Apply?* https://indiancountrytoday.com/archive/what-is-indigenous-self-determination-and-when-does-it-apply-xmO_BGShT0mVMpLh7IC-c (last visited July 25, 2020).

Indigenous Data Working Group, *Recommended Practice for Provenance of Indigenous Peoples' Data* https://development.standards.ieee.org/myproject-web/public/view.html#pardetail/8382 (last visited November 30, 2020).

International NGO Conference on Discrimination against Indigenous Populations in the Americas, Geneva, Switzerland, (1977).

JDSUPRA USACE, *Nationwide Permit 12 Vacated: What You Need to Know,* https://www.jdsupra.com/legalnews/usace-nationwide-permit-12-vacated-what-17066/ (Last visited 18 November 2020).

Lindsay Kingston, *The Destruction of Identity, Cultural Genocide and Indigenous Peoples* Journal of Human Rights 14 (1) (2015).

Tahu Kukutai and John Taylor, Data Sovereignty for Indigenous peoples: Current Practice and future needs in indigenous data sovereignty: toward an agenda 1,7, Kau Kukutai and John Taylor eds., (2016).

Edward C Luck, *Cultural Genocide and the Protection of Cultural Heritage,* J. PAUL getty trust occasional papers in cultural heritage policy 2 (2018).

Memorandum on Government-to-Government Relations with Native American Tribal Governments, 30 Weekly Comp. Pres. Doc. 936 (May 2, 1994).

Moving America's Energy: The Dakota Access Pipeline https://daplpipeline facts.com/ (last visited June 21, 2020).

Narragansett Indian Tribe v. Warwick Sewer Auth., 334 F.3d 161, 166 (1st Cir. 2003).

National Historic Preservation Act Section 106.

National Historic Preservation Act, 54 U.S.C. §§ 300101-307108 (1966).

National Parks Conservation Ass'n v. Semonite, 916 F.3d 1075, 1082 (D.C. Cir. 2019).

Native Voices, *Congress seeks to abolish tribes, relocate Indian Americans,* https://www.nlm.nih.gov/nativevoices/timeline/488.html (last visited November 18, 2020).

Elisa Novic, *From 'Genocide' to 'Persecution': 'Cultural Genocide' and Contemporary International Criminal Law in Cultural Rights as Collective Rights,* Studies in Intercultural Human Rights, (2016).

Fransesca Panzironi, *Indigenous Peoples Right to Self Determination and Development Policy* (Thesis submitted to fulfil the requirements for the award of Doctor of Philosophy Faculty University of Sydney).

Frank Przetacznik, *The Basic Collective Human Right to Self Determination of Peoples and Nations as a Prerequisite for Peace,* 8 NYLS Journal of Human Rights: 1 (1990).

Presidential Memorandum Regarding Construction of the Dakota Access Pipeline (Jan 24, 2017).

RDA COVID-19 Indigenous Data WG, *Data sharing respecting Indigenous data sovereignty.* In RDA COVID-19 Working Group (2020). Recommendations and guidelines on data sharing. Research Data Alliance. https://doi.org/10.15497/rda00052 (Last visited November 30, 2020).

Research Data Alliance, International Indigenous Data Sovereignty Interest Group, *CARE Principles for Indigenous Data Governance,* (September 2019), https://static1.squarespace.com/static/5d3799de845604000199cd24/t/5d79c383e904c741c9e9cd86/1568260995760/CARE+Principles+for+Indigenous+Data+Governance_FINAL_Sept+06+2019.pdf (last visited November 26, 2020).

D. Rodriguez-Lonebear and S.C. Rainie S.C, *US Indigenous Data Sovereignty founding documents,* (2016), http://usindigenousdata.arizona.edu/about-us-.

Bas Rombouts, *The Evolution of Indigenous Peoples' Consultation Rights Under the ILO and UN Regimes: A Comparative Assessment of Participation, Consultation, and Consent Norms Incorporated in ILO Convention No. 169 and the UN Declaration on the Rights of Indigenous Peoples and Their Application by the Inter-American Court of Human Rights in the Saramaka and Sarayaku Judgments,* 53 Stan. J. Int'L L. 169,197-200 (2017).

S.J Rombouts, Having a Say: Indigenous Peoples, International Law and Free, Prior and Informed Consent, Wolf Legal Publishers, 414-15 (2014).

Stephanie Russo, *et al, The CARE Principles for Indigenous Data Governance,* Data Science Journal, 19(1), at 43 (2020).

Stephanie Russo Carroll and Jane Anderson, *Working with the CARE Principles: Operationalizing Indigenous Data Governance,* https://www.adalovelaceinstitute.org/operationalising-indigenous-data-governance/ (last visited November 29, 2020).

Dr. Rudolf C. Ryser, Amelia Marchand, and Deborah Presentation, *Cultural Genocide CLE,* World Peace through Law Section of the Washington State Bar Association, (April 3 2020), https://search.informit.com.au/documentSummary;dn=273886063150734;res=IELIAC;type=pdf.

Secretarial Order No. 3342.

Sierra Club v. FERC, 867 F.3d 1357, 1379 (D.C. Cir. 2017).

Special Message to Congress on Indian Affairs, 213 Pub. Papers 564 (July 8, 1970).

Standing Rock Sioux Tribe v. U.S. Army Corps of Eng'rs, No. 16-1534 (JEB) (D.D.C. Aug. 4, 2016)

Standing Rock Sioux Tribe v. United States Army Corps of Eng'rs, 440 F. Supp. 3d 1, ¶ 13. (D.D C. 2020)

Standing Rock Sioux Tribe v. *U.S. Army Corps of Eng'rs* (Standing Rock IV), 282 F. Supp. 3d 91, 109 (D.D.C. 2017).

Standing Rock Sioux Tribe v. U.S *Army Corps of Engineers,* Case No. 1:16-cv-1534-JEB: Declaration of Tim Mentz Support of Motion for Injunction.

Walter E. Stern, *"Black Snakes" Or Essential Infrastructure: Dakota Access Pipeline, Standing Rock Sioux Tribe V. U. S. Army Corps of Engineers, The Federal Government's Tribal Consultation Obligations, and Why This Matters,* Modrall Sperling (2018).

The Standing Rock Sioux tribe Impacts of an Oil Spill from the Dakota Access Pipeline on the Standing Rock Sioux Tribe. A report was prepared under the direction of Mike Faith, Jr., Chairman of the standing rock tribe. (February 21 2018).

Taxpayers of Mich. Against Casinos v. Norton, 433 F.3d 852 (D.C. Cir. 2006).

George Tinker E, Missionary Conquest: The Gospel and Native American Cultural Genocide (1993).

Rebecca Tsosie, *Governance and Informational Privacy: Constructing "Indigenous Data Sovereignty",* 80 Mont. L. Rev. 229 (2019) at 242.

Treaty of Fort Laramie with Sioux, Etc., Sept. 17, 1851, 11 Stat. 749.

Tribal Consultation, 74 Fed. Reg. 57,881 (Nov. 5, 2009).

United States Government Accountability Office (GAO) *Tribal Consultation, Additional Actions Needed for Infrastructure Projects* Gao-19-22 (March 2019).

UNPFII, *Rep. of the International Workshop on Methodologies Regarding Free, Prior and Informed Consent and Indigenous Peoples,* U.N. Doc. E/C.19/2005/3 (Feb. 17, 2005) (presented at the fourth session of the United Nations Permanent Forum on Indigenous Issues in New York on May 16–27, 2005).

The United Nations Educational, Scientific and Cultural Organization (UNESCO) Basic Texts of the 2003 Convention for the Safeguarding of the Intangible Cultural Heritage.

UN General Assembly, Convention on the Prevention and Punishment of the Crime of Genocide, 9 December 1948, United Nations, Treaty Series, vol. 78, p. 277.

UN General Assembly, International Covenant on Civil and Political Rights, 16 December 1966, United Nations, Treaty Series, vol. 999, 171, Art 1.

UN General Assembly, International Covenant on Economic, Social and Cultural Rights, 16 December 1966, United Nations, Treaty Series, vol. 993, p. 3, Art 15.

UN General Assembly, Universal Declaration of Human Rights, 10 December 1948, 217 A (III) Art 27(1).

UN General Assembly, United Nations Declaration on the Rights of Indigenous Peoples: resolution / adopted by the General Assembly, 2 October 2007, A/RES/61.

US Department of the Interior Bureau of Land Management Tribal Consultation https://www.blm.gov/services/tribal-consultation (last visited December 13, 2020).

United States Environmental Protection Agency; *National Environmental Policy Act Review Process,* https://www.epa.gov/nepa/national-environmental-policy-act-review-process (last visited on October 23, 2020).

Ana Filipa Vrdojak, *Human Rights and Genocide: The Work Lauterpacht and Lemkim in Morden International Law* 20 EJIL 1163-94. 4 (2009).

Wild Horse Preservation Campaign v. Perdue, 873 F.3d 914, 932 (D.C. Cir. 2017).

Williston Basin Interstate Pipeline Co. v. FERC, 519 F.3d 497, 504 (D.C. Cir. 2008).

Chapter 7

Ecosystem Destruction in the Kole Wetlands in India

Dr. Dayana Maliyekkal Kunjachan

Government Law College, Ernakulam

Abstract: India has diverse environmental landscapes and ecosystems from the Himalayas to the sea coast of Kanyakumari. Due to the differences in environmental landscape, states within India have different approaches to environmental protection. The Indian legacy of living along with nature has given way to the destructive attitude of the present day.[1] Environmental destruction in India has now reached a stage that if further destruction continues, it will lead to certain unforeseen consequences such as mass destruction of ecosystems, species populations, and the eradication of certain land forms. This is evident by the shrinking wetland ecosystems.[2]

This chapter focuses on Kole Wetlands,[3] a specific ecosystem which is in Kerala, India. It extends through various districts[4] of Kerala. The role played by

---

[1] DTE, *How green is the country? Check out our State of India's Environment Report 2019 In Figures*, DOWN TO EARTH (June 4, 2019), https://www.downtoearth.org.in/news/climate-change/how-green-is-the-country-check-out-our-state-of-india-s-environment-report-2019-in-figures-64915.

[2] Gaurav Kumar et al, *Study on Status and Health of Wetlands in India: A Geographical Analysis*, OUR HERITAGE, (Aug.4, 2019), 10.6084/m9.figshare.11684394.

[3] Neil Adger and Cecilia Luttrell, *Property Rights and the Utilisation of Wetlands*, ECOLOGICAL ECONOMICS (2000), https://www.academia.edu/5103033/Property_rights_and_the_utilisation_of_wetlands.

[4] ENCYCLOPEDIA BRITANNICA, *Kerala*, https://www.britannica.com/place/Kerala (last visited August 5, 2020).

them in the protection of ecology in Kerala is noteworthy.[5] The most important problem faced by this ecosystem is land grab that leads to land-use change by the builders and various infrastructure projects in the land, which leads to ecocide.

This specific ecosystem protects the climate and renders the climate equable for the people of Kerala, and its unprecedented changes will lead to the eradication of a beautiful state of Kerala, which is known as "God's Own Country." The author argues that India needs to incorporate the crime of ecocide in its national legislation.[6] Ecocide, its history and current status within international criminal law have already been introduced to the reader. In this chapter, the author will focus specifically on how it should be incorporated into national legislation. Further, the author argues that the concept of criminal liability rather than civil liability would do much better in cases involving environmental destruction in India.

Keywords: Kole Wetlands, reclamation, ecocide, wise use, Ramsar Convention, Kerala, India, National Green Tribunal.

***

I. Introduction

At the creation of the world, God had invested on earth whatever was necessary for the sustenance of every creation. Certain functions were cast up on each and every component. Wetlands occupy a prime position as they help keep life moving. Wetlands were treated as wastelands worldwide until the scientific community found them to be the most important ecosystems with

---

[5] Ravender Singh, et al. *Crop diversification through land modification in canal irrigation command of Eastern India,* SAARC JOURNAL OF AGRICULTURE (June 1, 2003), https://www.researchgate.net/publication/305999554_Crop_diversification_through_land_modification_in_canal_irrigation_command_of_Eastern_India/citation/download.

[6] Kübra Kalkandelen and Darren O'Byrne, *On ecocide: toward a conceptual framework,* DISTINCTION: JOURNAL OF SOCIAL THEORY, 18:3, 333-49, (2017) DOI: 10.1080/1600910X.2017.1331857.

unique features.[7] Data establishes that they occupy only six percent of the land area on the entire earth.[8] Wetlands are:

> vital parts of hydrological cycle, are highly productive, support exceptionally high biological diversity and provide a wide range of ecosystem services such as waste assimilation, water purification, flood mitigation, erosion control, ground water recharge, micro climate regulation, aesthetic simultaneously supporting enhancement of the landscape while many significant recreational, social and cultural activities, besides being a part of the cultural heritage.[9]

The kole nilam is associated with the cultivation of paddy. [10] The word "kole" is associated with the yield of the land. These areas were said to make bumper yield[11], and hence they occupied prime position among the various types of paddy fields. Reference to these areas could be seen in the implementation of the historic Kerala Land Reforms Act, 1963.[12] The average annual rainfall is 3,200 mm, and temperature varied from 28°C to 31°5°C. The peculiar area extends from Chalakkudy River on the South to Bharathapuzha River in the north, and mainly to Ponnani taluk.[13] This area acts as a natural drainage

---

[7] G. Agoramoorthy and M.J. Hsu, *Biodiversity Surveys are crucial for India*, CURR. SCI., 82, 244-45 (2002) https://www.researchgate.net/publication/41396457_Bioconcentration_of_heavy_metals_in_selected_medicinal_plants_of_India.

[8] J.R. Dixon, et al, *Tracking Global Change in Ecosystem Area: The Wetland Extent Trends Index*, BIOLOGICAL CONSERVATION Vol. 193 (Nov. 19, 2016), https://doi.org/10.1016/j.biocon.2015.10.023.

[9] MINISTRY OF ENVIRONMENT, FOREST AND CLIMATE CHANGE, GOVERNMENT OF INDIA, *Wetlands conservation and management rules 2017*, http://moef.gov.in/wp-content/uploads/2020/01/final-version-and-printed-wetland-guidelines-rules-2017-03.01.20.pdf.

[10] ENCYCLOPEDIA BRITANNICA, *Hydroponics*, (May 22, 2019), https://www.britannica.com/topic/hydroponics.

[11] A.S. Binilkumar and A. Ramanathan. *Valuing Wetland Attributes Using Discrete Choice Experiments: A Developing Country Experience*, 17TH ANNUAL CONFERENCE OF THE EUROPEAN ASSOCIATION OF ENVIRONMENTAL AND RESOURCE ECONOMISTS, Vrije Universiteit (VU University) Amsterdam, The Netherlands.(June 24-27, 2009).

[12] K.N.Raj and M. Tharakan., *Agrarian reform in Kerala and its impact on the rural economy–a preliminary assessment*. AGRARIAN REFORM IN CONTEMPORARY DEVELOPING COUNTRIES: A STUDY PREPARED FOR THE INTERNATIONAL LABOUR OFFICE THE FRAMEWORK OF THE WORLD EMPLOYMENT PROGRAMME, 1 at 31, (2010) https://www.google.co.in/books/edition/Agrarian_Reform_in_Contemporary_Developi/b4wqQgl0HVYC?hl=en&gbpv=1&pg=PA31&printsec=frontcover.

[13] MERRIAM WEBSTER DICTIONARY, "*Taluk*", https://www.merriam webster.com/dictionary/taluk.

system for these districts, and they are connected through a network of canals and ponds.[14] Thus the different parts of Kole Wetlands remain interconnected to rivers which then drain to the Arabian Sea. Most of the lands under paddy cultivation are low-lying areas or Kole Wetlands.[15] Paddy cultivation requires more water, and most of the Kole Wetlands adopt a unique method of cultivation is adopted for paddy cultivation in these areas.[16] This is a very challenging activity. It should be noted that in bygone days the kole lands were reclaimed from the Kayal area by putting up temporary earthen bunds.[17] Farmers undertook the cultivation of rice in these areas during the summer period from December to May.[18] The practice of paddy cultivation in the kole land has evolved over the years.[19] Along with this, the host of climatic, ecological, institutional, socio-economic and technological factors have played their role well to make these wetlands multipurpose in use.[20]

---

[14] PO Nameer, *Wetlands and waterfowl conservation in Kerala with special reference to Ramsar sites*, Ambat B (Ed.) PROCEEDINGS OF KERALA ENVIRONMENT CONGRESS, CENTRE FOR ENVIRONMENT AND DEVELOPMENT, Thiruvananthapuram. 97-112, (2005), https://zoo sprint.zooreach.org/ZooPrintJournal/2006/August/2350-2355.pdf.

[15] P. Thomas, *Agricultural performance in Kerala*, in Prakash, B.A., KERALA'S ECONOMIC DEVELOPMENT: ISSUES AND PROBLEMS. Sage Publications Pvt. Ltd. (1999) https://journals. sagepub.com/doi/abs/10.1177/2277976014530232.

[16] E.B. Barbier, *Valuing environmental functions: tropical wetlands. Land economics*, 155-73, (1994) https://scholar.google.co.in/scholar?q=Barbier,+E.+B.+(1994).+Valuing+ Environmental+Functions:+Tropical+Wetlands.+Land+Economics,+70+(2)+155-74.&hl=en&as_sdt=0&as_vis=1&oi=scholar.

[17] Sarath Chandran, et al. HISTORY OF RECLAIMED KAYALS IN KUTTANAD WETLAND AND ASSOCIATED SOCIAL DIVIDE IN ALAPPUZHA DISTRICT, KERALA (2018) https://www.research gate.net/publication/326682004.

[18] N. Karunakaran, *Relative contribution of different elements to the growth of principal crop output in Kerala*, INDIAN DEVELOPMENT REVIEW, Vol. 11, No. 2 at 155-65. (2013) https://www.researchgate.net/publication/280499587_Karunakaran_N_Relative_contri bution_of_different_elements_to_the_growth_of_principal_crop_output_in_Kerala_Ind ian_Development_Review_Vol_11_No_2_pp_155-165.

[19] K.P. Mani, *Cropping pattern in Kerala– Spatial inter-temporal analysis*. In K. Rajan (Ed.), KERALA ECONOMY: TRENDS DURING THE POST-REFORM PERIOD, 64–84, New Delhi, India: Serials Publications. (2009) http://springer.nl.go.kr/chapter/10.1007%2F978-981-15-4611-2_10.

[20] A.S. Binilkumar, *Heterogeneity Across Stakeholders' Preferences for Wetland Attributes: The Case of Kole Wetland in India*, PROCEEDINGS OF THE FOURTH WORLD CONGRESS OF ENVIRONMENTAL AND RESOURCE ECONOMISTS, (June 27 to July 2, 2010) Montreal, Canada. (cited in Nufaisa M et al, *Analysis of Production and Marketing of Paddy in Thrissur-Ponnani Kole wetlands*, INTERNATIONAL JOURNAL OF CURRENT ADVANCED RESEARCH, 08(07), 19387-91. (2019), DOI: http://dx.doi.org/10.24327/ijcar.2019.19391.3738.

II. Kole Wetlands and kayal reclamation[21]

A large portion of land in Kerala was immersed underwater for a long period. These areas came under reclamation. This land reclamation was mainly comprised of kayal sites, backwaters, and other water-logged areas. This reclamation work in the kayals has a long history.[22] It is very difficult to ascertain the period of its origin. Based on the available records, this process is said to have started in 1883.[23] The first area that came under large-scale reclamation was the Kuttanad region which is located in the southern part of the state.[24] These reclaimed areas achieved profitable paddy cultivation. Enticed by the successful reclamation work and profitable paddy cultivation in these areas, landlords slowly turned their attention to similar water-logged areas comprising a number of kayals in the Thrissur district. The reclaimed lands in Thrissur later come to be known as kole lands. The main kayals brought under reclamation work from the Kole area were the Enamakkal and Mangara in Thrissur, Muriyad in Mukundapuram, and Kattakampalin Thalappilly taluks.[25] The majority of farmers cultivate rice in a single crop season. Farmers in the Kole are arranged under an institutional arrangement called padasekharams,[26] which is a cluster of farms. During 1975-1976, southern kole land alone had the total area under rice was 8.76 lakh hectares. By 2007-2008 the area was declined to 2.29 lakh hectares. There was an overwhelming decline of nearly seventy-four percent over a span of three decades.[27] As against the general trend observed, the loss of rice is comparatively low in kole lands, largely owing to its submergence for almost six months in a year.

The Thrissur Municipal Corporation is a city corporation, and it covers an area of 101.42 km, and there exists a high population density.[28] The city does not have a systematic and planned drainage facility to dispose of the wastewater as well as excess water during monsoons. Most of the drainage canals are connected to the irrigation canals of Kole Wetland. The city's

---

[21] Chandran, *supra* note 17.

[22] *Id.*

[23] *Id.*

[24] *Id.*

[25] Raj, *supra* note 12.

[26] The Kerala Land Development Act, 1964.

[27] Karunakaran, *supra* note 18.

[28] World Population Review, *World Urbanization Prospects*, United Nations population estimates and projections of major Urban Agglomerations. (2020) https://worldpopulationreview.com/world-cities/thrissur-population.

drinking water source and the surrounding areas largely depend on the Kole Wetland due to the same groundwater recharge properties. As the local paddy fields of Thrissur Corporation have been reclaimed for residential and industrial purposes due to increasing population pressure, the Wetland became essential for the urban society to drain its wastewater and excess water during the heavy monsoon months. During the summer, the presence of water in the Wetland helps retain groundwater level to a great extent.[29]

On the whole, kole lands are a unique wetland ecosystem whose characteristics are determined by the volume and duration of flooding and the silt brought in by the floodwater. This Wetland comes under the 'Central Asian- Indian Flyway'[30] and serves as a 'stepping stone' for the trans-continental migrant birds. It is found that the wetland system supports 20,000 residential as well as migratory water birds.[31] These wetlands support diverse fauna, including a large variety of fish, prawns, clams, reptiles, and birds. It is a complex ecological system that is submerged underwater half of the year, giving it both the properties of terrestrial and water generating substantial benefits to the society.

The kole land is a designated Ramsar site since 2002.[32] In 2004, the kole land was designated as the Important Bird Area. In 2009, the Kole Wetland was designated as High Value Biodiversity Area, and the Ministry of Environment and Forest and Climate Change treated the Kole Wetlands and Vembanad lake as two separate entities. A Biodiversity Conservation Plan was prepared separately for these areas.

The most important challenges posed towards the Kole are actions by individuals and by corporations. Various reasons are considered as challenges towards the original form of Kole Wetlands as these activities run against the natural features of this ecosystem. This is caused by state action through its policy and private individuals and companies to grab more resources.[33] The most important challenge faced by the Kole is population growth. This has led

---

[29] Binilkumar, *supra* note 20.

[30] CONVENTION ON THE CONSERVATION OF MIGRATORY SPECIES OF WILD ANIMALS, *Central Asian Flyway Action Plan for Waterbirds and their Habitat Country Report – INDIA*, https://www.cms.int/raptors/sites/default/files/document/inf_04_13_India_0.pdf.

[31] *Id.*

[32] Binilkumar, *supra* note 11.

[33] Jeena T. Srinivasan, *Agriculture-wetland interactions and sustainability of rice cultivation in the Kole land, Kerala*, INDIAN JOURNAL OF AGRICULTURAL ECONOMICS, Vol. 67(2) pp.213-224. (2012), http://14.139.116.20:8080/jspui/bitstream/10603/163270/8/17_bibliography.pdf.

to pressures on land resources for more food and housing needs. This results in the decline of land area under the kole. Production of rice also falls. Pursuant to the Kerala Land Reforms Act of 1963,[34] the large kole fields were fragmented, and the later policies of the state called for the intensification of agriculture through the strategies adopted under the green revolution, which led to the decline of land capability and natural existence of the Wetlands.[35] The national priority of food self-sufficiency has made the focus on the exploitation of a single provisioning service. For example, an improvement to the kole cultivation was achieved by storing part of the pumped water in the adjacent high lying lands where no crop was taken.[36] Also, with the commissioning of the Peechi reservoir and the Chimmony dam, efforts were made to stabilize kole cultivation and to bring the entire area under punja crop.[37] The mechanization of cultivation started around the 1960s, and the introduction of an improved variety of seeds further intensified the cultivation in kole.[38]

Mechanization coupled with the increased use of pesticides adversely affected the ecological sustainability of the area. Traditional fisheries and fishing communities gave way to the fishing farming practices in certain parts of the kole.[39] This introduced non-fishing communities to fisheries activities. This had an impact of a profit-driven, capital-intensive system driving away traditional communities from such activities. This also led to increased pollution in the area. Research studies conducted in this area show the

---

[34] This legislation was passed in pursuance of greater objective of land to the tiller and in order to provide equity in the holdings concept of ceiling on land holding was introduced in s. 82 of the Act. This resulted in the fragmentation of agriculture holding.

[35] R. Rajinikanth and T.V Ramachandra, *Restoration of Lakes in Bangalore based on Status and Socio-economic aspects of wetlands*, PROJECT REPORT, (November 2000), http://wgbis.ces.iisc.ernet.in/energy/water/paper/economic_valuation/ecodoc2004.pdf.

[36] *Id.*

[37] Jayan Jose Thomas, *Paddy Cultivation in Kerala*, REVIEW OF AGRARIAN STUDIES, vol. 1, no. 2, (2011) http://ras.org.in/paddy_cultivation_in_kerala.

[38] P.K. Muraleedharan, *Resource Use Efficiency in Kole Lands in Trichur District (Kerala)*, INDIAN JOURNAL OF AGRICULTURAL ECONOMICS, INDIAN SOCIETY OF AGRICULTURAL ECONOMICS, vol. 42(4), (October 1987), https://ideas.repec.org/a/ags/inijae/271920.html.

[39] A Parvathy. *Fish Diversity, Abundance and Traditional Fish Harvesting Methods at Kole Wetlands of Thrissur, Kerala*. INTERNATIONAL JOURNAL FOR RESEARCH IN APPLIED SCIENCE AND ENGINEERING TECHNOLOGY. 6. 1852-1857. (2018), 10.22214/ijraset.2018.1287. https://www.researchgate.net/publication/323872209_Fish_Diversity_Abundance_and_Traditional_Fish_Harvesting_Methods_at_Kole_Wetlands_of_Thrissur_Kerala.

presence of fluorides, chlorides, phosphates, nitrate, sulphate, ammonium, iron, chromium etc., is above the permissible limit.[40]

An influx of money from the Gulf region countries attracted the construction industry, and many parts of the kole got converted for the same.[41] The government policies of building roads and canals for intensifying agriculture paved the way for the conversion of these areas on a large scale due to the increase of infrastructural facilities.[42] These policies, coupled with the introduction of a ceiling on the landholdings, led to subdivision and fragmentation, given the nature of kole farming.[43] The holding size became uneconomical to cultivate. Along with this increase in demand for land for non-agricultural uses also augmented opening up land markets.

All this led to the ecosystem process and water flow changes. Agricultural intensification has been observed in the kole lands. This is evident from the efforts made to facilitate double cropping on kole lands by way of various types of engineering interventions aimed at improved drainage and water management. This intensification has both positive and negative aspects. It could bring more yields from the shrunken areas due to the various reasons listed. But it has led to the loss of originality of the kole, and the pollution and groundwater quality is also under threat.[44] Changes in the quantity and quality of soil and water are more evident. Non-scientific and increased use of chemical fertilizers and pesticides increased the acidity of the soil.

Moreover, water logging due to incomplete or faulty designs of bunds and canals and siltation and the presence of water hyacinths is adversely affecting water flow are some of the common problems. There is an increasing trend of kole lands lying as fallow lands. This is due to a multitude of factors like high

---

[40] B.I. Joseph., *Impact of Pesticides and Fertilizers on Quality of Water in Wetlands (Kole) and Neighbouring Areas of Division 43 of Thrissur Corporation,* PROJECT REPORT, St. Aloysius College, Elthuruth, Thrissur, Kerala. http://aloysius.in/joseph_project_abstract.pdf.

[41] Adger, *supra* note 3.

[42] E. L. Danielson and J. A. Leitch, *Private versus Public Economics of Prairie Wetland Allocation.* JOURNAL OF ENVIRONMENTAL ECONOMICS AND MANAGEMENT. (1986) in Jeena T Srinivasan, *Agriculture-wetland Interactions: A Case Study of the Kole land Kerala,* (July, 2011), https://cess.ac.in/wp-content/uploads/2019/10/Monograph-No.19.pdf. *See also* DISTRICT SPATIAL PLANNING, *Thrissur District Plan: Part 1, Vol1,* http://townplanning.kerala.gov.in/town/wp-content/uploads/2019/04/dsp_thrissur.pdf.

[43] The Kerala Land Reforms Act, 1963, §. 81 and §. 82 talks about ceiling area. This fixes the extend of land which can be owned by an adult individual person and a family consisting of five adult members. It is limited to 20 acres.

[44] Thomas, *supra* note 39.

wage rates and lack of availability of labor, low price of paddy, difficulty in using mechanized farming in some fields due to which paddy cultivation has become uneconomical. Loss of biodiversity that can undermine the ecosystem's ecological character and resilience is a common trade-off associated with the intensification of agricultural activities. A decrease in farmer-friendly microorganisms and other birds and reptiles is reported. It is reported that frogs, snakes and owls, which used to destroy crop-damaging organisms, have almost disappeared.[45] Increased mining activities have not only rendered the mined lands unsuitable for any agricultural activities but also led to the creation of nearby lands as fallow lands.[46]

This represents an overall trade-off in economic benefits and livelihoods rather than transformations of livelihoods themselves (that is, traditional fishing communities themselves becoming commercial fish farmers). Mining backed by a thriving construction industry provided livelihoods to many during the late 1970s and 1980s.[47] However, it was not sustained as a major source of livelihood. Often the miners were migrants from other places, had only business interests while extracting the resources, and were not concerned about sustainable extraction.[48] This effectively gave rise to competition for the resource and conflicts with other resource users. In some cases, this competition and conflicts stem from intensification and expansion in one or both activities and increased claims over the available resource. The pits that remained after the mining of clay and sand were not suitable for cultivation, which resulted in water stagnation and created pollution even to the surrounding wells used for drawing water for drinking and other domestic uses.[49]

---

[45] Joseph, *supra* note 42.

[46] W.N. Adger, C. Luttrell. *Property rights and the utilisation of wetlands*, ECOLOGICAL ECONOMICS, 35(1), 75-89 (2000).

[47] E. Matthews, I. Fung, *Methane emission from natural wetlands: Global distribution, area, and environmental characteristics of sources*, GLOBAL BIOGEOCHEMICAL CYCLES, 1(1), 61-86 (1986).

[48] L.E. Danielson, J.A. Leitch. *Private vs public economics of prairie wetland allocation*, JOURNAL OF ENVIRONMENTAL ECONOMICS AND MANAGEMENT, 13(1), 81-92 (1986).

[49] S.E. John, et al, *Environmental degradation of a tropical estuary due to human interferences—a case studies from southern Kerala, SW India*, ARABIAN JOURNAL OF GEOSCIENCES, 10(16), 352 (2017).

Another factor that is impacting the Kole Wetlands is increasing tourism.[50] In addition, the implementation of new power and energy projects[51] poses threats to the very delicate nature of this protected area. For example, the Central Government is planning to construct windmills in Kole Wetlands. The preliminary survey and other related activities are going to be operated under the auspices of the Agency for Nonconventional Energy and Rural Technology (ANERT). The estimated project cost of a single windmill is 4 crore, and about 10 acres of land is needed for one windmill. So, if more windmills are going to get established in Kole Wetlands, many of Kole Wetlands will be fallowed, and the windmills may adversely affect birds' migration.[52]

Another challenge is waste dumping. As there are more restrictions for waste dumping in towns, these wastes are now dumped into nearby kole lands. Moreover, after drinking liquors near the kole lands, anti-socials throw empty glass bottles into paddy fields and canals. These broken glass pieces cause difficulties to both paddy farmers and fish farmers when carrying out their work.[53]

III. Legal Regime on the Kole Wetlands

The area of Kole Wetlands assumes the characteristics of both water and land; hence the legislation bearing on the subject becomes complex. Legislation in India emanates from the Constitution of India, which follows a quasi-federal structure. Legislative lists are categorized into three, and the second list covers the areas coming under state jurisdiction.[54] Land and water and matters

---

[50] Mini Muringatheri, *Kole fields to attract tourists in hordes*, THE HINDU, (Nov. 29, 2017), https://www.thehindu.com/news/national/kerala/kole-fields-to-attract-tourists-in-hordes/article21127834.ece. In 2012, a private group allied '*Kayaloram* tourist boating' has started in *Manalur* Kole lands. Now the oils spills from boats in the canals are less, but if the number of tourist boats increase, the oil spills also may increase, which may adversely affect the habitats of birds and other organisms. In *Vembanad* and*Alapuzha* wetlands, the oils spills from boats have polluted the water of lake and canals.

[51] Sivaperuman Chandrakasan, and Jayson Eluvathingal. *Birds of Kole wetlands, Thrissur*, ZOOS' PRINT JOURNAL, 10. 334-349, (2001), https://doi.org/10.11609/JoTT.ZPJ.15.10.344-9.

[52] John, *supra* note 51.

[53] Muringatheri, *supra* note 52.

[54] THE CONSTITUTION OF INDIA, (1950) Art. 246, schedule VII.

related to the same are under this list.[55] Thus every state has the flexibility to enact and adopt legislation according to their needs.[56]

At the same time, Central Government is vested with the power of protection and conservation of the environment[57] and implementation of international conventions and treaties to which India is a party.[58] Moreover, the Central Government can promulgate legislation on any subjects coming under the state if the matter acquires national importance and if any two or more states request for central legislation in that area.[59]

As a Ramsar site of India,[60] the Kole Wetlands needs to be protected under the guidelines of the Ramsar Convention, 1971.[61] This requires parties to make plans for the national treatment of their country's wetlands and the use of them wisely.[62] As already discussed, the Kole Wetlands revel in the rich biodiversity of those areas. Thus, a better arena for the Biological Diversity Convention[63] and the World Heritage Convention[64] in protecting these

---

[55] *Id* at Schedule VII List II item 17 and 18.

[56] Kerala was the first state to legislate on Wetlands among the states in India. The Kerala Conservation of Paddy land and Wetland Act, 2008 was enacted and latest amendment was in 2019 and hence the present Act dealing on this subject is Kerala conservation of paddy land and wetland (amendment) act 2019.

[57] The Environment (Protection) Act, 1986. s.3 Power of Central Government to take measures to protect and improve environment.

[58] A. A. Sengupta, A. Gaur, *Treaty-making and Implementation in India: A Constitutional Paradox.* INDIAN JOURNAL OF INTERNATIONAL LAW 57, 47–61 (2017). https://doi.org/10.1007/s40901-018-0074-y.

[59] John, *supra* note. 51 at Art. 252.

[60] SANDRP, *India Ramsar Wetlands in Crisis in 2020,* (Mar. 7, 2020), https://sandrp.in/2020/03/07/india-ramsar-wetlands-in-crisis-in-2020/.

[61] THE RAMSAR CONVENTION ON WETLANDS OF INTERNATIONAL IMPORTANCE ESPECIALLY AS WATERFOWL HABITAT, 1971, http://portal.unesco.org/en/ev.php-URL_ID=15398&URL_DO=DO_TOPIC&URL_SECTION=201.html. The Ramsar Convention, 1971 Art 3.1, enjoins the parties to the convention to formulate and implement their planning so as to promote the conservation of listed wetlands as far as possible and the wise use of wetlands in their territory.

[62] *Id.* (I-2 of the Additional Guidance). The review of legal and institutional issues related to wise use of wetlands is mandated further by the Additional Guidance for the implementation of the wise use concept.

[63] THE BIODIVERSITY CONVENTION 1992, 8.2.3 *Biodiversity, waterways and wetlands overlay code.* https://publicdocs.scc.qld.gov.au/hpecmwebdrawer/Record/6008371/File/document.

[64] R. McInnes et al. *Ramsar and World Heritage Conventions: Converging towards success.* RAMSAR CONVENTION SECRETARIAT (2017), https://whc.unesco.org/en/ramsar/.

Wetlands arises. Therefore, this area deserves special protection for humanity as a whole. In order to meet the requirement of national legislation, especially to deal with wetlands of India, the Central Government has enacted Wetland (Conservation) Rules, 2010, which was amended in 2016.[65] Now the Wetland (Conservation and Management) Rules 2017 is in force. These rules are enacted under the umbrella legislation of the Environment (Protection) Act, 1986. These rules put forward the guidelines of the Ministry of Environment Forest and Climate Change. The rule has formulated authorities, both at a national and state level, for carrying out the activities for the protection and conservation of wetlands. They also suggest to list out the wetlands of the country by making a comprehensive inventory, identify wetlands for notification as wetlands of national importance, methods of delineating them, wetland complexes and the zone of influence, developing a list of activities to be regulated and permitted as well as integrating the management plan for each wetland. The most important amendment brought under the 2017 rules is that irrespective of location, size, ownership, biodiversity or ecosystem services or values, those can be notified under the 2017 rules.[66] Certain specific wetlands such as river channels, human-made water bodies constructed for drinking water, paddy fields, aquaculture, salt production, recreation, and irrigation purposes are not covered under these rules, and they are specifically protected under the Indian Forest Act, 1927, the Forest (Conservation) Act, 1980, the Wildlife (Protection) Act, 1972 and the Coastal Regulation Zone Notification 2011.[67] Apart from this, there is pollution control legislation that bears on various aspects of the protection of Kole Wetlands.[68] Along with this, state legislation bearing on the subject also deserves analysis.[69]

Specific state legislation on wetland

Kerala began its history as an agricultural economy. When India achieved independence, the Indian economy, which is largely based on agriculture, was

---

[65] *Supra* note 58.

[66] Mayank Aggarwal, *India's guidelines on wetlands will allow states to decide what counts as prohibited activities*, THE SCROLL, (Jan 22, 2020), https://scroll.in/article/949988/indias-guidelines-on-wetlands-will-allow-states-to-decide-what-counts-as-prohibited-activities.

[67] *Id.*

[68] *Id.*

[69] EPA, *supra* note 59.

sought to be intensified through the land to the tiller policy.[70] Thus, the constitutional goals envisaged for an egalitarian society and equitable distribution of available resources among the toiling class.[71] In tune with the direction of the Central Government, the state introduced the Kerala Land Reforms Act, 1963. It was an enactment to boost agricultural production by putting an end to the feudal forms of land system practiced all over India. Kerala also had a *jenmi kudian*[72] system that left most of the farmers with no land of their own. By introducing changes in land ownership, Kerala tried to bring in the growth of agricultural productivity. Kerala's land reforms led to the subdivision of holdings. The long-term impact was the fragmentation of the agricultural holding. But the large holding is a requirement of kole cultivation. Subsequent to the introduction of this historical enactment, another order was issued by the state to prevent the conversion of paddy fields and to boost the cultivation of paddy.[73] Every paddy land in Kerala is a typical wetland, and most remain submerged in water most of the time. The conversion was prohibited to ensure food security. Any person who contravenes any of the provisions in the Kerala Land Utilization Order is punishable with imprisonment for a term that shall not be less than three months but may extend to seven years and shall also be liable to fine.[74] In this context, Section 8 of the Act is also relevant, and it provides, "any person who attempts to contravene, or abets the contravention shall be deemed to have contravened that order." The Act provides for the constitution of special courts[75] by the state government for the purpose of providing speedy trial of offenses under this Act.

But the massive conversion of paddy lands for various purposes led to the new legislation. The preamble states that the Act aims to conserve the paddy land and wetland and restrict the conversion or reclamation thereof to promote growth in the agricultural sector and sustain the ecological system in Kerala. The Act has recognized the indiscriminate and uncontrolled

---

[70] A slogan of the Indian National Congress during the Independence struggle, meaning land should belong to the people who toil on land.

[71] THE CONSTITUTION OF INDIA, Art. 39.

[72] Landlord/tenant relationship.

[73] The Kerala Land Utilisation Order, 1967 which was enacted under the power of Central Government Legislation The Essential Commodities Act, 1955 §. 3(a)(b)(ii), this aims to boost the cultivation in the paddy fields so that self-sufficiency in food production will be achieved in state. This order had strong provisions and greater sanctions under the Essential Commodities Act, http://legislative.gov.in/sites/default/files/A1955-10.pdf.

[74] *Id.* at §7(1)(a).

[75] *Id.* at 12A.

reclamation and massive conversion of paddy land and wetland are taking place in the State. The preamble also approves the absence of effective laws to prevent the conversion or reclamation of paddy land.[76]

The Act defines wetland and paddy lands, respectively. A wetland is defined under section 2 of the Act, and "paddy" is defined as "all types of land situated in the state where paddy is cultivated at least once in a year or suitable for paddy cultivation but uncultivated and left fallow, and includes its allied constructions like bunds, drainage channels, ponds, and canals.[77]

The Act puts a complete prohibition on the reclamation of wetlands.[78] Only the activities for the protection of ecological characteristics of the wetlands can be undertaken. The state government is vested with the discretionary power of conversion for public purposes alone.[79] This power is also subjected to the scrutiny of the state-level committee and the satisfaction of adequate measures for maintaining ecological conditions. Special reference of protection of Kole Wetlands can be seen in the Kerala Land Reforms Act, 1963 too. The policy of the Act is focused on resource management, for example, paddy land and wetland. But the sustainability of resources and livelihood protection of stakeholders are not taken care of. There is a wide gap between hope and reality. Moreover, the expectations of the farming community are not adequately met.[80] Good governance principles like participation, accountability, transparency, and legitimacy are not taken care of through the provisions.

Lack of focus on collective action and monitoring, and limited concern for the livelihoods of stakeholders and others, adds to the momentum of loss of paddy fields and cultivation. The Act has discarded a century's best practices of community management of paddy fields.

IV. Kole Wetlands and ecocide

The question being addressed is whether the ecosystem destruction due to the various reasons listed above and the loss of originality of the Kole Wetlands can be categorized as ecocide. If it can be categorized as ecocide, then can criminal sanctions be enforced against those who are destroying the Kole Wetlands?

---

[76] *Supra* note 58.
[77] The Kerala Conservation of Paddy Land and Wetland Act, 2008, §2.
[78] *Id.* at §3.
[79] *Id.* at §10.
[80] *Id.* §4.

Even though the existing legislation in the field of wetlands is silent on the concept of ecocide and criminal sanctions on the crimes committed against the Kole Wetlands, it can well be brought in by interpretations of the Indian judiciary. The power of the Indian judiciary in interpreting the constitutional provisions has brought life to environmental law in India. The Kerala High Court, while deciding a land conversion case from the Kole Wetlands,[81] took a bold step in directing the converted area to be brought to the original cultivable situation. The writ petition concerns an order passed by the District Collector, whereby the petitioner was directed to remove the entire earth or any other material used to convert the Wetland and restore the land to its original position and make it fit for paddy cultivation.[82] Important questions have been raised regarding the interpretation of Kerala Conservation of Paddy Land and Wetland Act and Rules, 2008.[83] In a nutshell, the findings of the District Collector are that the land involved is "kole land," a wetland used for paddy cultivation. These lands are declared as Ramsar sites which need conservation, and there is a total prohibition on reclamation of such wetland under the Act. All orders issued under the Kerala Land Utilization Order[84] have become inoperative after the Kerala Conversion of Paddy and Wet Land Act, 2008 came into force. The unauthorized conversion comes into force of the Act, and therefore the action is purely illegal, and the property is liable to be restored to its original position to make it fit for paddy cultivation.[85] The case arouses curiosity because it brings in fruitful discussion regarding the application of state legislation for the protection of wetlands. In between, the Court has emphasized the application of the Public Trust Doctrine to the case concerned.

This Doctrine has paved the way for the protection of various threatened areas in the country through various decisions.[86] These doctrines and decisions, in a way, tried to bring in the concept of ecocide and protection of the environment in India. Thus, the crime of ecocide as defined by the International Law Commission as "extensive damage to, of or loss of ecosystems of a given territory, whether by human agency or by other causes, to such an extent that peaceful enjoyment by the inhabitants of that territory

---

[81] Kaipadath Property Development v. State of Kerala WP(C). No. 10248 of 2010(E).

[82] *Id.*

[83] *Id.*

[84] *Supra* note 19.

[85] Kaipadth, *supra* note 83.

[86] M.C. Mehata v. Kamalnath AIR 2000 SC 1997.

has been or will be severely diminished" can well be incorporated into the environmental law and can be enforced through the courts."[87]

A. Ecocide defined

A comprehensive definition of ecocide is still to be found as crimes against the environment acquire new avenues day by day. The term can generally mean grave metaphors of destroyed landscapes. The crime of ecocide involves the "right to life of all the inhabitants" of the Earth, including human beings, flora, and fauna.[88] Ecocide is often not intended but is rather a crime of consequences.[89] This is because different aspects of environmental crimes such as air pollution, land destructions, crimes against non-human species, and water pollution act as the basis of this ultimate crime.[90] All these crimes are present in Kole Wetlands. This leads to ecosystem destruction and loss of originality to the Kole. This area of wetland is specifically important for humanity. Therefore, the criminalization demands for the protection and preservation of the area to prevent climate change and limit the emission of greenhouse gases. Criminal law can create ideological settings and mind-sets for all those who deal with this ecosystem.[91] The creation of legal doctrine makes certain concepts fundamentally unquestionable and indisputable. Law can thus act as a prevailing expansive standard in which ideologies are set and spread. This characteristic is especially important when addressing ecocide. Law can also create obedience by creating fear for legal punishments and sanctions. The reader has been introduced to these concepts previously in chapter one with Dr. Aliozi.

B. Ecocide in Indian Law

As Beatrice Hamilton points out in her chapter on the legal challenges to the inclusion of the crime of ecocide in the current international criminal code,

---

[87] Polly Higgins, ERADICATING ECOCIDE: LAWS AND GOVERNANCE TO STOP THE DESTRUCTION OF THE PLANET, London: Shepheard- Walwyn Ltd, (2010).

[88] Claudia Card, *Genocide and Social Death,* IN GENOCIDE'S AFTERMATH: RESPONSIBILITY AND REPAIR, ed. Claudia Card and Armen T. Marsoobian, 10-26, Malden: Blackwell Publishing, (2007).

[89] Lauren J. Eichler, *Ecocide Is Genocide: Decolonizing the Definition of Genocide,* GENOCIDE STUDIES AND PREVENTION 14, 2 (2020): 104-21, (2020), https://doi.org/10.50 38/1911-9933.14.2.1720.

[90] M.C. Mehata v. Union of India AIR 1988 SC 1037.

[91] Barry Weisberg, ECOCIDE IN INDOCHINA. Canfield Press, San Francisco (1970).

the term ecocide is not universally defined, which contributes to the legal challenges to the incorporation of an independent crime for ecocide in the Rome Statute. Indian law on ecocide is being developed and discussed at various levels.[92] Arguments at academic conferences and symposiums project the idea that ecocide is the sibling of genocide.[93] One author opines that the concept of this crime deserves incorporation under the legal arena for the protection of the environment.[94] The two significant concepts laid down under the Ramsar Convention are wetlands of international importance and the "wise use" of wetlands in the territory of each nation. These two principles act as the guiding light of contracting parties. Only a few wetlands, including the one we are discussing, are Ramsar sites of international importance. Hence, they need conservation for humanity as a whole. The Ramsar Convention's mandate is a constitutional obligation, and the state has implemented this through the legislation later.[95] While the Ramsar Convention parties met in Canada in 1987, they gave a precise definition to the wise use of wetlands. It means sustainable utilization for the benefit of mankind in a way compatible with the maintenance of the natural properties of the ecosystem. Sustainable utilization is further defined as human use of wetlands that may yield the greatest continuous benefit to present generations while maintaining its potential to meet the aspirations of future generations. The natural properties of the ecosystem that are to be maintained in the process of wise use of wetlands were also explained as those physical, chemical and biological components, such as soil, water, plants, animals and nutrients, and the interaction between them.[96]

These guidelines on wise use call upon India to review the existing legislation and institutional arrangements to deal with wetlands and incorporate better criminal sanctions to address the crime of ecocide.[97] Even

---

92 Prerna Bindra, THE VANISHING: INDIA'S WILDLIFE CRISIS, Penguin Random House, India, (2017).

93 Tord Björk, *The emergence of popular participation in world politics: United Nations Conference on Human Environment 1972*, DEPARTMENT OF POLITICAL SCIENCE, UNIVERSITY OF STOCKHOLM, (1996), http://www.folkrorelser.org/johannesburg/stockholm72.pdf.

94 See K. N. Chandrasekharan Pillai, *Criminal Sanctions and Enforcement of Environmental Legislation*, (1984) C.U. L.R. 201 at p. 208. The author however agrees on the need to apply the provision in section 133, Cr. P.C. injuncting the party from causing the criminal nuisance of environmental pollution; Chhatrapthi Singh, *Legal Policy for the Control of Environmental pollution*, [1984] C.U.L.R. 1 at 9.

95 Vishaka v. State of Rajasthan (1997) 6 SCC 241.

96 *Id.*

97 Vishaka, *supra* note 97.

though India does not have a separate definition and legislative provision to deal with this crime, the judiciary has indirectly referred to the same many times while dealing with wetland conservation.[98] One Judge made his conclusion by observing the importance of maintaining the wetlands as they are the bounty of nature. He denied the conversion of wetlands and said that environmental consciousness and a precautionary approach are needed. The rationale of the decision makes us remember that there is no sustainable alternative to ecological land use based on natural cycles that cause the least destruction to the vital resource like Kole Wetlands. Thus, the crime of ecocide needs to be connected to Indian legislation. [99]

C. Penalties and Punishments

It is clear from the facts presented that the Kole Wetland suffers from ecocide. This contributes to a serious disequilibrium in the earth-system. Due to the deteriorating ecological conditions of Kole Wetland, the traditional farming community is displaced from these places.[100] They lost their livelihood, and social status and they were trapped under the clutches of loan liabilities. There is also total negation on the part of authorities too. These are prima facie not treated as a crime as these elements do not fit under the strict definition. At the beginning of environmental protection, Indian remedies mostly concentrated on common law as India was a British Colony, and it still followed common law.[101] But it assumed greater heights according to society's needs, and new legislation brought newer types of crimes and punishments. The statute law enacted as seen above has many advantages over the common law. A statute can declare a certain action or inaction to be an offense and lay down deterrent sanctions, as well as effective remedies. The provision for complaints by citizens for criminal action against the offender enshrined in the Environment (Protection) Act, 1986 is a notable area under the statute law.[102] A similar provision was subsequently introduced by way of amendments to the laws relating to air and water.[103] But when we talk about crimes against the environment, the main sanctions are civil in nature, and

---

[98] People United for Better Living in Calcutta v. State of West Bengal AIR 1993 Cal 215.
[99] *Id.*
[100] George Chackacherry, *Participation of stakeholders in wetland conservation and management.* JOURNAL OF BASIC AND APPLIED BIOLOGY, 4(3) at 29-33 (2010).
[101] Julian Juergensmeyer, *Common Law Remedies and Protection of the Environment,* 6 U. BRIT. COLUM. L. REV. 215 (1971), https://core.ac.uk/download/pdf/234558946.pdf.
[102] EPA, *supra* note 59, § 19.
[103] Air (Prevention and Control of Pollution) Act, 1981, §. 43 and Water (Prevention and Control of Pollution) Act, 1974, §.49 introduced by 1987 and 1988 amendments respectively.

the courts dealing with the environmental offenses are vested with the power of civil courts in all respects.

The National Green Tribunal (NGT), discussed earlier in this volume by David Krott, is a specialized court established to deal with environmental cases and is treated at par with civil courts. Their jurisdiction and powers are well defined under the National Green Tribunal Act, 2010, constituting the Tribunal.[104] The NGT is not bound by the ordinary procedural law in India. It is bound by the principles of natural justice.[105] The scope of jurisdiction extends to forests, wildlife, the environment, climate change, and coastal protection.[106] The incorporation of provisions relating to the protection for the environment under the Constitution through the amendment in 1976 courts (including the apex court in India) has shown enthusiasm and devised several methods apart from something devised under the legislation to tackle the issues related to the environment.[107] Some new methods adopted by the Supreme Court are entertaining petitions on behalf of the affected party and inanimate objects, taking *suo-moto* action against the polluter, expanding the sphere of litigation,[108] expanding the meaning of existing Constitutional provisions,[109] applying international environmental principles to domestic environmental problems,[110] appointing an expert committee to give inputs and monitoring implementation of judicial decisions,[111] making spot-visits to assess the environmental problem at the ground level,[112] appointing amicus curiae to speak on behalf of the environment,[113] and encouraging petitioners

---

[104] The National green Tribunal Act, 2010 Preamble, https://greentribunal.gov.in/sites/default/files/act_rules/National_Green_Tribunal_Act, 2010.pdf.

[105] Avishek Chakraboty, *Principles of natural justice are principles of justice, equity and good conscience*, https://www.academia.edu/6307388/Equity_justice_and_good_conscience.

[106] Swait Bansal, *NGT gets strict over notification of wetlands*, INDIA WATER PORTAL (Jul. 30, 2016), https://www.indiawaterportal.org/articles/ngt-gets-strict-over-notification-wetlands.

[107] Himanshu Thakkar and Bhim Rawat, *India Wetlands Review 2017: Important Court Orders*, SANDRP (Feb. 3, 2018), https://sandrp.in/2018/02/03/india-wetlands-review-2017-important-court-orders/.

[108] Rural Litigation Kendra v. State of Uttar Pradesh AIR 1985 SC652, https://indiankanoon.org/doc/1949293/.

[109] F.K. Hussain v. Union of India AIR 1990 Ker 321, https://indiankanoon.org/doc/1965629/.

[110] M C Mehtha v. Kamalnath (1997)1 SCC 388, https://indiankanoon.org/doc/1514672/.

[111] Kerala Land Development Act, *supra* note 26.

[112] *Id.*

[113] T N Godavarman Thirumulkpad v. Union of India AIR 1998 SC 769 https://indiankanoon.org/doc/298957/.

and lawyers to draw the attention of Court about environmental problems through cash award.

Similarly, high courts are also showing activism in protecting and conserving the environment and devising methods to solve the issues relating to the environment in each state.[114] This is based on the constitutional guarantee of the right to life and the right to a clean environment. The establishment of NGT is also a judicial reform. The suggestion put forward in establishing the NGT can be helpful in carving out new arenas to protect the environment like Kole Wetlands too.[115]

It is worthwhile to add the development of public interest litigation here.[116] This area of litigation has its roots in the conservation and protection of the environment.[117] This idea is drawn from the U.S. decision in *Sierra Club v. Morton.*[118] Today a person acting *bona fide* and having sufficient interest can move the courts for redressing public injury, enforcing public duty, protecting social and collective rights and interest, and vindicating public interest.[119]

Another element to be mentioned is that the judicial remedies for environmental maladies will have effective results only if the remedies benefit those who are not parties to the litigation. This particular method of litigation has gained momentum among the Indian judiciary and paved the way for

---

[114] Garima Prashad, *Indian Judicial Activism on the 'Right to Environment': Adjudication and Locus Standing* (June 29, 2018), https://ssrn.com/abstract=3391846 or http://dx.doi.org/10.2139/ssrn.3391846.

[115] In Mehta v. India, the Supreme Court suggests: [T]o the Government of India that since cases involving issues of environmental pollution, ecological destruction and conflicts over natural resources are increasingly coming up for adjudication and these cases involve assessment and evolution of scientific and technical data, it might be desirable to set up Environmental Courts on a regional basis with one professional Judge and two experts drawn from the ecological sciences research group keeping in view the nature of the case and the expertise required for adjudication. There would of course be a right of appeal to this court from the decision of the Environment Court. *See* Eeshan Chaturvedi, *Green Courts: The Way Forward,* CORNELL POLICY REVIEW (Feb. 6, 2017), http://www.cornellpolicyreview.com/green-courts-the-way-forward/.

[116] Ravikiran, *Public Interest Litigation (PIL) in India: History, Significance, Issues,* IAS EXPRESS (May 12, 2020), https://www.iasexpress.net/public-interest-litigation-history-significance-issues/.

[117] Gauri Varun, *Public Interest Litigation in India: Overreaching or Underachieving?,* THE WORLD BANK, POLICY RESEARCH WORKING PAPER SERIES. (2009) 10.1596/1813-9450-510. https://www.researchgate.net/publication/46444168_Public_Interest_Litigation_in_India_Overreaching_or_Underachieving.

[118] *Sierra Club v. Morton,* 405 US 727.

[119] S.P Guptha and others v. Union of India AIR 1982 SC 149 at 192.

Supreme Court decisions for the protection and conservation of the environment. This method can be extended to bring criminal sanctions to enforce the protection of ecologically fragile landforms. As Prayank Jain has illustrated in this text, victims of green crimes may not always be humans. It is possible that the Kole Wetlands could have the standing to sue in court, although this particular litigation has not been pursued yet in India. As previously mentioned, there have been cases that have been decided by courts that gave people in *loco parentis* authority to act over rivers such as the Ganges. These cases have had limited success due to the intervention of the Indian Supreme Court. Criminal sanctions in appropriate instances are an effective tool to protect both human life and the environment. Criminal sanctions have to play their role in developing an eco-culture and a civic mode of economic development, which alone will lead to a healthy and enduring civilization. The Constitution of India reminds us that every citizen has a social obligation to protect and preserve the environment and keeping an ecological balance.[120]

Decisions relating to the environment are essentially based on many factors such as scientific material, highly technical data, socio-economic facts, health hazard aspects and ecological mores of the region. The government may lack insight into these aspects. Sometimes the experts may fall prey to the influence of bureaucratic and political elements. Thus, the traditional administrative mechanism on decision-making has become outdated. There are instances where the judiciary has taken a silent node towards administrative decisions even though there was strong evidence that those areas need conservation. [121]

---

[120] The Fundamental Duties of the citizens of India are enshrined in Article 51A (Part IV-A) of the Constitution. The Article was brought in by way of the 42nd Amendment of 1976 to bring the Indian Constitution in accordance with Article 29(1) of the Universal Declaration of Human Rights. While Fundamental Duties are unenforceable in courts, they are often resorted to in the interpretation of constitutional and other matters. In the context of animal rights, the relevant clauses of Article 51A read as follows: It shall be the duty of every citizen of India: . . . (g) to protect and improve the natural environment including forests, lakes, rivers and wildlife, and to have compassion for living creatures; (h) to develop the scientific temper, humanism and the spirit of inquiry and reform, https://indiankanoon.org/doc/867010/.

[121] *See* Sachidananda Pandey v. State of West Bengal and Ors, AIR 1987 SC 1109, https://indiankanoon.org/doc/497388/. *See also* Kaipadath Property Development Company v. State of Kerala, WP(C). No. 10248 of 2010(E), https://indiankanoon.org/doc/1372536/. See also M.C. Mehta v. Kamal Nath, *supra* note 110.

VI. Conclusion

The author argues that since the Kole Wetland area is a Ramsar site and considered a biodiversity hotspot, it deserves *in situ* conservation. Conservation here means something more than mere protection but the preservation of the basic characteristics and quality, as well as protecting the stakeholders who are traditionally associated with these specific Kole Wetlands. The Central Government should undertake the responsibility of assessing the services in every aspect offered by this particular area to the whole community of Kerala and hence to the country. Policies of Government, both Central and state, without keeping in mind the concept of sustainable development should be discarded. Because once the texture and quality are irreparably lost, it would not be possible to bring it back. This would not do justice either intra-generationally or inter-generationally. Thus, the present scale of degradation can well be fitted within the concept of ecocide to the Kole Wetlands and hence to humanity.

Bibliography

W.N. Adger, C. Luttrell. *Property rights and the utilisation of wetlands*, ECOLOGICAL ECONOMICS, 35(1), 75-89 (2000).

Mayank Aggarwal, *India's guidelines on wetlands will allow states to decide what counts as prohibited activities*, THE SCROLL, (Jan 22, 2020), https://scroll.in/article/949988/indias-guidelines-on-wetlands-will-allow-states-to-decide-what-counts-as-prohibited-activities.

G. Agoramoorthy and M.J. Hsu, *Biodiversity Surveys are crucial for India*, CURR. SCI., 82, 244-45 (2002) https://www.researchgate.net/publication/41396457_Bioconcentration_of_heavy_metals_in_selected_medicinal_plants_of_India.

Air (Prevention and Control of Pollution) Act, 1981.

Swait Bansal, *NGT gets strict over notification of wetlands*, INDIA WATER PORTAL (Jul. 30, 2016), https://www.indiawaterportal.org/articles/ngt-gets-strict-over-notification-wetlands.

E.B. Barbier, *Valuing environmental functions: tropical wetlands. Land economics*, 155-73, (1994) https://scholar.google.co.in/scholar?q=Barbier,+E.+B.+(1994).+Valuing+Environmental+Functions:+Tropical+Wetlands.+Land+Economics,+70+(2)+155-74.&hl=en&as_sdt=0&as_vis=1&oi=scholar.

Prerna Bindra, THE VANISHING: INDIA'S WILDLIFE CRISIS, Penguin Random House, India, (2017).

A.S. Binilkumar, *Heterogeneity Across Stakeholders' Preferences for Wetland Attributes: The Case of Kole Wetland in India*, PROCEEDINGS OF THE FOURTH WORLD CONGRESS OF ENVIRONMENTAL AND RESOURCE ECONOMISTS, (June 27 to July 2, 2010) Montreal, Canada. (cited in Nufaisa M et al, *Analysis of Production and Marketing of Paddy in Thrissur-Ponnani Kole wetlands*, INTERNATIONAL JOURNAL OF CURRENT ADVANCED RESEARCH, 08(07), 19387-91. (2019), DOI: http://dx.doi.org/10.24327/ijcar.2019.19391.3738.

A.S. Binilkumar and A. Ramanathan. *Valuing Wetland Attributes Using Discrete Choice Experiments: A Developing Country Experience,* 17TH ANNUAL CONFERENCE OF THE EUROPEAN ASSOCIATION OF ENVIRONMENTAL AND RESOURCE ECONOMISTS, Vrije Universiteit (VU University) Amsterdam, The Netherlands. (June 24-27, 2009).

THE BIODIVERSITY CONVENTION 1992, 8.2.3 *Biodiversity, waterways and wetlands overlay code.* https://publicdocs.scc.qld.gov.au/hpecmwebdrawer/Record/6008371/File/document.

Claudia Card, *Genocide and Social Death,* IN GENOCIDE'S AFTERMATH: RESPONSIBILITY AND REPAIR, ed. Claudia Card and Armen T. Marsoobian, 10-26, Malden: Blackwell Publishing, (2007).

George Chackacherry, *Participation of stakeholders in wetland conservation and management.* JOURNAL OF BASIC AND APPLIED BIOLOGY, 4(3) at 29-33 (2010).

Avishek Chakraboty, *Principles of natural justice are principles of justice, equity and good conscience,* https://www.academia.edu/6307388/Equity_justice_and_good_conscience.

Sarath Chandran, et al. HISTORY OF RECLAIMED KAYALS IN KUTTANAD WETLAND AND ASSOCIATED SOCIAL DIVIDE IN ALAPPUZHA DISTRICT, KERALA (2018) https://www.researchgate.net/publication/326682004.

Sivaperuman Chandrakasan, and Jayson Eluvathingal. *Birds of Kole wetlands, Thrissur,* ZOOS' PRINT JOURNAL, 10. 334-349, (2001), https://doi.org/10.11609/JoTT.ZPJ.15.10.344-9.

Eeshan Chaturvedi, *Green Courts: The Way Forward,* CORNELL POLICY REVIEW (Feb. 6, 2017), http://www.cornellpolicyreview.com/green-courts-the-way-forward/.

THE CONSTITUTION OF INDIA, (1950) Art. 246, schedule VII.

CONVENTION ON THE CONSERVATION OF MIGRATORY SPECIES OF WILD ANIMALS, *Central Asian Flyway Action Plan for Waterbirds and their Habitat Country Report – INDIA,* https://www.cms.int/raptors/sites/default/files/document/inf_04_13_India_0.pdf.

E. L. Danielson and J. A. Leitch, *Private versus Public Economics of Prairie Wetland Allocation.* JOURNAL OF ENVIRONMENTAL ECONOMICS AND MANAGEMENT. (1986) in Jeena T Srinivasan, *Agriculture-wetland Interactions: A Case Study of the Kole land Kerala,* (July, 2011), https://cess.ac.in/wp-content/uploads/2019/10/Monograph-No.19.pdf.

J.R. Dixon, et al, *Tracking Global Change in Ecosystem Area: The Wetland Extent Trends Index,* BIOLOGICAL CONSERVATION Vol. 193 (Nov. 19, 2016), https://doi.org/10.1016/j.biocon.2015.10.023.

DISTRICT SPATIAL PLANNING, *Thrissur District Plan: Part 1, Vol1,* http://townplanning.kerala.gov.in/town/wp-content/uploads/2019/04/dsp_thrissur.pdf.

DTE, *How green is the country? Check out our State of India's Environment Report 2019 In Figures,* DOWN TO EARTH (June 4, 2019), https://www.downtoearth.org.in/news/climate-change/how-green-is-the-country-check-out-our-state-of-india-s-environment-report-2019-in-figures-64915.

Lauren J. Eichler, *Ecocide Is Genocide: Decolonizing the Definition of Genocide,* GENOCIDE STUDIES AND PREVENTION 14, 2 (2020): 104-21, (2020), https://doi.org/10.5038/1911-9933.14.2.1720.

ENCYCLOPEDIA BRITANNICA, *Hydroponics,* (May 22, 2019), https://www.britannica.com/topic/hydroponics.

ENCYCLOPEDIA BRITANNICA, *Kerala,* https://www.britannica.com/place/Kerala (last visited August 5, 2020).

The Environment (Protection) Act, 1986.

S.P. Guptha and others v. Union of India AIR 1982 SC 149 at 192.

Polly Higgins, ERADICATING ECOCIDE: LAWS AND GOVERNANCE TO STOP THE DESTRUCTION OF THE PLANET, London: Shepheard- Walwyn Ltd, (2010).

F.K. Hussain v. Union of India AIR 1990 Ker 321, https://indiankanoon.org/doc/1965629/.

INTERNATIONAL LABOUR OFFICE THE FRAMEWORK OF THE WORLD EMPLOYMENT PROGRAMME, 1 at 31, (2010) https://www.google.co.in/books/edition/Agrarian_Reform_in_Contemporary_Developi/b4wqQgl0HVYC?hl=en&gbpv=1&pg=PA31&printsec=frontcover

S.E. John, et al, *Environmental degradation of a tropical estuary due to human interferences—a case studies from southern Kerala, SW India,* ARABIAN JOURNAL OF GEOSCIENCES, 10(16), 352 (2017).

B.I. Joseph., *Impact of Pesticides and Fertilizers on Quality of Water in Wetlands (Kole) and Neighbouring Areas of Division 43 of Thrissur Corporation,* PROJECT REPORT, St. Aloysius College, Elthuruth, Thrissur, Kerala, http://aloysius.in/joseph_project_abstract.pdf.

Julian Juergensmeyer, *Common Law Remedies and Protection of the Environment,* 6 U. BRIT. COLUM. L. REV. 215 (1971), https://core.ac.uk/download/pdf/234558946.pdf.

Kaipadath Property Development Company v. State of Kerala, WP(C). No. 10248 of 2010(E), https://indiankanoon.org/doc/1372536/.

Kübra Kalkandelen and Darren O'Byrne, *On ecocide: toward a conceptual framework,* DISTINCTION: JOURNAL OF SOCIAL THEORY, 18:3, 333-49, (2017) DOI: 10.1080/1600910X.2017.1331857.

N. Karunakaran, *Relative contribution of different elements to the growth of principal crop output in Kerala,* INDIAN DEVELOPMENT REVIEW, Vol. 11, No. 2 at 155-65. (2013) https://www.researchgate.net/publication/280499587_Karunakaran_N_Relative_contribution_of_different_elements_to_the_growth_of_principal_crop_output_in_Kerala_Indian_Development_Review_Vol_11_No_2_pp_155-165

Kerala Conservation of Paddy Land and Wetland Act, 2008.

Kerala Land Development Act, 1964.

Kerala Land Reforms Act, 1963.

Kerala Land Utilisation Order, 1967.

Gaurav Kumar et al, *Study on Status and Health of Wetlands in India: A Geographical Analysis,* OUR HERITAGE, (Aug.4, 2019), 10.6084/m9.figshare.11684394.

K.P. Mani, *Cropping pattern in Kerala– Spatial inter-temporal analysis.* In K. Rajan (Ed.), KERALA ECONOMY: TRENDS DURING THE POST-REFORM PERIOD, 64–84, New Delhi, India: Serials Publications. (2009) http://springer.nl.go.kr/chapter/10.1007%2F978-981-15-4611-2_10.

E. Matthews, I. Fung, *Methane emission from natural wetlands: Global distribution, area, and environmental characteristics of sources,* GLOBAL BIOGEOCHEMICAL CYCLES, 1(1), 61-86 (1986).

M.C. Mehata v. Kamalnath AIR 2000 SC 1997.

M.C. Mehata v. Union of India AIR 1988 SC 1037.

M.C. Mehta v. Kamal Nath and Ors, (1997)1 SCC 388, https://indiankanoon.org/doc/1514672/.

R. McInnes et al. *Ramsar and World Heritage Conventions: Converging towards success.* RAMSAR CONVENTION SECRETARIAT (2017), https://whc.unesco.org/en/ramsar/.

MINISTRY OF ENVIRONMENT, FOREST AND CLIMATE CHANGE, GOVERNMENT OF INDIA, *Wetlands conservation and management rules 2017,* http://moef.gov.in/wp-content/uploads/2020/01/final-version-and-printed-wetland-guidelines-rules-2017-03.01.20.pdf.

P.K. Muraleedharan, *Resource Use Efficiency in Kole Lands in Trichur District (Kerala),* INDIAN JOURNAL OF AGRICULTURAL ECONOMICS, INDIAN SOCIETY OF AGRICULTURAL ECONOMICS, vol. 42(4), (October 1987), https://ideas.repec.org/a/ags/inijae/271920.html.

Mini Muringatheri, *Kole fields to attract tourists in hordes,* THE HINDU, (Nov. 29, 2017), https://www.thehindu.com/news/national/kerala/kole-fields-to-attract-tourists-in-hordes/article21127834.ece.

P.O. Nameer, *Wetlands and waterfowl conservation in Kerala with special reference to Ramsar sites,* Ambat B (Ed.) PROCEEDINGS OF KERALA ENVIRONMENT CONGRESS, CENTRE FOR ENVIRONMENT AND DEVELOPMENT, Thiruvananthapuram. 97-112, (2005), https://zoosprint.zooreach.org/ZooPrintJournal/2006/August/2350-2355.pdf.

National Green Tribunal Act, 2010, https://greentribunal.gov.in/sites/default/files/act_rules/National_Green_Tribunal_Act, 2010.pdf

A. Parvathy, *Fish Diversity, Abundance and Traditional Fish Harvesting Methods at Kole Wetlands of Thrissur, Kerala.* INTERNATIONAL JOURNAL FOR RESEARCH IN APPLIED SCIENCE AND ENGINEERING TECHNOLOGY. 6. 1852-1857. (2018), 10.22214/ijraset.2018.1287. https://www.researchgate.net/publication/323872209_Fish_Diversity_Abundance_and_Traditional_Fish_Harvesting_Methods_at_Kole_Wetlands_of_Thrissur_Kerala.

People United for Better Living in Calcutta v. State of West Bengal AIR 1993 Cal 215.

K.N. Chandrasekharan Pillai, *Criminal Sanctions and Enforcement of Environmental Legislation,* (1984) C.U. L.R. 201.

Garima Prashad, *Indian Judicial Activism on the 'Right to Environment': Adjudication and Locus Standing* (June 29, 2018). https://ssrn.com/abstract=3391846 or http://dx.doi.org/10.2139/ssrn.3391846.

K.N. Raj and M. Tharakan., *Agrarian reform in Kerala and its impact on the rural economy–a preliminary assessment.* AGRARIAN REFORM IN CONTEMPORARY DEVELOPING COUNTRIES: A STUDY PREPARED FOR THE INTERNATIONAL LABOUR OFFICE THE FRAMEWORK OF THE WORLD EMPLOYMENT PROGRAMME, 1 at 31, (2010), https://www.google.co.in/books/edition/Agrarian_Reform_in_Contemporary_Developi/b4wqQgl0HVYC?hl=en&gbpv=1&pg=PA31&printsec=frontcover.

R. Rajinikanth and T.V Ramachandra, *Restoration of Lakes in Bangalore based on Status and Socio-economic aspects of wetlands,* PROJECT REPORT, (November 2000), http://wgbis.ces.iisc.ernet.in/energy/water/paper/economic_valuation/ecodoc2004.pdf.

THE RAMSAR CONVENTION ON WETLANDS OF INTERNATIONAL IMPORTANCE ESPECIALLY AS WATERFOWL HABITAT, 1971, http://portal.unesco.org/en/ev.php-URL_ID=15398&URL_DO=DO_TOPIC&URL_SECTION=201.html.

Ravikiran, *Public Interest Litigation (PIL) in India: History, Significance, Issues,* IAS EXPRESS (May 12, 2020), https://www.iasexpress.net/public-interest-litigation-history-significance-issues/.

Rural Litigation Kendra v. State of Uttar Pradesh AIR 1985 SC652, https://indiankanoon.org/doc/1949293/.

SANDRP, *India Ramsar Wetlands in Crisis in 2020,* (Mar. 7, 2020), https://sandrp.in/2020/03/07/india-ramsar-wetlands-in-crisis-in-2020/.

Sachidananda Pandey v. State of West Bengal and Ors, AIR 1987 SC 1109, https://indiankanoon.org/doc/497388/.

A. A. Sengupta, A. Gaur, *Treaty-making and Implementation in India: A Constitutional Paradox.* INDIAN JOURNAL OF INTERNATIONAL LAW 57, 47–61 (2017). https://doi.org/10.1007/s40901-018-0074-y.

Sierra Club v. Morton, 405 US 727.

Ravender Singh, et al. *Crop diversification through land modification in canal irrigation command of Eastern India,* SAARC JOURNAL OF AGRICULTURE (June 1, 2003), https://www.researchgate.net/publication/305999554_Crop_diversification_through_land_modification_in_canal_irrigation_command_of_Eastern_India/citation/download.

Jeena T. Srinivasan, *Agriculture-wetland interactions and sustainability of rice cultivation in the Kole land, Kerala,* INDIAN JOURNAL OF AGRICULTURAL ECONOMICS, Vol. 67(2) pp.213-224. (2012), http://14.139.116.20:8080/jspui/bitstream/10603/163270/8/17_bibliography.pdf.

Himanshu Thakkar and Bhim Rawat, *India Wetlands Review 2017: Important Court Orders,* SANDRP (Feb. 3, 2018), https://sandrp.in/2018/02/03/india-wetlands-review-2017-important-court-orders/.

Jayan Jose Thomas, *Paddy Cultivation in Kerala,* REVIEW OF AGRARIAN STUDIES, vol. 1, no. 2, (2011) http://ras.org.in/paddy_cultivation_in_kerala.

P. Thomas, *Agricultural performance in Kerala,* in Prakash, B.A., KERALA'S ECONOMIC DEVELOPMENT: ISSUES AND PROBLEMS. Sage Publications Pvt. Ltd. (1999) https://journals.sagepub.com/doi/abs/10.1177/2277976014530232.

T. N. Godavarman Thirumulkpad v. Union of India AIR 1998 SC 769 https://indiankanoon.org/doc/298957/.

Gauri Varun, *Public Interest Litigation in India: Overreaching or Underachieving?.* THE WORLD BANK, POLICY RESEARCH WORKING PAPER SERIES. (2009) 10.1596/1813-9450-510, https://www.researchgate.net/publication/46444168_Public_Interest_Litigation_in_India_Overreaching_or_Underachieving.

Vishaka v. State of Rajasthan (1997) 6 SCC 241.

Barry Weisberg, ECOCIDE IN INDOCHINA. Canfield Press, San Francisco (1970).

WORLD POPULATION REVIEW, *World Urbanization Prospects,* United Nations population estimates and projections of major Urban Agglomerations. (2020) https://worldpopulationreview.com/world-cities/thrissur-population.

Chapter 8

Crouching Tiger, Hidden Dragon: Hydropower and Crimes against Humanity

Regina Menachery Paulose

International Criminal Law Attorney

Abstract: The Introduction to the volume introduced the reader to the ongoing situation involving the Sardar Sarovar Dam in the Narmada River Valley. In 2000, the World Commission on Dams issued a report outlining how the international community could course-correct some of the negative impacts of hydropower dams. This chapter will focus on hydropower projects that have been initiated by India and China in the Himalaya Region. After discussing the situations in Sikkim and Tibet, respectively, the author will analyze whether the conduct and impacts involving the building and maintenance of dams amount to crimes against humanity. This chapter concludes with recommendations to stop repeat human rights violations and ecosystem damage in the context of green energy projects, like hydropower dams.

Keywords: Hydropower Dams, Himalayas, UNDRIP, UN Guiding Principles on Business and Human Rights, Crimes against Humanity, forced displacement, World Commission on Dams, FPIC, accountability, Sikkim, India, Tibet, China.

***

I. Introduction

Dams have had historical significance and use in Mesopotamian, Greek, and Roman civilizations.[1] The first hydroelectric project in 1882 ushered in a new

---

[1] Paul Neibrzydowski, *Top Ten Origins: Dams*, ORIGINS: CURRENT EVENTS IN HISTORICAL PERSPECTIVE (January 11, 2016), http://origins.osu.edu/connecting-history/top-ten-origins-dams.

era of what is considered "clean energy."[2] Hydropower plants have a three-part system: a power plant, a dam, and a reservoir.[3] Another type of hydropower plant is called the run of river (ROR), and it uses a small dam in order to create a small reservoir (pondage).[4] Hydropower is often touted as a leading source of renewable energy.[5] Since 1965, the global consumption of hydroelectric power has steadily increased.[6] It is reported that countries such as Norway, Paraguay, Bhutan, and Ethiopia obtain most of their share of electricity from hydropower.[7]

This chapter focuses on the construction and operation of hydroelectric dams, which have led to significant human rights violations, ecosystem destruction, and the erasure of indigenous peoples (Peoples). The author begins with a focused synthesis on the World Commission on Dams report, published in 2000. The World Commission on Dams (WCD) report provided policy guidelines and considerations for states when embarking on hydroelectric projects. Next, the author will present cases involving dam projects in the Himalayas, led by India and China. In the last section of the chapter, the author will discuss whether the acts involved in planning, building and maintaining hydro dams meet the elements of crimes against humanity (CAH). The author concludes with ways to move forward.

II. Rewind: From Gland to The World Commission on Dams

The WCD was born out of a growingly antagonistic debate between those who saw the benefits of hydropower projects and those opposed to them because of its negative impact on the environment and human rights. The WCD was an effort initiated by the World Bank in order to increase transparency around its own projects.[8] The World Bank and the World Conservation Union (IUCN)

---

[2] Christina Nunez, *Hydropower, Explained*, NATIONAL GEOGRAPHIC (May 13, 2019), https://www.nationalgeographic.com/environment/global-warming/hydropower/.

[3] *Id.*

[4] CLIMATE TECHNOLOGY CENTRE AND NETWORK, *Run of river hydropower*, https://www.ctc-n.org/technology-library/renewable-energy/run-river-hydropower (accessed November 26, 2020).

[5] WORLD COMMISSION ON DAMS (WCD), *Dams and Development A New Framework for Decision – Making*, Earthscan Publications 14 (November 2000), http://awsassets.panda.org/downloads/wcd_dams_final_report.pdf.

[6] Hayley Moller, *Hydropower Continues Steady Growth*, EARTH POLICY INSTITUTE, (June 14, 2012), http://www.earth-policy.org/data_highlights/2012/highlights29.

[7] *Id.*

[8] Asmal, Kader, *Introduction: World Commission on Dams Report, Dams and Development*, AMERICAN UNIVERSITY INTERNATIONAL LAW REVIEW 16, no. 6, 1411-1433, 1417, (2001).

co-hosted a meeting in Gland, Switzerland, in 1997 and invited interested groups to review issues related to dams. This meeting eventually led to the creation of the WCD.

The WCD gathered pertinent information from stakeholders over a series of meetings.[9] The WCD believed that their final report represented a milestone because it was the first "global and independent review" of dams; it focused on options assessment, equitable sharing of resources, and the "rights-and-risks" approach.[10] The WCD created a framework based on seven strategic principles, which were: 1) gaining public acceptance; 2) comprehensive options assessment; 3) addressing existing dams; 4) sustaining rivers and livelihoods; 5) recognizing entitlements and sharing benefits; 6) ensuring compliance; and 7) sharing rivers for peace, development, and security.[11] The WCD believed that the "key element" to dam projects was the "sustainable improvement of human welfare."[12] Many were happy with the final report because it brought much-needed attention to dams.[13]

For the purposes of this chapter, the author will focus on the WCD analysis regarding displacement and accountability measures. For contextual purposes, the WCD's report focused mainly on large dams. The WCD found that "large dams affect critical, life-sustaining resources, such as land, fisheries and the quality and allocation of freshwater, an increasingly scarce and coveted resource."[14] In case studies, they also found a "systematic bias towards underestimation of the capital costs of large dams."[15] Further, the building of large dams has "led to the impoverishment and suffering of millions..."[16] The WCD noted construction of dams brings in employment opportunities and more services which connect localities to national markets. However, they concluded that such benefits were "short-lived."[17]

It appears the hyper-focus on large dams in the report led to less air time for small dams to be evaluated. In this chapter, the author takes the position that small dams can be just as problematic as large dams, particularly when there

---

[9] *Id.* at 1426 – 1427.
[10] WCD, *supra* note 5, xxxvii.
[11] *Id.* at xxxiv and xxxv.
[12] *Id.* at 2.
[13] Kader, *supra* note 8, 1427.
[14] WCD, *supra* note 5 at 20.
[15] *Id.* at 41.
[16] *Id.* at xxxi.
[17] *Id.* at 99-100.

are multiple dams built along the same river.[18] These are generally the ROR projects, which in fact, have significant consequences.[19]

The WCD discussed displacement of communities as a result of these projects. The WCD found that both physical displacement and livelihood displacement/deprivation was taking place and that "all too often this physical displacement is involuntary and involves coercion and force – in a few cases even killing."[20] The WCD highlighted some tragic situations where people who vocalized their opposition to dams were met with state-sponsored violence:

> ...in Mexico, the Papaloapan River Commission set fire to the houses of indigenous Mazatecs who refused to move for the Miguel Aleman dam. In 1978 police killed four people when they fired at an anti-resettlement rally at Chandil dam in the state of Bihar in India. In Nigeria in April 1980, police fired at people blocking roads in protest against the Bakolori dam. And in 1985, 376 Maya Achi Indians, most of them women and children, were murdered in the course of clearing the area to be submerged by the Chixoy dam in Guatemala.[21]

When dams are given clearance to be built, states generally will provide resettlement and compensation packages. The WCD appeared dismayed to find that "pervasive and systematic failure" existed around the examination of the range of negative impacts, mitigation, resettlement, and development programs for displaced peoples.

Another major area assessed in the report was accountability.[22] The WCD proposed a "rights-based" approach[23] which is intended to ensure that the

---

[18] The WCD noted, "although seldom analyzed, cumulative impacts occur when several dams are built on a single river. They affect both the physical (first-order) variables, such as flow regime and water quality, and the productivity and species composition of different rivers." *Id.* at 88.

[19] Jeff Opperman, *Crocodiles Are Not Geckos: The Realities of Run-Of-River Hydropower,* FORBES, (June 6, 2019), https://www.forbes.com/sites/jeffopperman/2019/06/06/crocodiles-are-not-geckos-the-realities-of-run-of-river-hydropower/.

[20] WCD *supra* note 5 at 102-03.

[21] *Id.* at 18.

[22] *Id.* at 192.

[23] *Id.* at 200.

rights of all people are respected throughout the development process.[24] Further, the WCD recommended that "an appropriate legal and policy environment, accompanied by clear political will to act" can ensure that people who are impacted by dams "share in the benefits generated by such projects."[25] The Commission articulated potential avenues for accountability, which included a focus on appropriate reparations and "fair, open, and transparent" mechanisms for conflict resolution.[26] On a broader level, the Commission recommended an external review process and an international certification system.[27]

Since the launch of the 2000 report, it would be remiss to say that nothing has been done.[28] Founded in 1928, the International Commission on Large Dams issued a World Declaration on Dam Safety in 2019.[29] The World Declaration covers some of the issues highlighted in the final report. It is unclear how the 100 member countries in the organization will implement the Declaration, launched nineteen years after the WCD report. Civil society stakeholders continue to monitor and raise awareness of dams. They utilize the information to empower communities around the world and to remind states of the recommendations made.[30]

---

[24] This appears inspired by the 1986 UN Declaration on the Right to Development which applies human rights in approaches to development. The WCD specifically highlighted that the Declaration on the Right to Development upholds the right of peoples to exercise "complete sovereignty over all their natural wealth and resources" and "the right to self-determination." *Id.* at 200-01.

[25] *Id.* at 129.

[26] *Id.* at 207.

[27] *Id.* at 228-30 and 246. It appears that each country may have its own certification process, although this particular topic falls more into the compliance side of dam building. Of particular note is the International Hydropower Association which is a nonprofit organization that works with states and third parties mentioned in this report.

[28] *See* C. Schulz and WM Adams, *Debating Dams: The World Commission on Dams 20 years on.* WIREs WATER. (2019); 6:e1396. https://doi.org/10.1002/wat2.1369.

[29] INTERNATIONAL COMMISSION ON WORLD DAMS, *World Declaration on Dam Safety,* (October 18, 2019), https://www.icold-cigb.org/userfiles/files/World%20declaration/World%20Declaration%20on%20Dam%20Safety_ICOLD_A3.pdf.

[30] *See* Zachary Hurwitz, *Dam Standards: A Rights-Based Approach,* INTERNATIONAL RIVERS, (January 2014), file:///F:/WCD%20reports%20and%20commentary/intlrivers_dam_standards_final.pdf.

Have players in the dam business learned anything from the WCD 2000 report? The author now turns her attention to the Himalayan Region and will focus on dam projects led by India and China. In this next section, the author will examine these projects and other factors surrounding dams that highlight the need for accountability. Twenty years after the WCD's groundbreaking initiative, states have continued damming rivers, destroying Peoples, their cultures, and ecosystems.

III. The Himalayan Region: Countdown to destruction?

The Himalayan Region (HR) is famous for its picturesque mountain ranges – particularly one of its peaks, Mount Everest. The HR runs through India, Pakistan, Afghanistan, China, Bhutan, and Nepal. This "cryosphere" or "third pole" has the largest freshwater reserves outside of the North and South Pole.[31] The HR is known for its diverse and rich biodiversity[32] and also plays a significant role in shaping the climate of surrounding countries.[33]

The HR is also the source of the largest rivers in Asia, such as the Ganga, Indus, Mekong, Brahmaputra, the Yangtze, and Yellow Rivers.[34] These rivers, which provide resources for over a billion people,[35] have become a focal point for hydropower projects. "The cumulative hydropower potential of the Himalayan Rivers is reported to exceed 500 gigawatts."[36] Dam building in the HR appears to have started in the 1970s with Bhakra Nangal Dam, built by India, followed closely with two more by Pakistan, and some small to medium

---

[31] *See* Mahima A. Jain, *Glacier Research is Particularly Treacherous at the 'Third Pole'*, ATLAS OBSCURA, (May 5, 2020), https://www.atlasobscura.com/articles/glacier-research-at-the-third-pole#.

[32] *See* J. Xu, et al., *Sustaining Biodiversity and Ecosystem Services in the Hindu Kush Himalaya* in: Wester P., Mishra A., Mukherji A., Shrestha A. (eds) THE HINDU KUSH HIMALAYA ASSESSMENT, Springer, (2019).

[33] Marquest Hayes, *How The Himalayas Shape Climate in Asia*, WORLD ATLAS, (September 21, 2017), https://www.worldatlas.com/articles/how-the-himalayas-shape-climate-in-asia.html.

[34] L. Vemsani, *The Himalayan Ranges, Glaciers, Lakes and Rivers: An International Ecological, Economic and Military Outlook*, THE POLITICAL ECONOMY OF CONFLICT IN SOUTH ASIA, MJ Webb and A Wijeweera (eds), International Political Economy Series, Palgrave Macmillan, London, 172 (2015).

[35] Maharaj K. Pandit, et.al, *Dancing on the Roof of the World: Ecological Transformation of the Himalayan Landscape*, BIOSCIENCE, Vol 64, Issue 11, (November 2014), 980–92, https://doi.org/10.1093/biosci/biu152.

[36] *Id.* at 987.

projects by Nepal.[37] Since the HR became a popular area for hydroelectric expansion, surrounding countries built 6,200 miles of road in order to allow dam builders to access the areas.[38] There are a large number of dams that are scheduled to be built[39] even though scientists and environmentalists note the "young" mountain range is still undergoing geological changes. Therefore, "the risks of constructing and operating large hydro projects in the Himalayan region are 'very well known' because landslides and geological instability due to tectonic activity…"[40] Environmentalists continue to harp on the fact that "the cumulative destructive force of dams to river systems is becoming undeniable in India, Bangladesh and Pakistan. Entire ecosystems [are] shrinking to the point of complete dysfunction [and are] becoming the norm in these south Asian river deltas."[41]

The impact climate change has on the HR should not be ignored. Although scientists have stated that the HR has experienced climate changes in the past, it is the future that is of great concern.[42] Glacier melting has "accelerated," and "land once used for growing vegetables has become barren."[43] The Government of India's Ministry of Earth Sciences (MES) released a report discussing climate change in the HR. The MES found, among

---

[37] Shripad Dharmadhikary, *Mountains of Concrete: Dam Building in the Himalayas*, INTERNATIONAL RIVERS, (2008), pg 6, https://www.internationalrivers.org/sites/default/files/attached-files/ir_himalayas_rev.pdf.

[38] Sunil Amrith, *The Race to Dam the Himalayas*, NEW YORK TIMES, (December 1, 2018), https://www.nytimes.com/2018/12/01/opinion/himalayas-mountains-dams.html.

[39] Pandit, *supra* note 35, 987-88. However, the COVID -19 pandemic, which continues at the time of the writing of this chapter, appears to be impacting financing of these projects. See Jack Board, Southeast Asia's hydropower boom grinds to a halt as COVID-19 stalls projects, CNA ASIA, (April 22, 2020), https://www.channelnewsasia.com/news/asia/southeast-asia-hydropower-boom-covid-19-coronavirus-12652202.

[40] Rishika Pardikar, *Himalayan dams become economic burdens: lessons for Etalin*, THIRDPOLE.NET, (July 7, 2020), https://www.thethirdpole.net/2020/07/07/lessons-for-etalin-himalayan-dams-economic-burdens/.

[41] Clare Harrison, *The Great Walls Damming Tibet*, TIBET NATURE ENVIRONMENTAL CONSERVATION NETWORK, (June 16, 2018), https://tibetnature.net/en/great-walls-damming-tibet/.

[42] R. Krishnan, et al., *Unravelling Climate Change in the Hindu Kush Himalaya: Rapid Warming in the Mountains and Increasing Extremes* in eds. Wester P., Mishra A., Mukherji A., Shrestha A. (eds) THE HINDU KUSH HIMALAYA ASSESSMENT, Springer, (January 5, 2019), https://doi.org/10.1007/978-3-319-92288-1_3.

[43] Bhadra Sharma and Kai Schultz, *As Himalayas Warm, Nepal's Climate Migrants Struggle to Survive*, NEW YORK TIMES, (April 5, 2020), https://www.nytimes.com/2020/04/05/world/asia/nepal-himalayas-glacier-climate.html.

other devastating impacts, that "accelerated anthropogenic warming over this ice-covered mountain peaks and valleys of the HKH have profound impacts such as loss in glacier mass and snow cover which can directly affect agriculture food production."[44] The impact of climate change is significant and detrimental to the lives of the millions of people who reside in the area.

The climate change discussion also underscores two important factors linked to the building of dams. The first factor is water. Climate change patterns in the HR means that there will likely be a decline in water availability which "changes in water flow regimes have implications for hydropower generation…"[45] The MES stated, "while global climate change significantly affects the environment over the high mountain regions of Asia, its impact on the Himalayan cryosphere is a major threat to the regional water resources."[46] In another field study, researchers noted, "villagers complained about a water shortage, it was often due to a management problem and/or to a damaged network, to a diversion of water towards a hydropower turbine…"[47] The second factor is greenhouse gases. Greenhouse gas emissions are warming the planet; dams emit greenhouse gases, thus accelerating any warming that may already be occurring in the HR.[48] With these two factors, one has to continue to wonder what are the real benefits to dams.

a. Sikkim

In the far northeastern corner of India, sandwiched between Nepal and Bhutan, lays the Indian state of Sikkim. Sikkim is considered to be the original homeland of the Rong[49] peoples, who also reside in Nepal and the forest area

---

[44] T.P. Sabin and R. Krishnan, *Climate Change Over the Himalayas* in Eds. Krishnan, et. al., ASSESSMENT OF CLIMATE CHANGE OVER THE INDIAN REGION, Springer, (2020), 217, https://doi.org/10.1007/978-981-15-4327-2.

[45] Krishnan, *supra* note 42.

[46] Sabin, *supra* note 44.

[47] Joëlle Smadja, et al, *Climate change and water resources in the Himalayas*, JOURNAL OF ALPINE RESEARCH, 103-2 (2015), http://journals.openedition.org/rga/2910; DOI: https://doi.org/10.4000/rga.2910.

[48] INTERNATIONAL RIVERS, *Greenhouse Gas Emissions from Dams FAQ*, (May 1, 2007), https://www.internationalrivers.org/resources/greenhouse-gas-emissions-from-dams-faq-4064#.

[49] TRIBAL RESEARCH AND CULTURAL INSTITUTE, *Lepcha*, https://trci.tripura.gov.in/lepcha (accessed July 25, 2020). *See also* Heleen Plaisier, *A Brief Introduction to Lepcha Orthography and Literature*, BULLETIN OF TIBETOLOGY, (2005), 8, http://himalaya.socanth.cam.ac.uk/collections/journals/bot/pdf/bot_2005_01_02.pdf.

of Bhutan.[50] The Rong peoples have an endangered verbal and written language that is still spoken today. [51]

Also located in Sikkim is Dzongu (Koakaram Faokram), which is an incredibly important sacred area to the Rong.[52] The Rong, to this day, protect and preserve Koakaram Faokram. As one Rong leader writes,

> Dzongu is where God created Nazaong (the first Lepcha man) and Nyooking (the first Lepcha woman). Located in North Sikkim in India, Dzongu is the destination of an annual Lepcha pilgrimage. The region has plenty of sacred sites: caves where Guru Rinpoche meditated, the Keshong Lake, the Kongsa hot springs, and the Tholung temple, which is not only revered by Lepchas, but by all the Buddhists of Sikkim. Dzongu represents the last bastion of the Lepcha cultural heritage and the only place where we feel free to follow our distinctive cultural and religious traditions.[53]

In addition to this area, the Teesta River is also considered sacred to the Rong peoples, as it is their belief that the river is the "path to salvation for their departed in the afterlife."[54] The Rong also have a special connection to the Khangchendzonga National Park (KNP), which was recognized by UNESCO as a world heritage site in 2016. KNP contains a "unique diversity of plains, valleys, lakes, glaciers and spectacular, snow-capped mountains covered with ancient forests, including the world's third highest peak, Mount Khangchendzonga."[55] Further, KNP is an herbal and wildlife haven; it "has 422

---

[50] JOSHUA PROJECT, *Rongkup in India*, https://joshuaproject.net/people_groups/13041/IN (accessed July 25, 2020).

[51] Bhavya Venkatesh, *Reviving Lepcha*, THE HINDU, (August 4, 2018), https://www.thehindu.com/education/reviving-lepcha/article24601118.ece.

[52] *See generally*, BBC NEWS, *India's Lepcha tribe may lose Kanchenjunga ritual*, (November 7, 2011), https://www.bbc.com/news/world-asia-15626993#.

[53] Lyansong Tamsang and Biswajit Chakraborti, *The Dwellers of the Valley: A Community Profile from West Bengal*, CULTURAL SURVIVAL QUARTERLY MAGAZINE, (December 2020), https://www.culturalsurvival.org/publications/cultural-survival-quarterly/dwellers-valley-community-profile-west-bengal.

[54] Nikhil Roshan, *Troubled Waters: Why the Lepcha Community in Sikkim is Resisting Its Government's Attempts to Build Dams Over the River Teesta*, THE CARAVAN, (November 26, 2015), https://caravanmagazine.in/vantage/troubled-waters-why-the-lepcha-community-in-sikkim-is-resisting-its-governments-attempts-to-build-dams-over-the-river-teesta.

[55] UNESCO, *Khangchendzonga National Park*, http://whc.unesco.org/en/list/1513, (accessed July 25, 2020).

species of medicinal plants and is home to a diverse array of wildlife, including the big cats."[56]

Although the Dongzu has been a protected area by royal decree since 1956,[57] the Rong peoples face enormous threats to their existence because of existing and planned dams. According to the Affected Citizens of Teesta (ACT), there are thirty-one proposed dams to be built in the Teesta River Basin and five which are ongoing projects.[58] In 2003, the Sikkim government had made plans for the construction of several dams along the Teesta River.[59] There are several dams, and all of them are at different stages of development. All of these projects have met fierce resistance from the Rong peoples, who have argued that damming the rivers would "result in a complete alteration of their ecosystem – loss of fishing habitats, lack of water for irrigation and the depletion of a host plan, insect and bird species that thrive close to the riverbed."[60] The Rong's complaints have been ignored as dam development continues. Prior to the 2016 KNP UNESCO designation, the Rong peoples were concerned that the designation would not stop the proposed dam projects.[61] They were correct.

In 2005 the government of Sikkim and Himgiri Hydro Energy planned the construction of the Panan hydroelectric dam, which would submerge parts of Dongzu.[62] The Panan dam is a ROR project, and the Panan dam works with the hydropower plants located on the same river, "designed together to function as

---

[56] Uttara Gangopadhyay, *Khangchendzonga National Park: A Peek into Sikkim's Magnificence*, OUTLOOK TRAVELLER, (November 20, 2019), https://www.outlookindia.com/outlooktraveller/explore/story/70052/khangchendzonga-national-park-a-peek-into-sikkims-magnificence. In 2019 a camera caught for the first time an Indian tiger and the ever-elusive snow leopard using the same areas. This was the first time a tiger had been seen in Sikkim, at least since the 1980's. See Dechen Lachungpa, In a first, tiger spotted at 9,500 feet in Sikkim, DOWN TO EARTH, (January 9, 2019), https://www.downtoearth.org.in/news/wildlife-biodiversity/in-a-first-tiger-spotted-at-9-500-feet-in-sikkim-62755.

[57] Roshan, *supra* note 54.

[58] ACT, *ACT – Project Map*, http://www.actsikkim.com/map.html (accessed July 25, 2020).

[59] Roshan, *supra* note 54.

[60] *Id.*

[61] Aadil Brar, *In India not all are pleased by a national park's World Heritage status*, DEVEX, (December 4, 2017), https://www.devex.com/news/in-india-not-all-are-pleased-by-a-national-park-s-world-heritage-status-91139.

[62] Roshan, *supra* note 54.

an integrated project."[63] The Panan Project is located approximately 10 kilometers from KNP.[64]

The project faced opposition by groups, particularly the Rong, who asserted that the "project will affect the culture, demography, and social fabric of the [Rong] people….and affect the fragile ecology of the place."[65] The Rong people presented several issues from project developers not obtaining appropriate clearance from the National Board of Wildlife to incorrect statements in the EIA.[66] Although there were meetings held with the community, the Panan dam builders and the Rong people have different versions of what happened.[67] By 2007 the Rong peoples took part in a hunger strike that lasted 915 days until the project was scrapped.[68] As a result of opposition from the Rong people and given the financial status of Himgiri Company, the Panan project was not able to start.[69] Despite this, PTC India Financial Services has continued seeking bids for the Panan project as of 2019.[70]

Another project taking place on the Teesta River is the Teesta-IV[71] project by National Hydroelectric Power Corporation (owned by India), which is halfway completed.[72] The project started back in 2009, but Lanco Teesta Hydro Power could not resolve its financial situation to complete the project. Starting in 2012, the government held meetings in order to give clearance for the project

---

63 UNFCCC/CCNUCC, *Project Design Document (PDD)*, (May 31, 2012), 8, https://cdm.unfccc.int/filestorage/g/x/.
64NE Now News, *Sikkim: Renewed bids for Panan Hydropower Project sought*, (October 9, 2018), https://nenow.in/north-east-news/sikkim/sikkim-renewed-bids-for-panan-hydropower-project-sought.html.
65 *Id.*
66 Dawn Lepcha, *Comments on Proposed CDM status for 300 MW Panan Hydro Power Project*, https://cdm.unfccc.int/Projects/Validation/DB/2FN6ZLKQZWUA2LTTIRAH73FERKHE0M/view.html. (accessed July 29, 2020). More discrepancies were pointed out by International Rivers, *Comments on the Panan Hydro-Electric Project (India)*, (August 18, 2012), https://www.internationalrivers.org/resources/comments-on-the-panan-hydro-electric-project-india-7639.
67 International Rivers, *supra* note 66.
68 *Id.*
69 NE News Now, *supra* note 64.
70 *Id.*
71 The Teesta IV is a "Run of the River" dam. Harrison, *supra* note 41.
72 NS Energy, *Teesta – VI Hydropower Project, Sikkim*, https://www.nsenergybusiness.com/projects/teesta-vi-hydropower-project-sikkim/ (accessed July 26, 2020).

to be built.[73] In 2014 official communications were issued by the Government of India's Ministry of Environment and Forests (MEF). The Expert Appraisal Committee "recommended for grant of Environmental Clearance" the Teesta-IV project subject to certain conditions.[74]

That same year the Rong peoples pursued legal action against the Government of India over the Teesta IV project in the National Green Tribunal[75] on the grounds that the project would violate their "religious and traditional rights."[76] The 2017 appellate court decision was not favorable to the Rong peoples. The court noted that the MEF "scrapped" the Teesta I and Teesta II projects as a result of environmental studies and reports which had been conducted.[77] The court appeared tone-deaf to the damage dams cause, given prominent examples of hydropower throughout India – notably in the Narmada.[78] The court did not take into account the cultural and religious practices of the Rong people, who will be severely impacted. The Rong argued that the court's cost-benefit analysis was "based on anthropocentric approach without considering factors like ecosystems and environment."[79] The court utilized the "Principles of Sustainable Development, Polluters Pay and Precautionary Principles"[80] (Principles) in order to come to its decision.[81] The purpose of the Principles is to "strike a balance between development and environmental protection to facilitate economic growth and protection and preservation of the environment."[82] The court held that there was information

---

73 For example, *see* Expert Appraisal Committee, *Minutes of the 64 th Meeting of the Expert Appraisal Committee for River Valley and Hydroelectric Projects constituted under the provisions of EIA Notification 2006*, (February 1-2, 2013), http://environment clearance.nic.in/writereaddata/Form-1A/Minutes/24_riverminutes.pdf.

74 B.B. Barman, *Subject: Teesta-IV HEP (520 MW) project in North Sikkim District of Sikkim by M/s. NHPC Ltd – for Environmental Clearance – regarding.* (January 9, 2014), No. J-12011/67/2008-IA-1.

75 For general reading about the National Green Tribunal *see* S. Shrotria, S., *Environmental justice: Is the National Green Tribunal of India effective?* ENVIRONMENTAL LAW REVIEW, 17(3), 169–88 (2015), https://doi.org/10.1177/1461452915595548.

76 *Lepcha v. Union of India*, Appeal No. 11/2014/PB/5/EZ, (2017), ¶3.

77 *Id.* ¶ 22.

78 *Id.* ¶ 83.

79 *Id.* ¶ 34.

80 For a short introduction and commentary regarding the Principles *see* LEXLIFE INDIA, *The 'Polluter Pays' principle: challenges to the NGT in securing environmental justice*, (September 12, 2019), https://lexlife.in/2019/09/12/the-polluter-pays-principle-challen ges-to-the-ngt-in-securing-environmental-justice/.

81 Lepcha *supra* note 76, 82.

82 *Id.* ¶ 82.

missing but did not "quash" the Environmental Clearance completely, but only in part, subject to certain conditions to be completed before commencement.[83] By 2018, the National Hydroelectric Power Corporation took over the finances for the project and now seeks to have the Teesta IV dam operating by 2024.[84]

b. Tibet

China is no stranger to the hydropower enterprise. Under the leadership of Chairman Mao, China embarked on an ambitious policy, "The Great Leap Forward," to build dams, irrespective of the impact it had on people (mass starvation) and wildlife.[85] Despite the horrible impact this had within China, China has not curbed its appetite to build dams. In fact, within the last twenty years,

> China already counts about half the world's large dams within its borders. It has paid a huge price for this development. Chinese dams have displaced an estimated 23 million people, and dam breaks have killed approximately 300,000 people. Scientific evidence suggests that the Zipingpu Dam may have triggered the devastating earthquake in Sichuan of 2008. Dams have also taken a huge toll on China's biodiversity, causing fisheries to plummet, threatening the endangered giant Chinese sturgeon, and driving species such as the *baiji*, or Yangtze River Dolphin, to extinction.[86]

China's dam ambitions have moved beyond its own borders and have started wreaking havoc throughout Asia. In 2011, Sinohydro (owned by China) began clearing forest areas for a dam in Indonesia.[87] The dam is scheduled to be built in the Batang Toru ecosystem, which is home to a rare species of Tapanuli orangutans.[88] The construction of the dam will fragment the orangutan population. In addition, it will destroy the surrounding ecosystem,

---

[83] *Id.* ¶ 85.
[84] NS Energy, *supra* note 72.
[85] For a full history *see* Frank Dikotter, MAO'S GREAT FAMINE, Bloomsbury USA, (2010).
[86] INTERNATIONAL RIVERS NETWORK, *Chinese Government Proposes New Dam Building Spree*, (February 28, 2011), https://www.internationalrivers.org/resources/china%E2%80%99s-government-proposes-new-dam-building-spree-3419.
[87] Jeremy Hance, *World's newest great ape threated by Chinese dam*, THE GUARDIAN, (April 23, 2018), https://www.theguardian.com/environment/radical-conservation/2018/apr/23/worlds-newest-great-ape-threatened-by-chinese-dam.
[88] *Id.*

emit greenhouse gases, and radically alter the lives of those who live downstream.[89] It is estimated that Sinohydro currently has "486 projects under construction in more than 72 countries."[90]

China's plan for hydropower growth also includes the fragile HR. In 2014 China began building the Lalho Hydel hydroelectric project on the Brahmaputra River (known in China as the Yarlung Zangbo River), which is near Sikkim.[91] According to the Chinese government, the goal of the project was to store water and assist with irrigating farmland.[92] Therefore, this dam, unlike the Panan and Teesta IV dams, will be a "storage reservoir" and take water out of the river.[93] The dam is being built in the upper stream of the Brahmaputra, which means that the lower stream or downriver states, India, Bangladesh, and Nepal, have concerns about water flowing into their countries.[94] Some experts have dismissed these concerns arguing that "China has little capacity to hold the water back."[95] However, there is no treaty between India and China, which means there is potential for water disputes to take place and remain unresolved.[96] The other possible negative impact of the Lalho dam is desertification in Tibet.[97] Tibet is "a geologically unstable region," and the Tibetan plateau "remains ecologically sensitive and seismically active"; therefore, all dams built will also be subjected to Mother

---

[89] Wettsein and Buckland, *Damming Evidence*, (May 2018), 2,4, https://www.orangutans-sos.org/content/uploads/2018/05/Damming-Evidence.pdf.

[90] INTERNATIONAL HYDROPOWER ASSOCIATION, *Power China*, https://www.hydropower.org/companies/powerchina# (accessed July 27, 2020).

[91] Sutirtho Patranobis, *China blocks Brahmaputra tributary, impact on water flow in India is not clear*, HINDUSTAN TIMES, (October 1, 2016), https://www.hindustantimes.com/india-news/china-blocks-brahmaputra-tributary-impact-on-water-flow-in-india-not-clear/story-QVAYbO2iOBFUSynwwpyneN.html.

[92] *Id.*

[93] Nihkar Gokhale, *Ignore the scaremongering. China can't turn off Brahmaputra even if it wants*, CATCHNEWS, (February 10, 2017), http://www.catchnews.com/india-news/china-can-t-block-brahmaputra-but-india-still-faces-a-threat-from-its-own-dams-1476452286.html.

[94] Ibu Sanjeeb Garg, *Why India should be worried about China's Lalho dam*, LIVEMINT, (October 18, 2016), https://www.livemint.com/Opinion/u143w6gzzfwkQs3t1wBu3O/Why-India-should-be-worried-about-Chinas-Lalho-dam.html.

[95] Gokhale, *supra* note 93.

[96] Anushka Saraswat, *Dragon in the Himalayas: China's Water Hegemony*, DIPLOMATIST, (June 3, 2020), https://diplomatist.com/2020/06/03/dragon-in-the-himalayas-chinas-water-hegemony/#.

[97] Harrison, *supra* note 41.

Nature's fury.[98] The environmental implications in Tibet are enormous,[99] and this is in addition to the significant challenges, crimes, and rights violations that Tibetans are subjected to under Chinese Community Party rule.[100]

It is unclear whether China has conducted any EIA for this dam or any others it is building within the HR. It has been alleged that the Chinese EIA process is riddled with corruption and is more of a "marginalizes and decorative process."[101] There is a lack of evidence as to whether or not Tibetan people have been incorporated into the pre-construction process of any project and/or that they have been notified of the tremendous risks they face.[102] Chinese secrecy regarding state-run projects and the lack of information sharing will continue to prove detrimental.[103]

c. State Relations (or the lack thereof)

The relationships between states in the region are a factor that must be considered when one examines dams. The states within Asia have complicated relationships and histories. Water is a coveted resource across the region, and given the number of people who need it, it automatically adds an extra social and political charge to each situation.[104] Dams have proven themselves to be unfashionable and costly[105] and also complicate state relations. For example, in 2000, "a dam burst in Tibet causing flash floods downstream in Arunachal Pradesh. The floods resulted in 30 casualties and

---

98 Dechen Palmo, *Tibet's Rivers Will Determine Asia's Future*, THE DIPLOMAT, (November 1, 2019), https://thediplomat.com/2019/11/tibets-rivers-will-determine-asias-future/.

99 *See* Dr. Simon Bradshaw, *Tibet An Environmental Challenge*, AUSTRALIAN TIBET COUNCIL, (2015), https://drive.google.com/file/d/0BznuJeH49IWRaW54WkpfMjR2TEU/view.

100 Frida Ghitis, *While All Eyes were on Hong Kong, China Just Ended Hopes for a 'Free Tibet*, WORLD POLITICS REVIEW, (July 23, 2020), https://www.worldpoliticsreview.com/articles/28934/while-all-eyes-were-on-hong-kong-china-just-ended-hopes-for-a-free-tibet. See also Michael C. Davis, China and the UN Declaration on the Rights of Indigenous Peoples: The Tibetan Case, E-INTERNATIONAL RELATIONS, (May 27, 2014), https://www.e-ir.info/2014/05/27/china-the-un-declaration-on-the-rights-of-indigenous-peoples-the-tibetan-case/.

101 Peter Bosshard, *Dam Nation*, FP, (March 8, 2011), https://foreignpolicy.com/2011/03/08/dam-nation/.

102 Palmo, *supra* note 98.

103 THE ECONOMIST, *If China won't build fewer dams, it could at least share information*, (May 14, 2020), https://www.economist.com/leaders/2020/05/14/if-china-wont-build-fewer-dams-it-could-at-least-share-information.

104 Saraswat, *supra* note 96.

105 FRED PEARCE, WHEN THE RIVERS RUN DRY, Granta Publishing, pg 14, (2018).

seriously damaged Indian infrastructure."[106] China, the upstream beneficiary of the dam, did not give information to the Indian government, which may have been able to avert casualties. By 2002, both countries signed a Memorandum of Understanding (MOU) to share information regarding three specific hydro stations so that India could monitor the water levels to avert further catastrophe.[107]

In 2006 both countries created an Expert Level Mechanism aimed at sharing information regarding trans-boundary rivers.[108] In 2008 and 2010, both countries signed pacts that shared rainfall data for the dams in Tibet.[109] However, in 2017, China's construction on the Brahmaputra was alleged to have turned the water black.[110] Yet, no data was shared with India as a result of political tensions.[111]

It is clear both countries need *neutral* mechanisms in order to assist in resolving disputes between them. The lack of fair and appropriate agreements and mechanisms impacts a large number of people. Fred Pearce states, "dam construction generates international tension when the rivers they block do not have functioning water-sharing agreements."[112] Current river agreements are extremely weak. They are "restricted to narrow data-sharing or technocratic remits…"[113] Some researchers and scholars have suggested creating a coalition of countries who share the rivers so that there is a mutually agreed-upon

---

[106] Madeleine Lovelle, *Co-operation and the Brahmaputra: China and India Water Sharing*, FUTURE DIRECTIONS INTERNATIONAL, (March 15, 2016), http://www.futuredirections.org.au/wp-content/uploads/2016/03/Co-operation-and-the-Brahmaputra-China-and-India-Water-Sharing.pdf.

[107] Dipanjan Roy Chaudhury, *River data to flow again as India, China defuse conflicts*, ECONOMIC TIMES, (March 8, 2018), https://economictimes.indiatimes.com/news/defence/river-data-to-flow-again-as-india-china-defuse-conflicts/articleshow/63224015.cms?from=mdr.

[108] *Id.*

[109] TNN, *Why India is worried about China's dam projects on the Brahmaputra river*, THE ECONOMIC TIMES, (October 5, 2016), https://economictimes.indiatimes.com/news/politics-and-nation/why-india-is-worried-about-chinas-dam-projects-on-the-brahmaputra-river/articleshow/54691589.cms?utm_source=contentofinterest&utm_medium=text&utm_campaign=cppst.

[110] FP Staff, *China's hand suspected in River Siang turning black: Beijing has always targeted Brahmaputra and its tributaries*, FIRSTPOST, (November 30, 2017), https://www.firstpost.com/india/chinas-hand-suspected-in-river-siang-turning-black-beijing-has-always-targeted-brahmaputra-and-its-tributaries-4234951.html.

[111] *Id.*

[112] Pearce, *supra* note 105, 167.

[113] *Id.* 167.

approach to utilizing the waters.[114] Most of these countries, with the exception of India and China, have bilateral treaties that govern their use of the river basins, but no multilateral treaty exists between all of them.[115] Other scholars suggest that a water treaty may also alleviate some problems.[116] Treaties that already exist might provide a glimpse of the challenges that lay ahead if a new one were to be created. In 1997 the UN adopted the Watercourses Convention. It asked countries to agree to a "sustainable and equitable use of shared rivers."[117] The Convention did not enter into force until August 2014 and to date has few signatories.[118] China voted against it.[119] India also has not ratified the Convention, given China's position.[120] As Michael Kugelman from the Wilson Center perfectly summed up:

> Many South Asian states are mired in deep cross-boundary water disputes, and they aren't ready to commit to the measures proposed by this Convention, especially as these provisions could be harmful to some states. For example, the Convention says states can't govern their water in ways that harm other states. This means, in effect, that an upstream state building a run of the river dam that nonetheless decreases river flows downstream, could be construed as a violation.[121]

While the author is skeptical of yet another water treaty coming into fruition, one success story is the Indus Water Treaty, which is enforced by the

---

[114] G.G. Dewdi, *China's Dam Building Spree in Tibet: Strategic Implications and India's Options*, MANOHAR PARRIKAR INSTITUTE FOR DEFENCE STUDIES AND ANALYSES, (October 21, 2016), https://idsa.in/idsacomments/china-dam-building-spree-in-tibet_ggdwivedi_211016.

[115] Dr. Gopal Siwakoti, *Trans-boundary River Basis in South Asia: Options for Conflict Resolution*, INTERNATIONAL RIVERS, (2011), pghttps://www.internationalrivers.org/sites/default/files/attached-files/transboundaryriverbasins.pdf.

[116] Saraswat, *supra note* 96. *See also* Ambika Vishwanath, *Tensions with China – Pakistan can derail fragile water treaties, but India won't talk about it*, THE PRINT, (July 6, 2020), https://theprint.in/opinion/tensions-with-china-pakistan-can-derail-fragile-water-treaties-but-india-wont-talk-about-it/455196/.

[117] Pearce, *supra* note 105, 169.

[118] CONVENTION ON THE LAW OF THE NON-NAVIGATIONAL USES OF INTERNATIONAL WATERCOURSES, A/Res/51/229, (May 21, 1997).

[119] Pearce, *supra note* 105, 167.

[120] Beth Walker, *China and India ignore UN watercourses convention*, CHINA DIALOGUE, (August 18, 2014), https://chinadialogue.net/en/climate/7229-china-and-india-ignore-un-watercourses-convention/.

[121] *Id.*

World Bank who refuses to give new loans unless the parties keep up with the agreed provisions.[122] The WCD had suggested the need for agreements so as to keep the peace between regional players. As more countries become ambitious with their water plans,[123] it may be inevitable that a regional treaty with a strong dispute resolution mechanism is created.

d. The State as a corporation and other third-party players

Corporate actors play a large role in the construction of dams; specifically, they "play a critical role in many of these infrastructure development[s], including those to mitigate and reduce the risks of natural hazards, such as the construction of flood protection embankments or reservoirs to mitigate drought risks."[124] Stakeholders suggest businesses should be more involved in the EIA and Strategic Environment Assessments.[125] Unfortunately, it is evident that state-sponsored corporations will likely be involved in the project, which means that there is a lack of diverse perspectives and solutions brought to most dam projects. However, even if a state is disguised as a corporation, it would still be bound by various international rights treaties and conventions such as the United Nations Convention against Corruption. Important non-binding instruments include the 2007 UNDRIP and also the UNGPBHR, which will now be discussed.

India voted in favor of the UNDRIP with the caveat that all people in India are indigenous.[126] India does have laws and provisions that aim to protect and preserve tribal and Adivasi peoples, including specific provisions in the Indian Constitution.[127] The UNDRIP was promptly supported and then disavowed by

---

122 Pearce, *supra* note 105, 169.

123 India has launched its ambitious River Linking Project which may have some benefits. However, it does include what appears to be the building of more dams. Mayank Bhardwaj, *Narendra Modi's $87 billion river linking project set to take off as floods hit India,* MINT, (September 1, 2017), https://www.livemint.com/Politics/CXOomlTqJMoDYIXPrLVrNP/Narendra-Modis-87-billion-riverlinking-project-set-to-tak.html.

124 Jyotiraj Patra and Christina Hill, *Rethinking business and human rights in transboundary river governance in South Asia,* OXFAM, (June 11, 2020), https://asia.oxfam.org/latest/blogs/rethinking-business-and-human-rights-transboundary-river-governance-south-asia.

125 *Id. See also* Brahma Chellaney, *Hydro-hegemony: Will China turn off Asia's tap?* THE JAPAN TIMES, (December 27, 2020), https://www.japantimes.co.jp/opinion/2020/12/27/commentary/world-commentary/china-asia-water/.

126 IWGIA, *Indigenous World 2019: India,* (April 24, 2019), https://www.iwgia.org/en/india/3455-iw2019-india.html.

127 *Id.*

China, stating there were no indigenous[128] peoples in China.[129] UNDRIP Article 7 provides that indigenous peoples have the right to life (which is also contained in the ICCPR and the ICESCR). This right is clearly violated over and over again with the development of hydropower dams, given water scarcity, food scarcity, and forced displacement. UNDRIP Article 8 provides that states "shall provide effective mechanisms for prevention… (b) any action which has the aim or effect of dispossessing them of their lands, territories, and resources."[130] India's EIA consultation sessions and the National Green Tribunal or public interest petitions in Indian courts mean such mechanisms exist; however, in China, it appears these mechanisms are blatantly absent. Furthermore, with China building dams outside its territories, there are no mechanisms created by companies to hear allegations regarding rights violations.

One key provision in the UNDRIP is FPIC which has been discussed in Leo Mukosi's chapter about the DAPL. The WCD also took note of FPIC in its final report. FPIC has been emphasized and repeated in UN committee decisions as well as regional and national courts.[131] At the same time, it has been noted that "the gap between what is increasingly accepted to be a requirement of international law and actual practice is still very wide."[132] It is clear FPIC is not a consideration in the cases highlighted here, particularly in the case of the Rong peoples, and as the ongoing situation in

---

[128] It should be noted that there was no formal adoption of a definition of indigenous peoples. However, there are characteristics that may identify whether a group is indigenous, which was discussed in the Final Report of Special Rapporteur Jose Martinez Cobo, *Study of the Problem of Discrimination against Indigenous Populations*, Chapter V, E/CN.4/Sub.2/1982/2/Add.6, (June 20, 1982), https://www.un.org/esa/socdev/unpfii/documents/MCS_v_en.pdf.

[129] *See* Michael C. Davis, *China and the UN Declaration on the Rights of Indigenous Peoples: The Tibetan Case*, E-INTERNATIONAL RELATIONS, (May 27, 2014), https://www.e-ir.info/2014/05/27/china-the-un-declaration-on-the-rights-of-indigenous-peoples-the-tibetan-case/.

[130] UN GENERAL ASSEMBLY, UNITED NATIONS DECLARATION ON THE RIGHTS OF INDIGENOUS PEOPLES: resolution / adopted by the General Assembly, (October 2, 2007), A/RES/61/295, available at: https://www.refworld.org/docid/471355a82.html.

[131] *See generally* J. Cariño and M. Colchester, *From dams to development justice: Progress with 'free, prior and informed consent' since the World Commission on Dams*, WATER ALTERNATIVES, 3(2): 423-437, (2010), http://www.water-alternatives.org/index.php/alldoc/articles/vol3/v3issue2/102-a3-2-25/file.

[132] *Id.*

the Mekong River Basin indicates, FPIC does not appear to be taken seriously generally by most states.[133]

Dam projects do not tend to show the intended strength of the UNDRIP. As Engle noted in her article, "by subjecting the rights contained in the declaration to the vague standards of 'international human rights obligations' and 'justice, democracy, respect for human rights, equality, non-discrimination, good governance and good faith', the provisions offer states a way to define certain indigenous claims out of these categories, and to deny them accordingly."[134]

The UNGPBHR has a significant role to play in the dam context because it contains specific provisions related to state-owned corporations. In 2008 Special Representative John Ruggie proposed a framework comprised of three pillars. These pillars were incorporated and became the basis of the UNGPBHR. The UNGPBHR gives clear guidance that governments must "protect" human rights, corporations must "respect" human rights, and victims should be given "remedy" for human rights abuses.[135]

Under Article 6 of the UNGPBHR, states are to ensure awareness, protection, and respect for human rights. Under Article 4, state-owned enterprises are to take "additional steps to protect against abuses that are committed." The UNGPBHR calls attention to the fact that states should facilitate grievance systems when human rights are violated (Article 28), and mechanisms should be "legitimate, accessible, predictable, equitable, transparent…" (Article 31).[136] Organizations such as the International Hydropower Association and the International Commission on Large Dams could play a critical role in ensuring that businesses (states) involved in hydropower are, in fact, upholding their commitments under the UNGPBHR. The number of

---

[133] The Mekong River Basin deserves its own chapter because of the dynamics between states. *See* EARTH RIGHTS INTERNATIONAL, *Indigenous Futures Submerged by Dams,* (November 12, 2014), https://earthrights.org/blog/indigenous-futures-submerged-by-dams/. *See also* Maureen Harris, *A Matter of Rights in the Future of the Mekong,* INTERNATIONAL RIVERS, (December 22, 2016), https://www.internationalrivers.org/blogs/721/a-matter-of-rights-in-the-future-of-the-mekong.

[134] Karen Engle, *On Fragile Architecture: The UN Declaration on the Rights of Indigenous Peoples in the Context of Human Rights,* EUROPEAN JOURNAL OF INTERNATIONAL LAW, Vol 22, Issue 1, (February 2011), 141–163, https://doi.org/10.1093/ejil/chr019.

[135] John Ruggie, *UN Guiding Principles,* https://scholar.harvard.edu/john-ruggie/un-guiding-principles (accessed on July 31, 2020).

[136] For a full analysis *see* Regina M. Paulose, et. al, *Navigating Business and Human Rights in South Asia,* THE COMMON GOOD FOUNDATION, (November 28, 2020), https://www.actwithus.org/report-navigating-business-and-human-rights-in-south-asia/.

hydropower companies appears to be growing,[137] and emphasizing these principles is important in achieving an appropriate "rights-risk" balance. The author could not locate any concrete examples of corporations or governments in Asia providing a *specialized mechanism* for communities impacted by dams.

Finally, third parties such as the World Bank and the Asian Development Bank have been instrumental in allowing dam construction. Even though communities have successfully pressured financiers away from projects, third parties must be examined in this context and held accountable for their actions in funding these environmental disasters. The WCD raised concerns about third parties as well:

> ...on paper the World Bank has a comprehensive set of policies dealing with large dam projects. More recently the International Finance Corporation and the Inter-American, Asian and African Development Banks have adopted similar guidelines. Despite these changes, the banks' policies, like the national regulatory systems are more concerned with project planning, design and financial management than with options assessment or with the operational phase of a large dam project.[138]

Despite the policies and mechanisms created to bring communities to the table, financiers walk away with blood on their hands with these investments. In 2018 a dam collapsed, killing at least 27 people and displaced approximately 6,600, not including the 25,000 people in Cambodia who had to be evacuated because of the flooding. [139] A day after the accident, 1,494 people in Laos had to be evacuated to emergency shelters.[140] The companies involved, two South Korean firms and one state-owned Laotian company, had differing accounts of the events, and so warnings were not adequate to help those who lived downstream.[141] Experts considered the dam to be a "slow moving humanitarian and ecological disaster."[142] The World Bank, alongside the Asian Development Bank, had financed the billion-dollar dam and in 2017

---

[137] Pearce, *supra* note 105, 102.

[138] WCD, *supra* note 5, 188.

[139] Mike Ives, *A Day Before Laos Dam Failed, Builders Saw Trouble*, NEW YORK TIMES, (July 26, 2018), https://www.nytimes.com/2018/07/26/world/asia/laos-dam-collapse.html.

[140] *Id.*

[141] *Id.*

[142] *Id.*

turned control of the dam over to the Laotian government.[143] This mistake of financing sham construction projects in the name of sustainable development had been repeated earlier by the World Bank in Thailand's Pak Mun dam.[144] Third-party financiers must be included as potential parties to be held accountable for rights violations and environmental damage.

IV. International Crimes: CAH

Communities, particularly Peoples, have no recourse for the plundering, destruction, razing of their lands, resources, and environment because of dam projects. Hydropower dams pose an interesting challenge for international criminal law practitioners because the victims are a combination of Peoples and ecosystems.

The two major countries written about in this chapter have not ratified the ICC's Rome Statute;[145] therefore, it is best to discuss CAH using the draft articles of the proposed Treaty on Prevention and Punishment of Crimes against Humanity (Treaty) which at the time of writing is in the preparatory phase.[146] The Treaty will encourage states to adopt and incorporate crimes against humanity into their national legal frameworks and encourage inter-state cooperation to address these prohibited acts. This is consistent with most crime-based conventions. The definition of CAH will seem familiar to those who are versed in international criminal law as the definition is identical to the one found in the Rome Statute.

The author now examines different ways in which dams could constitute CAH. The author will first examine forcible displacement as CAH, given the impact dams have on Peoples. The author will then examine violations of human rights that amount to "other inhumane acts" as CAH. Finally, the author will consider the question of environmental personhood, which is

---

[143] Kelli Rogers, *In Laos, a World Bank 'model' dam and the myth of sustainable hydropower*, DEVEX, (October 24, 2018), https://www.devex.com/news/in-laos-a-world-bank-model-dam-and-the-myth-of-sustainable-hydropower-93716.

[144] *Id.*

[145] *See* Takemura H. *The Asian Region and the International Criminal Court* in: Nakanishi Y. (eds), CONTEMPORARY ISSUES IN HUMAN RIGHTS LAW, Springer, Singapore (2018).

[146] The author is aware of another draft set of articles of the CAH floating around. For the purposes of this chapter, she utilizes the ILC's draft articles and commentary. INTERNATIONAL LAW COMMISSION, ***Draft articles on Prevention and Punishment of Crimes Against Humanity***, YEARBOOK OF THE INTERNATIONAL LAW COMMISSION, Vol II, Part Two, (2019), https://legal.un.org/docs/?path=../ilc/texts/instruments/english/draft_articles/7_7_2019.pdf&lang=EF.

referred to throughout this book and specifically written about in the chapter by Prayank Jain.[147] The author will begin with a general overview of each element and then proceed to the analysis thereafter.

Utilizing the proposed Convention,[148] under Article 2, crimes against humanity "means any of the following acts when committed as part of a widespread or systematic attack directed against any civilian population, with knowledge of the attack:

> (d) deportation or forcible transfer of population;
>
> (k) other inhumane acts of a similar character intentionally causing great suffering, or serious injury to body or to mental or physical health."[149]

The Commentaries of the ILC note that the term *widespread or systematic* has been defined in several cases. The ICTR, ICTY, and the ILC commentary to

---

[147] Leo Mukosi has discussed how the Dakota Access Pipeline has led to cultural genocide. In this instance, the author believes that indigenous groups in this chapter could make the same claims, consistent with the original interpretation presented by Raphael Lemkin, regarding dams. In addition, the crime of ecocide discussed by Beatrice Hamilton and Dr. Dayana Maliyekkal Kunjachan also would apply to this situation. Further the WCD report discusses in passing the crime of corruption. The author has decided to solely examine CAH as she believes it is an under-utilized crime among what is often labeled the "core crimes." However, the author has previously argued how transnational crimes should be incorporated into the Rome Statute and the crime of corruption was included in that analysis. *See* Regina M. Paulose, *Beyond the Core: Incorporating Transnational Crimes into the Rome Statute,* CARDOZA JOURNAL OF INTERNATIONAL AND COMPARATIVE LAW, Vol. 21, No 1 (Fall 2012).

[148] China and India are not parties to the Rome Statute. China had objections to the definition of crimes against humanity. *See* Dan Zhu, China, *Crimes Against Humanity and the International Criminal Court,* JOURNAL OF INTERNATIONAL CRIMINAL JUSTICE, Volume 16, Issue 5, December 2018, 1021-41, https://doi.org/10.1093/jicj/mqy036. India also had an objection to the definition of the crime in the Rome Statute. *See* Usha Ramanathan, *India and the ICC,* JOURNAL OF INTERNATIONAL CRIMINAL JUSTICE, Volume 3, Issue 3, (July 2005), Pages 627–34, https://doi.org/10.1093/jicj/mqi055. For reactions to the current treaty by India, China, and other countries, *see also* WHITNEY R. HARRIS WORLD LAW INSTITUTE, *Compilation of Government Reactions to the UN International Law Commission's Work on Crimes against Humanity 2013- 2019,* (July 2020), https://law.wustl.edu/wp-content/uploads/2020/08/Compilation-of-6th-Committee-Responses-to-CAH-2013-2019.pdf.

[149] ILC, *supra* note 146 at Article 2, 27.

the 1996 Draft Code of Crimes against Peace and Security of Mankind indicates that only one of the conditions needs to be met, *widespread* or *systematic*, for this particular criteria to be met under CAH.[150] The tribunals appear to consistently conclude that isolated acts of violence do not meet the criteria for *widespread*, but while there should be a "multiplicity" in victims, there is no definitive number required.[151] Second, international tribunals have interpreted the geographic area under *widespread* to be broad.[152] Similarly, the approach by international tribunals towards the element of *systematic* has been narrowed to the "organized nature of the acts of violence and improbability of their random occurrence."[153]

Under the proposed Treaty text, an *attack directed against any civilian population* means "a course of conduct involving the multiple commissions of acts referred to in paragraph 1."[154] Courts have found that the attacks against the civilian population should not be incidental, but rather civilians are the direct target of the attack.[155] Evelyne Schmid noted in her text that the element *attack* is not specifically defined in international criminal law treaties and is not limited to violent attacks.[156] In fact, Schmid points out that in *Prosecutor v. Akayesu* and in the Commission of Inquiry on Human Rights for the Democratic People's Republic of North Korea that an *attack* could be non-violent, as identified in these situations.[157] In *Karadzic*, the ICTY held an attack "may encompass any mistreatment of the civilian population."[158]

An *attack directed* poses a different challenge for CAH analysis with relation to dams. The Treaty states that the *attack* must be *directed* in furtherance of a state or organizational policy (this is consistent with the Rome Statute).[159] The

---

[150] *Id.* at 31, ¶10. The Rome Statute takes a slightly different view.

[151] *Id.* at 32-33, ¶12.

[152] *Id.* 33, ¶13.

[153] *Id.* 34, ¶16, *citing Prosecutor v. Ahmad Muhammad Harun and Ali Muhammad al abd-al-Rahman*, Case No. ICC02/05-01/07, Decision on the prosecution application under Article 58(7) of the Statute, (April 27, 2007), PRE-TRIAL CHAMBER I, INTERNATIONAL CRIMINAL COURT, ¶62. https://legal.un.org/docs/?path=../ilc/texts/instruments/english/commentaries/7_7_2019.pdf&lang=EF.

[154] *Id.* at 27, Article 2.

[155] *Id.* at 34, ¶18.

[156] Evelyne Schmid, TAKING ECONOMIC, SOCIAL, AND CULTURAL RIGHTS SERIOUSLY IN INTERNATIONAL CRIMINAL LAW, Cambridge, 76- 80 (2015).

[157] *Id.* at 76- 80.

[158] *Prosecutor v. Radovan Karadžić*, Case No. IT-95-5/18-T, Public Redacted Version of Judgement Issued on 24 March 2016 – Volume I of IV (TC), (March 24, 2016), ¶47.

[159] ILC, *supra* note 146 at 28, ¶2(a).

policy does not need to be formalized, nor does it require "pre-established plans," it can be implemented by action or inaction, and the policy can be inferred from the circumstances.[160] There are no lingering questions about whether the policies with regards to dams belong to the state, as it is clear they control every aspect of the process.

Interestingly, Schmid points out that the UN Commission of Inquiry on Human Rights in the Democratic Republic of Korea stated, "it is not necessary that the policy pursues the objective to harm the population."[161] She explains,

> a state could have a general policy to harass certain groups or a policy to do whatever it takes to achieve a certain outcome (achieve foreign investment, construct major infrastructure, etc.) without necessarily having a policy...as long as perpetrators are aware of the casual relationship between the policy and the harm done, it is not required that the policy aims at violating [economic, social, and cultural rights]."[162]

In the context of dams, it is important to note that several groups of people must be kept in mind when we think about the element of a *civilian population*. The easiest groups to identify are the communities that will be removed from specific locations in order to build the dams. Similarly, communities that depend on forest resources will be forced to relocate because of related submergence issues. As the WCD commented,

> In the case of communities dependent on land and the natural resources base, this often results in the loss of access to traditional means of livelihood, including agricultural production, fishing, livestock grazing, fuelwood gathering and collection of forest products, to name a few. Not only does this disrupt local economies, it effectively displaces people – in a wider sense – from access to a series of natural resource and environmental inputs into their livelihoods. This form of livelihood displacement deprives people of their means of production and dislocates them from their existing socio-cultural milieu.[163]

---

160 *Id.* at 39, ¶26.
161 Schmid, *supra* note 156, at 83.
162 Schmid, *supra* note 156, at 84.
163 WCD, *supra* note 5, 103.

Another group of civilians are those who reside "downstream" from the construction or structure. Downstream communities are impacted by dams because "the most common and most threatening impact is the loss of food security that stems from changes in the flow regime – especially the loss of seasonal flooding."[164] Downstream communities are often forgotten because they are forced to migrate as a result of these impacts. Finally, communities that are impacted when there are hydropower accidents (dam collapse) or natural disasters should be considered and included.

Finally, the *mens rea* element *with knowledge* continues to be shaped by international courts. Courts appear to agree that a perpetrator's general knowledge suffices, as opposed to the perpetrator having precise details. In addition, knowledge could be inferred from the circumstances.[165] Dams are created at the direction of higher-level state authorities, and as the author has already indicated, there are many cases throughout Asia where the project developers and financiers are the state. That leads to the question; do governments engaged in these projects have the requisite knowledge? It could be argued that they have knowledge as to what is at stake with dam construction because of the WCD report. Even prior to the WCD report, states surely would have had knowledge of what dams do if they took a moment to look down from their glass castles to see that communities were forced to relocate or were forcibly displaced under government-created schemes.

a. Forced Displacement

The Treaty has interpreted the prohibited act of *deportation or forcible transfer of a population* to mean "forced displacement of the persons concerned by expulsion or other coercive acts from the area in which they are lawfully present, without grounds permitted under international law."[166] It appears that this interpretation is taken from the ICTY, which used "forcible displacement" to cover both deportation and forcible transfer.[167] The late and brilliant Professor M. Cherif Bassiouni argued that the two prohibited acts are distinct as deportation involves forcibly removing people from one country to another, whereas the latter act would be the "compulsory" movement of people from one area to another (same state).

---

[164] B.D. Richter, et. al, *The downstream human consequences of dams*, WATER ALTERNATIVES, 3(2): 14- 42, (2010), available at: http://www.water-alternatives.org/index.php/volume3/v3issue2/80-a3-2-3/file.

[165] ILC, *supra note* 146, at 42, ¶34-35.

[166] *Id.* at 28, ¶1 (d).

[167] M. Cherif Bassiouni, CRIMES AGAINST HUMANITY, Cambridge Publishers, 393, (2011).

The ICTY has held that it is "the absence of 'genuine choice' that makes a given act of displacement unlawful."[168]

Do dams lead to the forcible transfer of a population? The WCD highlighted multiple times instances of displaced peoples, and in some cases, violence to forcibly displace peoples from their homes and territories in order to build dams. Generally, "the construction of large dams has led to the displacement of some 40 to 80 million people worldwide…Many of them have not been resettled or received adequate compensation, if any."[169] The WCD also highlighted this tidbit:

> The world's two most populous countries – China and India, have built around 57% of the world's large dams – and account for the largest number of people displaced. In the late 1980s China officially recognised some 10.2 million people as 'reservoir resettlers', though other sources suggest the figure may be substantially higher.[170]

Given the proliferation of dams since the WCD final report in 2000 and the increase in population in both countries, it is extremely likely that the number of displaced persons because of dams would have - using a conservative estimate - increased well over the figures the WCD presented.

This behavior is not lawful under international human rights law. The ICCPR provides under Article 12 states that people who are lawfully within a state[171] have the right to freedom of movement and to freely choose their homes.[172] This also means that people are to be protected against "all forms of forced internal displacement."[173] Although the state can place restrictions, those restrictions cannot "impair the essence of the right."[174] The UNDRIP states under Article 8 that Peoples should "not be subjected to forced assimilation or destruction of their culture." As the Rong court case proved,

---

168 *Id.* citing *Krnojelac v. Prosecutor*, Case No. IT-97-25-A, Judgment, ¶218, 222-224, (September 17, 2003) and *Prosecutor v. Simic et al.*, Case No IT-95-9, Trial Judgment, ¶123-24, (October 17, 2003). It is possible that the lack of FPIC would lead one to conclude that there is a lack of genuine choice in most of these cases.

169 WCD, *supra note* 5, 16-17.

170 WCD, *supra note* 5, 17.

171 In the situations mentioned there has been no disagreement about whether the populations impacted by the construction of dams in the HR are there lawfully.

172 Office of the High Commissioner for Human Rights, *CCPR General Comment No. 27: Article 12 (Freedom of Movement)*, CCPR/C/21/Rev.1/Add.9, (November 2, 1999), ¶4.

173 *Id.* at ¶7.

174 *Id.* at ¶13.

despite facts to the contrary, courts still will give clearance for dams to be built. The states are aware that the peoples in question are lawfully present where they are, and this constitutes a widespread or systematic (pick your poison) attack directed against a civilian population.

b. Other Inhumane Acts

Prohibited acts under this category have been interpreted to include acts where victims have inflicted on them "great suffering, or serious injury to body or to mental or physical health, by means of inhumane act."[175] The ICC's interpretation is once again consistent with the interpretations put forward by the ICTY and ICTR. The two tribunals appeared interested in matters that were of "similar seriousness" to the acts in the ICTY and ICTR articles.[176] The Cambodia and Sierra Leone tribunals have used "other inhumane acts" to prosecute acts such as forced marriage.[177]

Schmid indicates that "there is absolutely no element indicating that [economic, social, and cultural rights] violations could not amount to 'other inhumane acts' and this is clearly confirmed in the case law."[178] One example she uses to emphasize this point are the cases in the Nuremberg Military Tribunal where defendants were tried and found guilty of conducting medical experiments.[179]

There are two other types of impacts that states create as a result of these dam projects. These are detrimental health impacts and starvation of civilian populations. The WCD reported Peoples found "their lands and livelihoods threatened by forces beyond their experience or control. Similarly, existing settlements at construction sites have found themselves subject to increased health problems (including malaria, sexually transmitted diseases, and HIV-AIDS) and a loss of social cohesion with the large influx of outsiders."[180] This chapter has also highlighted that downstream communities suffer significantly as fisheries are impacted by large dams. Food and other resources will dwindle already as a result of climate changes, and dams will only stand to make things worse.

---

175 This interpretation is from the Rome Statute. ILC, *supra note* 146, 44, at ¶39. https://legal.un.org/docs/?path=../ilc/texts/instruments/english/commentaries/7_7_2019.pdf&lang=EF.

176 Bassiouni, *supra* note 167, 407.

177 *Id.* at 408-09.

178 Schmid, *supra note* 156, 164.

179 *Id.* at 163.

180 WCD, *supra* note 5, 100.

c. CAH and Environmental Personhood: A Philosophical Query

The environmental impact to dams cannot be overstated. The WCD found "large dams generally have a range of extensive impacts on rivers, watersheds and aquatic ecosystems – these impacts are more negative than positive and, in many cases, have led to irreversible loss of species and ecosystems."[181] The question presented in this section is whether or not environmental personhood could be utilized in the context of dams to pursue CAH cases.

In 2014 the Indian judiciary ordered three Uttarakhand officials to act *in loco parentis* and "protect, conserve and preserve the Rivers Ganga and Yamuna and their tributaries."[182] The officials were further ordered to "promote the health and well-being of the Rivers," which have extreme religious significance to Hindu peoples.[183] In another case, the Uttarakhand High Court then adjudicated a case brought by a private citizen who petitioned to prevent "the further recession of the Gangotri and Yamunotri Glaciers, as well as an order to protect nearby forests."[184] The Court noted that India had made international commitments under the 1968 Stockholm Declaration and the 1992 Rio Declaration and therefore has a duty to protect the environment. The Court formally declared the Himalayan ecosystem to be a "full legal person with rights equivalent to those of human beings" and appointed persons who would act *in loco parentis.*[185] While many environmentalists celebrated, the Indian Supreme Court swiftly stayed the decision of the Uttarakhand court, concerned about civil liability issues.[186]

In the international criminal legal realm, the current concept of environmental personhood appears to provide few answers and more questions. An appropriate test would be to see if an *in loco parentis* doctrine can work for a river that has dams. In the case of the Rong, the Teesta holds religious significance as the Ganga does for Hindu peoples, but as noted earlier, the National Green Tribunal did not incorporate that in its final decision.

---

[181] WCD, *supra* note 5, xxxi.

[182] INTERNATIONAL RIVERS, et. al, *Rights of Rivers*, 44, https://www.internationalrivers.org/resources/reports-and-publications/rights-of-river-report/ (accessed November 27, 2020).

[183] *Id.* at 44.

[184] *Id.* at 45.

[185] *Id.* at 45.

[186] THE INDIAN EXPRESS, *SC stays Uttarakhand HC order on Ganga, Yamuna living entity status*, (July 8, 2017), https://indianexpress.com/article/india/sc-stays-uttarakhand-hc-order-on-ganga-yamuna-living-entity-status-4740884/.

d. Last thoughts

Finally, it is worth calling attention to the *without prejudice* clause in the proposed CAH Convention. The ILC commentary states, "...this definition does not affect any broader definitions provided for in international instruments, customary international law or national law."[187] The *without prejudice* clause leaves room for possibly more prohibited acts to be considered under CAH, assuming it also meets the other elements.

Professor Bassiouni noted that a more progressive definition of CAH would extend the *ratione materiae* beyond harms against people and incorporate "other protected interests that may have effects or consequences on the life, health, and well-being of persons."[188] He continued, "there are a number of relevant international conventions for the protection of the environment but they seldom include criminal sanctions..."[189] Paying more attention to how international criminal law can be proactive in the dam arena may be the first step in creating this reality.

V. Steps forward to preventing green crimes

The callous behavior exhibited by states that build dams and ignore long-term repercussions needs to be addressed through accountability measures. Consideration of dams under the lens of green crimes is overdue. Public activism has been a significant deterrent on some level in Dongzu and Tibet. Given all the issues surrounding hydropower dams all over the world, the current solutions lie in repeating a little bit of dam history.

It is time for another global meeting of the WCD. Since 2000, many significant changes not only to international human rights law but also to international criminal law have taken place. The two instruments discussed in this chapter, the UNDRIP and the UNGPBHR, must be given focused attention should another meeting occur. In addition, the WCD has an opportunity to now ask pointed questions of governments engaged in building dams and how they have incorporated these legal instruments into their policies. Further, pointed questions should be asked about what mechanisms exist to allow people to remedy their situations appropriately. Further, it is time to incorporate international criminal law into the discussions.

With all the attention around climate change, we cannot ignore the creation of infrastructures that are new forms of "green colonialism." That is, they are

---

187 ILC, *supra* note 146, at 28, ¶1.

188 Bassiouni, *supra* note 167, 14.

189 *Id* at 14.

supposedly built to address sustainable development and climate change. These projects are leading to violations of basic human rights and causing further environmental destruction. Peoples, in particular, are constantly made a footnote in the expansion of green projects. Peoples need to be given *equal decision-making power* when projects are constructed on territories that are central to their cultural heritage.[190] Using international criminal law to shift frameworks may be a key aspect of the discussion that is needed. If not, as other authors in this volume suggest, perhaps it is time for international environmental criminal law to take hold and a dedicated international environmental criminal court to come into existence.

VI. Conclusion

In most cases involving hydropower dams, it is often Peoples who suffer violations of their basic human rights. This chapter has focused on two notable players in the dam game, but there are many more situations like this that have occurred or are occurring all over the world. The ICC Prosecutor should be encouraged to look at situations where forced displacement and other inhumane acts are taking place where jurisdictional requirements are met. At the same time or alternatively, regional mechanisms can be implemented to independently review these situations and states themselves should ensure the human dignity and security of their own peoples in conjunction with environmental protection.

International criminal law cannot be cleanly inserted into these discussions. The time has come to consider marrying international crimes with green crimes, as in some instances, they are intertwined. Whether one agrees with whether this can adequately work, the reality is, more needs to be done to hold states accountable for the damage caused to Peoples and the environment in the name of green energy and sustainable development.

---

[190] At the time of publication, the Congress of Nations and States has launched. The Congress of Nations and States "is expected to convene in 2022 to demonstrate the historical convergence of nations' delegations meeting with states' delegations on an equal political plane to jointly formulate and adopt methods for constructively conducting relations to maximize peaceful resolution of disputes and facilitate beneficial cooperation and mutual coexistence." THE CONGRESS OF NATIONS AND STATES, https://cnsint.org/about-cns/ (accessed on November 26, 2020). Whether the Congress will take up the issue of hydropower dams remains to be seen.

Bibliography

ACT, *ACT – Project Map*, http://www.actsikkim.com/map.html (accessed July 25, 2020).

Sunil Amrith, *The Race to Dam the Himalayas*, NEW YORK TIMES, (December 1, 2018), https://www.nytimes.com/2018/12/01/opinion/himalayas-mountains-dams.html.

B.B. Barman, *Subject: Teesta-IV HEP (520 MW) project in North Sikkim District of Sikkim by M/s. NHPC Ltd – for Environmental Clearance – regarding.* (January 9, 2014), No. J-12011/67/2008-IA-1.

M. Cherif Bassiouni, CRIMES AGAINST HUMANITY, Cambridge Publishers, 393, (2011).

BBC NEWS, *India's Lepcha tribe may lose Kanchenjunga ritual,* (November 7, 2011), https://www.bbc.com/news/world-asia-15626993#.

Mayank Bhardwaj, *Narendra Modi's $87 billion river linking project set to take off as floods hit India,* MINT, (September 1, 2017), https://www.livemint.com/Politics/CXOomlTqJMoDYIXPrLVrNP/Narendra-Modis-87-billion-river linking-project-set-to-tak.html.

Jack Board, Southeast Asia's hydropower boom grinds to a halt as COVID-19 stalls projects, CNA ASIA, (April 22, 2020), https://www.channelnewsasia.com/news/asia/southeast-asia-hydropower-boom-covid-19-coronavirus-12652202.

Peter Bosshard, *Dam Nation,* FP, (March 8, 2011), https://foreignpolicy.com/2011/03/08/dam-nation/.

Dr. Simon Bradshaw, *Tibet An Environmental Challenge,* AUSTRALIAN TIBET COUNCIL, (2015), https://drive.google.com/file/d/0BznuJeH49IWRaW54WkpfMjR2TEU/view.

Aadil Brar, *In India not all are pleased by a national park's World Heritage status,* DEVEX, (December 4, 2017), https://www.devex.com/news/in-india-not-all-are-pleased-by-a-national-park-s-world-heritage-status-91139.

J. Cariño and M. Colchester, *From dams to development justice: Progress with 'free, prior and informed consent' since the World Commission on Dams,* WATER ALTERNATIVES, 3(2): 423-437, (2010), http://www.water-alternatives.org/index.php/alldoc/articles/vol3/v3issue2/102-a3-2-25/file.

Dipanjan Roy Chaudhury, *River data to flow again as India, China defuse conflicts,* ECONOMIC TIMES, (March 8, 2018), https://economictimes.indiatimes.com/news/defence/river-data-to-flow-again-as-india-china-defuse-conflicts/articleshow/63224015.cms?from=mdr.

Brahma Chellaney, *Hydro-hegemony: Will China turn off Asia's tap?* THE JAPAN TIMES, (December 27, 2020), https://www.japantimes.co.jp/opinion/2020/12/27/commentary/world-commentary/china-asia-water/.

CLIMATE TECHNOLOGY CENTRE AND NETWORK, *Run of river hydropower,* https://www.ctc-n.org/technology-library/renewable-energy/run-river-hydropower (accessed November 26, 2020).

Jose Martinez Cobo, *Study of the Problem of Discrimination against Indigenous Populations,* Chapter V, E/CN.4/Sub.2/1982/2/Add.6, (June 20, 1982), https://www.un.org/esa/socdev/unpfii/documents/MCS_v_en.pdf.

CONVENTION ON THE LAW OF THE NON-NAVIGATIONAL USES OF INTERNATIONAL WATERCOURSES, A/Res/51/229, (May 21, 1997).

Michael C. Davis, China and the UN Declaration on the Rights of Indigenous Peoples: The Tibetan Case, E-INTERNATIONAL RELATIONS, (May 27, 2014), https://www.e-ir.info/2014/05/27/china-the-un-declaration-on-the-rights-of-indigenous-peoples-the-tibetan-case/.

G.G. Dewdi, *China's Dam Building Spree in Tibet: Strategic Implications and India's Options*, MANOHAR PARRIKAR INSTITUTE FOR DEFENCE STUDIES AND ANALYSES, (October 21, 2016), https://idsa.in/idsacomments/china-dam-building-spree-in-tibet_ggdwivedi_211016.

Shripad Dharmadhikary, *Mountains of Concrete: Dam Building in the Himalayas*, INTERNATIONAL RIVERS, (2008), 6, https://www.internationalrivers.org/sites/default/files/attached-files/ir_himalayas_rev.pdf.

Frank Dikotter, MAO'S GREAT FAMINE, Bloomsbury USA, (2010).

EARTH RIGHTS INTERNATIONAL, *Indigenous Futures Submerged by Dams*, (November 12, 2014), https://earthrights.org/blog/indigenous-futures-submerged-by-dams/.

THE ECONOMIST, *If China won't build fewer dams, it could at least share information*, (May 14, 2020), https://www.economist.com/leaders/2020/05/14/if-china-wont-build-fewer-dams-it-could-at-least-share-information.

Karen Engle, *On Fragile Architecture: The UN Declaration on the Rights of Indigenous Peoples in the Context of Human Rights*, EUROPEAN JOURNAL OF INTERNATIONAL LAW, Vol 22, Issue 1, (February 2011), 141–163, https://doi.org/10.1093/ejil/chr019.

EXPERT APPRAISAL COMMITTEE, *Minutes of the 64 th Meeting of the Expert Appraisal Committee for River Valley and Hydroelectric Projects constituted under the provisions of EIA Notification 2006*, (February 1-2, 2013), http://environmentclearance.nic.in/writereaddata/Form-1A/Minutes/24_riverminutes.pdf.

FP Staff, *China's hand suspected in River Siang turning black: Beijing has always targeted Brahmaputra and its tributaries*, FIRSTPOST, (November 30, 2017), https://www.firstpost.com/india/chinas-hand-suspected-in-river-siang-turning-black-beijing-has-always-targeted-brahmaputra-and-its-tributaries-4234951.html.

Uttara Gangopadhyay, *Khangchendzonga National Park: A Peek into Sikkim's Magnificence*, OUTLOOK TRAVELLER, (November 20, 2019), https://www.outlookindia.com/outlooktraveller/explore/story/70052/khangchendzonga-national-park-a-peek-into-sikkims-magnificence.

Ibu Sanjeeb Garg, *Why India should be worried about China's Lalho dam*, LIVEMINT, (October 18, 2016), https://www.livemint.com/Opinion/u143w6gzzfwkQs3t1wBu3O/Why-India-should-be-worried-about-Chinas-Lalho-dam.html.

Frida Ghitis, *While All Eyes were on Hong Kong, China Just Ended Hopes for a 'Free Tibet*, WORLD POLITICS REVIEW, (July 23, 2020), https://www.worldpoliticsreview.com/articles/28934/while-all-eyes-were-on-hong-kong-china-just-ended-hopes-for-a-free-tibet.

Nihkar Gokhale, *Ignore the scaremongering. China can't turn off Brahmaputra even if it wants*, CATCHNEWS, (February 10, 2017), http://www.catchnews.

com/india-news/china-can-t-block-brahmaputra-but-india-still-faces-a-threat-from-its-own-dams-1476452286.html.

Takemura H. *The Asian Region and the International Criminal Court* in: Nakanishi Y. (eds), CONTEMPORARY ISSUES IN HUMAN RIGHTS LAW, Springer, Singapore (2018).

Jeremy Hance, *World's newest great ape threated by Chinese dam*, THE GUARDIAN, (April 23, 2018), https://www.theguardian.com/environment/radical-conservation/2018/apr/23/worlds-newest-great-ape-threatened-by-chinese-dam.

Maureen Harris, *A Matter of Rights in the Future of the Mekong*, INTERNATIONAL RIVERS, (December 22, 2016), https://www.internationalrivers.org/blogs/721/a-matter-of-rights-in-the-future-of-the-mekong.

Clare Harrison, *The Great Walls Damming Tibet*, TIBET NATURE ENVIRONMENTAL CONSERVATION NETWORK, (June 16, 2018), https://tibetnature.net/en/great-walls-damming-tibet/.

Marquest Hayes, *How the Himalayas Shape Climate in Asia*, WORLD ATLAS, (September 21, 2017), https://www.worldatlas.com/articles/how-the-himalayas-shape-climate-in-asia.html.

Zachary Hurwitz, *Dam Standards: A Rights-Based Approach*, INTERNATIONAL RIVERS, (January 2014), file:///F:/WCD%20reports%20and%20commentary/intlrivers_dam_standards_final.pdf.

ICC 02/05-01/07, Decision on the prosecution application under Article 58(7) of the Statute, (April 27, 2007), PRE-TRIAL CHAMBER I, INTERNATIONAL CRIMINAL COURT, ¶62. https://legal.un.org/docs/?path=../ilc/texts/instruments/english/commentaries/7_7_2019.pdf&lang=EF.

THE INDIAN EXPRESS, *SC stays Uttarakhand HC order on Ganga, Yamuna living entity status*, (July 8, 2017), https://indianexpress.com/article/india/sc-stays-uttarakhand-hc-order-on-ganga-yamuna-living-entity-status-4740884/.

INTERNATIONAL COMMISSION ON WORLD DAMS, *World Declaration on Dam Safety*, (October 18, 2019), https://www.icold-cigb.org/userfiles/files/World%20Declaration/World%20Declaration%20on%20Dam%20Safety_ICOLD_A3.pdf.

INTERNATIONAL HYDROPOWER ASSOCIATION, *Power China*, https://www.hydropower.org/companies/powerchina# (accessed July 27, 2020).

INTERNATIONAL LAW COMMISSION, *Draft articles on Prevention and Punishment of Crimes Against Humanity*, YEARBOOK OF THE INTERNATIONAL LAW COMMISSION, Vol II, Part Two, (2019), https://legal.un.org/docs/?path=../ilc/texts/instruments/english/draft_articles/7_7_2019.pdf&lang=EF.

INTERNATIONAL RIVERS, *Greenhouse Gas Emissions from Dams FAQ*, (May 1, 2007), https://www.internationalrivers.org/resources/greenhouse-gas-emissions-from-dams-faq-4064#.

INTERNATIONAL RIVERS, et. al, *Rights of Rivers*, 44, https://www.internationalrivers.org/resources/reports-and-publications/rights-of-river-report/ (accessed November 27, 2020).

INTERNATIONAL RIVERS, *Comments on the Panan Hydro-Electric Project (India)*, (August 18, 2012), https://www.internationalrivers.org/resources/comments-on-the-panan-hydro-electric-project-india-7639.

INTERNATIONAL RIVERS NETWORK, *Chinese Government Proposes New Dam Building Spree,* (February 28, 2011), https://www.internationalrivers.org/resources/china%E2%80%99s-government-proposes-new-dam-building-spree-3419.

Mike Ives, *A Day Before Laos Dam Failed, Builders Saw Trouble,* NEW YORK TIMES, (July 26, 2018), https://www.nytimes.com/2018/07/26/world/asia/laos-dam-collapse.html.

IWGIA, *Indigenous World 2019: India,* (April 24, 2019), https://www.iwgia.org/en/india/3455-iw2019-india.html.

Mahima A. Jain, *Glacier Research is Particularly Treacherous at the 'Third Pole',* ATLAS OBSCURA, (May 5, 2020), https://www.atlasobscura.com/articles/glacier-research-at-the-third-pole#.

JOSHUA PROJECT, *Rongkup in India,* https://joshuaproject.net/people_groups/13041/IN (accessed July 25, 2020).

Asmal, Kader, *Introduction: World Commission on Dams Report, Dams and Development,* AMERICAN UNIVERSITY INTERNATIONAL LAW REVIEW 16, no. 6, 1411-1433, 1417, (2001).

R. Krishnan, et al., *Unravelling Climate Change in the Hindu Kush Himalaya: Rapid Warming in the Mountains and Increasing Extremes* in eds. Wester P., Mishra A., Mukherji A., Shrestha A. (eds) THE HINDU KUSH HIMALAYA ASSESSMENT, Springer, (January 5, 2019), https://doi.org/10.1007/978-3-319-92288-1_3.

Dechen Lachungpa, In a first, tiger spotted at 9,500 feet in Sikkim, DOWN TO EARTH, (January 9, 2019), https://www.downtoearth.org.in/news/wildlife-biodiversity/in-a-first-tiger-spotted-at-9-500-feet-in-sikkim-62755.

Lepcha v. Union of India, Appeal No. 11/2014/PB/5/EZ, (2017), ¶3

Dawn Lepcha, *Comments on Proposed CDM status for 300 MW Panan Hydro Power Project,* https://cdm.unfccc.int/Projects/Validation/DB/2FN6ZLKQZWUA2LTTIRAH73FERKHE0M/view.html. (accessed July 29, 2020).

LEXLIFE INDIA, *The 'Polluter Pays' principle: challenges to the NGT in securing environmental justice,* (September 12, 2019), https://lexlife.in/2019/09/12/the-polluter-pays-principle-challenges-to-the-ngt-in-securing-environmental-justice/

Madeleine Lovelle, *Co-operation and the Brahmaputra: China and India Water Sharing,* FUTURE DIRECTIONS INTERNATIONAL, (March 15, 2016), http://www.futuredirections.org.au/wp-content/uploads/2016/03/Co-operation-and-the-Brahmaputra-China-and-India-Water-Sharing.pdf.

Hayley Moller, *Hydropower Continues Steady Growth,* EARTH POLICY INSTITUTE, (June 14, 2012), http://www.earth-policy.org/data_highlights/2012/highlights29.

NE NOW NEWS, *Sikkim: Renewed bids for Panan Hydropower Project sought,* (October 9, 2018), https://nenow.in/north-east-news/sikkim/sikkim-renewed-bids-for-panan-hydropower-project-sought.html.

Paul Neibrzydowski, *Top Ten Origins: Dams,* ORIGINS: CURRENT EVENTS IN HISTORICAL PERSPECTIVE (January 11, 2016), http://origins.osu.edu/connecting-history/top-ten-origins-dams.

Christina Nunez, *Hydropower, Explained*, NATIONAL GEOGRAPHIC (May 13, 2019), https://www.nationalgeographic.com/environment/global-warming/hydropower/.

NS ENERGY, *Teesta – VI Hydropower Project, Sikkim*, https://www.nsenergybusiness.com/projects/teesta-vi-hydropower-project-sikkim/ (accessed July 26, 2020).

OFFICE OF THE HIGH COMMISSIONER FOR HUMAN RIGHTS, *CCPR General Comment No. 27: Article 12 (Freedom of Movement)*, CCPR/C/21/Rev.1/Add.9, (November 2, 1999), ¶4.

Jeff Opperman, *Crocodiles Are Not Geckos: The Realities of Run-Of-River Hydropower*, FORBES, (June 6, 2019), https://www.forbes.com/sites/jeffopperman/2019/06/06/crocodiles-are-not-geckos-the-realities-of-run-of-river-hydropower/.

Dechen Palmo, *Tibet's Rivers Will Determine Asia's Future*, THE DIPLOMAT, (November 1, 2019), https://thediplomat.com/2019/11/tibets-rivers-will-determine-asias-future/.

Maharaj K. Pandit, et.al, *Dancing on the Roof of the World: Ecological Transformation of the Himalayan Landscape*, BIOSCIENCE, Vol 64, Issue 11, (November 2014), 980–92, https://doi.org/10.1093/biosci/biu152.

Jyotiraj Patra and Christina Hill, *Rethinking business and human rights in transboundary river governance in South Asia*, OXFAM, (June 11, 2020), https://asia.oxfam.org/latest/blogs/rethinking-business-and-human-rights-transboundary-river-governance-south-asia.

Sutirtho Patranobis, *China blocks Brahmaputra tributary, impact on water flow in India is not clear*, HINDUSTAN TIMES, (October 1, 2016), https://www.hindustantimes.com/india-news/china-blocks-brahmaputra-tributary-impact-on-water-flow-in-india-not-clear/story-QVAYbO2iOBFUSynwwpyneN.html.

Regina M. Paulose, *Beyond the Core: Incorporating Transnational Crimes into the Rome Statute*, CARDOZA JOURNAL OF INTERNATIONAL AND COMPARATIVE LAW, Vol. 21, No 1 (Fall 2012).

Regina M. Paulose, et. al, *Navigating Business and Human Rights in South Asia*, THE COMMON GOOD FOUNDATION, (November 28, 2020), https://www.actwithus.org/report-navigating-business-and-human-rights-in-south-asia/.

Rishika Pardikar, *Himalayan dams become economic burdens: lessons for Etalin*, THIRDPOLE.NET, (July 7, 2020), https://www.thethirdpole.net/2020/07/07/lessons-for-etalin-himalayan-dams-economic-burdens/.

Fred Pearce, WHEN THE RIVERS RUN DRY, Granta Publishing, pg 14, (2018).

Heleen Plaisier, *A Brief Introduction to Lepcha Orthography and Literature*, BULLETIN OF TIBETOLOGY, (2005), 8, http://himalaya.socanth.cam.ac.uk/collections/journals/bot/pdf/bot_2005_01_02.pdf.

Prosecutor v. Radovan Karadžić, Case No. IT-95-5/18-T, Public Redacted Version of Judgement Issued on 24 March 2016 – Volume I of IV (TC), (March 24, 2016), ¶47.

Usha Ramanathan, *India and the ICC*, JOURNAL OF INTERNATIONAL CRIMINAL JUSTICE, Volume 3, Issue 3, (July 2005), Pages 627–34, https://doi.org/10.1093/jicj/mqi055.

B.D. Richter, et. al, *The downstream human consequences of dams*, WATER ALTERNATIVES, 3(2): 14- 42, (2010), available at: http://www.water-alternatives.org/index.php/volume3/v3issue2/80-a3-2-3/file.

Kelli Rogers, *In Laos, a World Bank 'model' dam and the myth of sustainable hydropower*, DEVEX, (October 24, 2018), https://www.devex.com/news/in-laos-a-world-bank-model-dam-and-the-myth-of-sustainable-hydropower-93716.

Nikhil Roshan, *Troubled Waters: Why the Lepcha Community in Sikkim is Resisting Its Government's Attempts to Build Dams Over the River Teesta*, THE CARAVAN, (November 26, 2015), https://caravanmagazine.in/vantage/troubled-waters-why-the-lepcha-community-in-sikkim-is-resisting-its-governments-attempts-to-build-dams-over-the-river-teesta.

John Ruggie, *UN Guiding Principles*, https://scholar.harvard.edu/john-ruggie/un-guiding-principles (accessed on July 31, 2020).

T.P. Sabin and R. Krishnan, *Climate Change Over the Himalayas* in Eds. Krishnan, et. al., ASSESSMENT OF CLIMATE CHANGE OVER THE INDIAN REGION, Springer, (2020), 217, https://doi.org/10.1007/978-981-15-4327-2.

Anushka Saraswat, *Dragon in the Himalayas: China's Water Hegemony*, DIPLOMATIST, (June 3, 2020), https://diplomatist.com/2020/06/03/dragon-in-the-himalayas-chinas-water-hegemony/#.

Evelyne Schmid, TAKING ECONOMIC, SOCIAL AND CULTURAL RIGHTS SERIOUSLY IN INTERNATIONAL CRIMINAL LAW, Cambridge, 76- 80 (2015).

C. Schulz and WM Adams, *Debating Dams: The World Commission on Dams 20 years on.* WIREs WATER. (2019); 6:e1396. https://doi.org/10.1002/wat2.1369.

Bhadra Sharma and Kai Schultz, *As Himalayas Warm, Nepal's Climate Migrants Struggle to Survive*, NEW YORK TIMES, (April 5, 2020), https://www.nytimes.com/2020/04/05/world/asia/nepal-himalayas-glacier-climate.html.

S. Shrotria, S., *Environmental justice: Is the National Green Tribunal of India effective?* ENVIRONMENTAL LAW REVIEW, 17(3), 169–88 (2015), https://doi.org/10.1177/1461452915595548.

Dr. Gopal Siwakoti, *Trans-boundary River Basis in South Asia: Options for Conflict Resolution*, INTERNATIONAL RIVERS, (2011), pg https://www.internationalrivers.org/sites/default/files/attached-files/transboundaryriverbasins.pdf.

Joëlle Smadja, et al, *Climate change and water resources in the Himalayas*, JOURNAL OF ALPINE RESEARCH, 103-2 (2015), http://journals.openedition.org/rga/2910; DOI : https://doi.org/10.4000/rga.2910.

Lyansong Tamsang and Biswajit Chakraborti, *The Dwellers of the Valley: A Community Profile from West Bengal*, CULTURAL SURVIVAL QUARTERLY MAGAZINE, (December 2020), https://www.culturalsurvival.org/publications/cultural-survival-quarterly/dwellers-valley-community-profile-west-bengal.

TNN, *Why India is worried about China's dam projects on the Brahmaputra river*, THE ECONOMIC TIMES, (October 5, 2016), https://economictimes.indiatimes.com/news/politics-and-nation/why-india-is-worried-about-chinas-dam-projects-on-the-brahmaputra-river/articleshow/54691589.cms?utm_source=contentofinterest&utm_medium=text&utm_campaign=cppst.

TRIBAL RESEARCH AND CULTURAL INSTITUTE, *Lepcha*, https://trci.tripura.gov.in/lepcha (accessed July 25, 2020).

UNESCO, *Khangchendzonga National Park*, http://whc.unesco.org/en/list/1513, (accessed July 25, 2020).

UNFCCC/CCNUCC, *Project Design Document (PDD)*, (May 31, 2012), 8, https://cdm.unfccc.int/filestorage/g/x/.

UN GENERAL ASSEMBLY, United Nations Declaration on the Rights of Indigenous Peoples: resolution / adopted by the General Assembly, (October 2, 2007), A/RES/61/295, available at: https://www.refworld.org/docid/471355a82.html.

Bhavya Venkatesh, *Reviving Lepcha*, THE HINDU, (August 4, 2018), https://www.thehindu.com/education/reviving-lepcha/article24601118.ece.

L. Vemsani L, *The Himalayan Ranges, Glaciers, Lakes and Rivers: An International Ecological, Economic and Military Outlook*, THE POLITICAL ECONOMY OF CONFLICT IN SOUTH ASIA, MJ Webb and A Wijeweera (eds), International Political Economy Series, Palgrave Macmillan, London, 172 (2015).

Ambika Vishwanath, *Tensions with China – Pakistan can derail fragile water treaties, but India won't talk about it*, THE PRINT, (July 6, 2020), https://theprint.in/opinion/tensions-with-china-pakistan-can-derail-fragile-water-treaties-but-india-wont-talk-about-it/455196/.

Beth Walker, *China and India ignore UN watercourses convention*, CHINA DIALOGUE, (August 18, 2014), https://chinadialogue.net/en/climate/7229-china-and-india-ignore-un-watercourses-convention/.

Wettsein and Buckland, *Damming Evidence*, (May 2018), 2, 4, https://www.orangutans-sos.org/content/uploads/2018/05/Damming-Evidence.pdf.

WHITNEY R. HARRIS WORLD LAW INSTITUTE, *Compilation of Government Reactions to the UN International Law Commission's Work on Crimes against Humanity 2013- 2019*, (July 2020), https://law.wustl.edu/wp-content/uploads/2020/08/Compilation-of-6th-Committee-Responses-to-CAH-2013-2019.pdf.

WORLD COMMISSION ON DAMS, *Dams and Development A New Framework for Decision – Making*, Earthscan Publications 14 (November 2000), http://awsassets.panda.org/downloads/wcd_dams_final_report.pdf.

J Xu, et al., *Sustaining Biodiversity and Ecosystem Services in the Hindu Kush Himalaya* in: Wester P., Mishra A., Mukherji A., Shrestha A. (eds) THE HINDU KUSH HIMALAYA ASSESSMENT, Springer, (2019).

Dan Zhu, *China, Crimes Against Humanity and the International Criminal Court*, JOURNAL OF INTERNATIONAL CRIMINAL JUSTICE, Volume 16, Issue 5, December 2018, 1021-41, https://doi.org/10.1093/jicj/mqy036.

Chapter 9

To infinity and beyond: Finding an adequate approach to protect against Environmental Damages in Outer Space – prevention or remediation?

Tamara Blagojević

Independent Researcher

Abstract: The discovery of the space ecosystem has led to the accelerated development of the space industry, the commercialization of space, and in general, the growth of outer space activities, which are characterized as high-risk and presume the usage of large amounts of energy. The consequences that accompany these types of activities are excessive exploitation of natural space resources and pollution of the outer space environment. These consequences take the shape of environmental damages on Earth, which have many similarities with space damages; since they both imply the risk of pollution, all their effects cannot always be predicted in advance but also both reflect on ecosystems. When compared with environmental law, space law, being a young branch of law, is underdeveloped and lacks not only precise primary norms but also secondary norms. The existing secondary norms of space law cannot be properly applied due to issues with interpretation and application of vague primary norms. The impossibility of supervision and tracking due to the lack of appropriate mechanisms and bodies for dispute resolution and prosecution of potential breaches of space law and the consequent non-transparency of space activities further enables the monopoly of space forces and excludes underdeveloped countries from the "game." This has opened the possibility of the illegitimate undertaking of a wide range of activities that lead to space damages that can also affect the Earth's environment. That is why most of the space debris leftovers from space activities have not been addressed or cleaned up properly and exactly the reason why we must consider other sources of international law, especially environmental law, in order to fill the gaps and interpret the vague terms in space law better.

The question remains - should these damages incur civil or criminal liability? Which approach to sanctioning and remedying environmental damages is the most appropriate and efficient? Is the application of international criminal law to the damages in outer space possible and appropriate? This chapter will first identify and define the existing issues in the outer space environment and the relevant environmental laws parameters that may be compared and transplanted to outer space regulations. It will then take relevant components of space law and examine how they apply to space damages and could they fall under the scope of "green crimes." This also implies the ultimate purpose of this chapter is to contribute to clarifying existing controversies and problems in the field of outer space policy and how they should be handled in the context of international environmental law and other appropriate and related areas of law.

Keywords: Space law, space debris, Moon Agreement, Lugano Convention, environmental damages, Polluter Pays Principle, arbitration, dispute resolution, Outer Space Treaty.

***

I. Introduction

As of now, the Earth's orbit and nearby space represent the most endangered parts of space, both due to the lack of a clear line of demarcation of the air and outer space boundary and the significant amount of space waste circulating there and its distance from Earth. Therefore, environmental damage, as a product of the scientific and technological development that required the excessive use of Earth's natural resources, became the unfortunate link between these two branches of law. For these reasons, environmental awareness is a necessary basis for further sustainable development, both on Earth and in outer space.

Environmental law is certainly more developed and precise. As the most frequent and dangerous type of space damages, space waste has significant similarities with environmental damages on Earth regarding their scope and effects on ecosystems. Therefore, using well-established environmental parameters and applying them to the analysis and interpretation of main space law sources is of utmost importance.

On the other hand, space law, being a young branch of law colored with politics and international relations, ended up full of imprecise primary norms, abstract, vague terms, and legal gaps. This has further led to the impossibility of adequate application of secondary norms and lack of will of space-faring nations to develop formal and obligatory mechanisms for dispute resolution. This can be proved by the numerous cases of space debris left unaddressed until this day.

This chapter, through the analysis of the common problems and the relevant regulations of both branches of law, aims to prove that the actions that would enable remedying the current state of the outer space environment certainly include a qualitative transformation of laws towards a multidisciplinary and preventive approach.

II. Space Debris as the nexus between environmental law and space law

Space law and international environmental law are almost equally young branches of law, but due to the delicacy of the very substances they regulate, they initially developed in isolation from each other. Such isolation can be disastrous for branches of law that have such broad subjects of regulation: two geographically distant and unequally explored areas that both represent goods of a higher value of importance for all humanity. Specifically, the background of the emergence of space law was quite different, as it actually originated at the international level and was not properly developed by states.

Namely, the first flights into space took place in a period when there was no indication of the emergence of the outer space legal regime, which led to certain controversies over the legal qualification of outer space.[1] However, even after the relatively early acceptance of the non-appropriation of outer space and its consequent formal proclamation as *res communis omnium*,[2] its boundaries and outer space itself have remained undefined.[3] Even to this day, there has not been a precise legally binding boundary between airspace and

---

[1] Obrad Račić, *Basic Principles of Outer Space Law*, IMPP, Belgrade, at 34 -35 (1972).

[2] The Outer Space Treaty has proclaimed outer space as the Province of all mankind, which means states no longer have any sovereign right there.

[3] *See* Obrad Račić, *Collection of Documents on the Legal Regulation of Research and Use of the Cosmos*, Manuscript, IMPP, Belgrade, 31-33, (1969), available in the library of the Faculty of Law, University of Belgrade.

outer space, but in practice, it is accepted that the approximate limit ranges from 100-110 km above sea level.[4]

The "Space Age" officially began with the launch of the first artificial Soviet satellite - Sputnik, in October 1957. Since then, about 5450 rocket launches have been successfully performed, and about 8950 satellites have been launched into Earth orbit.[5] From then on, the accelerated development of the space industry and the accompanying pollution led to environmental damage, becoming an unfortunate link between environmental and space law.

The current climate crisis requires finding alternative ways to rationalize the use of natural resources and the improvement of international cooperation in the field of scientific research.[6] Turning to technologies that use energy from renewable sources should lead to a noticeable reduction of harmful gas emissions and the prevention of further environmental degradation.[7] Other alternative energy sources on Earth may be the sun and wind, which produce solar and kinetic energy; however, the possibility of using these sources is not as accessible in outer space as it is on Earth.[8] There is a great distance of certain space missions from the sun, so solar systems work well for orbital missions and those moving towards the sun, but as the satellite moves away from the sun, the developed energy drops drastically, making solar energy impractical.[9] On the other hand, fuel and chemical batteries have a limited lifespan and cannot produce the large amounts of energy needed to support the entire mission into space.[10] For these reasons, there has been an increased use of nuclear energy sources, precisely because they are characterized by high power capacity, long life, compactness, and the ability to function independently of solar energy.[11] However, they pose a significant risk if

---

[4] Karman's line is an imaginary line that represents the lower limit of space, somewhere between 100 and 110 km above sea level, accepted by the International Aviation Federation. This line is not only the line of separation of two natural wholes, but at the same time the line of separation of two different legal regimes.

[5] EUROPEAN SPACE AGENCY (ESA), *Space Debris By the Numbers*, (Jan. 2019), https://www.esa.int/Safety_Security/Space_Debris/Space_debris_by_the_numbers.

[6] Sarab Entesar, *The Importance of Environmental Standards and Environmental Management for the Sustainable Development of Libya*, Belgrade, at 5, (2018), https://futura.edu.rs/wordpress/wp-content/uploads/2018/12/SARAB-ENTESAR-MASTER-RAD_FINAL_05122018.pdf.

[7] *Id.* at 5.

[8] *Id.*

[9] *Id.*

[10] *Id.*

[11] *Id.*

nuclear fuel falls back to Earth or other celestial bodies and causes significant environmental damage.[12]

This is important because sustainability and impact assessments were not properly done or were not considered prior to some projects related to space in the past. Particularly, one of the most famous examples of this was former US President Ronald Regan's Strategic Defense Initiative (SDI),[13] known as Star Wars, inspired by the scientist Edward Teller, who predicted that climate modifications would be the main reason for the last war on Earth.[14] Allegedly, SDI was supposed to protect the US from potential ballistic missile attacks from USSR, but it was later proven that USSR did not have the technology advanced enough to make such weapons and instead went into bankruptcy trying to prepare for protection from the USA.[15]

A similar idea was recently explored by Donald Trump, who declared to form the Space Force as the sixth branch of the US military. He signed the Space Policy Directive (SPD-4) and ordered the Pentagon to execute his decision.[16]

Even today, when environmental awareness is growing worldwide, so is technological development and the ambitions of private entrepreneurs to explore outer space and go even beyond the boundaries explored now.

Namely, there have been ongoing projects by Elon Musk and Jeff Bezos to not only explore Mars but plan human space travel there, and even future settlements. Seemingly it appears they do not have enough regard for basic

---

[12] *Id.*

[13] John R. Blackburn Jr, *President Reagan's Nuclear Policy From 1981 To 1983: The Effects on National Defense, Foreign Policy and Society*, FACULTY OF THE GRADUATE COLLEGE OF THE OKLAHOMA STATE UNIVERSITY, Oklahoma Christian University, Oklahoma, (May, 1999), https://shareok.org/bitstream/handle/11244/11685/Thesis-1999-B628p.pdf?sequence=1.

[14] Howard. J. Taubenfeld, *International Environmental Law: Air and Outer Space*, NATURAL RESOURCES JOURNAL, at 323, (April 1973), https://digitalrepository.unm.edu/nrj/vol13/iss2/9.

[15] Adam Augustyn, *Strategic Defense Initiative - United States Defense System*, ENCYCLOPEDIA BRITANNICA, (March 27, 2019). https://www.britannica.com/topic/Strategic-Defense-Initiative.

[16] Mike Wall, *Trump Signs Directive to Create a Military Space Force, SPACE.COM*, (Feb. 27, 2019), (October 30, 2020) https://www.space.com/president-trump-space-force-directive.html.

international law requirements and principles.[17] This might become a very worrying issue since neither of them are government officials and are not suitable to bring such rushed decisions that could potentially influence the wellbeing of all of humankind and the potential of our sustainable future. This is especially having in mind the fact Musk's plans of terraforming, or in other words, to nuke Mars in order to create atmospheric environment,[18] without certain and proven scientific research and information on how Mars's tectonic plate would react, or how that would affect its course, shape or any potential forms of microorganisms or life, however embryonic and basic it might be.

As of now, SpaceX is launching sets of 60 satellites every couple of weeks and has already received approval for 12,000 Starlink satellites. SpaceX is seeking approval for 30,000 more, and other companies are not far behind.[19] The Starlink mega-constellation itself would increase the number of active satellites more than tenfold. There are around 3,000 active satellites in orbit; current Starlinks are brighter than 99% of them because they are in lower orbits and more reflective than Starlink engineers predicted. Light pollution is a potential threat to discoveries of hazardous near-Earth asteroids because of Starlinks confusing their targets, leaving Earth more vulnerable to world-altering impacts.[20]

With 10,000 new satellites approved for launch and no laws on orbit crowding or space cleanup, the stage is set for the disastrous possibility of "Kessler Syndrome," a runaway cascade of debris that could destroy most satellites in orbit and prevent launches for decades.[21]

Therefore, the main cause of pollution in space is the emission of waste materials and parts of space objects, as a consequence of undertaking the activities of the space industry and the use of mobile space objects in performing space activities. Such "space waste," otherwise known as space

---

[17] Stacy Liberatore, *SpaceX declares independence: Elon Musk's firm says they will not recognize Earth laws in planned Mars colony and says 'free planet' will adopt 'self-governing principles'*, DAILYMAIL.CO.UK, (October 30, 2020), https://www.dailymail.co.uk/sciencetech/article-8897601/Elon-Musks-SpaceX-says-not-recognize-Earth-laws-planned-Mars-colony.html.

[18] Jackie Wattles, *Colonizing Mars could be dangerous and ridiculously expensive. Elon Musk wants to do it anyway*, CNN BUSINESS, (September 8, 2020), https://edition.cnn.com/2020/09/08/tech/spacex-mars-profit-scn/index.html.

[19] Samantha Lawler, *SpaceX's Starlink satellites are about to ruin stargazing for everyone*, THE CONVERSATION, Nov. 17, 2020 10.21pm GMT, available at: https://theconversation.com/spacexs-starlink-satellites-are-about-to-ruin-stargazing-for-everyone-149516.

[20] *Id.*

[21] *Id.*

debris, "represents all people-made objects, including their fragments and elements (remnants of dysfunctional satellites and spacecraft, bodies of old rockets, as well as fragments formed during their subsequent collision) in earth orbit or re-entering into the atmosphere, which are no longer functional."[22]

However, there is a significant discrepancy between official and public data on the amount of space debris. The data on NASA's website dates from 2011-13 and indicates that even then, there were more than 500,000 pieces of space debris, between 1 and 10 cm in diameter, while the number of particles smaller than 1 cm probably exceeds tens of millions.[23] Of that number, the U.S. Space Surveillance Network monitors only 22,000 objects larger than 10 cm, including about 1,000 operational spacecraft, while the rest are orbital debris.[24] Most of such space debris is located 2,000 km from the Earth's surface, but the highest concentrations are in low Earth orbit, where the waste orbits at a speed of as much as 7-8 km/s,[25] enough for even a relatively small remnant to damage the space object.[26] The higher the altitude, the longer the debris will remain in Earth orbit; so at altitudes below 600 km in orbit, the debris usually falls to Earth in a few years, while at altitudes above 1,000 km, it can orbit the Earth for a century or more.[27]

However, a significant amount of debris burns during re-entry,[28] and the surviving components are thought to be most likely to fall into bodies of water or sparsely populated regions, probably because they make up over two-thirds of the Earth's surface.[29] According to NASA's data over the past 50 years, an average of one piece of waste falls back to Earth daily with no serious injuries or significant property damage observed.[30] The latest data from the European Space Agency (ESA) indicates that out of about 5,000 objects in

---

[22] INTER-AGENCY SPACE DEBRIS COORDINATION COMMITTEE, *IADC Space Debris Mitigation Guidelines*, at 5, (Sep. 2007), https://www.unoosa.org/documents/pdf/spacelaw/sd/IADC-2002-01-IADC-Space_Debris-Guidelines-Revision1.pdf.

[23] NASA, *News and Features*, ed. Holly Zell, (Sep. 2, 2011), https://www.nasa.gov/news/debris_faq.html.

[24] *Id.*

[25] *Id.*

[26] NASA, *Space Debris and Human Spacecraft*, ed. Mark Garcia, (Sep. 27. 2013), https://www.nasa.gov/mission_pages/station/news/orbital_debris.html.

[27] Zell, *supra* note 23.

[28] *Id.*

[29] P. Manikowski, *Examples of space damages in the light of international space law*, ECONOMICS AND BUSINESS REVIEW EBR 6.1: 54-68.at 65, (2006), https://www.ebr.edu.pl/pub/2006_1_54.pdf.

[30] Zell, *supra* note 23.

space with a total mass of 8,400 t, around 1,950 are functional, 34,000 objects are estimated by statistical data, and there are 900,000 items smaller than 10 cm and 128 million items smaller than 1 cm.[31]

Although the transparency, accuracy, and timeliness of this data can certainly be questioned, it can be said that there are roughly millions of pieces of remains so tiny that they cannot be detected by monitoring and tracking.[32] If we take into account the fact that even small paint stains can damage the spacecraft when traveling at high speeds and that the average speed of collision of space debris with another space object is approximately 10 km/s, it can be concluded that even collisions with smaller debris involve a significant amount of energy. Therefore, space debris can pose a risk of environmental damage.[33]

However, recently, different agencies and organizations have made certain efforts to remove such space debris by various technological and robotic creations, which either destroy the trash by laser beams or collect it with nets or prolonged robotic hands. Even SpaceX plans to potentially task its Starship with collecting and de-orbiting big and troublesome pieces of space junk.[34] Starlink satellites can also allegedly perform collision-avoiding maneuvers autonomously, using information from the US Department of Defense's debris-tracking system, at least according to the SpaceX Starlink page.[35]

Again, the question remains as to whether that will be efficient enough to remove all the trash and where that trash would be stored, as it is quite obvious that such projects are only experiments and are in their initial testing phase of development. Testing things in an unknown environment triggers the question of how that environment would react and what could all potential consequences be like.

Since it is now obvious that environmental damages represent a common issue for both space and environmental law, we must also take a look into the environmental law approach to this phenomenon.

---

[31] ESA, *supra* note 5.

[32] NASA ORBITAL DEBRIS PROGRAM OFFICE, *Orbital Debris Quarterly News*, (Sep. 2018), https://www.orbitaldebris.jsc.nasa.gov/quarterly-news/pdfs/odqnv22i3.pdf.

[33] NASA, *supra* note 23.

[34] Mike Wall, *SpaceX's Starship may help clean up space junk*, SPACE, (Oct. 2020), https://www.space.com/spacex-starship-space-junk-cleanup.

[35] *Id.*

III. Environmental Law approach and relevant parameters

Bearing in mind that the object of protection against pollution in the field of space law are parts of the outer space environment, it is necessary to connect the relevant branches of law and find common solutions to similar problems by clarifying the relevant environmental principles, concepts, and definitions related to liability for environmental damages.

Generally speaking, environmental damage occurs due to the reduction of the value of resources or their utilization,[36] in other words, it can occur as a consequence of the qualitative or quantitative negative change of natural goods and resources or pollution or degradation of the environment.

One of the basic characteristics of environmental damages is their unbreakable connection with undertaking numerous economic and industrial activities, which is why minor damages are tolerated if they do not exceed some expected usual limits.[37] That is why the question of compensation is raised only for those damages that exceed the allowed limits, producing greater harmful consequences (injury or death of a person, large material damages, significant environmental damage, high costs of repairing damages, etc.).[38]

Another important feature of environmental damages concerns how they occur, as they usually arise from permitted, socially beneficial activities that involve the risk of environmental damage, while the action itself is usually permissible.[39] As a rule, the occurrence of environmental damage doesn't depend exclusively on the will of the wrongdoers: he is usually aware of the risk of damage that may occur due to his actions, but the occurrence of damage is not always a predictable event.[40] "If the one who undertakes generally dangerous activities, intentionally violates the technical and legal standards of conduct, that would enable the establishment of the classic types of legal liability of the tortfeasor for a civil tort or criminal offense committed with guilt."[41] In such a case, we could even talk about applying a definition of green crimes if interpretation allowed subsuming space damages under such definition, having in mind the gravity and characteristics of the effects they would have on the environment. But as Dr. Zoi Aliozi illustrated in Chapter 1,

---

[36] Entesar, *supra* note 6 at 14.
[37] Mrvić-Petrović, *supra* note 37, at 89.
[38] *Id* at 89.
[39] *Id.*
[40] *Id.*
[41] *Id.*

we need to understand that green crimes at this moment refer to wrongdoing forbidden by law which means that if an action is not codified by law, then it cannot be classified as a green crime.

The third feature of environmental damages refers to the way they are caused since, in practice, it happens that "omissions occur from entities engaged in risky activities."[42] In such conditions, the effect of several causes of environmental accidents is acquired, so it is difficult to determine the responsibility of only one subject, which is why the "rules on joint and several liability of multiple polluters are most often applied."[43] The cooperation of different causes also implies the problem of defining environmental damage, since "the extent of harmful consequences can hardly be influenced by the one who causes the damage because the damages are often immeasurable."[44] Even when they can be determined, it is difficult to see all their effects, because "they can occur cumulatively, gradually, and even late, which makes the institute of compensation for damages useless, since, in normal circumstances, it should correspond to the total extent of the damage suffered, for the compensation to be fair."[45]

International environmental law contains various definitions of environmental damage and has developed many rules of liability for it. These are contained in conventions that protect different ecosystems.

The Lugano Convention (1993), for example, states that "damage is the injury of a person or loss of human life and damage to human property, but excludes damage to a plant or property managed by a carrier of environmentally hazardous activities."[46] This definition shows partial anthropocentrism by conditioning the sanctioning of environmental damage with the existence of human rights violations.

---

[42] *Id.*

[43] *Id.*

[44] Entesar, *supra* note 6, at 14.

[45] Mrvić-Petrović, *supra* note 37, at 90.

[46] M. Drenovak-Ivanovic; S.Đorđević; S. Važić, *Legal instruments of environmental protection - civil and criminal law protection,* Belgrade, OSCE, OSCE MISSION TO SERBIA, at 29 (2015).

As defined by the EU Directive 2004/35/EC on Liability for Environmental Damage[47], environmental damage is defined as "a measurable negative change in a natural good or a measurable weakening of its functions, which may occur as a direct or indirect consequence of a certain activity."[48] It applies only to explicitly listed damages and provides for an additional condition for damages caused to protected species and natural habitats, waters, and land that the "damage has a significant adverse effect on the condition and/or to the potential of the natural resource or that it poses a significant risk to the object of protection."[49] However, air pollution in itself is excluded from the scope of the Directive since it represents only a method of polluting other ecosystems, which in no way contributes to the need for urgent and preventive action.

The definition of nuclear damage is provided by the Paris Convention on Third Party Liability in the Field of Nuclear Energy,[50] the Vienna Convention on Civil Liability[51] for Nuclear Damage, and the Convention on Supplementary Compensation for Nuclear Damage,[52] the latter of which provides an expanded definition. All three mentioned conventions accept the basic principles of nuclear law: the principle of exclusive liability of the user of a nuclear installation, the principle of causal liability, the principle of limited liability and the principle of the jurisdiction of the court of the state on whose territory the nuclear accident occurred.[53] The basic environmental law

---

47 *European Parliament and Council, Directive 2004/35/CE on environmental liability with regard to the prevention and remedying of environmental damage,* OFFICIAL JOURNAL OF THE EUROPEAN UNION, (Apr. 21, 2004), https://eur-lex.europa.eu/LexUriServ/LexUriServ.do?uri=OJ:L:2004:143:0056:0075:en:PDF.

48 Drenovak-Ivanovic, *supra* note 46, at 55.

49 *Id*, at 55.

50 PARIS CONVENTION ON THIRD PARTY LIABILITY IN THE FIELD OF NUCLEAR ENERGY, 1960, NUCLEAR ENERGY AGENCY, https://www.oecd-nea.org/jcms/pl_20196/paris-convention-on-third-party-liability-in-the-field-of-nuclear-energy-paris-convention-or-pc .

51 VIENNA CONVENTION ON CIVIL LIABILITY, 1963, INTERNATIONAL ATOMIC ENERGY AGENCY, https://www.iaea.org/publications/documents/infcircs/vienna-convention-civil-liability-nuclear-damage .

52 THE CONVENTION ON SUPPLEMENTARY COMPENSATION FOR NUCLEAR DAMAGES (CSC), INTERNATIONAL ATOMIC ENERGY AGENCY, https://www.iaea.org/topics/nuclear-liability-conventions/convention-supplementary-compensation-nuclear-damage.

53 Petra Amidžić-Jelovčić; I. Perković, *Liability of Carriers for Nuclear Damage with Special Reference to the Convention on Supplementary Compensation for Nuclear Damage,* PROCEEDINGS OF THE FACULTY OF LAW IN SPLIT (hereinafter cited as PFS), Split, 45, at 378 and 379, (February 2008), https://www.pravst.unist.hr/dokumenti/zbornik/200888/zb200802_377.pdf.

principle of compensation for damage was provided for by the Vienna Convention on Civil Liability for Nuclear Damage from 1963 and was explicitly included in the Stockholm and Rio Declarations for the first time.[54] According to this principle, each state is obliged to ensure that "activities within its borders or under its control do not cause damage to the environment on its territory, but also the territory of other states."[55] Although the Vienna Convention refers only to civil liability, thus shifting the problem from the field of interstate liability of international public law to the level of individuals, regulated by private international law, the definition of nuclear damage applies in both fields.[56]

Thus, for the purposes of Article 1 of the Supplementary Compensation Convention, nuclear damage means:

1. Death or personal injury;
2. Loss or damage to property;
3. Profits lost due to death or bodily injury, i.e., due to loss or damage to property;
4. Costs of measures taken to restore the natural environment, unless the damage is negligible;
5. Profit lost due to environmental damage; or
6. Costs of preventive measures, as well as other subsequent losses and damages caused by those measures; Any other losses that are recognized under the general rules on civil liability of the state competent to adjudicate in a dispute over nuclear damage.[57]

---

[54] Bojan Pajtić, *Environmental Protection - Prevention and Compensation of Damages*, PROCEEDINGS OF THE PFNS, 2/2011, Novi Sad, at 255 (2011).
[55] *Id.*
[56] Alexander Kiss, *Responsibility for nuclear damage, Conference on the Human Right to a Safe and Healthful Environment and the Responsibility under International Law of Operators of Nuclear Facilities*, at 80, (2008), http://djilp.org/wp-content/uploads/2011/08/State-Responsibility-Liability-Alexandre-Kiss.pdf.
[57] Amidžić-Jelovčić, *supra* note 53, at 380-81.

All these types of damages, except for the costs of preventive measures, "must be the result of ionizing radiation to be recognized as a basis for compensation."[58]

If we take into account that space activities are permitted but generally dangerous high-risk industrial activities, where entrepreneurs of such activities certainly agree to implied risks, since space exploration presumes the impossibility for complete and exact prior knowledge of all potential causes of dangers and their effects, this unequivocally speaks in favor of *space damage being a type of environmental damage.* Similarly, we can also conclude that such space damages could equally be subsumed under the definition of *green crimes* if the elements of such damages would constitute a crime by international law.

State liability for environmental damage is specific because it implies the broadest forms of original liability for illegal actions against foreign countries at the international level and for all administrative errors that cause damage from environmental accidents, and therefore must be based on some principles other than basic Roman law principle *neminem laedere.*[59] Many international regulations on the liability for environmental damages include and specify these principles in their operational provisions: sustainable development (knowns as *umbrella norm,* defined by the International Court of Justice as "the need to reconcile economic development and environmental protection");[60] the "Polluter Pays" and "User Pays Principle;" the principle of compensation for damage; the precautionary principle and the principle of prevention; the principle of impact assessment; and the principle of ecological information and public participation.

Concerning environmental damage, international acts often provide for vicarious responsibility of the state for everything that happens on the territory of the state in question.[61] As can be seen, the importance of protecting the legal interest in a healthy environment imposes the need to establish additional mechanisms in the form of accountability at the international level in two fields: within international commercial law and

---

[58] *Id.* at 381.

[59] Nataša Mrvić-Petrović, Z. Petrović, *State Responsibility for Environmental Damages,* ECOLOGY AND LAW, ed. Čavoški and Knežević, INSTITUTE FOR COMPARATIVE LAW, Faculty of Law, UNION University, Belgrade, at 91 (2012).

[60] Case concerning the Gabčikovo-Nagymaros Project, Judgement, ICJ REPORTS 1997, 78. ¶ 140, available at: https://www.icj-cij.org/files/case-related/92/092-19970925-JUD-01-00-EN.pdf.

[61] *Id* at 92.

international public law.[62] Regarding international commercial law, it is a system of state liability for damages within international agreements, established by accepting the risk of damages that can have regional, transnational, and even planetary proportions.[63] In the domain of public law, the state has obligations to other states to respect international agreements in the field of environmental protection but also to guarantee its citizens the protection of environmental rights.[64] Provisions from international documents, especially the EU, formally belong to international commercial law, but also affect the field of public law, so we witness the tendency of unusual integration of civil and public liability of the state, the result of which is the regime of parallel responsibilities of the operator who causes damage by undertaking dangerous activities or using dangerous goods, and the state that should control such activities or the use of dangerous goods.[65] This division of responsibilities between the state and the operator indicates the wide acceptance of the risk management model in the regulation of environmental damage.[66] Risk dispersion is necessary because the damage caused by environmental pollution can be so large that neither the injured party nor the person responsible for the damage could bear it with their entire property.[67] In essence, this type of environmental responsibility is aimed at creating an insurance system that would ensure that the costs of protection in this area are borne by those who cause pollution and that when taking into account and making strategic planning policy, they are required to quantify external costs.[68] For these reasons, this is where the "polluter pays" and "user pays" principles take effect, as they are based on the idea that a polluter or a user pays a fee for environmental pollution when his activities cause or may cause damage to the environment,[69] which means that everyone who uses natural resources is obliged to pay an appropriate price as a part of the tax burden.[70]

---

[62] *Id.*

[63] *Id.*

[64] *Id.*

[65] *Id.*

[66] *Id.*

[67] *Id.*

[68] Predrag Stojanović, Ilija Zindović, *Legal responsibility for environmental damage and environmental protection,* ANNALS OF THE THE BELGRADE FACULTY OF LAW, LXIII, 1/2015, Belgrade, at 45, http://ojs.ius.bg.ac.rs/index.php/anali/article/view/66/243, https://anali.rs/.

[69] Alexandra Chavoshki, et al., Environment in the European Union, *Environmental Handbook - International Law and Environment,* OSCE MISSION TO SERBIA, 2010, at 27.

[70] *Id.* at 27.

Precisely because of the broad understanding of the concept of the environment and given the unpredictability of the scope and effects of human actions on nature, the activities of environmental preservation must move towards prevention due to frequent failure to completely remedy the subsequent multiple consequences.[71] Instead of remediation, in the form of compensation for complementary and compensatory damage, prevention is extended to imply the costs of preventive measures taken to protect the existing situation, as well as to measures taken to re-establish the disturbed environment.[72] This is why the principle of prevention, which arose in parallel with the establishment of the duty to avoid environmental damage and the principle of reducing waste pollution at the international level,[73] is of utmost importance in this area.

For example, both the Stockholm and Rio Declarations mention environmental damage in a preventive form without a deeper concretization of its concept through an appeal to states to reduce the possibility of environmental incidents and improve their legislation.

The Lugano Convention[74] proclaims the concept of strict liability, i.e., "liability without guilt for environmental damage caused by undertaking dangerous activities or using dangerous things."[75] The primary responsibility lies with the operator responsible for the environmental damage that occurs during the performance of the hazardous activity or during the period when he was obliged to supervise such activity.[76] On the other hand, "the responsibility of the state arises from the non-application or inadequate application of preventive measures or failure to supervise the operator of hazardous activities."[77]

In this Convention, priority is given to the risk management model because risk dispersion also enables the application of the institute of joint and several

---

[71] Bojana Čučković, *The notion of environmental damage in international environmental law*, LEGAL LIFE, at 406 (September 2010).

[72] Stojanović, Zindović, *supra* note 68, at 45.

[73] B. Pajtić, *Environmental Protection - Prevention and Compensation of Damages*, PROCEEDINGS OF THE FACULTY OF LAW in Novi Sad, 2/2011, Novi Sad, at 255 (2011).

[74] CONVENTION ON CIVIL LIABILITY RESULTING FROM DANGEROUS ACTIVITIES FOR THE ENVIRONMENT, ETS No. 105, Lugano, COUNCIL OF EUROPE, 2013, https://rm.coe.int/168007c079. [hereinafter ETS No. 105].

[75] Mrvić-Petrović, *supra* note 37, at 95.

[76] *Id* at 94.

[77] *Id.*

liability of multiple operators.[78] Additionally, the contracting parties can provide liability insurance for operators or other methods of financial security for the caused damage.[79]

Compensation for damage here includes the damage caused to the quality of the environment related to lost profits and which includes the value of the costs of measures necessary to prevent damage and measures of environmental restoration, but also compensation for actual damage directly inflicted on persons and their property.[80]

The Directive 2004/35/EC on Liability for Environmental Damage defines the "operator's strict liability for damage to certain parts of the environment, arising from activities which he manages or controls, to finance the remediation of a damaged natural resource and its functions."[81] It is reactive because it deals with the consequences of damage, yet preventive because the high costs of remediation can direct the behavior of the operator to take preventive measures and introduce safer techniques and technologies.[82]

Therefore, "in the case of damage that occurs in the performance of dangerous professional activities or those that poses a potential danger to the environment and human health there can be strict liability."[83] In contrast, "subjective liability will exist in the event of a potential risk of damage or for the damage caused to animal and plant species or their natural habitats when the existence of intent or negligence is required."[84] In addition to imposing the obligation to eliminate the damage, the competent authority may also impose a measure prohibiting activities that pose a potential danger.[85] Also, "the competent authority can act on the request of any legal or natural person, who, in case of failure of the authority to act on that request, can sue the competent authority for its own omission" which shows that the directive does not specify the type of liability, rather that these can be all liability types, namely: civil, criminal (including misdemeanors and economic offenses) and administrative.[86]

---

[78] *Id.*

[79] *Id.*

[80] ETS 105, *supra* note Art. 2, ¶ 7, items C and D.

[81] Pajtić, *supra* note 255 and 256.

[82] *Id.*

[83] A. Čavoški, et al., *Environment in the European Union, Environmental Handbook - International Law and Environment,* OSCE MISSION TO SERBIA, 32 (2010).

[84] *Id.* at 32.

[85] *Id.*

[86] *Id.*

In cases when primary reparation of natural resources is impossible, the responsible person has the obligation of complementary reparation, i.e., the polluter must invest a value equivalent to the irreparable part of the damage in the improvement of a similar resource.[87]

Contrary to the Lugano Convention, this Directive excludes the application of compensation for personal injury, property, or actual damage, and also states that it does not affect the exercise of the right to compensation for ordinary damage under civil law or the right to compensation for damages arising from other international agreements governing civil liability for damages.[88] This indicates the interrelationship between the Directive and the Lugano Convention, even though they originate from two different legal systems, the EU and the COE, which can have a negative effect on countries that have not adopted both.

The Supplementary Compensation Convention stipulates that "a state is obliged to insure itself through the International Public Fund prior to the occurrence of nuclear damage."[89] The annex to the Convention provides for "strict liability for nuclear damage caused outside the site of the nuclear installation in which the nuclear accident occurred, the exclusive liability of the user of the nuclear facility for the nuclear damage, and joint and several liability for damage caused by multiple users of the nuclear facility."[90]

The Basel Convention on the Control of Transboundary Movements of Hazardous Wastes and Their Disposal of 1992, despite not entering into force, is important because it deals with the control, supervision, information, and cooperation of states, and only calls on its members to provide preventive measures in their national legal systems and punish illegal trafficking.[91] The Protocol on Liability and Compensation for Damage contains rules on compensation for damage to people and their property, damage to the economic interest in the use of natural values, the cost of measures necessary to restore the environment before the damage, as well as the cost of preventive measures.[92] The holder of the obligation to compensate for the damage is "the person who manages and controls the transport of hazardous waste or its

---

[87] Stojanović; Zindović, *supra* note 49, 68.

[88] Drenovak-Ivanović, *supra* note 55.

[89] Amidzic-Jelovčić, *supra* note 53, at 385-386.

[90] *Id.*

[91] M. Drenovak-Ivanović, S. Đorđević, S. Važić, *Legal Instruments of Environmental Protection - Civil and Criminal Protection*, OSCE, OSCE MISSION TO SERBIA, Belgrade, 46 (2015).

[92] *Id.* at 47

disposal."[93] A novelty in the protocol is the obligation to "insure the person responsible for compensation for damage as a consequence of transboundary movement and disposal of hazardous waste."[94] Unlike the Basel Convention, the Protocol extends the issue of compensation to the case where the exporting or the importing countries are not members of the Convention.[95]

The coinciding characteristics of space and environmental damages speak in favor of the fact that the integration of Public and Commercial Law, division of responsibilities, application of risk management models, and emphasis on prevention meet the requirements of the liability for space damage.

As we can already see here, there is no rationale to wait to apply the international criminal law mechanisms, as it is well known to be the last resort, and since penalizing the perpetrator would bring no greater benefit to the environment long after it had already been "broken." That, of course, does not mean that prevention and remediation exclude each other, as they are not applied in the same timeframe and are not necessarily pointed towards the same results. Criminal law mechanisms serve well as general prevention but tend to be much more anthropocentric regarding the results, while preventive mechanisms, achieved mostly through other legal and economic means of sanctioning, are pointed more towards the protection of nature and are therefore more ecocentric.

The transplantation of economic principles into the regulation of legal institutes indicates positive results of combining solutions of related scientific disciplines and areas of law in cases of insufficient development of the branch of law that regulates similar phenomena. Such results are most easily observed through multidisciplinary and comparative analysis, which is why a deeper analysis of environmental law regulations of liability for environmental damage was necessary in order to form the basis for the angle of observation of space law norms.

IV. The critical analysis of relevant space law regulation

The main sources of Space Law are the five main treaties: the Treaty on the Principles Governing the Activities of States in the Exploration and Use of

---

93 *Id.*

94 *Id.*

95 *Id.*

Space, including the Moon and Other Celestial Bodies (the OST),[96] the Treaty on the Rescue of Astronauts and their Safe Return (Rescue Treaty);[97] Convention on International Liability for Space Objects (Liability Convention); Convention on the Registration of Space Objects (Registration Convention);[98] and the Agreement Governing the Activities of States on the Moon and other Celestial Bodies (Moon Agreement).[99] All of these treaties call on the elaboration of basic space principles, as well as the elaboration and continuation of the regulation of the previous treaty, together forming a coherent network of rules for space activities.

The 1967 OST is the first legally binding treaty popularly called the Magna Carta or the Outer Space Constitution,[100] which, by incorporating the principles of space law, creates certain legal units, more thoroughly elaborated in operational provisions, and subsequently adopted contracts. Similarly, the OST preamble already extends the objectives and principles of the UN Charter to outer space,[101] with a more precise but correspondingly explicit operational provision.[102]

The most similar provisions to the OST are contained in the lastly adopted Moon Agreement, which, although not yet entered into force, consists of more

---

96 TREATY ON PRINCIPLES GOVERNING THE ACTIVITIES OF STATES IN THE EXPLORATION AND USE OF OUTER SPACE, INCLUDING THE MOON AND OTHER CELESTIAL BODIES, Volume-610-I-8843, Oct. 10th 1967, available at: https://treaties.un.org/doc/Publication/UNTS/Volume%20610/volume-610-I-8843-English.pdf.

97 AGREEMENT ON THE RESCUE OF ASTRONAUTS, THE RETURN OF ASTRONAUTS AND THE RETURN OF OBJECTS LAUNCHED INTO OUTER SPACE, Volume-672-I-9574, May 15th, 1969. Preambule, available at: https://treaties.un.org/doc/Publication/UNTS/Volume%20672/volume-672-I-9574-English.pdf.

98 CONVENTION ON REGISTRATION OF OBJECTS LAUNCHED INTO OUTER SPACE, Ch_XXIV_1, VOL-2, Chapter XXIV. Outer Space, New York, 12 Nov. 1974, available at: https://treaties.un.org/doc/Publication/UNTS/Volume%201023/volume-1023-I-15020-English.pdf.

99 AGREEMENT GOVERNING THE ACTIVITIES OF STATES ON THE MOON AND OTHER CELESTIAL BODIES, Vol. 1363, No. 23002, GENERAL ASSEMBLY OF THE UNITED NATIONS on 5 Dec. 1979, Available at: https://treaties.un.org/doc/Publication/UNTS/Volume%201363/volume-1363-I-23002-English.pdf.

100 Ajey Lele, *Fifty Years of the Outer Space Treaty: Tracing the Journey Institute for Defence Studies and Analyses*, Pentagon Press, ISBN 978-81-8274-948-1, New Delhi, 13 (2017).

101 MOON TREATY, *supra* note 96, Preamble.

102 *Id.* article 3.

progressive environmentally-oriented provisions.[103] Given such congruence of their regulation, many of the provisions from the Moon Agreement can be seen as customary Space Law and serve for clarifying other treaties.[104]

---

[103] Common Provisions of the Moon Agreement and OST Application of International Law and the UN Charter to Outer Space or the Moon; International cooperation; Peaceful use; Prohibition of testing of any weapons, setting up nuclear weapons, military bases, stations and establishing and undertaking military maneuvers; Informing the UN Secretary-General and the public about space activities; Freedom of scientific research and staff exchange; Declaring astronauts envoys of humanity and informing states and the UN Secretary-General of any phenomenon that may endanger their lives or health and providing them with the necessary assistance in the event of an accident, danger or unintentional landing; Non-interference in the space activities of other State Parties; Prohibition of national appropriation by sovereignty, occupation or in any other way; Retaining jurisdiction and control over staff and facilities; International responsibility of states for national activities; Prior notification and consultations regarding visits, in order to control mutual activities; Peaceful means of resolving disputes through diplomatic channels, appropriate to the circumstances and nature of the dispute and, in the event of failure, the assistance of the UN Secretary-General, without the consent of the other State Parties; Mediation by a third country or the UN Secretary-General in the absence of diplomatic relations; Extension of provisions relating to States (with the exception of Articles 17, 18, 19, 20 and 21 of OST) to International Intergovernmental Organizations, if they accept the obligations of the Treaty and if the majority of the member organizations are also parties to the OST. UNITED NATIONS OFFICE FOR OUTER SPACE AFFAIRS, *United Nations Treaties and Principles on Outer Space*, UNITED NATIONS PUBLICATION, Vienna, 23-30. (2002), https://www.unoosa.org/pdf/publications/ST_SPACE_51E.pdf.

[104] Such common provisions of the OST and the Moon Agreement are: Application of International Law and the UN Charter to Outer Space or the Moon; International cooperation; Peaceful use; Prohibition of testing of any weapons, setting up nuclear weapons, military bases, stations and establishing and undertaking military maneuvers; Informing the UN Secretary-General and the public about space activities; Freedom of scientific research and staff exchange; Declaring astronauts envoys of humanity and informing states and the UN Secretary-General of any phenomenon that may endanger their lives or health and providing them with the necessary assistance in the event of an accident, danger or unintentional landing; Non-interference in the space activities of other State Parties; Prohibition of national appropriation by sovereignty, occupation or in any other way; Retaining jurisdiction and control over staff and facilities; International responsibility of states for national activities; Prior notification and consultations regarding visits, in order to control mutual activities; Peaceful means of resolving disputes through diplomatic channels, appropriate to the circumstances and nature of the dispute and, in the event of failure, the assistance of the UN Secretary-General, without the consent of the other State Parties; Mediation by a third country or the UN Secretary-General in the absence of diplomatic relations; Extension of

Similarly, to other space treaties, the OST has its model treaty: the 1959 Antarctic Treaty.[105] Additionally to the existence of certain necessary differences between their regulations, conditioned by the characteristics of protected natural areas, there are many similarities reflected in their goals and principles. Therefore, the Antarctic Treaty can be taken as an indirect source of space law and serve for interpreting imprecise but comparable provisions of space sources.

For example, the OST proclaims the principle of peaceful space exploration in the Preamble, referring to UN General Assembly Resolution 1884, which "prohibits the installation of nuclear and other weapons of mass destruction in Earth orbit, or its installation on celestial bodies," as well as the UN General Assembly resolution 110 (II) which "condemns propaganda designed to provoke or support threats to peace, violations of peace or acts of aggression."[106] A better solution of the Antarctic Treaty is that it also prohibits the disposal of radioactive waste,[107] while in space law, there is no legally binding protection from space waste. Similarly, the Moon Agreement goes beyond the OST and prohibits "any threat or use of force or any other hostile act or such threat on the Moon, including the use of the Moon for those purposes in relation to the Earth, the Moon, spacecraft, personnel or space objects."[108] If the OST prohibition of the installation of facilities with nuclear weapons or any other weapons of mass destruction[109] is read in the light of the prior prohibition, such interpretation might extend its scope to the prohibition of the use of nuclear weapons and other weapons of mass destruction. However, as with the OST, the use of military personnel, equipment or facilities for scientific research or other peaceful purposes is not prohibited in the Moon Agreement either.[110]

Furthermore, Article 9 of the OST states that "States Parties shall undertake space exploration so as to avoid harmful pollution and adverse changes resulting from the introduction of extraterrestrial matter into the Earth's

---

provisions relating to States (with the exception of Articles 17, 18, 19, 20 and 21 of OST) to International Intergovernmental Organizations, if they accept the obligations of the Treaty and if the majority of the member organizations are also parties to the OST.

105 THE ANTARCTIC TREATY, Washington, D.C, USA, Dec. 1st, 1959, article. 1, https://treaties.un.org/doc/Publication/UNTS/Volume%20402/volume-402-I-5778-English.pdf.

106 MOON TREATY, *supra* note 96.

107 THE ANTARCTIC TREATY, *supra* note 105, article 5.

108 *Id.*, article 3, ¶ 1, i 2.

109 *Id.* article 4,

110 *Id.* article 3, ¶ 3

environment and, adopt measures when necessary."[111] If a "State Party has reason to believe that a planned activity or experiment in space could cause potentially harmful interference with the activities of other State Parties in the peaceful exploration and use of space, it shall undertake appropriate international consultations before proceeding with them."[112] On the other hand, the Moon Agreement, in addition to providing that "States Parties, during exploration and use of the Moon, shall take measures to prevent disturbances to the existing balance of the Moon's and Earth's natural environment by introducing adverse changes through harmful contamination by extraterrestrial matter or otherwise,"[113] also envisages "informing the UN Secretary-General of the measures adopted by the States, as well as informing, as far as possible, of all the placement of radioactive materials on the Moon and the reasons for it."[114] Furthermore, the environmental orientation is visible in the "obligation to inform the UN Secretary-General, the public and the international scientific community of any indications of organic life and any phenomena discovered by States Parties in space and on the Moon that could endanger human life or health."[115] After anticipating the "equal and just enjoyment of the freedom of scientific research, the right to collect, remove and dispose of samples of mineral and other substances of the Moon for scientific purposes,"[116] it envisages "informing the UN Secretary-General, the public, and the international scientific community of the potential discovery of natural resources on the Moon by a State Party."[117] Another good solution is the mutual reporting of the state parties and the UN Secretary-General on "areas of special scientific interest on the Moon, in order to declare such areas international scientific reserves and to agree on special protection arrangements in consultation with the competent UN bodies."[118]

Additionally, the Moon Agreement even incorporates the principle of sustainability by foreseeing that "attention should be paid to the interests of present and future generations, as well as to the need for promoting higher life standards and conditions of economic and social progress in accordance with the UN Charter."[119] Furthermore, the Agreement takes into account the

---

[111] *Id.* article 9.
[112] *Id.*
[113] *Id.* article 7, ¶ 1.
[114] *Id.* article 7, ¶ 2.
[115] *Id.* article 5.
[116] *Id.* article 6.
[117] *Id.* article 11, ¶ 6.
[118] *Id.* article 7, ¶ 3.
[119] *Id.* article 4, ¶ 1.

development of the space industry, anticipating the "need to establish an international regime and procedures for managing the exploitation of natural resources on the Moon," which regime and procedures shall be subject to periodic revision following the scientific and technological development.[120] The goals of establishing an international regime are orderly, safe, and rational development and management of Moon's natural resources, as well as their fair distribution among all States Parties, taking into account, especially, the interests and needs of developing countries and the efforts of the countries that have contributed to the exploration of the Moon.[121]

Although both the OST and the Moon Agreement provide for consultations when disagreements arise between state parties and the use of peaceful means of resolving international disputes,[122] only the Antarctic Treaty provides for the jurisdiction of the International Court of Justice, as a last resort.[123] However, since all space treaties were adopted by the UN General Assembly and UNCOPUOS, the assumption is that UN mechanisms are implied. Similarly, we can conclude that resolving practical issues through a UN member state is an alternative[124] and may imply third-party mediation as a possibility.

The OST addresses the responsibility of States by stating that "States Parties bear international responsibility for national activities in space including the Moon and other celestial bodies[125] whether such activities are carried out by government agencies or non-governmental organizations, and for guaranteeing that national activities will be carried out in accordance with the treaty provisions."[126] Also, the "activities of non-governmental entities in space require

---

[120] *Id.* article 11, ¶ 5.

[121] *Id.* article 11, ¶ 7, a), b), c) and d).

[122] *Id.* article 9,12 i 13.

[123] THE ANTARCTIC TREATY, *supra* note 105, Article 11,

[124] MOON TREATY, *supra* note 96.

[125] Since the Treaty on Principles Governing the Activities of States in the Exploration and Use of *Outer Space, including the Moon and Other Celestial Bodies,* implies the expansion of its validity to the Moon and other Celestial bodies, most of its provisions also expand their value to the Moon and other Celestial bodies, and for that reason it wouldn't be practical to mention them every time when Space is mentioned. However, in OST, one of the main issues is the sporadic mentioning of the Moon in some provisions and then leaving it out in others, but that is not the main topic of concern for this chapter. Therefore, hereinafter, whenever OST mentions activities, responsibility or liability in space, the Moon and other celestial bodies are included.

[126] MOON TREATY, *supra* note 96, article 6.

the approval and continuous supervision of the State Parties."[127] As for the space activities of international intergovernmental organizations, "the responsibility for respecting the Treaty will lie with both the international organization and its member states."[128] Having in mind the goal of these provisions and the time when they were drafted, this should be interpreted as to include other ways of organizing or other legal entities, as well as private entrepreneurs and individuals, if they fall under the jurisdiction, sovereignty and laws of the state of their registry or nationality.

The following article clarifies the basis of international liability of states for damage from a space object or its components on Earth, in airspace or outer space, including the Moon and other celestial bodies, to another State Party or its natural or legal persons, by tying it to the action of launching, securing launch, the territory or the object used for launching.[129] This provision correctly covers liability in a wider area (Earth, airspace, and outer space), which avoids the issues related to the unclear line of separation of different liability regimes. Finally, as the type of damage is not specified, then the ambiguity of this provision allows subsuming environmental damages and thus enables the potential application of the definition of green crimes.

But if the previous two articles are read comparatively, linguistic interpretation already shows terminological inconsistencies,[130] as Article 6 uses the term "responsibility" while Article 7 uses the term "liability."[131] Despite the fact that these terms are not defined by space law, in practice, "liability" is activated when the launching state fails to execute its responsibilities, which as a consequence generates damages to space objects.[132] In other words, responsibilities are tied to the state based on the nationality principle[133] and therefore specify the standard of due diligence.

---

[127] *Id.*

[128] *Id.*

[129] *Id* article 7.

[130] *See* Joyeeta Chatterjee, *Reflections on the Concepts of 'Liability' and 'Responsibility' in a Privatised Atmosphere*, NEW PERSPECTIVES ON SPACE LAW - PROCEEDINGS OF THE 53RD IISL COLLOQUIUM ON THE LAW OF OUTER SPACE, eds. Mark J. Sundahl, V. Gopalakrishnan, International Institute for Space Law, 183-201, (2011), https://www.iislweb.org/docs/NewPerspectivesonSpaceLaw.pdf.

[131] P. Manikowski, *supra* note 29, at 58.

[132] *Id.* at 59.

[133] L. Kovudhikulrungsri, D. Nakseeharach, *Liability Regime of International Space Law: Some Lessons from International Nuclear Law*, 4 JOURNAL OF EAST ASIA AND INTERNATIONAL LAW AND INT'L L. 291, 298, (2011), https://heinonline.org/HOL/LandingP.?handle=hein.journals/jeasil4&div=30&id=&p.=&t=1556925702.

The formal incorporation of the principle of retaining ownership over space objects and their staff[134] not only provides protection against possible unfounded occupation or other claims of sovereignty but also reduces the possibility of isolating the state from liability by claiming that it lacks effective control over its personnel and facilities. This proves that the launching state is responsible and liable for the actions of any organization, individual or entity, regardless of whether they are explicitly listed in the OST or other space agreements.

The Rescue Agreement, the second-most ratified agreement, envisages rights and obligations related to "providing all possible assistance to astronauts in the event of an accident, danger, emergency and unintentional landing, as well as the urgent and safe return of astronauts and spacecraft."[135] By conditioning the application of the agreement from the existence of the risk of accidents and dangers, it extends its scope to harmful consequences, which reflects its connection with secondary norms on liability for space damages.

The main issue in this agreement is reflected in the determination of the "launching state as the state to which the space object is returned,"[136] as opposed to a different definition of the OST, which provides for the "return of the object to the state of registration."[137] Such a contradiction can lead to problems in the application of the principle of *lex specialis*, especially if this provision is read in the light of the next article, which provides for a different definition of the launching state, although introduced only for the purpose of this Agreement. This special definition also includes "International Intergovernmental Organizations, if they declare that they accept the rights and obligations provided by this Agreement."[138]

On the other hand, a good solution is reflected in the fact that the causes of dangers and accidents[139] are not explicitly enumerated, so such provisions can extend to the prevention of environmental damages and emphasizing the principles of emergency response and disclosure of information[140] also meets the environmental requirements.

"Space damage" itself is defined only by the Liability Convention, which states that "damage" means "loss of life, personal injury or other damage to health, or

---

134 MOON TREATY, *supra* note 96, article 8.
135 ASTRONAUTS, *supra* note 97, Preamble.
136 *Id.* article 4.
137 MOON TREATY, *supra* note, 96, article 5.
138 ASTRONAUTS, *supra* note 97, article 6.
139 *Id.* article 1.
140 *Id.* article 2.

loss or damage to property of the state or its natural or legal persons or property of international intergovernmental organizations."[141] Additionally, it clarifies other relevant terms, therefore "launch" "includes an attempted launch"[142] and "launching State" includes "the State initiating or securing the launch of a space object, and the State from whose territory or object the space object is launched." Meanwhile, the term "space object" "includes the components of a space object as well as its launching vehicle and parts thereof."[143]

The definition of the liable state of this convention was elaborated within the Registration Convention by adding the condition of "registration of the space object with the launching state, for establishing liability."[144] This confirms that the responsibility of the launching state derives from the affiliation of the space object over which it has jurisdiction and control, which, having in mind the principle of retaining ownership over the space object, also facilitates proving the causal link and attributing the action that causes damage to the state, regardless whether such an action comes from entities, entrepreneurs or individuals not explicitly listed in these conventions. They all still fall under the laws of their government and international law, and the states exercise control and due diligence over the activities of their nationals, objects or entities.

Still, the first noticeable shortcoming of the definition of space damage from the Liability Convention is reflected in the fact that it does not extend its scope to anybody's property (*terra nullius*).[145] Additionally, due to the anthropocentric approach and explicit enumeration of the consequences that must occur on certain goods, the possibility of sanctioning for environmental damages is indisputable only when there are also direct consequences on explicitly protected goods. Similarly, humanity as a whole could not fall under the definition of space damage because it doesn't represent a legal entity.[146] However, the inclusion of common goods could potentially be enabled with the general clause "other damage to health" if the term were interpreted more broadly so that it also referred to the well-being of humanity. Furthermore,

---

[141] CONVENTION ON INTERNATIONAL LIABILITY FOR DAMAGE CAUSED BY SPACE OBJECTS, Ch_XXIV_1, VOL-2, Chapter XXIV. Outer Space, New York, 12 Nov. 1974, https://treaties.un.org/doc/Treaties/1976/09/19760915%2003-08%20AM/Ch_XXIV_01p.pdf.

[142] Ana Mikulec, *The Outer Space Law*, LAWYER, LAW AND SOCIETY REVIEW, Vol. 49 Issue 99, 105-127, 23, (2016), https://hrcak.srce.hr/index.php?show=toc&id_broj=12777.

[143] CONVENTION ON INTERNATIONAL LIABILITY, *supra* note 141, article. 1.

[144] *Id.*

[145] Mikulec, *supra* note 142, at 23.

[146] Manikowski, *supra* note 29, at 60.

having in mind the definition of the space object, it is obvious that the definition of damage can be extended to space waste, although the sole creation of space waste cannot be considered as isolated damage unless property damage is also inflicted.

Additionally, there is no consensus in legal doctrine as to whether indirect and moral damages are also covered.[147] Finally, although during the formulation of the definition of damage, there were proposals that included nuclear damages in the term, the explicit and formal inclusion did not happen, but through the practice of states and subsequent adoption of principles in the field of nuclear energy in space, the scope of the definition is extended to them as well. Additionally, as nuclear damages are a specific type of environmental damage, *argumentum a fortiori* allows us to presume that space damages must include environmental damages as a more general type.

The justification for the restrictive interpretation of the terms in the convention is that only State Parties give them a special meaning, and if they do not, they cannot be interpreted arbitrarily because it could be contrary to the intention of those states.[148] On the other hand, since interpretation in good faith dictates that certain types of damages should not be excluded, rather, that definitions from this convention should be interpreted in their usual linguistic meaning and, in accordance with the convention objectives, narrow interpretation cannot be adequately applied due to unclear terminology.[149] In addition, the fact that the primary goal of the convention is to protect the citizens of non-space-faring nations from the potential and covert undertaking of dangerous activities by space forces, suggests that a restrictive interpretation conflicts with this convention. Therefore, since this convention seems to focus primarily on casualties, a broader interpretation of the definition of space damage would be entirely justified.[150]

For these reasons, it is necessary to turn to evolutionary interpretation based on the assumption that contractual provisions are developed and adapted to the new norms of international law, on the basis of which it can be concluded that the contracting parties adopted a vague and open definition, to allow the concept of space damage to evolve following the development of

---

147 *Id.*

148 Cohen E. Carpanelli, *Interpreting "Damage Caused by Space Objects" under the 1972 Liability Convention*, PROCEEDINGS OF THE INTERNATIONAL INSTITUTE OF SPACE LAW (2013), Eleven International Publishing, 4, (2014), https://iislweb.org/docs/Diederiks2013.pdf.

149 *Id* at 4.

151 *Id.*

150 *Id.* at 4 and 5.

the space industry.[151] This interpretation not only enables the sanctioning of both environmental and nuclear damages but also justifies the application of the institute of green crimes in the context of space law.

Evolutionary interpretation is formally justified at the very end of the Convention, in an article stating that in cases of damages caused to space objects, which pose a great danger to human life or serious interference with the living conditions of the population, or functioning of vital centers, State Parties should investigate the possibility of providing appropriate, effective, and prompt assistance to the affected State, at its request.[152] Despite the fact that this enables a wider interpretation of explicitly stated actions that cause damage, this provision still primarily concerns international cooperation and legal assistance.[153] This is probably to prevent the states from calling on the principle of non-interference in their internal affairs.

The Liability Convention further provides for the absolute responsibility of the launching State for the payment of compensation to the damaged State, but only for the damage caused by that State's space object on the surface of the Earth and on the aircraft in flight.[154] In addition, the convention regulates the collision of space objects elsewhere above the Earth's surface, providing for the strict liability of the state that causes the collision or if the collision is caused by persons for whom it is responsible, and damage occurs to the space object or personnel of such object.[155] However, the State may be exempted from absolute liability to the extent that it proves that the damage is wholly or in part the result of gross negligence or willful misconduct or omission done in intent to cause damage, of the claiming State or its natural or legal persons.[156] On the other hand, there can be no exemption if the damage is caused by activities that violate the rules of international law, especially the UN Charter and the OST.[157] Given that the institute of strict liability (with fault) is included in the convention, and the previous provision directly refers to the UN Charter, this justifies the application of international criminal law and the definition of green crimes.

Furthermore, if mutually independent launches together cause damage to personnel or a space object of a third State above the surface of the Earth,

---

[151] *Id* at 9.

[152] CONVENTION ON INTERNATIONAL LIABILITY, *supra* note 141, article. 21.

[153] *Id.* article 21.

[154] *Id* article. 2.

[155] *Id.* art. 3.

[156] *Id.* art. 6.

[157] *Id.* art. 6.

those two launching States shall be liable for the damage individually, jointly, and severally to the third State.[158] The burden of compensation is then determined based on the degree of guilt, and in case it cannot be determined, it will be distributed to both states equally, with the injured third state still able to claim compensation from either of the two responsible states, since they both have the right to pursue each other for contribution.[159] Individual and joint liability also exists in the case when two states jointly launch a space object which also applies to the state from whose territory the space object was launched.[160]

This Convention also incorporates the principle of *volenti non fit iniuria*[161] by stipulating that the Convention is not applicable if the space object of the launching state causes damage to its own nationals or foreign nationals, invited by the launching state to participate in the operation of that spacecraft, from the time of launch until the landing or during the time they are in the immediate vicinity of the planned take-off or recovery area.[162] This enables the application of the national criminal laws of states, and with it, the formulation of standards of domestic courts in the field of space damages. Therefore, this also compensates for the fact that a claim for damages can be filed only by the state (injured state, and if it does not, then the state in whose territory the damage occurred, and if it does not, then the state whose residents have suffered the damage),[163] through diplomatic channels, and if they do not exist, then through another state or the UN Secretary-General.[164] The Convention does not exclude the possibility for a State to claim compensation before the courts, administrative tribunals, or agencies of the launching State, but it is prohibited to simultaneously submit a claim authorized by this Convention while a claim for the same damage is already pending before such authorities and agencies.[165] A good solution is not requiring the exhaustion of local remedies prior to filing claims for damages authorized by the Convention.[166] This is in accordance with the principles of process efficiency.

---

[158] *Id.* art. 4.
[159] *Id.* art. 4.
[160] *Id.* art. 5.
[161] Mikulec, *supra* note 142, at 23.
[162] CONVENTION ON INTERNATIONAL LIABILITY, *supra* note 141, article. 7.
[163] *Id.* art. 8, ¶ 1, 2 i 3.
[164] *Id.* art. 9.
[165] *Id.* art. 11, ¶ 2, point 2.
[166] *Id.* article, 11, ¶ 2, point 1.

The Convention also provides for the possibility of establishing a three-member Commission when the settlement of demands from compensation claims does not arrive through diplomatic channels, or in other ways, provided by the Convention, within one year from the date of notification.[167] The Commission decides on the amount of the request and the merits, and its decision must be reasoned and public, but final and binding only if the parties so agree, while otherwise, it has the form of a recommendation that is respected in good faith.[168]

Furthermore, providing that compensation takes the form of restitution, and that is measured in accordance with international law and the principles of fairness and equality,[169] not only meets the requirements of environmental damages but also enables the application of relevant principles of environmental and criminal law to damages in space.

Despite the fact that this Convention practically appeals to states to adopt other agreements related to liability for damage to space objects that would specify, confirm, or expand the rules of the Convention, it also states that it does not affect treaties already in force between states,[170] without demanding their harmonization which complicates the relationship between the principles of *lex generalis and lex specialis*. On the other hand, the Moon Agreement also leaves the possibility of concluding more detailed arrangements on states' liability for damage on the Moon, in addition to the provisions of the OST and the Liability Convention, but also adds that such arrangements will be revised in line with the progress of scientific and technological development after a certain period after their entry into force.[171]

The already-mentioned Registration Convention is also of importance because the preamble calls for the concretization and expansion of the provisions in the Liability Convention.[172] In order to achieve the objectives of the Convention, the preamble also emphasizes the need to establish a central public registry run by the UN Secretary-General,[173] as well as the obligation of

---

[167] *Id.* article, 14.
[168] *Id.* article 18.
[169] *Id.* article, 12.
[170] *Id.* article 23, ¶ 1 i 2.
[171] *Id.* article 14, ¶ 2, and article 18.
[172] CONVENTION ON REGISTRATION OF OBJECTS LAUNCHED INTO OUTER SPACE, Preamble, Ch_XXIV_1, VOL-2, Chapter XXIV. Outer Space, New York, 12 Nov. 1974, https://treaties.un.org/doc/Treaties/1976/09/19760915%2003-08%20AM/Ch_XXIV_01p.pdf.
[173] *Id.* Preamble.

states to inform the Secretary-General about the launch of registered and marked facilities and the removal of dysfunctional facilities.[174]

Of particular importance for preventing space damages is the provision which states that if the conventional mechanisms appear insufficient for identifying a space object which causes damage to the state or its natural or legal persons or may be dangerous or harmful in nature, the state may turn to other State Parties which obtain objects for space monitoring, for assistance in object identification, or to transmit information about the object to the UN Secretary-General to assist in object identification under fair and reasonable conditions.[175] Since causing damage to natural or legal persons of such state is only set as an alternative, the prevention of environmental damage is set more explicitly compared to any other provision of previous conventions. The fact that this provision also concerns harmful or dangerous characteristics of the space object itself speaks in favor of the extension of preventive protection to space waste as dysfunctional parts of the space object.

As can be seen, the Registration Convention is perhaps the only space treaty that provides a somewhat clearer and more precise concretization of the provisions from the Liability Convention, and by doing so, it facilitates attributing damages to the state.

On the other hand, the main shortcomings of the main space law sources are already noticeable in the linguistic interpretation of the used expressions. Namely, all of them are characterized by imprecise, unclear, and inconsistent terminology, formulations of provisions, and writing techniques. Despite the fact that each subsequent contract refers to the previous one, the regulations of most of them are not mutually harmonized, and this can make it difficult to apply the principle of *lex specialis* to contradictory provisions. Due to the number of legal gaps and ambiguities, all contracts may be subject to arbitrary interpretation, either too broad or too narrow, which may further lead to the abuse of rights and legal uncertainty.

Despite the fact that the Moon Agreement regulates comparable matter in more detail and goes further than other space agreements, especially in terms of environmentally-oriented regulation, it mainly applies to the Moon and other celestial bodies. It has its controversial points and has not entered into force. Additionally, the importance of environmental protection in space and Earth's orbit is only being established in principle without any corresponding strict obligations. Aside from that, it is clear that no space agreement has a

---

174 *See* CONVENTION ON REGISTRATION OF OBJECTS, *supra* note 174, Articles: 3, 4 i 5.

175 *Id.*

sufficiently developed legally binding primary norm in the field of the prevention of space waste generation. Therefore, the environment is not explicitly and directly protected in almost any contract, but its protection can be achieved, and equally bypassed, based on the subjective interpretation of state signatories. Environmental legal principles of sustainable development, precaution, prevention, environmental information, and public participation are rare principles whose incorporation has been made by a somewhat adequate adaptation to damages in outer space. However, the same cannot be said with equal certainty for other environmental principles of a procedural nature, which are of the utmost importance for liability for environmental damage. The effectiveness of the principle of compensation has been relativized by making it dependent on diplomatic relations between states and the balance of powers in international relations, due to the lack of impartial and independent supervisory bodies and mandatory dispute resolution mechanisms in space. In fact, there are no norms that foresee such mechanisms whatsoever in any outer space regulation.

These shortcomings are exacerbated by the insufficiently strict emphasis on the duties of the contracting parties in space contracts, by formulating obligations in the form of possibilities or conditioning certain duties only by the existence of requests of other states, reciprocity, and the existence of factual possibilities for their realization. Such underdevelopment and ambiguity of the primary norms further complicate the interpretation, elaboration, and application of the few secondary norms of the OST, the Liability Convention, and the Moon Agreement, and consequently, their further development.

All such emphasized ambiguities of the main outer space treaties could certainly be removed by their amendment and harmonizing their regulation. However, since no extensive changes have been made in the last few decades, due to the reluctance of most space forces to introduce legally binding and strict obligations in the field of arms race prevention and liability, in order to understand vague terms, standards, and definitions, space agreements should be interpreted in the light of comparable solutions from the indirect sources of space law.

For example, the Treaty on the Prohibition of Experiments on Nuclear Weapons in the Atmosphere, Outer Space and Underwater[176] and the Convention on the Prohibition of Military or Any Other Hostile Use of

---

[176] TREATY BANNING NUCLEAR WEAPON TESTS IN THE ATMOSPHERE, IN OUTER SPACE AND UNDER WATER, MOSCOW, Vol. 480, No. 6964, Aug. 5th, 1963, Preamble, https://treaties.un.org/doc/Publication/UNTS/Volume%20480/volume-480-I-6964-English.pdf.

Environmental Modification Techniques,[177] which link these branches of law by linking their basic principles of peaceful exploration of outer space, sustainable development, the principles of humanity, military necessity, distinction, and proportionality, also formally extend their scope to outer space. Since the term "peaceful" is not precisely defined in the main sources of space law, its interpretation can be made by combining the aforementioned principles.

Despite the noticeable coincidence of the characteristics of environmental and space damages, and the introduction of certain comparable rules on joint and several liability, the similarity of obligations of states to apply due diligence to the national space activities, even such rules are not strict enough and not credibly transferred from the environmental law agreements.

Likewise, despite the similarities between the nuclear and space sectors (high-risk and dangerous activities and serious consequences), there is a significant difference between their liability regimes, as nuclear law provides for strict civil liability of private operators, while space law imposes absolute liability on the state. So, unlike laws pertaining to air, sea, and nuclear energy, space law places the responsibility on the state. Given that the participation of private actors in space activities is becoming more frequent, it would be expedient to shift responsibility from the state to the field of civil responsibility. Following the example of nuclear law, there would be three pillars of responsibility: the first would be financed by the responsible operator, the second by the public funds of the states, while the third would include the contribution of all member states. Shifting a part of the responsibility to private actors in space law could be achieved by requiring insurance for undertaking space activities as a mandatory precondition, which is becoming an increasingly common phenomenon in the practice of states.

A good nuclear law solution can also be seen in the inclusion of economic losses in the new definition of nuclear damage of the Vienna Convention, and an appropriate change should be formally made in the Convention on the Liability of Space Law.

Similarly, the Protocol to the Basel Convention in the rules on compensation, in addition to the damage to people and their property, includes damage to the economic interest in the use of natural resources, but also the costs of environmental remediation and preventive measures. The

---

177 CONVENTION ON THE PROHIBITION OF MILITARY OR ANY OTHER HOSTILE USE OF ENVIRONMENTAL MODIFICATION TECHNIQUES, Ch_XXVI_1, VOL-2, Chapter XXVI. Disarmament, New York, Dec. 10th 1976, Preamble, https://treaties.un.org/doc/Treaties/1978/10/19781005%2000-39%20AM/Ch_XXVI_01p.pdf.

similarity of the matter of regulating these sources speaks in favor of the need for a comparable extension of the definition of space damage.

A similar alternative to making profound changes to the basic agreements would be to interpret them in the light of the corresponding precise provisions of soft law, in which way such provisions would gradually grow into customary rules. Environmental principles of prevention and precaution, and the principle of peaceful exploration and use of outer space, are more thoroughly specified in the soft law sources. They specify numerous preventive measures that fall under the scope of the standard of due diligence that obliges states even when a certain issue does not directly concern them. The existence of separate Principles Relevant to the Use of Nuclear Power Sources in Outer Space[178] somewhat compensates for the fact that the Safety Framework for the Application of Nuclear Energy Sources[179] does not expand the protection of people and the natural environment to outer space, especially if we take into account that these principles were adopted much earlier to bring the definition of nuclear damage under the framework of the Liability Convention. The Code of Conduct against Ballistic Missile Proliferation[180] and the Code of Conduct for Space Activities[181] connect the problems of the arms race and environmental damage in space, and the latter code, aside from referencing all the Space law sources, also refers to the Space Debris Mitigation Guidelines,[182] which makes them the only documents that explicitly regulate space waste. However, the fact remains that soft law is not legally binding but also that strict formulations of obligations are lacking here as well.

---

[178] UNGA, *Principles Relevant to the Use of Nuclear Power Sources In Outer Space - With Introductory Note,* Resolution 47/68, Dec. the 14th, 1992, https://aerospace.org/sites/default/files/policy_archives/Principles%20on%20Nuclear%20Power%20Sources%20in%20Space.pdf.

[179] UN COPUOS and IAEA, *Safety Framework for Nuclear Power Source Applications in Outer Space,* (2009), https://fas.org/nuke/space/iaea-space.pdf.

[180] INTERNATIONAL CODE OF CONDUCT AGAINST BALLISTIC MISSILE PROLIFERATION, A/57/724, UNITED NATIONS GENERAL ASSEMBLY, Feb. 2003, https://www.hcoc.at/documents/Hague-Code-of-Conduct-A_57_724-English.pdf.

[181] Sergio Marchisio, *The Draft Code of Conduct for Outer Space activities, Activities of States in Outer Space in Light of New Developments: Meeting International Responsibilities and Establishing National Legal and Policy Frameworks,* SAPIENZA UNIVERSITY OF ROME, EUROPEAN CENTRE FOR SPACE LAW, 16-19, (Nov. 2010), https://www.unoosa.org/pdf/pres/2010/SLW2010/02-10b.pdf.

[182] UN COPUOS, *Space Debris Mitigation Guidelines of the Committee on the Peaceful Uses of Outer Space,* UNOOSA, (2010) https://www.unoosa.org/pdf/publications/st_space_49E.pdf .

This brings us to the unfortunate conclusion that space law, even if helped by a broader interpretation from the angle of environmental principles and soft law, remains underdeveloped in terms of the possible application of international criminal law, which requires precision, clarity, and strictness. Since space law is more inclined to have preventive mechanisms and since it is hard enough to enable the inclusion of environmental damages per se, the idea of applying the institution of green crimes, for now, stays only theoretically possible, at least until space law develops enough to reach a certain degree of precision and strictness. Until that day comes, preventive mechanisms seem to be the best approach.

V. Deficiencies of potential mechanisms for resolving disagreements regarding space activities

Insufficient strictness of primary norms of substantive law, in light of the non-existence of provisions on mandatory judicial settlement of disputes in the main sources of space law, leads to a significantly reduced effectiveness of space law in general.[183] Due to the underdevelopment of secondary norms, and thus procedural space law, more attention is focused on conflict prevention than on resolving already existing conflicts and disputes,[184] which further has its implications on the lack of case law.

Apart from the general possibility of invoking Article 7 of the UN Charter in case of threats to peace, violations of peace and acts of aggression, as well as Article 6 in conditions of peace, space law has no other independent and specific means of resolving international disputes.[185] There are only three space treaties that contain provisions for resolving disagreements: the OST, the Liability Convention, and the Moon Agreement, which can all be reduced to consultations, good services, mediation, conciliation, arbitration, and appeals commissions.[186] Thus, within the space agreements, the only mention of resolving international disputes related to space activities is the method of "world consultations," which consists of three contractual obligations: obligation of advance notification on space activities, the right of

183 Gérardine Meishan Goh, *Dispute Settlement in International Space Law: A Multi-Door Courthouse for Outer Space*, Universitet Lajden, 19, 20, (2007), https://openaccess.leidenuniv.nl/bitstream/handle/1887/11860/Thesis.pdf?sequence=10.

184 *Id.* at 18.

185 *Id.* at 22.

186 *Id.* at 23.

the injured state to request consultations, and the obligation of the state-wrongdoer to engage in them.[187]

Appropriate provisions providing for more specific means of resolving disputes can be found only in the preparatory documents for draft space treaty proposals. Article 11 of the U.S. draft Space Treaty provided that "any disputes arising out of the interpretation or application of the treaty, any Contracting Party may refer to the International Court of Justice," while the Soviet draft provided for immediate joint consultations.[188] Unfortunately, there was no agreement between the states on the final version of this provision, and none of the mentioned proposals was accepted.[189]

In line with such proposals would be the suggestion to establish a chamber for outer-space disputes within the ICJ. This would be similar to the chamber for environmental matters created back in 1993.[190] But, the environmental chamber of the ICJ has not heard a single case because no state filed a claim there.[191]

Another option could be the appeal of legal academics and experts to amend the European Convention on Human Rights and Freedoms (ECHR),[192] to formally incorporate the Right to a Healthy Environment, as well as to the adequate formal extension of the case-law of the European Court of Human Rights to environmental damage *per se*. This view is justified by the fact that despite that neither the ECHR nor the European Social Charter includes the right to a safe, quiet and healthy environment among other basic human rights, the European Court of Human Rights has begun to develop practice in matters concerning the environment over time.[193] This progress has been made because the violation of certain rights explicitly provided for in the

---

[187] *Id.* at 24.

[188] *Id.* at 21.

[189] *Id.*

[190] George Khoukaz: *ADR That is Out of This World: A Regime for the Resolution of Outer Space Disputes*, 2018 J. DISP. RESOL. at 274, https://scholarship.law.missouri.edu/jdr/vol2018/iss1/16.

[191] *Id*, at 274.

[192] *See European Convention on Human Rights*, EUROPEAN COURT OF HUMAN RIGHTS, COUNCIL OF EUROPE, 4. Nov., 1950, Rome, https://www.echr.coe.int/Documents/Convention_ENG.pdf%23p.=9 .

[193] COUNCIL OF EUROPE, *Manual on Human Rights and the Environment*, (2012), at 7 https://www.echr.coe.int/librarydocs/dh_dev_manual_environment_eng.pdf.

ECHR[194] includes environmental damage. Given that the Liability Convention only authorizes states to claim space damages, filing a petition with this court by individuals whose human rights are compromised as a result of damage caused by space activities would be an effective complement to such a shortcoming.

Some of the relevant cases mostly concern violations of the right to life, property, and an effective remedy due to environmental damage caused by nuclear and similar radioactive explosions or polluting emissions from nearby factories and plants. Such cases are *Öneryıldız v. Turkey*,[195] *The L.C.B. v. the United Kingdom*,[196] *Athanassoglou and Others v. Switzerland*,[197] and the case of *McGinley et Egan c. Royaume-Uni*.[198] In most of these cases, the court found no violation of these rights, and in others, the application was rejected because the condition of "significant damage" was not met. Therefore, even these few cases of environmental damages that could have potentially been used as a model for decision-making in future space disputes did not result in formed standards in this area. Regarding criminal procedures, one can only think of national criminal courts, since claiming damages in front of the ICC would not only require all the space forces to sign the Rome Statute but also the crime to be committed during war or to fall under the definition of the crimes against humanity. Aside from that, the ICC is a court of last resort, as mentioned in previous chapters in this volume.

Multiple authors in this volume have also called attention to the 2016 policy paper of the Office of the Prosecutor, calling attention to the possible examination of environmental crimes. However, it is not realistic to expect

---

194 Some of the rights provided by the ECHR that may involve damage to the environment are: the right to property (Article 1), the right to life (Article 2), the prohibition of torture, inhuman and degrading treatment (Article 3), the right to liberty and personal security (Article 5), the right to respect for private and family life (Article 8), freedom of expression (Article 10) and freedom of assembly (Article 11). However, in addition to these rights, the right to a fair trial (Article 13), the right to a remedy (Article 6) and the prohibition of discrimination (Article 14) are often emphasized in violation of other human rights under the Convention and may entail sanctioning environmental damages.

195 *Öneryıldız v. Turkey*, petition nu: 48939/99, ECHR Judgement Nov. 30th 2004, available at: https://hudoc.echr.coe.int/eng#{%22itemid%22:[%22002-4094%22]}.

196 *L.C.B. v. the United Kingdom, petition nu. 23413/94*, ECHR Judgement, June 9th 1998, available at: https://hudoc.echr.coe.int/eng#{%22itemid%22:[%22001-58176%22]}.

197 *Athanassoglou and Others v. Switzerland*, petition nu. 27644/95, ECHR Judgement, Apr. 6th 2000, available at: http://hudoc.echr.coe.int/eng?i=002-6883 .

198 *McGinley et Egan c. Royaume-Uni*, petition nu. 23413/94, ECHR Judgment, 9.6.1998, available at: http://hudoc.echr.coe.int/eng?i=002-6861 .

that jurisdiction will be expanded to include such crimes in outer space in the near future. Aside from that, there are notable absences among State Parties of the Rome Statute – namely big greenhouse gas emitters such as the U.S, China, India, and Russia.[199]

Therefore, due to the significant permeation of space law with the policies and interests of a small number of space powers, and the consequent difficulty of achieving a formally uniform *opinio iuris* that would lead to more precise norms, the two most accepted ways to prevent conflicts related to space activities remain institutional mechanisms of international and regional organizations[200] and establishing multilateral cooperative space projects.[201]

The agreements on the establishment of such organizations envisage various legal procedures for resolving international disputes, which range from negotiations to mandatory arbitration.[202] The European Space Research Organization (ESRO) and ESA stand out as rare examples of organizations dealing with space issues, which have accepted mandatory court *or* arbitration dispute resolution as an option.[203] ESA is a successor of the organization ELDO, established by the 1962 Convention on the Establishment of a European Space Vehicle Development, which provides for the establishment of an arbitral tribunal, with binding decisions, if the dispute is not resolved before the council of the organization.[204] On the other side, in such a situation, the ESRO Convention provides for disputes to be referred to the ICJ.[205] However, since the US is the main partner of ESA, the standard practice between ESA and NASA has become the introduction of mutual

---

199 *ICC To Focus On Environmental Crimes: A Landmark Move For International Environmental Law*, Alessandra Lehmen, Juchem Advocacia, Brazil, (21/03/2017) https://www.expertguides.com/articles/icc-to-focus-on-environmental-crimes-a-landmark-move-for-international-environmental-law/arljgbwe.

200 Such examples of international and regional organizations established for the purpose of rationalizing the allocation of space resources and avoiding conflict situations are: the International Satellite Telecommunications Organization (INTELSAT), the International Maritime Satellite Organization (INMARSAT), the Program for Cooperation in Peaceful Space Exploration (INTERSPACE), International Space Communications System and Organization (INTERSPUTNIK), European Space Agency (ESA), Arab Satellite Communications Organization (ARABSAT) and European Satellite Telecommunications Organization (EUTELSAT).

201 Goh, *supra* note 185.

202 *Id.* at 46.

203 *Id.* at 50.

204 *Id.*

205 *Id.*

indemnity clauses in case of damage resulting from the violation of the provisions of the relevant agreements in order to prevent conflict.[206]

Most international environmental conventions do not impose mandatory dispute resolution. Exceptions to this include the 1954 Convention on the Prevention of Oil Pollution from Ships, the 1978 Convention on the Prevention of Pollution from Ships, the IAEA Convention on Early Notification of a Nuclear Accident and the IAEA Convention on Assistance in the Event of a Nuclear Accident or Radiological Emergency.[207] It was not until the 1980s that international environmental agreements began to include more far-reaching dispute settlement mechanisms, offering the option of mandatory dispute settlement with third parties.[208] Three such conventions are the 1985 Convention for the Protection of the Ozone Layer and its 1987 Montreal Protocol on Substances that Deplete the Ozone Layer, the 1992 Convention on Biological Diversity and the UN Framework Convention on Climate Change.[209]

The lack of legally binding dispute resolution mechanisms conditioned the reaction in the legal doctrine in the form of proposing new mechanisms that would correspond to the peculiarities of space law. Thus, the concept of the "multi-door courthouse" emerged, based on the mechanisms of alternative ways of resolving international disputes.[210] The basis for proposing a multi-purpose umbrella court is found in the UN General Assembly statement from Resolution 1721 (XVI) B that states: "The United Nations should provide a central point of international cooperation in the peaceful exploration and use of space."[211] Specifically, in theory, the "central point of international cooperation" is interpreted as an appeal for an establishment of a special multi-level institutionalized quasi-judicial body by adopting a Protocol to the OST, based on elements of the Liability Convention, the final draft of the 1998 UNCLOS Convention on the Settlement of Space Law Disputes (ILC Final Draft Convention on Settlement of Space Law Disputes), the WTO Dispute Settlement Understanding and other international dispute settlement instruments.[212] A similar basis as an agreement for establishing an international multifunctional

---

[206] *Id.*
[207] *Id.* at 195.
[208] *Id.* at 197.
[209] *Id.*
[210] *Id.* at 7.
[211] UN GENERAL ASSEMBLY RESOLUTION 1721 B (XVI) - INTERNATIONAL CO-OPERATION IN THE PEACEFUL USES OF OUTER SPACE, UNITED NATIONS OFFICE FOR OUTER SPACE AFFAIRS, 20. Dec, 1961, https://www.unoosa.org/oosa/en/ourwork/spacelaw/treaties/resolutions/res_16_1721.html.
[212] Goh, *supra* note 285, at 12.

environmental court for resolving disputes regarding the protection of the environment has already been introduced to the reader in David Krott's chapter on an international court for the environment.

Institutionalization of various mechanisms for peaceful settlement of disputes and disagreements under one roof would form a single framework of mechanisms, which would lead to savings and greater efficiency, but also have a reciprocal impact on legitimizing alternative ways of resolving international disputes.[213] As some of the functions of the court, the legal doctrine emphasizes the division of duties and responsibilities for: space activity that causes damage, resolving conflicts in space activities and determining the amount of compensation or the appropriate form of reparation.[214] Access to this court would extend the doctrine to non-state actors, intergovernmental organizations, non-governmental organizations, private entities, and even individuals.[215] Multifunctionality, comprehensiveness, broad competencies, non-binding jurisdiction, and the necessary specialization within this court, meet the requirements of the cross-border and interdisciplinary character of space disputes and give legitimacy to this mechanism. However, since the idea of this court seems to be ambitious in the context of the current balance of powers, it would be more realistic to consider some comparable, appropriate solutions.

Of course, for most of these proposals, it would be necessary, at least, to revise the primary norms within the conventions to provide for appropriate mechanisms for resolving disagreements, which is why these examples confirm the effect of the shortcomings of the basic sources of Space Law. Insufficiency and inadequacy of mechanisms for resolving disputes regarding space damages, as well as the absence of competent courts, indicate an obvious lack of case law in this area. All of the above confirms the need to focus on prevention and strengthen the preventive mechanisms in this area.

VI. Examples of Space Damages and the lack of case law

Although in the current state that space law regulation is in, it is quite obvious that the subsequent lack of case law must follow, that does not mean that there are no examples of damages and incidents related to space. In fact, there are various such outer space-related cases; however, the states were not so eager to resolve them by formal, judicial means.

---

213 *Id.* at 9.
214 *Id.* at 10.
215 *Id.*

The most recent cases of leaving clouds of space debris were related to China's and India's Anti-Satellite tests.[216] Specifically, in January, China's Fengyun-1C weather satellite was destroyed by an anti-satellite (ASAT) device, also launched by the Chinese, which created a mess of fragments fluttering through space.[217] The satellite's destruction is now being viewed as the most prolific and severe fragmentation in the course of five decades of space operations.[218] Still, many similar cases happened earlier in the past that also left a significant amount of space waste, which makes this a recurring and ongoing issue.

On NASA's website, it is reported three "catastrophic" collisions resulted in space damage caused by traveling space debris: the first was in 1996, where a French satellite was hit and damaged by the remains of a French rocket that exploded a decade earlier. The second was on February 10, 2009, where a dysfunctional Russian satellite struck and destroyed a U.S. functional commercial satellite, Iridium 33, and the said collision added more than 2,000 visible pieces of space debris. Finally, another incident took place in 2007 where a Chinese anti-satellite test, which used a rocket to destroy an old meteorological satellite, added more than 3,000 pieces of space debris.[219] The latest data of ESA states that in 2018, there was an observation of over 500 fractures, explosions, collisions, or unusual events that resulted in fragmentation.[220]

In the 1960s, two space cases provoked a significant scientific reaction. One of them was the US West Ford Project, which was an attempt to place copper needles in the Earth's orbit in 1961 and 1963, while the other referred to a series of high-altitude nuclear explosions, carried out before the 1963 Nuclear-Test-Ban Treaty.[221] The West Ford project has been attacked by scientists in several countries, as well as numerous government officials, as a potential disruption to radio astronomy and other observation techniques,

---

[216] Doris Elin Urrutia, *India anti-satellite test significance - India's Anti-Satellite Missile Test Is a Big Deal. Here's Why.* SPACE.COM, (Mar. 30, 2019), https://www.space.com/india-anti-satellite-test-significance.html.

[217] Leonard David, *China's Anti-Satellite Test: Worrisome Debris Cloud Circles Earth,* (Feb. 2, 2007), https://www.space.com/3415-china-anti-satellite-test-worrisome-debris-cloud-circles-earth.html.

[218] *Id.*

[219] Garcia, *supra* note 26.

[220] ESA, *supra* note 5.

[221] *See* Howard J. Taubenfeld, *International Environmental Law: Air and Outer Space,* 13 NAT. RESOURCES J. 315 (1973). https://digitalrepository.unm.edu/nrj/vol13/iss2/9.

and as a precursor to scientifically undesirable space congestion.[222] Similarly, high-altitude nuclear explosion experiments have been opposed by some scientists because of possible distortions in the Van Allen Belt and making it difficult to study the Earth's natural environment, as it would interfere with satellites in orbit and pose a danger to humans in space.[223] The Soviet bloc called such experiments acts of aggression contrary to international law, the UN Charter, and UN Resolutions.[224] Even if no specific harm was done to the nation or individuals in these cases, they were widespread enough to indicate a general interest worldwide in protecting the environmental status quo,[225] which is proven by the fact that they were followed by the introduction of environmentally-oriented provisions in the OST.

However, for the subject matter of this chapter, cases of crashes or collisions of space objects and spacecraft are of greater importance, as such cases, in addition to human casualties, speak more directly about the accompanying environmental damage in space or the Earth's atmosphere.

Due to the fact that the Liability Convention excludes from its application damages incurred in the territory of the launching state, when only national law of the state can apply to such damages, states are increasingly concluding agreements containing provisions on liability insurance. In such agreements, the State Parties either disclaim liability or assign the term "Launching state" to a particular Contracting Party, on the basis of which the Liability Convention is again given a basis for application. A good example of such a practice is the case concerning the space launch complex of the city of Baikonur in Kazakhstan. Namely, in that case, the Baikonur launch complex was managed by the Russians, but it was located on the territory of Kazakhstan, so here, based on the Liability Convention, Kazakhstan would be considered the launching country.[226] Therefore, if the damage were done in the territory of Kazakhstan by a space object launched from Baikonur, the Liability Convention would not be applicable.[227] However, the lease agreement provided that in the event of damage to the Baikonur launch complex in connection with Russian space programs, Russia would be liable as a launching state under the Liability Convention, without Kazakhstan

---

[222] *Id.* 318.

[223] *Id.* 319.

[224] *Id.*

[225] *Id.*

[226] Manikowski, *supra* note 29, at 61.

[227] *Id.* at 61.

being considered a joint participant.[228] The result of such a contractual arrangement enabled Kazakhstan to request compensation from Russia.[229] This is, therefore, one of the many examples in which the instruments of economics complement legal instruments, enabling their more efficient application, which is why insurance arrangements are becoming more common when undertaking space activities.

A frequent occurrence in the field of space activities are also damages caused to third parties who do not participate in space activities. Such damages, however, occur on the Earth's surface much more often than in flight, and the most dangerous accidents occur on the launching platform itself or during the launch and take-off of a space object.[230] One such case occurred in 1986 when the Titan rocket exploded at an altitude of only 240 meters, destroying both the platform and the launch facilities, and the material damage was higher than $40,000,000.[231]

The case of the Thor Able Star rocket falling on the territory of Cuba, which killed a cow on that occasion, is also interesting, and the outcome was the obligation of the American government to pay Cuba $2,000,000 in compensation, on the basis of which the unfortunate cow remained known as one of the most expensive cows in history.[232]

However, in addition to cases of environmental damage where the victims are animals, there are also cases with a significant number of human victims. Thus, for example, the unsuccessful launch of the Long March 3B rocket on February 14, 1996, due to a deviation from the trajectory before leaving the launch tower, resulted in a collision, which killed at least 100 people and accidentally destroyed the Intelsat 708 satellite.[233] A comparable case concerns the explosion of a VLS-3 rocket on a Launchpad in August 2003 in Brazil, which resulted in at least 21 human casualties.[234]

Without disputing the significance of the prior types of damages, the most relevant case for this chapter is the crash of the USSR satellite, the so-called

---

[228] *Id.* at 62.

[229] *Id.*

[230] *Id.*

[231] *Id.*

[232] *Id.*

[233] *Id.* at 63

[234] *Id.*

Cosmos 954.[235] This case marked the first time in history of the return and fall of nuclear matter back to Earth and the first legal test in the practice of secondary norms of the Liability Convention.[236]

The satellite crash occurred on January 24th, 1978, in the early morning, in a sparsely populated area of Canada.[237] However, despite the fact that the final and complete disintegration of the Soviet satellite took place in an almost uninhabited area, space debris from the spacecraft spread over a much wider area northwest of there.[238] Although it is obvious that the entry of Cosmos 954 satellite into Canadian airspace and the deposition of hazardous, radioactive satellite debris in its territory constitute a violation of Canadian sovereignty, the problem was the interpretation of the terms of the Liability Convention, as it does not explicitly regulate damage resulting from radioactive radiation of nuclear matter.[239]

The omission of the USSR, which provided the basis for responsibility, was reduced to the lack of prior notification of the satellite crash, as well as to the untimely submission of complete and accurate information, even after the timely and repeated request of the Canadian government.[240] Even the official information given by the Soviet ambassador to the Ministry of Foreign Affairs was inadequate and inaccurate, as it boiled down to the assessment that the satellite crash could only lead to "insignificant local pollution," for which they claimed was easily removable.[241]

When the statement is compared to research conducted by the Nuclear Research Center in Canada, whose results showed that almost all the fragments were radioactive and that some of them even posed a danger to life, the discrepancy between the published data and the actual situation becomes obvious. The only adequate action of the Soviet authorities at that time was the

---

[235] *See* Alexander F. Cohen, *Cosmos 954 and the International Law of Satellite Accidents*, YALE JOURNAL OF INTERNATIONAL LAW, Vol. 10, Issue 1, Article 7, (1984), https://digitalcommons.law.yale.edu/cgi/viewcontent.cgi?referer=https://www.google.com/&httpsredir=1&article=1316&context=yjil.

[236] William B. Wirin, *The Sky is Falling: Managing Space Objects*, DOCUMENTS ON OUTER SPACE LAW, University of Nebraska, 146, (1985), https://digitalcommons.unl.edu/spacelawdocs/8/.

[237] *Id.* at 146.

[238] *Id.*

[239] *Id.*

[240] *See* Settlement of Claim between Canada and the Union of Soviet Socialist Republics for Damage Caused by "Cosmos 954", 2.4.1981, point. 7.-case facts, available at: https://www.jaxa.jp/library/space_law/chapter_3/3-2-2-1_e.html.

[241] Wirin, *supra* note 232, at 146.

recognition of the satellite's affiliation, as well as the confirmation that nuclear and radioactive material originated from it.[242] The facts of the case also indicate the failure of the Soviet authorities to make any contribution to reducing the damage from the fall of the satellite, let alone eliminating it. On the other hand, within the "Morning Light" operation and with the help of the U.S., the Canadian authorities took all necessary measures provided for in Article 6 of the Convention in order to eliminate the damage and radioactive material.[243]

The applicable law in the case included Article 7 of the Outer Space Treaty, Article 2 of the Liability Convention, as well as the general legal principles of justice and fairness.[244] Since both states were members of the conventions, it was concluded that there is an absolute liability of the USSR and that the separation of hazardous, radioactive waste from satellites over a large area of Canada and the presence of that waste in an environment that makes part of that property unsuitable for use represents "damage to property" within the meaning of the Convention.[245] The outcome of the case was an out-of-court settlement of the dispute by peaceful means, without the need for establishing the Commission provided in the Convention.[246] Based on established facts and legal principles, the Government of Canada requested payment from the USSR in the amount of $6,041,174.70, reserving the right to request additional compensation in case of future damages and additional consequences, as well as the right to all potential future costs in case possible needs for the establishment of a Commission for deciding on requests.[247]

The significance of this case is attributed to the subsequent adoption of principles in the field of nuclear energy sources and the concretization of certain terms and obligations provided by the Liability Convention. Therefore, this was a turning point in the development of space law because by accepting nuclear damage as damage protected by the Convention, the path for the evolutionary development of space law opened in the direction of more environmentally-oriented protection.

Nevertheless, from these few examples of damages, the reluctance of states to turn to court dispute resolution in the field of space activities becomes obvious. Until recently, space activities were undertaken almost exclusively by states; in cases where the damage was within state borders, these events were

---

242 Settlement, *supra* note 242, ¶12.

243 Wirin, *supra* note 232, at 146.

244 Settlement, *supra* note 242, Point 14, 15, 19, i 20.

245 *Id.* ¶ 15.

246 *Id.*

247 *Id.* ¶ 24 and 25.

considered issues of national interest exclusively. Additionally, due to the lack of a specific international court or body responsible for resolving disputes over space activities, as well as the terminological inaccuracy of the Liability Convention, cases of damages in this area are usually resolved amicably, i.e., through diplomatic channels, so the case law is scarce.

VII. Conclusion

The scientific achievements have taken us far, but since law has not followed them in a timely and adequate manner, that has led to a modern environmental crisis that takes its form in transboundary environmental damage and becomes the unfortunate link between outer space and the Earth.

The imbalance in power relations and the monopoly of space forces indicates the non-transparency of space activities, the unequal participation of other countries in the creation of space law, and the illegitimacy of many norms in this area. The impossibility of finding a compromise among the space forces led to a greater focus on substantive space law, which for the most part retained its principled character in the binding legal instruments, while it was more adequately elaborated and specified only by soft law. The principled character of imprecise primary norms indicates the impossibility of adequate application of the few secondary norms. This situation is further aggravated by the reluctance of states to resolve disagreements in space through judicial mechanisms or at least adopt binding secondary norms that would form the procedural space law.

In such circumstances, as we are unable to adequately apply the traditional civil and criminal law mechanisms, we should turn to soft law and preventive mechanisms, as well as the multidisciplinary approach and transplantation of well-founded principles of related branches of law, which in this case is environmental law, but also partially nuclear law. Due to the underdevelopment of space law, the only way to create a counterbalance to the politics of space forces can be through confirming general principles in the sources of soft law. The reaction of the world population to climate change and global warming speaks in favor of the potential emergence of a new civil revolution through activism and the formation of collective consciousness globally. Thus, we come to a contradictory situation - that anthropocentrism, fear of the unknown and the desire to survive took us to outer space, and that the same, by force of chance, will bring us back to Earth.

Bibliography

AGREEMENT GOVERNING THE ACTIVITIES OF STATES ON THE MOON AND OTHER CELESTIAL BODIES, Vol. 1363, No. 23002, GENERAL ASSEMBLY OF THE UNITED NATIONS on 5 Dec. 1979, https://treaties.un.org/doc/Publication/UNTS/Volume%201363/volume-1363-I-23002-English.pdf.

AGREEMENT ON THE RESCUE OF ASTRONAUTS, THE RETURN OF ASTRONAUTS AND THE RETURN OF OBJECTS LAUNCHED INTO OUTER SPACE, Volume-672-I-9574, May 15th, 1969. Preamble, https://treaties.un.org/doc/Publication/UNTS/Volume%20672/volume-672-I-9574-English.pdf.

Petra Amidžić-Jelovčić; I. Perković, *Liability of Carriers for Nuclear Damage with Special Reference to the Convention on Supplementary Compensation for Nuclear Damage*, PROCEEDINGS OF THE FACULTY OF LAW IN SPLIT (hereinafter cited as PFS), 2/2008. year, 2008, Split, 45, at 378 and 379, https://www.pravst.unist.hr/dokumenti/zbornik/200888/zb200802_377.pdf.

ANTARCTIC TREATY, Washington, D.C, USA, Dec. 1st, 1959, https://treaties.un.org/doc/Publication/UNTS/Volume%20402/volume-402-I-5778-English.pdf.

Athanassoglou and Others v. Switzerland, petition nu. 27644/95, ECHR Judgement, Apr. 6th 2000, : http://hudoc.echr.coe.int/eng?i=002-6883.

Adam Augustyn, *Strategic Defense Initiative - United States Defense System*, ENCYCLOPEDIA BRITANNICA, 3/27/2019. https://www.britannica.com/topic/Strategic-Defense-Initiative.

John R. Blackburn Jr, *President Reagan's Nuclear Policy From 1981 To 1983: The Effects On National Defense, Foreign Policy and Society*, FACULTY OF THE GRADUATE COLLEGE OF THE OKLAHOMA STATE UNIVERSITY, Oklahoma Christian University, Oklahoma, May, 1999, : https://shareok.org/bitstream/handle/11244/11685/Thesis-1999-B628p.pdf?sequence=1.

Case concerning the Gabčikovo-Nagymaros Project, Judgement, ICJ REPORTS 1997, 78. ¶ 140, https://www.icj-cij.org/files/case-related/92/092-19970925-JUD-01-00-EN.pdf.

Cohen E. Carpanelli, *Interpreting "Damage Caused by Space Objects" under the 1972 Liability Convention*, PROCEEDINGS OF THE INTERNATIONAL INSTITUTE OF SPACE LAW (2013), Eleven International Publishing, 2014, p. 4, : https://iislweb.org/docs/Diederiks2013.pdf.

A. Čavoški, et al., *Environment in the European Union, Environmental Handbook - International Law and Environment*, OSCE MISSION TO SERBIA, 2010, at 32.

Alexandra Chavoshki, et al., *Environment in the European Union, Environmental Handbook - International Law and Environment*, OSCE MISSION TO SERBIA, 2010, at 27.

Joyeeta Chatterjee, *Reflections on the Concepts of 'Liability' and 'Responsibility' in a Privatised Atmosphere*, NEW PERSPECTIVES ON SPACE LAW - PROCEEDINGS OF THE 53RD IISL COLLOQUIUM ON THE LAW OF OUTER SPACE, eds. Mark J. Sundahl, V. Gopalakrishnan, International Institute for Space Law, 183-201, 2011, https://www.iislweb.org/docs/NewPerspectivesonSpaceLaw.pdf.

Alexander F. Cohen, *Cosmos 954 and the International Law of Satellite Accidents*, YALE JOURNAL OF INTERNATIONAL LAW, Vol. 10, Issue 1, Article 7, 1984 : https://digitalcommons.law.yale.edu/cgi/viewcontent.cgi?referer=https://www.google.com/&httpsredir=1&article=1316&context=yjil.

CONVENTION ON THE PROHIBITION OF MILITARY OR ANY OTHER HOSTILE USE OF ENVIRONMENTAL MODIFICATION TECHNIQUES, Ch_XXVI_1, VOL-2, Chapter XXVI. Disarmament, New York, Dec. 10th 1976, Preamble : https://treaties.un.org/doc/Treaties/1978/10/19781005%2000-39%20AM/Ch_XXVI_01p.pdf.

CONVENTION ON CIVIL LIABILITY RESULTING FROM DANGEROUS ACTIVITIES FOR THE ENVIRONMENT, ETS No. 105, Lugano, COUNCIL OF EUROPE, 2013, https://rm.coe.int/168007c079.

CONVENTION ON INTERNATIONAL LIABILITY FOR DAMAGE CAUSED BY SPACE OBJECTS, Ch_XXIV_1, VOL-2, Outer Space, New York, 12 Nov. 1974, https://treaties.un.org/doc/Treaties/1976/09/19760915%2003-08%20AM/Ch_XXIV_01p.pdf.

CONVENTION ON REGISTRATION OF OBJECTS LAUNCHED INTO OUTER SPACE, Ch_XXIV_1, VOL-2, Outer Space, New York, 12 Nov. 1974, https://treaties.un.org/doc/Publication/UNTS/Volume%201023/volume-1023-I-15020-English.pdf.

THE CONVENTION ON SUPPLEMENTARY COMPENSATION FOR NUCLEAR DAMAGES (CSC), INTERNATIONAL ATOMIC ENERGY AGENCY, https://www.iaea.org/topics/nuclear-liability-conventions/convention-supplementary-compensation-nuclear-damage.

Bojana Čučković, *The notion of environmental damage in international environmental law*, LEGAL LIFE 9/2010, at 406.

Leonard David, *China's Anti-Satellite Test: Worrisome Debris Cloud Circles Earth*, Feb. 2nd, 2007, *https://www.space.com/3415-china-anti-satellite-test-worrisome-debris-cloud-circles-earth.html*.

M. Drenovak-Ivanović, S. Đorđević, S. Važić, *Legal Instruments of Environmental Protection - Civil and Criminal Protection*, OSCE, OSCE MISSION TO SERBIA, Belgrade, 2015, at 46.

M. Drenovak-Ivanović; S. Đorđević; S. Važić, *Legal instruments of environmental protection - civil and criminal law protection*, Belgrade, OSCE, OSCE MISSION TO SERBIA 2015, at 29.

Sarab Entesar, *The Importance of Environmental Standards and Environmental Management for the Sustainable Development of Libya*, Belgrade 2018 at 5, https://futura.edu.rs/wordpress/wp-content/uploads/2018/12/SARAB-ENTESAR-MASTER-RAD_FINAL_05122018.pdf.

European Parliament and Council, Directive 2004/35/CE on environmental liability with regard to the prevention and remedying of environmental damage, OFFICIAL JOURNAL OF THE EUROPEAN UNION, Apr. 21st, 2004., : https://eur-lex.europa.eu/LexUriServ/LexUriServ.do?uri=OJ:L:2004:143:0056:0075:en:PDF.

EUROPEAN CONVENTION ON HUMAN RIGHTS, EUROPEAN COURT OF HUMAN RIGHTS, COUNCIL OF EUROPE, 4. Nov., 1950, Rome, https://www.echr.coe.int/Documents/Convention_ENG.pdf%23p.=9.

EUROPEAN SPACE AGENCY (ESA*), Space Debris By the Numbers*, Jan. 2019, https://www.esa.int/Safety_Security/Space_Debris/Space_debris_by_the_numbers.

Gérardine Meishan Goh, *Dispute Settlement in International Space Law: A Multi-Door Courthouse for Outer Space*, Universitet Lajden, 19. Apr. 2007. at 20, https://openaccess.leidenuniv.nl/bitstream/handle/1887/11860/Thesis.pdf?sequence=10.

INTER-AGENCY SPACE DEBRIS COORDINATION COMMITTEE, *IADC Space Debris Mitigation Guidelines*, Sep. 2007. at 5, https://www.unoosa.org/documents/pdf/spacelaw/sd/IADC-2002-01-IADC-Space_Debris-Guidelines-Revision1.pdf.

INTERNATIONAL CODE OF CONDUCT AGAINST BALLISTIC MISSILE PROLIFERATION, A/57/724, UNITED NATIONS GENERAL ASSEMBLY, Feb. 2003, https://www.hcoc.at/documents/Hague-Code-of-Conduct-A_57_724-English.pdf.

George Khoukaz: *ADR That is Out of This World: A Regime for the Resolution of Outer Space Disputes*, 2018 J. Disp. Resol. 274, https://scholarship.law.missouri.edu/jdr/vol2018/iss1/16.

Alexander Kiss, *Responsibility for nuclear damage, Conference on the Human Right to a Safe and Healthful Environment and the Responsibility under International Law of Operators of Nuclear Facilities*, 2008, at 80, http://djilp.org/wp-content/uploads/2011/08/State-Responsibility-Liability-Alexandre-Kiss.pdf.

L. Kovudhikulrungsri, D. Nakseeharach, *Liability Regime of International Space Law: Some Lessons from International Nuclear Law*, 4 JOURNAL OF EAST ASIA AND INTERNATIONAL LAW AND INT'L L. 291 (2011), at 298, https://heinonline.org/HOL/LandingP.?handle=hein.journals/jeasil4&div=30&id=&p.=&t=1556925702.

Samantha Lawler, *SpaceX's Starlink satellites are about to ruin stargazing for everyone*, THE CONVERSATION, Nov. 17, 2020, https://theconversation.com/spacexs-starlink-satellites-are-about-to-ruin-stargazing-for-everyone-149516.

Stacy Liberatore, *SpaceX declares independence: Elon Musk's firm says they will not recognize Earth laws in planned Mars colony and says 'free planet' will adopt 'self-governing principles'*, DAILYMAIL.CO.UK, 10/30/2020 https://www.dailymail.co.uk/sciencetech/article-8897601/Elon-Musks-SpaceX-says-not-recognize-Earth-laws-planned-Mars-colony.html.

L.C.B. v. the United Kingdom, petition nu. 23413/94, ECHR Judgement, June 9th 1998, https://hudoc.echr.coe.int/eng#{%22itemid%22:[%22001-58176%22]}.

Alessandra Lehmen, *ICC To Focus On Environmental Crimes: A Landmark Move For International Environmental Law*, JUCHEM ADVOCACIA, Brazil, 21/03/2017 https://www.expertguides.com/articles/icc-to-focus-on-environmental-crimes-a-landmark-move-for-international-environmental-law/arljgbwe.

Ajey Lele, *Fifty Years of the Outer Space Treaty: Tracing the Journey Institute for Defence Studies and Analyses*, Pentagon Press, ISBN 978-81-8274-948-1, 2017. New Delhi, at 13.

P. Manikowski, *Examples of space damages in the light of international space law*, ECONOMICS AND BUSINESS REVIEW EBR 6.1 (): 54-68. 2006. at 65 https://www.ebr.edu.pl/pub/2006_1_54.pdf.

MANUAL ON HUMAN RIGHTS AND THE ENVIRONMENT, COUNCIL OF EUROPE, 2012, at 7 https://www.echr.coe.int/librarydocs/dh_dev_manual_environment_eng.pdf.

Sergio Marchisio, *The Draft Code of Conduct for Outer Space activities, Activities of States in Outer Space in Light of New Developments: Meeting International Responsibilities and Establishing National Legal and Policy Frameworks*, SAPIENZA UNIVERSITY OF ROME, EUROPEAN CENTRE FOR SPACE LAW,

16-19 Nov. 2010. Bangkok, Thailand, https://www.unoosa.org/pdf/pres/2010/SLW2010/02-10b.pdf.

McGinley et Egan c. Royaume-Uni, petition nu. 23413/94, ECHR Judgment, 9.6.1998, http://hudoc.echr.coe.int/eng?i=002-6861.

Ana Mikulec, *The Outer Space Law*, LAWYER, LAW AND SOCIETY REVIEW, 2016, Vol. 49 Issue 99, 105-127. at 23, 111 pages, https://hrcak.srce.hr/index.php?show=toc&id_broj=12777.

Nataša Mrvić-Petrović, Z. Petrović, "State Responsibility for Environmental Damages", ECOLOGY AND LAW, ed. Čavoški and Knežević, INSTITUTE FOR COMPARATIVE LAW, Faculty of Law, UNION University, Belgrade, 2012 at 91.

NASA, *News and Features*, ed. Holly Zell, Sep. 2, 2011, https://www.nasa.gov/news/debris_faq.html.

NASA, *Space Debris and Human Spacecraft*, ed. Mark Garcia, Sep. 27. 2013, https://www.nasa.gov/mission_pages/station/news/orbital_debris.html.

NASA ORBITAL DEBRIS PROGRAM OFFICE, *Orbital Debris Quarterly News*, (Sep. 2018), https://www.orbitaldebris.jsc.nasa.gov/quarterly-news/pdfs/odqnv22i3.pdf.

Öneryıldız v. Turkey, petition nu: 48939/99, ECHR Judgement Nov. 30th 2004, https://hudoc.echr.coe.int/eng#{%22itemid%22:[%22002-4094%22].

Bojan Pajtić, *Environmental Protection - Prevention and Compensation of Damages*, PROCEEDINGS OF THE PFNS, 2/2011, Novi Sad, 2011, at 255.

PARIS CONVENTION ON THIRD PARTY LIABILITY IN THE FIELD OF NUCLEAR ENERGY, 1960, NUCLEAR ENERGY AGENCY, https://www.oecd-nea.org/jcms/pl_20196/paris-convention-on-third-party-liability-in-the-field-of-nuclear-energy-paris-convention-or-pc.

Principles Relevant to the Use of Nuclear Power Sources In Outer Space - With Introductory Note, UNGA Resolution 47/68, Dec. the 14th, 1992, https://aerospace.org/sites/default/files/policy_archives/Principles%20on%20Nuclear%20Power%20Sources%20in%20Space.pdf.

Obrad Račić, *Basic Principles of Outer Space Law*, IMPP, 1972, Belgrade, at 34 - 35.

Obrad Račić, *Collection of Documents on the Legal Regulation of Research and Use of the Cosmos*, Manuscript, IMPP, Belgrade, 1969, 31-33, available in the library of the Faculty of Law, University of Belgrade.

Safety Framework for Nuclear Power Source Applications in Outer Space, Jointly published by the United Nations Committee on the Peaceful Uses of Outer Space Scientific and Technical Subcommittee and the International Atomic Energy Agency, IAEA, UN COPUOS, Vienna, Austria, 2009, : https://fas.org/nuke/space/iaea-space.pdf.

Settlement of Claim between Canada and the Union of Soviet Socialist Republics for Damage Caused by "Cosmos 954", 2.4.1981, point. 7.-case facts, : https://www.jaxa.jp/library/space_law/chapter_3/3-2-2-1_e.html.

Predrag Stojanović, Ilija Zindović, *Legal responsibility for environmental damage and environmental protection*, ANNALS OF THE THE BELGRADE FACULTY OF LAW, LXIII, 1/2015, Belgrade, at 45, http://ojs.ius.bg.ac.rs/index.php/anali/article/view/66/243, https://anali.rs/.

Howard. J. Taubenfeld, *International Environmental Law: Air and Outer Space*, NATURAL RESOURCES JOURNAL, Apr. 1973, at 323, , https://digitalrepository.unm.edu/nrj/vol13/iss2/9.

TREATY BANNING NUCLEAR WEAPON TESTS IN THE ATMOSPHERE, IN OUTER SPACE AND UNDER WATER, Moscow, Vol. 480, No. 6964, Aug. 5th, 1963, https://treaties.un.org/doc/Publication/UNTS/Volume%20480/volume-480-I-6964-English.pdf.

TREATY ON PRINCIPLES GOVERNING THE ACTIVITIES OF STATES IN THE EXPLORATION AND USE OF OUTER SPACE, INCLUDING THE MOON AND OTHER CELESTIAL BODIES, Volume-610-I-8843, Oct. 10th, 1967, https://treaties.un.org/doc/Publication/UNTS/Volume%20610/volume-610-I-8843-English.pdf.

UN COPUOS, *Space Debris Mitigation Guidelines of the Committee on the Peaceful Uses of Outer Space*, UNOOSA, Vienna, 2010, https://www.unoosa.org/pdf/publications/st_space_49E.pdf.

UNITED NATIONS OFFICE FOR OUTER SPACE AFFAIRS, *United Nations Treaties and Principles on Outer Space*, UNITED NATIONS PUBLICATION, Vienna, 2002, at 23-30. https://www.unoosa.org/pdf/publications/ST_SPACE_51E.pdf.

UN GENERAL ASSEMBLY RESOLUTION 1721 B (XVI) - INTERNATIONAL CO-OPERATION IN THE PEACEFUL USES OF OUTER SPACE, UNITED NATIONS OFFICE FOR OUTER SPACE AFFAIRS, 20. Dec, 1961, https://www.unoosa.org/oosa/en/ourwork/spacelaw/treaties/resolutions/res_16_1721.html.

Doris Elin Urrutia, *India anti-satellite test significance - India's Anti-Satellite Missile Test Is a Big Deal. Here's Why.* SPACE.COM, Mar. 30, 2019, https://www.space.com/india-anti-satellite-test-significance.html.

VIENNA CONVENTION ON CIVIL LIABILITY, 1963, INTERNATIONAL ATOMIC ENERGY AGENCY, https://www.iaea.org/publications/documents/infcircs/vienna-convention-civil-liability-nuclear-damage.

Mike Wall, *Trump Signs Directive to Create a Military Space Force, SPACE.COM*, Feb. 27, 2019. : https://www.space.com/president-trump-space-force-directive.html.

Mike Wall, *SpaceX's Starship may help clean up space junk*, SPACE, Oct. 2020, https://www.space.com/spacex-starship-space-junk-cleanup.

Jackie Wattles, *Colonizing Mars could be dangerous and ridiculously expensive. Elon Musk wants to do it anyway*, CNN BUSINESS, 9/8/2020, https://edition.cnn.com/2020/09/08/tech/spacex-mars-profit-scn/index.html.

William B. Wirin, *The Sky is Falling: Managing Space Objects*, DOCUMENTS ON OUTER SPACE LAW, University of Nebraska, 1985, at 146, https://digitalcommons.unl.edu/spacelawdocs/8/.

Index

A

actus reus, 4, 16, 23, 28, 29, 95, 96, 131, 165, 167, 168
African Court of Justice and Human and Peoples' Rights (ACJHR), 84, 91, 92, 96, 97, 98
African Criminal Court, 70, 91, 92, 93, 95, 97, 101
African Union (AU), xi, 66, 91, 92, 94
Agreement Governing the Activities of States on the Moon and other Celestial Bodies. *See* Moon Agreement
Antarctica, 149, 162, 164
Australia, 71, 73, 100, 115, 166, 180, 210

B

Bangladesh, 46, 51, 52, 61, 64, 263, 270
  National River Protection Commission (NRPC), 51
Bolivia, 46, 47, 48, 56, 62
Brazil, 19, 45, 82, 105, 142, 180, 332, 337, 343
  Court of Environment and Agrarian Issues, 19

C

CAH. *See* crimes against humanity
Cambodia, ix, 277, 284
  Extraordinary Chamber in the Courts of Cambodia (ECCC), 80
Canada, 125, 139, 164, 175, 210, 234, 247, 252, 338, 339, 344
CARE principles, 184, 216, 219, 220, 221, 222
Central African Republic, 66, 86
Cheyenne River Sioux Tribe, 199, 203
China, 55, 257, 258, 262, 269, 270, 271, 272, 273, 274, 275, 279, 283, 288, 289, 290, 291, 292, 293, 294, 332, 335, 342
climate change, 264, 293
Colombia, 50, 144
Congo, Democratic Republic of, 66, 67, 75, 80, 86, 95, 96, 100, 103, 106
Congress of Nations and States, 287
Convention on International Trade in Endangered Species of Fauna and Flora (CITES), 11, 18
Convention on the Prevention and Punishment of the Crime of Genocide (Genocide Convention), 87, 88, 204, 205
Cote d'Ivoire, 77, 86, 94
crimes against humanity, 66, 258, 278, 279, 280, 285, 286, 294
Crimes Against the Peace and Security of Mankind. *See* Rome Statute

D

Dakota Access Pipeline (DAPL), 164, 184, 185, 186, 187, 190, 191, 192, 193, 196, 197, 198, 199, 200, 201, 202, 203, 207, 208, 216, 220, 221, 222, 223, 224

E

ecocide, vi, 2, 3, 12, 28, 31, 32, 108, 114, 123, 127, 134, 135, 138, 139, 142, 159, 166, 181, 232, 246, 253, 254, 256
Ecuador, 46, 56, 58
EIA. *See* environmental impact assessment
environmental crimes, ix, 1, 5, 7, 10, 15, 16, 19, 22, 23, 26, 28, 65, 67, 69, 76, 77, 84, 97, 99, 107, 109, 132, 133, 135, 137, 141, 142, 143, 145, 146, 148, 150, 151, 152, 154, 156, 157, 158, 159, 160, 161, 162, 164, 165, 166, 167, 168, 169, 170, 171, 172, 173, 175, 176, 178, 179, 180, 246, 331
environmental impact assessment (EIA), xi, 56, 180, 267, 268, 271, 274, 275, 289
environmental personhood, 35, 36, 46, 59, 63, 285
European Commission, 10
European Convention of Human Rights, xi, 26, 153, 330, 331, 341, 343, 344
European Court of Human Rights, xi, 57, 153, 330, 342
European Union, xi, 10, 11, 17, 18, 31, 109, 152, 170, 176, 180, 305, 308, 310, 311, 341, 342
Europol, 10, 17, 31

F

Financial Action Task Force (FATF), 17, 31
forced displacement, vii, viii, 77, 79, 80, 89, 90, 257, 275, 278, 279, 282, 283, 287

G

Geneva Convention(s), 66, 70, 71, 74, 104, 112, 133, 139
  Additional Protocol(s), 66, 70, 73, 104, 112, 133, 139
genocide, ix, 3, 12, 28, 66, 67, 69, 71, 74, 79, 87, 88, 89, 90, 92, 107, 108, 109, 110, 116, 118, 134, 139, 157, 159, 162, 164, 166, 183, 184, 203, 204, 205, 207, 208, 224, 247
  cultural genocide, 90, 91, 184, 205, 207, 208
geocide. *See* ecocide
Germany, 54, 55, 63, 151, 153
global commons, 112, 125, 126, 138, 142, 149
Greece, 6, 8, 9, 13, 14, 29, 32, 94, 110
green crimes. *See* environmental crimes
greenwashing, 12
Guatemala, 260

H

Higgins, Polly, vi, ix, 107, 109, 110, 127, 138, 142, 166, 181, 246, 254
Himalayas, 231, 257, 258, 262, 263, 264, 270, 288, 289, 290, 291, 293, 294
human rights, 257, 258, 261, 274, 276, 278, 283, 286, 287, 292

hydropower dams, vii, 55, 257, 258, 260, 262, 263, 264, 267, 268, 269, 270, 275, 276, 277, 278, 282, 286, 287, 288, 290, 291, 292, 293
International Commission on Large Dams, 261, 276
Panan hydroelectric dam, 266, 267, 270, 290, 291
run of river (ROR), 258, 260, 266

I

India, vii, 19, 30, 46, 49, 50, 51, 53, 55, 58, 62, 64, 131, 153, 154, 175, 176, 181, 231, 232, 233, 234, 236, 239, 240, 241, 242, 243, 245, 246, 247, 248, 249, 250, 251, 252, 253, 254, 255, 256, 257, 258, 260, 262, 263, 264, 265, 266, 267, 268, 270, 272, 273, 274, 279, 283, 285, 288, 289, 290, 291, 292, 293, 294, 332, 335, 345
Ganges River, 49, 50, 251
High Court of Uttarakhand, 49, 50, 51, 62, 63
Himalayas, 49, 50
Kerala, 231, 232, 233, 234, 235, 236, 237, 238, 239, 241, 242, 243, 244, 245, 249, 251, 252, 253, 254, 255, 256
Kole Wetlands, 154, 231, 232, 234, 235, 236, 237, 240, 241, 242, 244, 245, 246, 248, 250, 251, 252, 255
Land Reforms Act, 233, 237, 238, 243, 244, 254
National Green Tribunal, 19, 30, 142, 153, 154, 155, 175, 176, 181, 232, 249, 255
Rong peoples, 264, 265, 266, 267, 268, 275, 283, 285
Sikkim, 257, 264, 265, 266, 267, 268, 270, 288, 289, 291, 292, 293
Supreme Court of India, 49, 51, 62, 64
Teesta River, 265, 266, 267, 268, 269, 270, 285, 288, 292, 293
Yamuna River, 49, 50
Indigenous Peoples, v, vii, ix, 57, 61, 79, 83, 84, 90, 91, 92, 97, 98, 100, 101, 105, 183, 184, 188, 193, 197, 198, 200, 205, 206, 207, 208, 209, 210, 211, 212, 213, 214, 215, 216, 217, 218, 219, 220, 221, 222, 223, 224, 225, 226, 227, 228, 258, 260, 262, 271, 274, 275, 276, 278, 279, 283, 284, 287, 289
data sovereignty, 183, 184, 208, 211, 212, 214, 215, 216, 217, 221, 222, 224, 226, 227
Native Americans, 187, 188, 189, 193, 226, *See* Standing Rock Sioux Tribe, *See* Cheyenne River Sioux Tribe
United Nations Declaration on the Rights of Indigenous Peoples (UNDRIP), xi, 184, 197, 198, 206, 207, 209, 210, 211, 213, 215, 226, 229
Indonesia, v, 269
International Court for the Environment Coalition (ICE Coalition), 144, 145, 146, 147, 148, 150, 151, 153, 164, 178, 181
International Court of Justice, xi, 54, 55, 63, 113, 126, 137, 142, 143, 148, 151, 164, 174, 175, 177, 178, 180, 182, 213, 307, 317, 330, 332, 341
International Court of the Environment Foundation (ICEF), 141, 144, 149, 150

International Covenant on Civil and Political Rights, xi, 212, 229
International Covenant on Economic, Social and Cultural Rights (ICESCR), xi, 25, 32, 57, 82, 206, 212, 229
International Criminal Court, vi, viii, xi, 3, 16, 23, 28, 32, 66, 107, 108, 117, 119, 120, 124, 129, 131, 132, 136, 137, 139, 142, 146, 148, 157, 158, 159, 162, 169, 175, 177, 178, 179, 180, 181, 185, 226, 278, 279, 280, 290, 294, 331, 332, 343
  Office of the Prosecutor, viii, 23, 28, 32, 77, 78, 79, 81, 97, 108, 129, 139, 331
    Policy paper on case selection and prioritisation, viii, 23, 65, 68, 79, 97, 98, 129
International Criminal Tribunal for Rwanda, xi, 66, 69, 88, 98, 179
International Criminal Tribunal for the Former Yugoslavia, xi, 179
International Labor Organization Convention 169, 209, 210, 211, 214
International Law Commission, xi, 107, 110, 111, 112, 113, 114, 115, 116, 121, 122, 125, 132, 134, 138, 139, 245, 278, 279, 290, 294, 333
Interpol, 7, 10, 11, 15, 17, 18, 32
Irish Supreme Court, 26

K

Katanga, Germain, 67, 76, 81, 104
Kenya, 70, 77, 84, 85, 86, 100, 101, 102
Kyoto Protocol, 145, 147

L

Liberia, 66, 75, 95, 96, 106
Lugano Convention, 296, 304, 309, 311

M

Malabo Protocol, 65, 66, 69, 84, 91, 92, 93, 95, 97, 99, 100, 101, 104
mens rea, 4, 9, 16, 20, 23, 28, 29, 73, 79, 83, 90, 115, 117, 128, 131, 135, 165, 168, 169, 282
Mexico, 142, 174, 260

N

Narmada Bachao Andolan, vii, viii
Narmada River Valley, vii, viii, 257
NASA, 301, 302, 332, 335, 344
Nepal, 262, 263, 264, 270, 293
Netherlands, The, v, vi, 233, 253
New Zealand, 46, 48, 49, 50, 53, 56, 58, 61, 142, 153, 155, 167, 175, 176, 210
  Environment Court, 154
    Resource Management Act, 154, 155, 176
  Te Urewera, 48, 63
  Treaty of Waitangi, 48
Nigeria, 12, 32, 77, 79, 80, 84, 86, 90, 96, 99, 101, 105, 260
  Niger Delta, 80, 84
Nuremberg, 111, 116, 179

O

OAU. *See* African Union (AU)
Ogoni, 84
outer space, v, 4, 23, 24, 42, 149, 163, 164, 295, 296, 297, 298, 299, 303, 313, 314, 317, 318, 320, 324, 326, 328, 329, 330, 332, 333, 334,

335, 338, 339, 340, 341, 342, 343, 344, 345
Liability Convention, 313, 319, 320, 321, 322, 324, 325, 326, 328, 329, 331, 333, 336, 338, 339, 340, 341
Moon Agreement, 296, 313, 314, 315, 316, 317, 324, 325, 326, 329
Outer Space Treaty (OST), 313, 314, 315, 317, 319, 322, 324, 326, 329, 333, 336
Rescue Agreement, 319

P

Pakistan, 25, 26, 32, 262, 273, 294
Papua, v, vi
pillage, 75, 76, 97
Polluter Pays Principle, 51, 56, 268, 296, 307
Precautionary Principle, 56, 268
Protocol on the Statute of the African Court of Justice and Human Rights. *See* Malabo Protocol
Pulp Mills Case (2006), 147, 175

R

Ramsar Convention, 232, 234, 236, 241, 245, 247, 252, 255, 256
res communis, 40, 41, 42, 297
res nullius, 39, 41, 42
rights of nature, 15, 35, 43, 44, 45, 46, 48, 51, 52, 53, 55, 56, 58, 60, 61
Rohingya, 79
Rome Statute, viii, 3, 23, 31, 68, 71, 72, 73, 74, 76, 77, 78, 79, 80, 81, 82, 85, 86, 87, 88, 93, 98, 99, 101, 102, 104, 105, 106, 107, 117, 118, 119, 120, 121, 124, 127, 128, 129, 130, 131, 132, 134, 135, 136, 137, 139, 157, 162, 166, 168, 169, 172, 180, 181, 182, 247, 278, 279, 280, 284, 331, 332
Article 28, 92, 93, 127
Article 6, 88, 134, 209, 318, 329, 331, 339
Rule of Law in Armed Conflicts (RULAC), 73
Ryser, Rudolph, 205

S

Sardar Sarovar Dam, vii, viii, 257
SCSL. *See* Special Court for Sierra Leone
Sierra Leone, 66, 75, 76, 95, 96, 105, 106
South America, 56
Special Court for Sierra Leone, 66, 69, 103
Standing Rock Sioux Tribe, 184, 185, 191, 193, 196, 199, 201, 202, 203, 225, 228
Standing Rock Reservation, 184
Stone, Christopher, 44
strict liability doctrine, 51
Sudan, 66, 78, 82, 88, 89, 101, 105
Al-Bashir, Omar, 88, 89, 90, 92, 103
Supreme Court of India, 285

T

Taylor, Charles, 75
Tibet, 257, 263, 269, 270, 271, 272, 273, 286, 288, 289, 290, 292
Tomuschat, Christian, 111, 113, 115, 132, 136, 138

Treaty on Prevention and Punishment of Crimes against Humanity, 278
Treaty on the Principles Governing the Activities of States in the Exploration and Use of Space, including the Moon and Other Celestial Bodies. *See* Outer Space Treaty

U

Uganda, 46, 52, 53, 61, 62, 64, 70, 80, 86, 96, 102, 103
United Nations, xi, 8, 17, 18, 20, 26, 32, 33, 36, 37, 48, 56, 57, 59, 61, 64, 108, 110, 111, 112, 113, 114, 115, 116, 125, 127, 134, 135, 138, 139, 144, 145, 146, 159, 163, 168, 171, 174, 177, 181, 182, 197, 204, 205, 206, 209, 212, 214, 216, 217, 222, 226, 227, 228, 229, 235, 247, 256, 274, 275, 294, 313, 314, 315, 316, 317, 322, 323, 324, 325, 328, 329, 333, 336, 341, 343, 344, 345
  Committee on Economic, Social and Cultural Rights (CESCR), 82
  General Assembly, xi, 57, 64, 108, 111, 121, 138, 139, 328, 343, 344
  Guiding Principles on Business and Human Rights, xi
  Harmony with Nature program, 48
  Interregional Crime and Justice Research Institute, xi, 11, 33
  Office of the High Commissioner for Human Rights, 96, 106
  Security Council, xi, 120, 144
  Special Rapporteur on Human Rights and Climate Change, 56
  UN Educational, Scientific and Cultural Organization (UNESCO), 206, 228, 265, 266
  United Nations Environmental Programme, xi, 11, 26, 33, 67, 83, 94, 106, 156, 171, 177, 181
United Nations Declaration on the Rights of Indigenous Peoples, 275, 294
United States, 46, 53, 125, 139, 151, 164, 175, 184, 185, 186, 187, 189, 193, 194, 196, 214, 216, 224, 228, 229, 299, 341
Universal Declaration of Human Rights, 25, 28, 205, 229, 251
User Pays Principle, 307

W

war crimes, 66, 74, 97, 105
World Bank, The, vii, 250, 256, 258, 274, 277, 278, 293
World Commission on Dams, 257, 258, 259, 260, 261, 262, 274, 275, 277, 279, 281, 282, 283, 284, 285, 286, 288, 290, 291, 293, 294

www.ingramcontent.com/pod-product-compliance
Lightning Source LLC
LaVergne TN
LVHW010722210926
848485LV00007B/1424/J
* 9 7 8 1 6 4 8 8 9 1 0 9 0 *